Palgrave Critical Studies of Antisemitism and Racism

Series Editor
David Feldman
Department of History, Classics & Archaeology
Birkbeck College – University of London
London, UK

Palgrave Critical Studies of Antisemitism and Racism considers antisemitism from the ancient world to the present day. The series explores topical and theoretical questions and brings historical and multidisciplinary perspectives to bear on contemporary concerns and phenomena.

Grounded in history, the series also reaches across disciplinary boundaries to promote a contextualised and comparative understanding of antisemitism. A contextualised understanding will seek to uncover the content, meanings, functions and dynamics of antisemitism as it occurred in the past and recurs in the present. A comparative approach will consider antisemitism over time and place. Importantly, it will also explore the connections between antisemitism and other exclusionary visions of society. The series will explore the relationship between antisemitism and other racisms as well as between antisemitism and forms of discrimination and prejudice articulated in terms of gender and sexuality.

More information about this series at
http://www.palgrave.com/gp/series/15437

David Feldman
Editor

Boycotts Past and Present

From the American Revolution to the Campaign to Boycott Israel

Editor
David Feldman
Department of History, Classics & Archaeology
Birkbeck College – University of London
London, UK

Palgrave Critical Studies of Antisemitism and Racism
ISBN 978-3-319-94871-3   ISBN 978-3-319-94872-0 (eBook)
https://doi.org/10.1007/978-3-319-94872-0

Library of Congress Control Number: 2018957121

© The Editor(s) (if applicable) and The Author(s) 2019
This work is subject to copyright. All rights are solely and exclusively licensed by the Publisher, whether the whole or part of the material is concerned, specifically the rights of translation, reprinting, reuse of illustrations, recitation, broadcasting, reproduction on microfilms or in any other physical way, and transmission or information storage and retrieval, electronic adaptation, computer software, or by similar or dissimilar methodology now known or hereafter developed.
The use of general descriptive names, registered names, trademarks, service marks, etc. in this publication does not imply, even in the absence of a specific statement, that such names are exempt from the relevant protective laws and regulations and therefore free for general use.
The publisher, the authors and the editors are safe to assume that the advice and information in this book are believed to be true and accurate at the date of publication. Neither the publisher nor the authors or the editors give a warranty, express or implied, with respect to the material contained herein or for any errors or omissions that may have been made. The publisher remains neutral with regard to jurisdictional claims in published maps and institutional affiliations.

Cover illustration: © Guy Corbishley / Alamy Stock Photo

This Palgrave Macmillan imprint is published by the registered company Springer Nature Switzerland AG
The registered company address is: Gewerbestrasse 11, 6330 Cham, Switzerland

Acknowledgements

This book has developed from the papers presented at a three-day conference on *Boycotts—Past and Present* held in June 2013 at Birkbeck, University of London. The conference was organised by the Pears Institute for the Study of Antisemitism on behalf of the International Consortium for Research on Antisemitism and Racism. I am thankful to everyone who presented papers at the conference, not all of whom are represented in this volume, and who contributed to a lively and remarkable event. I am especially grateful to my co-convenors Scott Ury (Tel Aviv University) and Michael Miller (Central European University) and to Jan Davison and Madisson Brown who took care of all administrative and practical arrangements.

David Feldman

Contents

1 Boycotts: From the American Revolution to BDS   1
  David Feldman

2 Consumer Boycotts in Modern History: States, Moral Boundaries, and Political Action   21
  Frank Trentmann

3 In Defense of the Nation: Protectionism and Boycotts in the Habsburg Lands, 1844–1914   41
  Michael L. Miller

4 The Enemy Within: The Anti-Jewish Boycott and Polish Right-Wing Politics in the Early Twentieth Century   53
  Grzegorz Krzywiec

5 Zionist "Buy National" Campaigns in Interwar Palestine   73
  Hizky Shoham

6 Picketing Jewish-Owned Businesses in Nazi Germany: A Boycott?   97
  Christoph Kreutzmüller

7 Boycott Campaigns of the Radical Left in Cold-War West Germany 115
   Alexander Sedlmaier

8 "The Onward March of a People Who Desire to Be Totally Free": The 1953 Baton Rouge Bus Boycott 139
   Derek Charles Catsam

9 The United Farm Workers Union and the Use of the Boycott Against American Agribusiness 157
   Lori A. Flores

10 Sanctions Against South Africa: Myths, Debates, and Consequences 175
   Yehonatan Alsheh

11 Sanctioning Apartheid: Comparing the South African and Palestinian Campaigns for Boycotts, Disinvestment, and Sanctions 197
   Lee Jones

12 A Collision of Frames: The BDS Movement and Its Opponents in the United States 219
   Sina Arnold

13 The British Summer of 2014: Boycotts, Antisemitism, and Jews 243
   Dave Rich

14 Palestine: Boycott, Localism, and Global Activism 261
   Philip Marfleet

15 The Boycott, Divestment, Sanctions (BDS) Movement
   and Radical Democracy   287
   John Chalcraft

16 Moral-Historical Questions of the Anti-Israel Boycott   311
   Jeremy Krikler

Index   333

Notes on Contributors

Yehonatan Alsheh is a member of the Faculty of Social Work, University of Toronto, Canada. He wrote his doctoral dissertation in the Tel Aviv University School of Historical Studies on the political and intellectual origins of the United Nations Genocide Convention. He has been a postdoctoral fellow at the University of the Free State in Bloemfontein South Africa and his book on the political history of South Africa appeared in Hebrew in 2014.

Sina Arnold is a social anthropologist and postdoctoral researcher at the Center for the Research on Antisemitism (Zentrum für Antisemitismusforschung—ZfA) in Berlin. She is also a member of the Berlin Institute for Integration and Migration Research (BIM) at Humboldt-Universität zu Berlin. She is the author of *Das unsichtbare Vorurteil. Antisemitismusdiskurse in der US-amerikanischen Linken nach 9/11* (2016) and *Der Fall Ethel und Julius Rosenberg. Antikommunismus, Antisemitismus und Sexismus in den USA zu Beginn des Kalten Krieges* (with Olaf Kistenmacher, 2016). Her recent research focuses on antisemitism in social movements and in migration societies, digital media and forced migration, and national and postnational forms of identity.

Derek Charles Catsam is Professor of History and the Kathlyn Cosper Dunagan Professor in the Humanities at the University of Texas of the Permian Basin and is a senior research associate at Rhodes University in Grahamstown, South Africa. He is the author of three books: *Freedom's Main Line: the Journey of Reconciliation and the Freedom Rides* (2009); *Beyond the Pitch: The Spirit, Culture, and Politics of Brazil's 2014 World*

Cup (2014); and *Bleeding Red: A Red Sox Fan's Diary of the 2004 Season* (2005). He is working on books on bus boycotts in the United States and South Africa in the 1940s and 1950s and on the 1981 Springbok rugby tour to the United States.

John Chalcraft is Professor of Middle East History and Politics at the London School of Economics and Political Science (LSE). He is the author of *The Striking Cabbies of Cairo and Other Stories: crafts and guilds in Egypt, 1863–1914* (2004), *The Invisible Cage: Syrian migrant workers in Lebanon* (2009), and *Popular Politics in the Making of the Modern Middle East* (2016). He is working on Gramscian approaches to social movements and transnational activism.

David Feldman is Director of the Pears Institute for the Study of Antisemitism at Birkbeck, University of London, where he is also Professor of History. He has written widely on the history of Jews and immigrants in Britain. His publications include *Englishmen and Jews: Social Relations and Political Culture* (1994) and most recently *Immigration and Antisemitism in Western Europe Today: Is there a connection?* (2018) He is an editor of *History Workshop Journal* and a founder member of International Consortium for Research on Antisemitism and Racism (ICRAR). He is writing a book on the history of the term 'antisemitism'.

Lori A. Flores is Associate Professor of History at the State University of New York at Stony Brook. She is the author of *Grounds for Dreaming: Mexican Americans, Mexican Immigrants, and the California Farmworker Movement* (2016) which was named Best History Book by the International Latino Book Awards, Best First Book by the Immigration and Ethnic History Society, and the winner of the Martin Ridge Book Award. In efforts to bring Latino history to wider audiences, she has written for publications such as *ColorLines/RaceForward*, *PopMatters*, and *The Detroit Free Press,* and helps host the New Books in Latino Studies podcast on the New Books Network. She is researching a new book project on the history of Latino food workers in the US Northeast from 1940 to the present day.

Lee Jones is Reader in International Politics in the School of Politics and International Relations at Queen Mary University of London and research associate at the Asia Research Centre, Murdoch University. He is the author of *ASEAN, Sovereignty and Intervention in Southeast Asia* (Palgrave Macmillan, 2012), *Governing Borderless Threats: Non-Traditional Security and the Politics of State Transformation* (2015, with

Shahar Hameiri), and *Societies Under Siege: Exploring How International Economic Sanctions (Do Not) Work* (2015).

Christoph Kreutzmüller joined the Jewish Museum Berlin in 2015. Before that he coordinated extensive research projects on the fate of Jewish-owned businesses in Berlin, 1930–1945, at the Humboldt-University (Berlin) and worked as a senior historian for the House of the Wannsee Conference. The former banker has written extensively on both the Holocaust and economic history. His publications include the acclaimed study: *Final Sale in Berlin: The Destruction of Jewish Commercial Activity* (2017). Together with Michael Wildt and Moshe Zimmermann he is also the co-editor of *National Economies: Volks-Wirtschaft, Racism and Economy in Europe between the Wars* (2015).

Jeremy Krikler is Reader in History at the University of Essex. He has long been concerned with questions of race and class, principally as these pertain to South African history, but also with respect to the Atlantic slave trade. In *Revolution from Above, Rebellion from Below* (1993) he explored the relationship of black peasants to their landowners and to British imperialism in South Africa. *White Rising* (2005) investigated an intense moment of rebellion and racial violence amongst white workers in South Africa. With Wulf Hund and David Roediger, he co-edited *Wages of Whiteness and Racist Symbolic Capital* (2010).

Grzegorz Krzywiec is a research associate at the Institute of History (Polish Academy of Sciences). He is preparing a book on the cultural history of fascism in Poland in the European context, 1919–1939. His articles on the history of Polish nationalism have appeared in various books, including: *Szowinizm po polsku, 1886–1905* (2009), which has also been published in English as *Chauvinism, Polish style: The Case of Roman Dmowski (Beginnings: 1886–1905)* (2016). Most recently he has published *Polska bez Żydów. Studia z dziejów idei, wyobrażeń i praktyk antysemickich na ziemiach polskich 1905–1914* [Poland without the Jews. Studies on the History of Anti-Semitic Ideas, Phantasms and Practices in the Polish Lands on the Early Twentieth Century (1905–1914)] (2017).

Philip Marfleet is an emeritus professor in the School of Social Sciences at the University of East London. He has written widely on globalisation, migration, refugee histories, racism and exclusion in Europe, and on contemporary social and political affairs in the Middle East. Publications include *Refugees in a Global Era* (Palgrave 2006); *Egypt* –

Contested Revolution (2016); and with Nira Yuval-Davis (eds.), *Racism, Secularism and the Politics of Belonging* (2012).

Michael L. Miller is Head of the Nationalism Studies Program at Central European University in Budapest. He holds his PhD in History from Columbia University, where he specialized in Jewish and Central European History. Michael's research focuses on the impact of nationality conflicts on the religious, cultural, and political development of Central European Jewry in the nineteenth century. His articles have appeared in *Slavic Review, Austrian History Yearbook, Simon Dubnow Institute Yearbook, Múlt és Jövő*, and *The Jewish Quarterly Review*. Miller's book, *Rabbis and Revolution: The Jews of Moravia in the Age of Emancipation*, was published in 2011. It appeared in Czech translation as *Moravští Židé v době emancipace* (2015). Michael is a founding member of the International Consortium for Research on Antisemitism and Racism.

Dave Rich is Head of Policy for the Community Security Trust (CST), a UK Jewish charity that provides security advice and assistance to the UK Jewish community and assists victims of antisemitic hate crime. He is also an associate research fellow at the Pears Institute for the Study of Antisemitism, Birkbeck, University of London, where he completed his PhD in 2015. His published work includes *The Left's Jewish Problem: Jeremy Corbyn, Israel and Anti-Semitism* (2016) and 'Global antisemitism', in *The Routledge International Handbook on Hate Crime*, eds. Nathan Hall, Abbee Corb, Paul Giannasi & John G. D. Grieve (2015). He has written about antisemitism, anti-Zionism, and extremism for *The New York Times, The Guardian, The New Statesman, The Huffington Post, Standpoint, World Affairs Journal, Haaretz, The Jerusalem Post, The Jewish Chronicle, Forward* and *Fathom*.

Alexander Sedlmaier is Reader in Modern History at Bangor University, Wales. He is presently Marie Skłodowska-Curie Research Fellow at the Institute for Social Movements at Ruhr-University Bochum. His publications include *Public Goods versus Economic Interests: Global Perspectives on the History of Squatting* [ed. with F. Anders, 2017] and *Consumption and Violence: Radical Protest in Cold-War West Germany* [2014, German translation 2018]. His current research looks at the political means employed by those who, for various reasons, resorted to protest during times of war in the period from the First World War to the Iraq War.

Hizky Shoham is a cultural historian of Zionism, the Yishuv, and Israel. He is a senior lecturer at the Interdisciplinary Program for Hermeneutics and Cultural Studies at Bar-Ilan University, Israel, and a research fellow in the Kogod Institute for Advanced Jewish Studies at the Shalom Hartman Institute in Jerusalem. His publications include *Carnival in Tel Aviv: Purim and the Celebration of Urban Zionism* (2014) and *Israel Celebrates: Festivals and Civic Culture in Israel* (2017).

Frank Trentmann is Professor of History at Birkbeck College, University of London, and an associate of the Consumer Society Research Centre, University of Helsinki. He is also a member of the EPSRC-ESRC research centre "DEMAND" (Dynamics of Energy, Mobility and Demand). His work has been in the history of consumption, civil society, and politics broadly defined, with a particular focus on food, water and energy. His publications include *Free Trade Nation: Commerce, Consumption and Civil Society in Modern Britain* (2008); *The Oxford Handbook of the History of Consumption* (editor, 2012); and *Empire of Things: How We Became a World of Consumers, from the Fifteenth Century to the Twenty-First* (2016), which has been translated into several languages.

Abbreviations

AAM	Anti-Apartheid Movement
AIPAC	American Israel Public Affairs Committee
ANC	African National Congress
AWOC	Agricultural Workers Organizing Committee
AZAPO	Azanian People's organization
BDS	Boycott, Divestment and Sanctions
BIN	Boycott Israel Network
BRICUP	British Committee for Universities of Palestine
COSATU	Congress of South African Trade Unions
CP	Conservative Party, South Africa
CUNY	City University of New York
CUPE	Canadian Union of Public Employees
CV	*Central-Verein deutscher Staatsbürger jüdischen Glaubens*
FBO	Faith-based organisation
IJAN	International Jewish Anti-Zionist Network
IMF	International Monetary Fund
INSS	Israel's Institute for National Security Studies
JVP	Jewish Voice for Peace
NCL	National Consumers' League
NFWA	National Farm Workers Association
NGO	Non-governmental organisation
NP	National Party, South Africa
PA/PNA	Palestinian National Authority
PACBI	Palestinian Academic and Cultural Boycott Initiative
PFLP	Popular Front for the Liberation of Palestine

PLO	Palestine Liberation Organisation
RZ	*Revolutionäre Zellen*
SACP	South African Communist Party
SANGOCO	South African Non-Governmental Organization Coalition
SA/SS	Sturmabteilung/Schutzstaffel
SJP	Students for Justice in Palestine
UDF	United Democratic Front
UDL	United Defense League
UFW	United Farm Workers
UFWOC	United Farm Workers Organizing Committee
UNWCAR	United Nations World Conference Against Racism
USACBI	US Campaign for the Academic and Cultural Boycott of Israel
WSF	World Social Forum
ZOA	Zionist Organization of America

CHAPTER 1

Boycotts: From the American Revolution to BDS

David Feldman

For more than a decade the drive for boycott, divestment, and sanctions (BDS) has been at the front of a global campaign directed against Israel. Formally launched on 9 July 2005 by more than 170 Palestinian non-governmental organisations, the movement's stated goals are: the end of Israel's occupation and colonisation of Arab lands, dismantling the security wall, full equality for Palestinian-Arab citizens of Israel, and recognition of the right of return for Palestinian refugees.[1] Most supporters of BDS cast their movement as the latest iteration of a boycott conducted in the cause of human rights and in opposition to racialised inequalities. The British charity War on Want explains its support for BDS citing the 'Israeli repression and human rights abuse' that Palestinians have suffered for

---

[1] The origins of the movement have been traced to the World Conference Against Racism, Racial Discrimination, Xenophobia, and Related Intolerance, held in Durban, South Africa in 2001, where the NGO forum called for the 'complete and total isolation of Israel as an apartheid state'. Kenneth Marcus, *The Definition of Antisemitism* (Oxford, 2015), 204.

D. Feldman (✉)
Department of History, Classics & Archaeology,
Birkbeck College – University of London, London, UK
e-mail: d.feldman@bbk.ac.uk

© The Author(s) 2019
D. Feldman (ed.), *Boycotts Past and Present*, Palgrave Critical Studies of Antisemitism and Racism,
https://doi.org/10.1007/978-3-319-94872-0_1

more than 60 years.² The campaign presents itself both as an expression of Palestinian civil society and as a legatee of the international campaign against apartheid in South Africa. BDS is 'the South Africa strategy for Palestine', one of the movement's founders, Omar Barghouti, asserts.³ In stark contrast, several of the movement's opponents denounce it as the most recent manifestation of antisemitism. Speaking in Jerusalem in March 2016, Ronald Lauder, the president of the World Jewish Congress, did just this, stating that 'BDS is nothing more than a dangerous new strain of an age-old disease. And that disease is anti-Semitism.'⁴ According to the prime minister of Israel, Benjamin Netanyahu, the letters B, D, and S, 'really stand for bigotry, dishonesty and shame', and represent 'simply the latest chapter in the long, dark history of anti-Semitism.'⁵

These divergent interpretations have shaped academic work on the boycott of Israel, yet it is precisely because these interpretations emerge directly from the battle over BDS that they are at once significant and limited.⁶ They reproduce the conflict as much as they illuminate it. They do not generate fresh questions or a new framework of analysis. If we are to move beyond this impasse, we should take account not only of the perspectives of the foes and advocates of BDS, but also try to move beyond them. Boycotts are neither an invention of European antisemitism nor of campaigns for racial equality. They have a history that antedates and extends beyond both these movements. This volume's premise, and the premise of this introductory chapter, is that by locating BDS within this larger history of political mobilisation we will be better placed to develop a productive understanding of the phenomenon.

Historically, boycotts have been remarkably diverse, both in the forms they take and the goals they pursue. We tend to think of boycotts as a form of activity that focuses on markets. These boycotts aim to banish goods, purchasing power, labour, or services associated with a particular target.

---

² http://www.waronwant.org/bds; https://www.alaraby.co.uk/english/blog/2016/12/10/university-of-manchester-must-follow-students-and-endorse-bds

³ Omar Barghouti, *BDS: Boycott, Divestment, Sanctions. The Global Struggle for Palestinian Rights* (Chicago, 2011), 63.

⁴ http://www.jpost.com/Opinion/BDS-is-the-modern-form-of-anti-Semitism-449415

⁵ http://www.haaretz.com/israel-news/1.577920

⁶ Joel S. Fishman, 'The BDS message of anti-Zionism, anti-Semitism, and incitement to discrimination', *Israel Affairs*, vol. 18, no. 3, (July 2012), 412–25; Gary Nelson and Gabriel Noah Brahm, *The Case Against Academic Boycotts of Israel* (Chicago, 2015); Maia Carter Hallward, *Transnational Activism and the Israeli-Palestinian Conflict* (New York, 2013).

Yet at other times boycotts have pursued other forms of exclusion. For example, some artists, musicians, and Green activists currently campaign for art galleries to refuse sponsorship from oil companies such as Shell and BP.[7] Not only do many boycotts operate within markets but sometimes they are pursued with the aim of changing the ways in which markets operate. In Chap. 9 of this book, Lori Flores' account of the consumer boycott of agricultural produce in the United States, instigated in support of a campaign for the unionisation of farmworkers, provides a narrative and analysis of one such boycott. However, in many cases, the goals of boycotts have been positioned beyond the marketplace. The boycotts of apartheid South Africa and of Israel, analysed in Chaps. 10, 11, 13, 14, 15 and 16, by Yehonatan Alsheh, Lee Jones, Dave Rich, Philip Marfleet, John Chalcraft, and Jeremy Krikler respectively, are instances of boycotts of this sort. Other boycotts have shared economic and political goals. The boycott of Jewish businesses in East European empires in the late nineteenth and early twentieth centuries ostensibly sought to improve the lot of the peasantry and of non-Jewish enterprises but, as Michael Miller and Grzegorz Krzywiec demonstrate in Chaps. 3 and 4, they were closely bound to nation-building political movements. The same hybridity is found in the initiatives in interwar Palestine inspired by Zionism and examined by Hizky Shoham in Chap. 5.

All the movements we have so far mentioned emerged from civil society, yet this defining feature does not mean that the state has been unimportant in the history of boycotts. As Alexander Sedlmaier reminds us in Chap. 7, the state, and specifically the law, plays an important role in determining what sorts of boycott activities are legitimate. More broadly, as Frank Trentmann argues in Chap. 2, 'the political space and ambition of boycotts have evolved in relation to the state's capacity to act on behalf of its citizens'. Yet we should distinguish boycotts generated from within civil society from actions that are initiated by the state and its agents.[8] From time to time, states impose sanctions upon other states that they seek to punish but occasionally, as Christoph Kreutzmüller shows in Chap. 6, they sponsor boycotts against their own subjects. The attack on Jewish businesses in Nazi Germany provides one notorious example of this sort

---

[7] https://www.theguardian.com/environment/2010/jun/24/artists-bp-protest-tate
[8] In this regard BDS is different from the boycott of Israel pursued by Arab states. Gil Feiler, *From Boycott to Economic Cooperation: The Political Economy of the Arab Boycott of Israel* (London, 1988).

of action. This campaign was not only violent but also, crucially, was supported and condoned by public agencies and parts of the apparatus of the governing National Socialist Party. As Kreuzmueller argues, it was not a boycott in the usual sense of the term.

The term 'boycott' was not coined until 1880. Nevertheless, the kind of collective action analysed in this volume can be traced to the eighteenth century and, most dramatically, to events that culminated in revolution, war, and the founding of the United States of America.[9] The most famous pre-revolutionary act of defiance became known to posterity as the Boston Tea Party. On the night of 16 December 1773, the Sons of Liberty boarded three ships and threw 342 chests of tea overboard. This was not only a highly theatrical rejection of British goods but was also just one episode in a longer history of the use of a boycott in the colonists' struggle with imperial authority. The role of boycotts in the American Revolution is well known. Our aim here is not to rehearse that narrative but to ask how these events can shed light on the subsequent history of boycotts.

The disposition to boycott was present from the very beginning of the crisis of colonial governance in North America. In 1765 the British parliament in London introduced the Stamp Act: a new tax on printed materials used in the British American colonies, including the legal documents and other papers that merchants required in order to import goods. It met with protest, riot, and widespread non-compliance. Campaigners argued that the new tax was a violation of the colonists' rights because it had been introduced without the consent of local legislatures.[10] Merchants joined the protest movement, first in New York and then elsewhere. They entered into agreements to retaliate against the Stamp Act by refusing to import British goods. In present-day parlance we would say they decided to boycott British goods. In March 1766 the British government repealed the Stamp Act, but further attempts to raise revenue from the colonies soon followed. In Feb 1768 the Massachusetts legislature sent a circular to 12 other colonies urging them to unite in protest against the new duties. The merchants in that colony signed an agreement vowing not to

[9] But not only in North America. See M. O'Dowd, 'Politics, Patriotism and Women in Ireland, Britain and Colonial America, 1700–80', *Journal of Women's History*, vol. 22, no. 4, (2010), 15–38; On the United States, see T.H. Breen, *The Marketplace of Revolution. How Consumer Politics Shaped American Independence* (2004).

[10] Laurel Thatcher Ulrich, 'Political Protest and the World of Goods', in: *The Oxford Handbook of the American Revolution*, eds. Edward Gray and Jane Kamensky, (Oxford, 2013), 75.

import anything from Britain except necessities. By the end of 1769 all the colonies, with the solitary exception of New Hampshire, had agreed to either the non-importation or the non-consumption of British-made goods.[11]

The tactics of non-importation, non-consumption, and non-exportation that developed in the late 1760s became more forceful in the following decade, and were proclaimed as policy by the First Continental Congress in October 1774. The Congress called for the creation of local associations to watch over and enforce the boycott. Policing the boycott brought political conflict and political identity into everyday life. As Tim Breen argues, 'the non-importers of the 1760s and 1770s were doing more than simply obstructing the flow of British-made goods. They were inviting the American people to reinvent an entire political culture.'[12] As far as the British government was concerned, the boycott was tantamount to treason. Within a few years it developed into a violent and ultimately successful revolution.

The anatomy of boycotts in the American Revolution reveals features that recurred in the centuries that followed. First, boycotts were both expressive and instrumental. Meetings of merchants, traders, and freeholders, as well as press reports and broadsides, represented these disparate protests as a single 'public' resisting 'enslavement' and promoting freedom. Boycotts were tactics pursued with the aim of achieving concessions from the imperial government, but at the same time the practice helped to constitute and consolidate a political identity. Second, boycotts provided a way to extend political mobilisation. It was a form of propaganda by deed that permitted anyone with spending power to express their political commitment in everyday life. Third, the boycott had an ambivalent relationship to the rule of law. It was enforced not only by argument and persuasion but also by intimidation and violence. Newspapers exposed merchants who refused to sign non-importation agreements or who, having signed them, subsequently broke their promise. The public humiliation of renegade merchants was essential if the embargo on British trade was to hold.[13] However, the pressure applied to merchants who

---

[11] Breen, *The Marketplace*, ch. 7.
[12] Breen, *The Marketplace*, xvii.
[13] Breen, *The Marketplace*, 254–67; Lawrence B. Glickman, *Buying Power. A History of Consumer Activism in America* (Chicago, 2009), 46–8.

broke the embargo, and who profited by continuing to trade with Britain, sometimes led to the destruction of property and interpersonal violence, including the application of feathers and tar. Fourth, boycotts were pursued in defence of the rights of local legislatures, and were promulgated by those legislatures, but nevertheless culminated in armed rebellion. This revolutionary dimension is not an essential feature of boycotts but, as we shall see, it is a recurrent one.

In the late eighteenth and early nineteenth centuries boycotts became part of the repertoire of protest, not least in Britain. Here, within a decade of the American Revolution, the tactic was used by campaigners against the institution of slavery and, in this particular sense, for the cause of racial equality. William Fox's pamphlet, *Address to the People of Great Britain, on the Propriety of Abstaining from West India Sugar and Rum*, first published in 1791, stimulated a boycott of West Indian sugar that involved 300,000 families. The focus on patterns of domestic consumption opened pathways through which women—as traditional guardians of morality, and the sex generally responsible for household consumption—were able to participate in the movement.[14] The anti-slavery campaign returned to the tactic of abstention three decades later. British participation in the slave trade had been banned by law in 1807, and by the 1820s the target had become the institution of slavery itself in British colonies.[15] Some supporters of the Chartist movement also used the boycott tactic in the 1830s and 1840s. They tried to use their power as consumers to promote a democratic suffrage by trading only with shopkeepers who were sympathetic to their cause and by promoting the boycott of others who were not.[16] None of these movements achieved its immediate goal but, as in the American colonies, boycotts infused mundane consumption with moral and political significance and provided a new form of political expression that helped to extend political mobilisation.

The social movements we have discussed up to this point were not named boycotts by contemporaries. That term was born in Ireland in 1880. Conquered and colonised by Britain in the sixteenth and seventeenth centuries, from 1801 Ireland was incorporated within a single

---

[14] Clare Midgely, *Women Against Slavery. The British Campaigns, 1780–1870* (London, 1992), 35–37.
[15] Midgley, *Women against Slavery*, 60–2, 103–4.
[16] Peter Gurney, 'Exclusive Dealing in the Chartist Movement', *Labour History Review*, vol. 74, no. 1, (April 2009), 90–110.

kingdom—the United Kingdom of Great Britain and Ireland. Conquest had profound religious and social dimensions. It led to the supremacy of a Protestant monarchy and its local agents over a predominantly Catholic population. Most land was owned by a narrow elite of Protestant landlords, having been confiscated from Catholics landowners and sold to families loyal to the Crown. It was in this context of political and economic domination that the Land War developed in the last years of the 1870s as the effects of agricultural depression hit rural Ireland.

From 1873 the price of agricultural produce fell globally. In Ireland the impact was worsened by a series of poor harvests beginning from 1877, which left many tenants unable to pay their rent or fearful they would be unable to do so. Falling prices and evictions for failure to pay rent not only brought personal hardships but were also ruinous for the rural economy. Tenant farmers and their supporters formed defence organisations, first in the west of Ireland but spreading to parts of the north and almost all of the south. The Irish Land League—an alliance which grew to encompass 500 branches—directed the associations. It mobilised mass support at a series of open-air meetings, and demanded reductions in rent, an end to evictions for failure to pay rent, and 'ownership of the soil by the occupiers.'[17] From the outset, the League's leaders encouraged supporters to isolate and refuse to have dealings with anyone who profited from the eviction of tenants from their home and farm. Speaking at Ennis on 19 September 1880, Charles Parnell, president of the Land League, exhorted the mass meeting in these terms:

> When a man takes a farm from which another had been evicted you must shun him on the roadside when you meet him, you must shun him in the streets of the town, you must shun him in the shop, you must shun him in the fair green and in the marketplace, and even in the place of worship, by leaving him alone….by isolating from the rest of his country as if he were the leper of old, you must show your detestation of the crime he has committed.[18]

Less than a week passed before Captain Charles Boycott, land agent for the third Earl of Erne's estates in County Mayo, and who also farmed more than 600 acres on his own account at Ballinrobe, was the target of

---

[17] R.C. Comerford, 'The land war and the politics of distress'. in: *In A New History of Ireland. VI Ireland Under the Union II*, ed. WE Vaughan, (Oxford, 1996), 28–45.

[18] T.W. Moody, *Davitt and the Irish Revolution 1848–82* (Oxford, 1982), 418–9.

precisely the sort of resistance Parnell had urged. The Earl of Erne had granted his tenants a 10 per cent reduction in rent, and all but two held out for a further 15 per cent cut. Erne refused, and Captain Boycott obtained eviction notices against 11 defaulting tenants.

Almost a month later, he wrote a letter to *The Times* in which he gives a vivid account of what happened after he issued tenants with notices to quit.

> On the ensuing day…the people collected in crowds upon my farm, and some hundred or so came up to my house and ordered off, under threats of ulterior consequences, all my farm labourers, workmen and stablemen, commanding them never to work for me again … My blacksmith has received a letter threatening him with murder if he does any more work for me, and my laundress has also been ordered to give up my washing… The shopkeepers have been warned to stop all supplies to my house, and I have just received a message from the post mistress to say that the telegraph messenger was stopped and threatened on the road when bringing out a message to me and she does not think it safe to send any telegrams which may come for me in the future … My farm is public property: the people wander over it with impunity. My crops are trampled upon, carried away in quantities and destroyed wholesale.[19]

At first sight, the events in Ballinrobe appear to have been the outgrowth of conflict in a localised, face-to-face society. The instructions from Parnell are in keeping with this impression. He made clear that one aim of the movement was to make Captain Boycott painfully feel the disapproval of his neighbours. But these personal interactions were not the only social relationships that mattered and to focus on them alone would lead us to overlook the modernity of what took place. The boycott was promoted by an association—the Land League—and its message was broadcast by the press to a growing political public. At the heart of the Land League were the local middle classes—tenant farmers, shopkeepers, priests, local lawyers, and journalists. Their refusal to deal with Captain Boycott was an outgrowth of Irish civil society and an organised movement of social and political protest.[20] Ballinrobe, moreover, was a market society, connected to national and international contexts by newspapers and by the telegraph.

---

[19] *The Times*, 18 October 1880, 6.
[20] Donnacha Seán Lucey, *Land, Popular Politics and Agrarian Violence in Ireland: The Case of County Kerry, 1872–1886* (Dublin, 2011).

The measures directed at Captain Boycott were designed not only to isolate him and his family personally but also to deny them access to the labour market, to local shopkeepers, and to communications.

As was the case in the American Revolution, the boycott movement in Ireland was expressive as well as instrumental. It was one way in which the Land League attempted to forge and build support for an Irish nationalist political identity. When the instigators and leaders of the League called for land to be returned to the people, their message promoted nationalist sentiment and ambition.[21] When the farmers, tradesmen, and labourers of Ballinrobe shunned Captain Boycott, they were expressing their political identity as Irish nationalists in a way that infused their behaviour with political meaning.[22]

The boycott carried several practical objectives. Most immediately, the movement was intended to punish its eponymous target. Additionally, however, the boycotters sent a warning to other landlords and agents. They aimed to discourage them, lest they follow the example of the Earl of Erne and Captain Boycott. There were larger political goals too. For Charles Parnell, who was not only the president of the League but also the leader of the Irish Members of Parliament in the House of Commons, the aim of the campaign was to bring pressure to bear on the Liberal government led by William Gladstone. The British government's willingness to bring, extend, and implement land reform, Parnell believed, would depend on the strength of the agitation in Ireland. From his standpoint, and that of his supporters, the boycott was one part of a strategy which combined mobilisation and intimidation with parliamentary, constitutional, and legal means.[23] For others, however, the Land League was the continuation of a revolutionary movement. Its formation comprised an alliance of reformers with Fenians whose past encompassed gun running, and who argued that moral suasion without armed force would never be sufficient.[24]

It was James Redpath, an American journalist, and Father John O'Malley, a local priest prominent in the campaign against Captain

[21] R.V. Comerford, 'The impediments to freehold ownership of land and the character of the Irish Land War', in: *Uncertain Futures: Essays about the Irish Past for Roy Foster*, ed. Senia Paseta, (Oxford, 2016), 60.

[22] Donald Jordan, *Land and Popular Politics in Ireland. County Mayo from the Plantation to the Land War* (Cambridge, 1994), 221, 226–7.

[23] R.F. Foster, *Modern Ireland, 1600–1972* (London, 1988), 405–13.

[24] Moody, *Davitt*, 377–81, 458.

Boycott, who were responsible for inventing the term that gave global resonance to an Irish conflict. According to Redpath, he and the priest, their minds lubricated by whisky, reflected one night on how best to encapsulate their campaign. They considered the term 'ostracism' but agreed it would not do. O'Malley wondered, 'How would it be to call it to boycott him?' Redpath agreed, and a new word had entered the political lexicon. Redpath employed the term 'boycott' in his syndicated newspaper column as well as on a speaking tour. His lecture, entitled 'Ireland's land war: what I know about boycotting', drew thousands in venues across the American Midwest, from Chicago to Louisville.[25] By 1882 'boycott' had entered Webster's Dictionary. More than this, it passed rapidly and without significant alteration into Dutch, French, German, Czech, Polish, Russian, and many other languages. Yet if the word 'boycott' did not change much as the term made its way around the globe, its meanings did mutate as the word was employed in a multitude of contexts and conflicts. As Frank Trentmann illustrates in Chap. 2, boycotts have been a protean form of social action. If we take an overview of boycott movements in the late nineteenth and early twentieth centuries, we find how diverse they were and how none of the movements that adopted the name 'boycott' looked quite the same as the movement in Ireland.

Reflecting on the boycott tactic in the 1890s, the American lawyer and writer Arthur Dudley Vinton proposed, 'we lent the policy to Ireland and she returned it to us with a name.'[26] In the United States, boycotts had figured in conflicts between workers and their employers since at least the 1830s but there was a surge of this activity from the 1880s, chiefly in an attempt to enforce the employment of union men.[27] The use of boycotts multiplied as unions demanded that the public should withhold services from the boycotted firm. In some cases, customers were threatened with a place on a 'black-list' if they continued to trade with the boycott's original target.[28] In New York there were 59 boycotts in 1885 alone, and there were 183 the following year. Once again, the goals of these boycotts were both instrumental and expressive. For the most part the instrumental goal was to reserve jobs for union men. But this economic aim was also attached to

---

[25] John McKivigan, *Forgotten Firebrand. James Redpath and the Making of Nineteenth-Century America* (Ithaca, 2008), 159.
[26] Glickman, *Buying Power*, 122–4.
[27] Leo Wolman, *The Boycott in American Trade Union* (Baltimore, 1916), 24–5.
[28] Harry Laidler, *Boycotts and the Labor Struggle* (New York, 1913), 58–94.

a set of normative claims. In this case, the boycott called upon the wider community to support the rights and values of organised labour.[29] Boycotts proliferated in the United States in the late nineteenth and early twentieth centuries. In addition to boycotts organised by trade unions, there were also boycotts directed at the point of consumption: against sweatshops, to promote ethical consumption and, in New York in 1902, Jewish women raided and boycotted butcher shops to force a reduction in the price of kosher meat.[30]

In Central and Eastern Europe boycotts emerged from the efforts to ameliorate the economic condition of peasants and small traders in the face of the capitalist transformation of the countryside. From the late nineteenth century social reformers proposed the formation of co-operatives and credit unions as a means to evade middlemen and to secure loans at advantageous rates. They promoted these new associations alongside a boycott of the ethnic groups that already dominated these services. Jews were one of a number of groups targeted in this way, as Michael Miller points out in Chap. 3. Beyond Europe, boycotts developed as a facet of anti-colonial movements in India, China, and Egypt. Here was a form of protest that could be utilised to advance a plethora of causes. Boycotts were associated with campaigns over land, and to promote the interests of organised labour and peasants; they could promote anti-colonial and nationalist political identities; their targets could be landlords, employers, middlemen, or colonial rulers. Each boycott pursued a particular goal but also conveyed and consolidated a political identity.

These late nineteenth and early twentieth century boycotts focused predominantly on local or proto-national goals. This type of activity did not fade after 1945. In Chap. 8, Derek Catsam's account of a bus boycott in 1953, which was directed against segregation on public transport in Baton Rouge, illustrates this point in one context. Nevertheless, in these same decades we find a growing concern with faraway evils. Boycott campaigns once again displayed an international perspective, as they had in the anti-slavery boycotts in the early nineteenth century. As Alex Sedlemaier shows, in the 1970s in the Federal Republic of Germany, boycott movements which focused on local transport and nuclear energy were pursued alongside other campaigns whose political vision extended to Chile and

---

[29] Glickman, *Buying Power*, 128–31.
[30] Paula Hyman, 'Immigrant women and consumer protest: The New York City kosher meat boycott of 1902', *American Jewish History*, vol. 70, no. 1, (September 1980), 91–105.

South Africa. In the United Kingdom the same tendency was evident in the development of transnational consumer activism which took the form of 'buycott' campaigns for fair trade, as well as in campaigns to abjure companies such as Nestlé.[31] These boycotts too were expressive as well as goal oriented. The campaign against Nestlé aimed both to protect third world mothers from the milk formula sold by an international corporation, and to constitute and mobilise a humanitarian global civil society dedicated to ameliorating suffering.[32] It was in this context, moreover, that activists promoted sports and cultural boycotts, as well as economic boycotts, in support of causes all over the world. These campaigns were in solidarity with Jews in the Soviet Union, blacks in South Africa, democrats and socialists in Chile, and Palestinians in the Middle East.

All of these campaigns were selective: necessarily so. Boycotts, typically, have been promoted by social movements and subaltern groups with limited resources and capacity. In the context of a specific campaign, therefore, a particular target is selected from a wider class of wrongdoers. Those merchants in the American colonies who were denounced, tarred, and feathered for trading with Britain were one such target, and Captain Boycott was another.[33] Inevitably, those individuals selected for punishment or boycott, sometimes for symbolic effect, have felt victimised and personally attacked. In his letter to *The Times*, Captain Boycott complained, 'my ruin is openly avowed as the object of the Land League.' Regardless of the motives of the boycotters, and the principled terms in which these motives have often been expressed, their actions are likely to be experienced by their targets as persecutory.

Selectivity arises in other ways too. Some boycott movements have attributed their grievance to the behaviour of members of an ethnic, national, or religious group. In these cases, the group as well as the grievance have sometimes become the target of protest. The boycott has been directed at people not only on account of their actions but also because of who they are seen to be. In such cases it is impossible for targets to

[31] Tehila Sasson, 'Milking the Third World? Humanitarianism, Capitalism and Moral Economy of the Nestlé Boycott', *American Historical Review*, vol. 121, no. 4, (October 2016), 1196–1224; Matthew Hilton, *Prosperity for All: Consumer Activism in an Era of Glaobalization* (Ithaca, 2009), ch. 5; Frank Trentmann, *Empire of Things: How We Became a World of Consumers from the Fifteenth Century to the Present* (London, 2016), 562–80.

[32] Sasson, 'Milking', 1217.

[33] This dimension to the practice of boycott was present from the earliest occasions, when we find collective action to restrict the markets of an individual or group of individuals as a way of effecting political or social change. Wollman, *The Boycott*, 12.

amend their behaviour and evade sanctions. One Indian advocate of a boycott of British-made goods was keenly aware of this danger. In 1929 he wrote that boycott 'is a method to show dislike for the attitude of the opponent and need not involve personal, racial or national hatred or enmity'.[34] In other cases, however, boycotts have not been pursued with this sort of ideological and emotional restraint. Instead they have promoted the racialisation of their target. This was the case with labour boycotts in the United States in the late nineteenth century. Here, in some cases, boycotts directed against the employment of non-union labour were, at the same time, targeted at the employment of immigrants. The first union label, introduced by cigar makers in 1875 was, in effect, a guarantee that cigars which bore that label were made by 'white'—and not by Chinese—labour. In 1885, boycotts against Chinese labour accounted for 40 of the 41 boycotts in the western states. In Portland, Oregon, the boycotts were organised by the Anti-Coolie Law and Order Association, and led to the dismissal of 400 Chinese working in 40 firms.[35]

This practice of boycotting a target that was at the same time racialised also arose in Central and Eastern Europe in the late nineteenth and early twentieth centuries. Here, as we have noted, some boycotts aimed to liberate peasants from dependence on Jewish traders and creditors. The goal of economic emancipation was often tied to anti-Jewish propaganda and policies.[36] In northwest Hungary, cooperatives and credit unions were promoted by conservative agrarians, Catholic politicians, and Slovak nationalists who created the People's Bank 'to protect Christian people from usurers'.[37] The manager, Julius Markovi, hoped the establishment of cooperatives and credit unions would drive Jews out of business. His antipathy extended further and encompassed 'Israelite doctors, traders, hucksters, innkeepers etc., because together they form an organic unit'.[38]

---

[34] Maneklal H. Vakil, *Boycott of British goods and foreign cloth*, (Bombay, 1930), 14.
[35] Laidler, *Boycotts*, 75.
[36] Torsten Lorenz, 'Introduction' 11, in: *Cooperatives in Ethnic Conflicts. Eastern Europe in the Nineteenth and early Twentieth Century*, ed. Lorenz, (Berlin, 2006).
[37] Miloslav Szabo, 'Because Words are not Deeds.' Antisemitic Practice and Nationality Politics in Upper Hungary around 1900, *Quest. Issues in Contemporary Jewish History, Journal of Fondazione CDEC*, no. 3, (July 2012), url: www.quest.cdecjournal.it/focus.php?id=299, 176.
[38] Szabo, 'Because Words', 179.

In Lithuania too nationalists called for emancipation from the Jews. Conservative Catholic nationalists wished for the creation of a merchant class to build the Lithuanian nation. In 1889 Jonas Berzanskis wrote in a programmatic article: 'The Lithuanian is sinking into poverty, but Shlomo is growing rich…Can our people not do the same as the Jew.'[39] Cooperatives were designed to promote the economic emancipation of the peasantry, but this was often yoked to a fantasy of rebuilding the nation, economy, and society on ethnic lines, without Jews. Indeed, in Congress Poland, as Grzegorz Krzywiec argues in Chap. 4, these priorities were reversed. Here the economic boycott of Jewish businesses was an outgrowth of a project for national revival that was expressed in the language of militant antisemitism.

The strategy of singling out a target for boycott intersected with race in new ways in the twentieth century. The boycott of Nazi Germany that was promoted by some Jewish organisations following the German elections in March 1933 is an early example of a boycott that was aimed at a state on account of its policy of racial discrimination.[40] Similarly, opposition to apartheid was manifested across the West in a movement to boycott South Africa. Here the regime's defenders accused the boycotters of double standards, and returned the charge of racism in kind. South Africa, they argued, was being judged by special criteria and not by the standards applied to other countries, least of all others in Africa. The anti-apartheid movement was racist, it claimed, because it singled out white South Africans and ignored the crimes of people of colour against both other people of colour and 'white' people.[41]

The movement for the boycott of Israel faces similar complaints. Why target Israel, some ask, when we can point to other states in the region, let alone in the world, which commit graver abuses?[42] In general, BDS presents itself as a universalist movement that promotes human rights. This very universalism, however, prompts the question of why Israel's

---

[39] Klaus Richter, 'Antisemitism, "Economic Emancipation" and the Lithuanian Co-operative movement Before World War 1', *Quest. Issues in Contemporary Jewish History, Journal of Fondazione CDEC*, no. 3, (July 2012), url: www.quest.cdecjournal.it/focus.php?id=300, 187.

[40] M. Gottleib, 'The anti-Nazi boycott movement in the United States: an ideological and sociological appreciation', *Jewish Social Studies*, vol. 35, no. 3–4, (July–October 1973), 198–227.

[41] James Sanders, *South Africa and the International Media, 1972–79* (London, 1999), 56.

[42] http://www.spiked-online.com/newsite/article/singling-out-israel-singling-out-the-jews/18904#.WuGteG4vxR0; Alan Dershowitz, *The Case Against BDS: Why Singling Out Israel is Anti-Semitic and Anti-Peace* (New York, 2018).

violations, and not those of others, should be targeted for action. If we examine BDS we find various arguments that aim to justify why Israel is singled out for criticism and boycott. For even if we agree that activists do not have the capacity to combat all human rights violators all over the world and so, therefore, some sort of choice has to be made, activists still face the task of justifying their choice in any particular case.

One answer to this challenge has been to point out that the BDS campaign is a response to the call made from Palestinian civil society.[43] However, this argument leaves the moral and political precedence of BDS dependent on the silence of other groups. In this way it penalises victim groups whose are so beleaguered that they find it impossible to organise and make a similar call for solidarity and help. A second argument is that the BDS strategy should be pursued because it will be effective and help the Palestinian people achieve their goals. This assumption rests on questionable foundations, as Yehonatan Alsheh and Lee Jones argue in Chaps. 10 and 11. Both contributors draw attention to specific conditions that marked the boycott of South Africa and, in particular, to the way in which boycott proceeded alongside armed struggle and a strategy clearly articulated by the African National Congress. By contrast, Jones suggests, BDS is a movement that lacks a defined strategy. In other words, one justification made for BDS is that it is a means to an end. The claim is not always convincing, even to people who support the Palestinian cause.

Other reasons for singling out Israel are expressive in character, in the sense that Israel is criticised in the name of a moral or political community. In this regard the boycott of Israel, like many earlier boycott movements, is intended to draw attention to injustice and mobilise support against it. In Chap. 12 Sina Arnold highlights the importance of opposition to racism and colonialism in the BDS movement. Chapters 14 and 15 by Phil Marfleet and John Chalcraft, also highlight how support for BDS draws powerfully from a repudiation of the legacy of European colonialism and racism. Here the unique circumstances of Israel's foundation are significant, as Jeremy Krikler argues in Chap. 16. Notwithstanding the fact that the creation of Israel in 1948 eventually required a struggle against the British imperial power, Zionism was also a product and a unique expression of European colonialism.[44] As Krikler points out, in the post-war decades

---

[43] Barghouti, *BDS*.

[44] Tara Zahra, 'Zionism, emigration and East European Colonialism', in: *Colonialism and the Jews*, eds. Lisa Moses Leff and Maud Mandel, (Bloomington, 2017), 166–92.

European colonisation increasingly was understood to be one of the great moral problems of the age. This distinctive history is significant because it helps to account for the exceptional status that Israel and the fate of the Palestinians holds for many on the Left and why Israel is singled out for condemnation. This insistence on Israel's colonial origins is expressed regularly when supporters of BDS characterise it as a settler-colonial state.[45] This conceptualisation does not convey the complexity of the state's origins and development but, equally importantly, it captures a central part of that history and one that it is re-enacted before a global audience that sees a continued policy of colonisation and displacement in territory occupied since 1967.[46]

As we noted at the start of this chapter, there is a different characterisation and analysis of the politics of singling out Israel for boycott. For some activists and scholars, the BDS movement is an antisemitic movement. This claim arises in two different ways: one line of argument focuses on what the supporters of BDS say and do, and the other focuses on outcomes. The former approach highlights speech acts and other actions carried out in support of BDS and finds they are suffused with antisemitic content. The other line of argument proposes that the very act of singling out Israel, the Jewish state, is functionally antisemitic.[47]

Since BDS is directed against Israel—which describes itself as a Jewish state whose existence is supported by the great majority of Jews worldwide—there is always an opportunity for supporters of BDS to fail to distinguish between Israel and Jews, and sometimes this does happen.[48] As Dave Rich demonstrates in Chap. 13, support for BDS has on occasion given rise to the abuse and harassment of Jews and even, more rarely, to violence. This is a phenomenon related to the presence of antisemitic stereotypes on the Left, the identification of economic and political power and covert influence with wealthy Jews, and the development of an antiracism that focuses on white privilege alone and tends to pass over the history of racialised exclusions within Europe itself.[49] Nevertheless,

---

[45] Maxim Rodinson, *Israel and the Arabs* (Harmondsworth, 1968) was important in establishing this formulation.

[46] Derek J Penslar, 'Zionism, Colonialism and Postcolonialism', *Journal of Israeli History*, vol. 20, no. 2–3, (2001), 84–98.

[47] Anthony Julius, *Trials of the Diaspora. A History of Anti-Semitism in England* (Oxford, 2010), 476–83.

[48] Marcus, *The Definition*, 207, 213.

[49] Marcus, *The Definition*, 207–9; David Feldman and Brendan McGeever, 'Labour and antisemitism: what went wrong and what is to be done?' https://www.independent.co.uk/

although antisemitic behaviour and rhetoric recurs in and around the BDS movement, even its opponents concede that it is not typical of the movement in general.[50]

For this reason, the characterisation of BDS as antisemitic ultimately depends not on its practice at any particular moment but on the argument that it is inherently so because of its impact on Jews. Kenneth Marcus has proposed that the offence BDS gives Jews is one crucial reason why the movement should be regarded as antisemitic.[51] It is certainly true, and evidenced by survey data, that most Jews consider an attachment to Israel to be central to their identity as Jews and this is one reason they tend to finds BDS offensive.[52] However, if we rest our identification of antisemitism on the subjective responses of Jews we will be left in an anarchic situation. The authority of Jews' subjectivity, inevitably, will face that of their detractors and we will have nothing to arbitrate between the two sides. We will be left without any way to adjudicate between the hurt feelings of Jews and those of the alleged perpetrators who deny they are antisemitic and who assert that they are falsely accused. Moreover, since there is a great deal of evidence that Jews differ widely over what antisemitism is, and also over when anti-Zionism becomes antisemitism, in this context any appeal to what Jews think and feel is bound to be inconclusive.[53] Jews' sense of offence, where it arises, is significant and should be reckoned with. However, this sort of recognition is not the same as elevating that experience of offence so that it becomes the touchstone for judging whether or not an action is antisemitic. In some cases the feeling of offence will be a sign that antisemitism is at work, but on its own it is insufficient.[54]

Since Jews' perceptions and experiences are not decisive in this matter, the key question is whether the very act of singling out Israel as a target for boycott is inherently antisemitic. Some writers and politicians have argued

---

news/long_reads/labour-party-antisemitism-jeremy-corbyn-jewish-left-wing-holocaust-a8306936.html

[50] Marcus, *The Definition*, 207.

[51] Marcus, *The Definition*, 181–5, 209.

[52] Stephen Miller, Margaret Harris, and Colin Shindler, *The Attitudes of British Jews Towards Israel* (London, 2015); European Union Agency for Fundamental Rights, *Discrimination and Hate Crime Against Jews in EU Member States: Perceptions and Experiences* (Luxembourg, 2013), 27.

[53] *Discrimination and Hate*, figure 1, p. 16.

[54] Marcus appears to concede this point: *The Definition*, 210.

that this is the case because BDS is continuous with other anti-Jewish boycotts.[55] This is unconvincing. There are key differences between earlier boycotts and BDS. One difference concerns the relationship of the different boycotts to state power. We have already noted that the Nazi boycott of Jews is a misnomer and bears no resemblance to BDS, precisely because it was supported by the state and the ruling party. Moreover, late nineteenth- and early twentieth century anti-Jewish boycott movements were directed at Jews in places where they were a vulnerable minority group, whereas BDS targets Israel where Jews are in the majority and hold state power. Finally, in this regard, as we have seen in Eastern Europe and in Germany, it is clear that Jews were singled out not only for what they did, but also for whom they were: radical nationalists imagined a country without Jews. In the case of BDS, when antisemitism emerges it usually does so in a different way: as a contingent feature of the movement but not as constitutive.

Controversy over antisemitism has drawn attention away from a more significant ambiguity within BDS. This concerns the relationship of the movement to the rule of law and social revolution. BDS supporters present themselves as taking part in a non-violent protest movement that aims to bring pressure to bear on the Israeli government and electorate. Whether this is realistic or not, they hope that BDS will make life uncomfortable for Israel, either politically or economically, and that this will contribute to a programme of change that will promote equal rights for Palestinians, both collectively and as individuals. However, if this is a possibly dominant strand in the boycott movement, there is also another. Writing in the academic journal *Social Text* in November 2016, Sunaina Maira proposes that 'while the boycott formally relies on a rights-based approach…the BDS principles [in her view] actually promote an anti-Zionist and decolonial paradigm for liberation'.[56] This dimension of BDS is elaborated in this volume by John Chalcraft in Chap. 15. He affiliates the movement to a multitude of other radical democratic mobilising projects that have developed across the globe in the last half-century. These movements, Chalcraft argues, aim 'to deconstruct dominant arrangements, and bring into being alternative systems of egalitarian (re)production and meaning which go well beyond the reformulation of the sphere of formal politics'. Phil Marfleet too, in Chap. 14, places BDS alongside a broader challenge to the dominant global order—one that privileges social

---

[55] https://www.theguardian.com/politics/2014/sep/09/gove-against-boycotting-israeli-goods-gaza-conflict; Julius, *Trials of the Diaspora*, 477–82.

[56] http://socialtextjournal.org/periscope_topic/the-academic-boycott-movement/

justice above the rule of law. These chapters highlight a significant tension within BDS, between its characterisation as an activist and reformist coalition engaged in pressure group politics and its identity as one facet of a revolutionary struggle.

This unresolved tension overlaps with another point of ambiguity that concerns the aims of the BDS movement. As Lee Jones points out, the movement contains supporters who accept the continued existence of the State of Israel within its internationally recognised boundaries, and others who in one form or another favour a 'one state solution' to the conflict. For Jones this confusion undermines BDS. My point here is different. In principle, commitment to a single state can proceed in tandem with a democratic strategy which recognises the importance of democratic practice.[57] However, when allied to a revolutionary movement that derogates the rule of law, the pursuit of a single state exacerbates the tension between BDS as a democratic movement allied to international law and a movement that aims at the removal of the State of Israel by revolutionary activism and people power.

As we have seen, over a period of 250 years boycott movements have carried within them tensions between constitutional and revolutionary aims, and between a drive towards substantive outcomes and a practice that has placed emphasis on forging new political cultures and identities. By placing the movement to boycott Israel in this long-term perspective we are able to perceive it in new ways and see the presence of these ambiguities. BDS, like many earlier boycott movements, is both instrumental and expressive: it aims not only to achieve a goal but also to consolidate and propagandise the different political identities that find a home within the movement. Further, supporters of BDS include some activists who look forward to the disappearance of Israel and others who do not. The question of whether the BDS movement is antisemitic is significant, not only for its opponents and supporters but also for anyone who aims to understand the phenomenon. Nevertheless, it is a question that often has crowded out others, of at least equal significance, that illumine the movement and enable us better to understand it.

---

[57] Bashir Bashir, 'Reconciling historical injustices: deliberative democracy and the politics of reconciliation', *Res Publica*, vol. 18, no. 2, (2012), 127–43.

CHAPTER 2

Consumer Boycotts in Modern History: States, Moral Boundaries, and Political Action

Frank Trentmann

In 1905, Chinese consumers across Asia decided to boycott American goods to protest against the US exclusion of Chinese immigrants, which had been US federal policy since 1882. Fourteen years later, in 1919, thousands of students walked through the Chinese section of Shanghai and burnt anything that looked to be of Japanese origin, in response to the "national humiliation" at the end of the First World War and the transfer of German rights in Shandong on the Yellow Sea to Japan. In 1925, it was British goods that became the target, after British-led soldiers from the International Settlement in Shanghai had fired on demonstrators who had gathered on Nanjing Road in protest at the death of a Chinese worker in a nearby Japanese textile factory. In Egypt, a British protectorate, Wafdist nationalism sparked a similar wave of protests in this period. In 1932 law students at Cairo University lit bonfires of fine European suits: "The silk

---

F. Trentmann (✉)
Birkbeck College, University of London, London, UK
e-mail: f.trentmann@bbk.ac.uk

© The Author(s) 2019
D. Feldman (ed.), *Boycotts Past and Present*, Palgrave Critical Studies of Antisemitism and Racism,
https://doi.org/10.1007/978-3-319-94872-0_2

garment is from your enemy, take it off and trample it. Light the fire and burn his old clothes in it."[1]

Boycotts—and buycotts, their more positive cousin—have made their appearance on the major battlegrounds of modern history, in fights over slavery, land rights, national sovereignty and imperial power, social justice, and, in recent years, animal rights. Many of these boycotts have been studied in their own right in the context of the politics and society at the time. In the historical literature especially, it has been the Anglo-American boycotts against slave-grown sugar in the late eighteenth century, and then the campaigns against sweatshop labour and sales conditions in the early twentieth century that have received the greatest attention and provide the main point of entry into the subject.[2] The resultant trajectory is a progressive one, highlighting the role of boycotts in battles for human rights and social justice and giving political voice to groups formally excluded from politics, women in particular. Recent interest in the growth of alternative, non-party, and transnational politics in late modernity has understandably seized on these earlier precursors, reinforcing this progressive trajectory.

This chapter cannot attempt to offer an encyclopaedic overview of boycotts, past and present, nor does it try to dispute or minimise the number of progressive causes fought (and sometimes won) by boycotters. Rather, it asks what happens to the story if we opt for a different starting point and give greater recognition to boycotts and

---

[1] Quoted in Nancy Young Reynolds, *Commodity Cultures: Interweavings of Market Cultures, Consumption Practices, and Social Power in Egypt, 1907–61* (Stanford PhD, 2003), 300. For China, see Karl Gerth, *China Made: Consumer Culture and the Creation of the Nation* (Cambridge, MA, 2003) esp. chs. 3–4.

[2] Charlotte Sussman, *Consuming Anxieties: Consumer Protest, Gender and British Slavery, 1713–1833* (Stanford, 2000). K. Kish Sklar, 'The Consumers' White Label Campaign of the National Consumers' League, 1898–1918', in: *Getting and Spending: European and American Consumer Societies in the Twentieth Century*, eds. Susan Strasser, Charles McGovern, and Matthias Judt, (Cambridge, 1998); Landon R. Y. Storrs, *Civilizing Capitalism: The National Consumer's League, Women's Activism, and Labor Standards in the New Deal Era* (Chapel Hill, 2000). Michele Micheletti, *Political Virtue and Shopping: Individuals, Consumerism, and Collective Action* (New York and Basingstoke, 2003). Sophie Dubuisson-Quellier, *La Consommation Engagée* (Paris, 2009). For the somewhat different role of boycotts as a space of action for social Catholics in early twentieth-century France, see Marie-Emmanuelle Chessel, *Consommateurs engagés à la Belle époque: La Ligue sociale d'acheteurs* (Paris, 2012).

causes that lie outside those of progressive social politics. Instead of pairing boycotts with civil society, I want to suggest a more triangular relationship, in which the state and national power have proved to be equally important. The shape of this triangle changed in the course of modern history, its contours determined not only by the relative strength of social movements and liberal traditions but by nationalism, state sovereignty, and power. The political space and ambition of boycotts have evolved in relation to the state's capacity to act on behalf of its citizens. In a weak state, boycotts could be attractive as an alternative instrument of power.

This chapter offers a brief, suggestive exploration of this neglected side of the relationship, with a focus on three dimensions. The first concerns the state itself, and will take us from situations in the early twentieth century, where state sovereignty was infringed and boycotts became substitute assertions of national power, to subsequent periods in the mid and late twentieth century where the state's growing ambition to improve its citizens' lives had the indirect effect of widening the terrain for "responsible" consumer activism. The second dimension revisits the idea of "moral economy" and asks about the spatial reach of boycotts: what has been the impact of the welfare state in the twentieth century and for the geographical imagination of boycotters and their objects of concern? How far does caring stretch? Third, and finally, we will look at changes in political subjectivity and practice.

In the Shadow of the State

One way to think of consumer boycotts is as alternatives to institutional force when formal state power is limited, constrained, or absent. In early twentieth-century China and Egypt—the examples with which we started—nationalists were unable to turn to a strong state and use taxes or trade barriers to punish a foreign enemy and its products. After the Opium War, the treaty of Nanjing (1842) forced China not only to open itself up to foreigners with a number of "treaty ports", it also lost tariff autonomy, that is, the power to decide what goods went in and out of the country. For societies that faced colonial dependence or a partial loss of sovereignty, boycotts of foreign goods attempted to fill that vacuum. It made it possible to wage an anti-colonial struggle without armies.

Clothing occupied an especially prominent place as both target and weapon. This was partly for economic reasons—textile manufacturing was the biggest global industry, and by 1900 it was still predominantly in the hands of British and European powers. Keeping foreign clothes out and building up a national garment industry were natural steps towards independence, although there was considerable slippage as to whether "national" clothes meant national manufacture, a national dress style, or nationals selling the clothes.

But clothes also played a central role because of their symbolic power: for aspiring nationalists they offered a highly visible informal uniform. Clothes literally made the nation, a phenomenon most powerfully promoted by Mahatma Gandhi, who made hand-spun khadi cloth simultaneously a defining practice and a politically symbolic appearance for the Indian National Congress in its fight for independence. In India as in Egypt, foreign clothes were among the first products boycotted or thrown onto bonfires.[3]

These repertoires of action did not suddenly disappear when colonies gained independence or states managed to shake off constraints and regained full sovereignty. Quite the contrary, states have turned to boycotts as a welcome addition to regular diplomacy, sometimes openly fanning the flames of consumers' anger at foreign nations. In China, there have been repeated calls for a boycott of Japanese cars, cosmetics, and electronic products since the Japanese Prime Minister Junichiro Koizumi started paying visits to the Yasukuni shrine in 2006—which honours all those who have died in service of the Japanese empire including a thousand convicted war criminals—a controversial ritual kept up by the incumbent prime minister, Shinzo Abe.[4]

---

[3] Lisa Trivedi, *Clothing Gandhi's Nation: Homespun and Modern India* (Bloomington, 2007); Reynolds, *Commodity Cultures in Egypt*. See also C.A. Bayly, 'The Origins of Swadeshi (Home Industry): Cloth and Indian Society, 1700–1930', in: *The Social Life of Things: Commodities in Cultural Perspective*, ed. Arjun Appadurai, (Cambridge, 1986), 285–321.

[4] P. Deans, 'Diminishing Returns? Prime Minister Koizumi's Visits to the Yasukuni Shrine in the Context of East Asian Nationalisms', *East Asia: An International Quarterly*, vol. 24, no. 3, (2007), 269–94.

> **THE BOMBAY CHRONICLE, SATURDAY, JULY 30, 1921.**
>
> ## BOYCOTT OF FOREIGN CLOTHES
>
> ## BONFIRE OF FOREIGN CLOTHES
>
> Shall take place at the Maidan near Elphinstone Mills Opp. Elphinstone Road Station on Sunday, 31st July, 1921.
>
> THE CEREMONY WILL BE PERFORMED BY
>
> ## MAHATMA GANDHIJI
>
> All are requested to attend in Swadeshi Clothes of Khadi. Those who have not given away their Foreign Clothes are requested to bring them to the Meeting.
>
> **SPECIAL ARRANGEMENT IS MADE FOR LADIES AND CHILDREN**
>
> IN MEMORY OF
>
> ## LOKMANYA TILAK
>
> PUBLIC MEETING AT CHAUPATI, 1st AUGUST 1921, AT 6-30 P. M.

Announcement of a bonfire of foreign clothes in Mumbai, 30 July 1921; note, the boycott meeting took place near the Elphinstone cotton mills, owned by the nationalist Umar Sobhani

The argument that boycotts filled the gap of limited formal powers must not be confused with the idea that boycotts were the weapon of choice only of the colonial underdog. There have also been historical situations where fiscal power was limited at the heart of the empire and boycotts became a popular vehicle for imperialists themselves. After the First World War, Britain was the largest empire on earth, but it was also still a Free Trade empire which refused to use its vast market at home and in the colonies to bargain for trade advantages with other countries. Until 1931, when Britain finally introduced a general tariff, there were no imperial preferences on any major commodities. Britain kept its door open to goods, regardless of their origin. Without the option of help from the state, in the mid and late 1920s imperial protectionists consequently turned to housewives, urging them to "buy British" and "buy Empire goods" in mass campaigns. These were not underdogs, seeking to throw off the shackles of empire; they were prosperous consumers hoping to strengthen imperial ties and hierarchies with the help of a "buycott", buying apples from their cousins in Canada and coffee from white farmers in Kenya.[5]

A second kind of magnetism between boycotts and the state has arisen in non-colonial settings, where the state itself served as a point of orientation for consumer activists. Here we are dealing not with a vacuum at the centre of power, but with states that have autonomy and capacities for action which boycotters seek to capture. This orientation has taken multiple forms. At its most basic, states and empires have helped structure the political imagination of activists, shaping their sense of the potential and legitimate space for political action, and its social and territorial limits. The early nineteenth-century anti-slavery movement in Britain is a good example. The campaign against consuming sugar grown by slaves was a strictly imperial affair. Activists targeted sugar from the colonial West Indies and the slave trade that involved British ships and colonies. The focus was on the British state and on stopping the traffic in imperial waters. The slave trade in other European empires was not targeted. For boycotters and anti-slavery activists this was primarily a British affair, politically and spiritually. The slave trade was sinful but it was Britain's sin specifically that mobilised British abolitionists. Their conscience was imperial. Their duty was to the slaves within the British empire and to their own souls as Britons, not to some apolitical or universal human entity. Their loyalty was to king and country. When the slave trade was abolished in the British empire in 1807, and slaves formally "emancipated" in 1833, the appetite for further consumer activism waned. Sin had been erased from the shores of the empire. That slavery continued in foreign empires was a matter for their own subjects.[6]

Today, boycotts are often cited for their supranational or global qualities, reaching fields of political action and social reform that lie outside the boundaries and capacities of nation-states. It is wrong to think that earlier

---

[5] Stephen Constantine, 'Bringing the Empire Alive': The Empire Marketing Board and Imperial Propaganda, 1926–33', in: *Imperialism and Popular Culture*, ed. John M. MacKenzie (1986), 192–231; Frank Trentmann, *Free Trade Nation: Commerce, Consumption, and Civil Society in Modern Britain* (Oxford, 2008), 228–40.

[6] Richard Huzzey, 'The Moral Geography of British Anti-Slavery Responsibilities', *Transactions of the Royal Historical Society, 6th series,* vol. 22, (2012), 111–39; Richard Huzzey, *Freedom Burning: Anti-Slavery and Empire in Victorian Britain* (Ithaca, 2012).

boycotts must have been stepping stones along the road to a global civil society. The Britons who boycotted slavery and its products would have been surprised by this. They operated within the territorial and mental limits of their imperial state. They were Britons, not cosmopolitans.

"East India Sugar not made by Slaves": a bowl used by abolitionists in the campaign against slavery, c. 1810–1820s. Wilberforce House Museum, Hull

In a third kind of relationship, consumer activism and the state developed something close to symbiosis. In the earlier cases, the state's capacities were mainly limited to war, taxation, and the regulation of trade. Boycotts, similarly, had limited functions, seeking to compensate for the lack of tariff autonomy and full state sovereignty. From the early twentieth century, the capacity and infrastructure of the modern state expanded dramatically, as states started to be actively involved in education, welfare, pensions, public health, waste management, and many other aspects of life. Many of the most basic aspects of consumption were regulated or reassessed by the state, from standards of hygiene and food safety all the way to key measurements such as the calorie, which rose to fame in the first half of the twentieth century and bore the mark of the American state and its nutritional research, military interests, and food diplomacy.[7] The

---

[7] Nick Cullather, 'The Foreign Policy of the Calorie', *The American Historical Review*, vol. 112, no. 2, (2007); John Burnett and Derek J. Oddy, eds., *The Origins and Development of Food Policies in Europe* (London, 1994); David F. Smith and Jim Phillips, eds., *Food, Science, Policy and Regulation in the Twentieth Century: International and Comparative Perspectives*

late nineteenth and early twentieth centuries, therefore, saw the rise not only of new forms of commercial branding and advertising but also of more extensive forms of public regulation, intervention, and propaganda. It was amidst these two forces that a new generation of consumer boycotts and buycotts sprang up: the black lists and white lists drawn up by the National Consumers League (NCL) in the United States, founded in 1899, and used by similar shopper leagues in Europe in their campaigns against sweatshops and retail stores with inhuman working conditions.

It needed incipient welfare states for activists to think that consumer boycotts might push governments to introduce tougher health and safety standards and improve working conditions. In the United States, the NCL under Florence Kelley did not so much try to raise consumer awareness for its own sake but did so in order to direct it at the state governments and the courts and abolish long working hours by law. Consumers, in this sense, were not doing good in the absence of the state, but were mobilised to push the state into doing more. In parts of Europe, the state was not only the target of buyer leagues, but sometimes was part of the family. In Imperial Germany, Martha von Bethmann-Hollweg, the president of the buyers' league founded in 1907, happened to be the wife of the Prussian Minister of the Interior and future Chancellor of Germany.

(London, 2000); Keir Waddington, *The Bovine Scourge: Meat, Tuberculosis and Public Health, 1850–1914* (Woodbridge, 2006); Heinz-Gerhard Haupt, *Konsum und Handel: Europa im 19. und 20. Jahrhundert* (Göttingen, 2002).

An exhibit of garments made by sweatshop labour, by the New York Consumers League, New York City, 1908. (Photographer: Lewis Wickes Hine; Source: Library of Congress)

The growing politicisation of consumer choice, then, was the result of a dialogue between state and civil society. Social movements used white lists and black lists to advance social reform and expand the reach of the state but, simultaneously, the state itself was becoming increasingly interested in modulating and disciplining what and how its citizens consumed. War made a major contribution to this process. In the First

World War, rationing was not ubiquitous but all belligerent states introduced salvage campaigns and war-time menus, exhorting citizens on the home front to change their habits in order to free up resources for their sons and brothers at the front. Savings campaigns preached individual discipline and "rational" consumption. The Second World War raised these interventions to a higher level, adding to the list the essential sources that powered daily practices: fuel and electricity. In Scandinavian countries, the state would also come to play a direct role in consumer advice and product testing.[8] Through war and welfare, the state thus played a critical role in opening up more and more aspects of private consumption to public view and subjecting them to "Dos and Don'ts". All this helped to extend the appeal and terrain of boycotts and buycotts, both directly, as with state-sponsored national products campaigns, and indirectly, by making private consumption a legitimate part of politics and popularising the notion that private consumers should think about the public consequences of their actions.

Moral Economy

The late twentieth century has seen a notable increase in the frequency and popularity of boycotts. In Denmark, for example, around one in five citizens was involved in one boycott or another in 1990. By 2004, every second person had joined one.[9] Such numbers and the growing support for particular causes, such as fair trade, have made it tempting to diagnose the coming of a new "moral economy", in which citizens use the power of their purse to inject ethics, reciprocity, and care into global neoliberal markets.[10] Globalisation here appears as the fertile ground for

---

[8] Iselin Theien, 'Planung und Partizipation in den regulierten Konsumgesellschaften Schwedens und Norwegens zwischen 1930 und 1960', *comparativ*, vol. 21, no. 3, 2011 67–78. Alain Chatriot, Marie-Emmanuelle Chessel, and Matthew Hilton, eds., *Au Nom du Consommateur: Consommation et politique en Europe et aux États-Unis au XX Siècle* (Paris, 2004).

[9] Magnus Boström, Andreas Føllesdal, Mikael Klintman, Michele Micheletti, and Mads P. Sørensen, *Political Consumerism: Its Motivations, Power, and Conditions in the Nordic Countries and Elsewhere* (København, 2005).

[10] See Gavin Fridell, 'Fair Trade and Neoliberalism: Assessing Emerging Perspectives', *Latin American Perspectives*, vol. 33, no. 6, (2006), 8–28; Gavin Fridell, *Fair Trade Coffee: The Prospects and Pitfalls of Market-Driven Social Justice* (Toronto, 2007). Cf. Frank Trentmann, 'Before "Fair Trade": Empire, Free Trade, and the Moral Economies of Food in the Modern World', *Environment and Planning D*, vol. 25, no. 6, (2007), 1079–1102.

transnational consumer activism, simultaneously weakening the state's reach and creating opportunities for ethical consumers to operate above and below the formal political arena of the nation-state.

How much is there in the link between globalisation and the moral economy of ethical consumers? A longer historical perspective can be useful. At first sight, the correlation is striking. The big eras in which boycotts took the stage were all periods marked by growing global integration: the late eighteenth-century boycotts against slave-grown sugar came on the heels of rapidly advancing trade in goods and people; the late nineteenth century completed the integration of a global food system and saw new transnational networks of finance and communication.

There is, however, a major difference between globalisation today and globalisation a century ago as far as the ethical horizon of caring consumers is concerned. In the two decades running up to the First World War, the primary concern of consumer leagues on both side of the Atlantic was local workers and shop assistants. Boycotts and buycotts targeted local factories and local shops. Caring was provincial. Today, by contrast, the main focus is on distant others. "5000 miles away a farmer is waiting to shake your hand," as a Fair Trade campaign poster puts it.[11] Coffee, cocoa, and bananas are the principal commodities that make up the fair trade shopping basket. Moral concern stretches from cafes in Stockholm and Zurich to farmers in Guatemala and Tanzania, although there is a debate whether it is possible to care for others across such distances.[12]

Of course, it might be argued that this migration of moral concerns from one's local community to distant others is only to be expected since earlier activism and reforms have rooted out sweatshops in the affluent North. Notwithstanding social legislation, however, this argument only holds partly true. The debate over a living wage continues in many affluent societies, and unhealthy working hours have been on the increase in the last two decades. The exploitation of migrant and seasonal workers has not vanished. With some notable exceptions—such as Sweden's debate about the poor condition of Eastern Europeans picking Swedish blueberries, or recent consumer boycotts in the United Kingdom against global

---

[11] See http://fairtrade.ca; http://www.thepowerofyou.org.nz/resources/, last accessed 24 January 2014.

[12] Joan C. Tronto, *Moral Boundaries: A Political Argument for an Ethic of Care* (New York, 1994).

corporations such as Amazon dodging local taxes[13]—these proximate links to a consuming lifestyle have been sidelined or altogether displaced by a concern for distant producers. Compared to the thousands of activities in the annual Fairtrade Fortnight, with people sporting banana suits, and visits from Central American farmers, there is remarkably little attention to injustices next door. Few diners use white lists or black lists for hotels and restaurants to improve the wage and working conditions of the people cleaning and cooking there.

To avoid misunderstanding, the point here is not to berate consumers in the North, let alone to ask them to shift their attention from distant others to close neighbours. It is rather to point to a remarkable shift in the horizon of consumer activists, and in the orientation and outlook of boycotts. How can we explain this transformation?

The literature on neoliberalism tends to portray globalisation as the withering away of the state, and it is certainly true that the power of the state is declining in the international economy, including the collapse of international quotas and commodity agreements in the 1980s which saw the shift to market-oriented, consumer-driven activism like fair trade. Even though frail or failing in its capacity, however, the welfare state of the mid-twentieth century continues to cast its shadow over core assumptions of social and political rights and responsibilities. Here lies a fundamental difference between boycotts in the early twentieth century and those today. The earlier generation was looking towards the state to help put things right at home, with welfare measures and legislation on wages and hours. Today's shoppers grew up after the welfare state and largely take for granted that such domestic social problems are (or should be) the domain of public policy, and not of consumer choice—it will be interesting to see how current austerity measures and cuts in social services might change this assumption. In the half-century since the Second World War, when welfare measures and public spending were expanding rapidly in the industrial West,[14] caring could be directed to fields further away where the power of the state did not reach. In this sense, Fair Trade added a new variation to consumer boycotts as substitutes of state power, by taking former battles to a supranational level. Welfarism thus left behind a new division of ethical labour between state and consumers.

[13] See http://www.ethicalconsumer.org/boycotts.aspx, last accessed at 10 September 2017.

[14] Peter H. Lindert, *Growing public: social spending and economic growth since the eighteenth century* (Cambridge, 2004).

All this does not mean that we should become nostalgic about some earlier progressive high-point in the history of boycotts. The focus on sweatshops and shop girls in the years around 1900 involved its own kind of forgetting and narrowing of moral concern. Significantly, the white label campaigns against sweatshops gathered momentum at the very time when globalisation was reaching its crescendo before the First World War. Never before had so many residents in New York, Paris, and London enjoyed so many benefits of cheap global commodities and materials, harvested and mined by cheap and exploited labour overseas. Yet few consumers in the rich North blinked an eye at violent and miserable working conditions in the poor South. In 1905, in *Harpers Monthly Magazine*, the radical journalist Henry Nevinson exposed the slave-like conditions on cocoa plantations in the Portuguese colonies of São Tomé and Príncipe, off the coast of West Africa. Unlike a century earlier, in the campaign against the slave trade, consumers did not rally to boycott chocolates made by Cadbury and Rowntree from cocoa from these islands. In the end, in 1909, it was the producers who took action and sourced their cocoa from other plantations.[15] Tea, coffee, rubber, and the many metals flowing into Europe from the colonies: none of these galvanised any consumer boycotts in this period, in spite of atrocious working conditions in mines and plantations. The closest Europeans came to any consumer boycott of colonial products was in imperial Germany, but here the anger was about coffee prices being too high, not too low.

The geographic narrowing of moral horizons happened alongside the local thickening of social caring and commitment in the transition from political to social citizenship. New progressive, communitarian, and social democratic ideals and actions stressed the mutual dependence and obligations between individual and community. Welfare reform and legislation were part of this local intensification. This process cannot simply be understood in terms of political culture, however, with commercial culture undergoing parallel shifts. Interestingly, these years also saw a European distancing from the exotic in the advertising, taste, and branding of overseas commodities. Instead of representing coffee and cocoa through exotic landscapes or non-European producers, and finding value in distance and rarity, European importers, refiners, and advertisers began to highlight the

---

[15] Henry Nevinson, *A modern slavery* (London, 1906); Lowell J. Satre, *Chocolate on trial: slavery, politics, and the ethics of business*, 1st ed. (Athens, 2005); Kevin Grant, *A Civilised Savagery: Britain and the New Slaveries in Africa, 1884–1926* (New York, 2005).

national qualities of chocolate and coffee, rebranding them with the help of national heroes like Arminius (who defeated Roman legions in 9 CE) and Barbarossa (Frederick I, the Holy Roman Emperor in the twelfth century) in Germany and Jeanne d'Arc (1412–1431) in France. It was Western manufacturing processes such as the extraction of cocoa butter and the creation of milk chocolate—rather than the foreign bean and its cultivation—that became the defining feature in an expanding mass market at home. Exotic cocoa was nationalised into "Swiss chocolate" and Cadbury's the "good old English cocoa" with pictures of the Swiss Matterhorn and a pastoral English countryside complete with shepherds. The growing importance of scientific quality control and health advertising in the food industries meant that when there were images of labour conditions they would increasingly be of healthy, vigorous English women in "Cadbury's garden factory" at Bournville, just outside Birmingham, and its workroom "with wide open windows that admit the fresh air from the well-kept gardens that surround it",[16] and not of plantations in Africa or Latin America. Non-European images never fully disappeared and retained some presence, especially in France. Still, advertising and marketing point to an increasingly provincial orientation and domestication of products that in the seventeenth and eighteenth centuries had been prized for their exotic origin, distance, and difference.[17]

POLITICAL ACTION

The idea of a new era of "moral economy" and consumer activism ushered in by globalisation in the late twentieth century often goes hand in hand with a narrative of "late-" or "post-modernity", where traditional party and parliamentary politics give way to lifestyle politics. For the sociologist

---

[16] Cadbury advert in *The Times*, 17 Oct. 1910, 6. For pastoral scenery, see *The Penny Illustrated Paper and Illustrated Times*, 4 Oct. 1902.

[17] For this argument, see Frank Trentmann, *Empire of Things: How We Became a World of Consumers, from the fifteenth century to the twenty-first* (London, 2016), ch. 3. For chocolate, see Roman Rossfeld, *Schweizer Schokolade: industrielle Produktion und kulturelle Konstruktion eines nationalen Symbols, 1860–1920* (Baden, 2007), for the English marketing of 'safe' Indian tea from the British Raj versus 'dirty' foreign Chinese tea, see Erika Rappaport, 'Packaging China: Foreign Articles and Dangerous Tastes in the Mid-Victorian Tea Party' in: *The Making of the Consumer: Knowledge, Power and Identity in the Modern World*, ed. Frank Trentmann, (Oxford and New York, 2006), 125–46, and now at length Erika Rappaport, *A Thirst for Empire: How Tea Shaped the Modern World* (Princeton, 2017).

Anthony Giddens, choice is the defining feature of the reflexive self in late modernity. The plurality of choice is the hallmark of everyday life: "we have no choice but to choose." Dress and diet, bodily regimes, and lifestyles thus produce a new kind of politics. "While emancipatory politics is a politics of life chances", Giddens writes, "life politics is a politics of lifestyle."[18] And, by extension, buycotts and boycotts emerge as dominant ways to express political voice and accomplish political objectives. Consumer activism is the beneficiary of this shift in politics from institutional structures to individual choice.

The thesis of late modernity has invited two opposed readings of the relationship between "new" and "traditional" modes of politics. One offers a positive interpretation. Lifestyle politics and boycotts here are emancipatory and inclusive, giving voice to citizen consumers who previously had little say in a political system organised around parties and collective producer interests, or who were excluded altogether. The other interpretation reaches a negative conclusion. Here boycotts and similar forms of lifestyle politics do not enrich politics but undermine it, by eroding trust in politicians and sapping interest in elections and parliamentary structures and procedures. Both these readings are historically doubtful.

Choice might have proliferated since the 1950s, but it is unhelpful to draw a sharp chronological break between modernity and late modernity and its styles of politics. As a political weapon, bodily sensitivity was highly developed in the late eighteenth century and was a widespread form of expression in the boycott of slave-grown sugar. The Baptist abolitionist William Fox in 1791 appealed to the people of Great Britain to abstain from using sugar grown by slaves, arguing that "in every pound of sugar used... we may be considered as consuming two ounces of human flesh."[19] Women were considered to have a particularly heightened sensibility, and the campaign appealed to their supposedly heightened sensitivity to feel disgust and outrage about such kinds of bodily contamination, indeed cannibalism. Similarly, body politics played its role in the campaigns against sweatshop labour in the years around 1900. Both these earlier boycott movements developed early kinds of transnational networks. This was not something that had to wait for "late modernity". There was a general rise in transnational movements and politics in the late nineteenth

---

[18] Anthony Giddens, *Modernity and Self-Identity* (Cambridge, 1991), quoted at pp. 81, 214.
[19] Quoted from Sussman, *Consuming Anxieties*, 155.

century, in tandem with the intensified global traffic in goods and peoples. At the level of boycotts, such movements had nationalist and imperialist programmes as well as progressive ones, as has been stressed previously. True, the main reference point was not individual lifestyle or a pluralism of subcultures, but this does not mean we should not recognise something like the hundred thousand conservative housewives setting up local "Buy British" stalls and campaigning to "buy empire goods" as a version of identity politics.

A second error is to assume that boycotts and "traditional" or formal politics must stand in a zero-sum relationship. The political scientists Dietlind Stolle, Marc Hooghe, and Michele Micheletti surveyed one thousand university students in Canada, Belgium, and Sweden. Two-thirds said that ethical considerations influenced their choice when buying food; for 40% it extended to clothing, for a third also to banks. Three out of four had boycotted or purchased a product specifically for ethical or political reasons. At the same time, they had a disproportionately high level of political engagement, read the newspaper, voted more frequently, and were more likely to belong to a party or help as a volunteer in an organisation. Many of them were critical of international organisations, like the United Nations, as well as of nation-states, but they were not alienated from politics as such.[20] Political consumption, these findings suggest, does not crowd out older forms of political commitment, nor does it pull previously silent or excluded citizens into new spaces of politics. Rather, there is a symbiotic relationship between new and old styles of politics: those who were most active in consumer boycotts were also more engaged in conventional forms of politics.

A final problem with the narrative of late modernity lies with its instinctive association of choice with personal lifestyle. The importance of choice, in this view, is a product of affluence after the Second World War and comes largely as a by-product of an enlarged assortment of goods and services which gave individuals new opportunities (and pressures) for creating their personal identity and finding their place in an ever more differentiated landscape of distinct groups and subcultures. Advertisers,

---

[20] M. Micheletti, D. Stolle, and M. Hoogh, 'Zwischen Markt und Zivilgesellschaft: Politischer Konsum als bürgerliches Engagement', in: *Zivilgesellschaft – national und transational*, eds. D. Gosewinkel, et al., (Berlin, 2003), 151–71. See also: Michele Micheletti and Dietlind Stolle, 'Swedish Political Consumers: Who They Are and Why They Use the Market as an Arena for Politics', in: *Political Consumerism: Its Motivations, Power, and Conditions in the Nordic Countries and Elsewhere*, eds. M. Boström, et al., (Oslo, 2005), 145–164.

corporations, and—from the 1970s—neo-liberal governments boosted the discourse of choice and naturalised it as part of public and private life. By the 1990s, ethical consumer movements like Fair Trade, too, had appropriated choice as a movement strategy, turning to individual consumers to effect global justice: "it is your choice".

Commercial and neo-liberal governmental pressures have certainly increased in the last few decades but, as a discourse and strategy of change, choice is older than affluence, with roots in liberal and progressive politics.[21] In the consumer and shopper leagues active on both sides of the Atlantic in 1900 and in the mass movement for free trade in Great Britain, the consumer was a citizen who made choices in the interests of the public good. "The consumer", the German social reformer Elisabeth von Knebel-Doeberitz explained in 1907, "was the clock which regulates the relationship between employer and employee". If the clock was driven by "selfishness, self-interest, thoughtlessness, greed, and avarice, thousands of our fellow beings have to live in misery and depression".[22] An individual's choice was connected to ways of living but also to an ethos of social duty—social Catholics and Christian reformers like von Knebel-Doeberitz played prominent roles in the buyers' leagues across Europe.

If the discourse of choice is older and richer than the recent neo-liberal strain, it is equally important not to confuse rhetoric with reality. Choice might dominate the discourse of fair trade and consumer boycotts, but often it is governments, public institutions, and firms which decide the success or failure of ethical consumer initiatives. Choice can be a marketing tool for campaigners to sign up individuals in support of fair trade initiatives and provide an appearance of democratic people power to local

---

[21] Frank Trentmann, 'The Modern Genealogy of the Consumer: Meanings, Identities and Political Synapses', in: *Consuming Cultures, Global Perspectives: Historical Trajectories, Transnational Exchanges*, eds. John Brewer and Frank Trentmann, (Oxford and New York, 2006), 19–69.

[22] Elisabeth von Knebel-Doeberitz, 'Die Aufgabe und Pflicht der Frau als Konsument', in: *Hefte der Freien Kirchlich-Sozialen Konferenz*, 40 (Berlin, 1907), 39, my translation. For the citizen consumer in the United States, see Lizabeth Cohen, *A Consumers' Republic: The Politics of Mass Consumption in Postwar America* (New York, 2003); Meg Jacobs, *Pocketbook Politics: Economic Citizenship in Twentieth-Century America* (Princeton, 2005); cf.: David Steigerwald, 'All Hail the Republic of Choice: Consumer History as Contemporary Thought', *The Journal of American History*, vol. 93, no. 2, (2006) 385–403. For Britain, see Matthew Hilton, *Consumerism in Twentieth-Century Britain* (Cambridge, 2003); Trentmann, *Free Trade Nation: Commerce, Consumption, and Civil Society in Modern Britain*.

authorities.²³ In many towns and canteens, fair trade coffee and other products have found their place thanks to changes in public provisioning, not individual decisions of shoppers at the till. Many companies, such as the British sugar giant Tate & Lyle, and public offices, like the Treasury, have made the decision for fair trade sugar or fair trade coffee for their employees and customers; in some instances, shoppers were not even aware the products they bought had switched to fair trade.²⁴ In Sweden, Germany, and the Netherlands, it has been municipalities that have been a crucial source of support for fair trade products. States thus remain vital allies for ethical consumerism in many contexts. Given the rhetorical ubiquity of choice, it is worth emphasising how, in the marketplace, individual consumer choice has never given more than a tiny support to ethical products and campaigns. In the last decade, fair trade products have enjoyed considerable growth each year, often in double figures, but starting out from a tiny share of the world market. The United Kingdom is now the biggest market for fair trade products in the world—in 2013, spending peaked at £1.8 billion. But this is still a miniscule fraction of consumer spending, amounting to barely £28 per person per year in Britain spent on fair trade coffee, bananas, roses, and all other fair trade products. To put this in perspective, the average household in Britain spent a hundred times that amount (£2880) in 2011 on food and non-alcoholic drinks alone.²⁵ Fairtrade sales fell to £1.6 billion in 2014 and 2015. In the other rich countries even less is spent on fair trade items.²⁶

On the eve of the First World War, the British feminist and socialist consumer advocate Teresa Billington-Greig, wrote that "[w]e are all more or less profiteers." Consumers loved cheap goods and were, in part, responsible for low wages and appalling working conditions. One hundred years and countless boycotts later, her diagnosis retains its troubling force.

---

²³ Alice Malpass, Clive Barnett, Nick Clarke, and Paul Cloke, 'Problematizing Choice: Responsible Consumers and Sceptical Citizens', in: *Governance, Citizens, and Consumers: Agency and Resistance in Contemporary Politics*, eds. Mark Bevir and Frank Trentmann, (Basingstoke, 2007), 231–56; Alice Malpass, Paul Cloke, Clive Barnett, and Nick Clarke, 'Fairtrade urbanism? The politics of place beyond place in the Bristol fairtrade city campaign', *International Journal of Urban and Regional Research*, vol. 31, no. 3, (2007), 633–45.

²⁴ Kathryn Wheeler, *Fair Trade and the Citizen-Consumer* (Basingstoke, 2012).

²⁵ Office for National Statistics, chapter 5 'Weekly household expenditure, an analysis of the regions of England and countries of the United Kingdom', 8 Feb 2013, available at http://www.ons.gov.uk/ons/dcp171766_297746.pdf, last accessed 22 January 2015.

²⁶ *The Guardian*, 3 Sept. 2014.

CONCLUSION

Consumer boycotts tend to be viewed through the lens of civil society, not least by their advocates today. This chapter has suggested an alternative view, locating consumer boycotts in relationship to the state. Today, boycotts often receive attention for operating in transnational spaces, above and beyond the level of the state. But in the course of modern history, they have at least as importantly looked towards the state, either fighting to bolster the incomplete power of a state or to capture state power from a rival. Scholarly interest in boycotts initially focused on their connection to new social movements—and, like other social movements before them, there has been an instinctive (and understandable) tendency towards hagiography, to tell a heroic story of the unfolding of a progressive present. After two decades of inquiry, we are now ready for more critical perspectives. The study of boycotts here can learn lessons from the scholarly debate about civil society, where the earlier interest in the pure essence of civil society as an independent domain outside the state gave way to a recognition of their multiple interactions and interdependence.[27] For the study of boycotts, retrieving such links between civil society and the state has the advantage of showing their entanglement in the structures of power in modern history. Boycotts, from this perspective, were not only reactions to power but also instruments of power, privileging some groups, territories and causes over others.

---

[27] John Keane, *Civil society and the state: new European perspectives* (London, 1988); John A. Hall, *Civil society: theory, history, comparison* (Cambridge, 1995); John A. Hall and Frank Trentmann, eds., *Civil Society: A Reader in History, Theory and Global Politics* (Houndmills, 2004); Nancy Bermeo and Philip Nord, eds., *Civil Society Before Democracy: Lessons from Nineteenth-Century France* (Lanham, 2000); Stefan-Ludwig Hoffmann, *Civil Society, 1750–1914* (Basingstoke, 2006).

CHAPTER 3

In Defense of the Nation: Protectionism and Boycotts in the Habsburg Lands, 1844–1914

Michael L. Miller

Any discussion of economic nationalism in Central and Eastern Europe must begin with Friedrich List (1789–1846), the nineteenth-century German economist who is best known for his advocacy of trade protectionism. In his magnum opus, *The National System of Political Economy* (1841–1844), List objected to the laissez-faire policies of economic liberalism, singling out free trade for particularly sharp criticism. Free trade, he argued, stimulated economic growth in countries with internationally competitive industrial sectors, but it actually impeded economic growth in countries whose "backward" economies were based on the export of agricultural goods. Unless something could be done to level the playing field, untrammeled free trade would only widen the economic gap between industrialized and agricultural countries, making it well-nigh impossible for the latter to "catch up." In an effort to correct the imbalance, List proposed that agricultural countries actively develop new branches of industry, using protective tariffs to shield these branches until they became internationally competitive. Known as infant-industry tariff protection,

M. L. Miller (✉)
Central European University, Budapest, Hungary
e-mail: millerm@ceu.edu

© The Author(s) 2019
D. Feldman (ed.), *Boycotts Past and Present*, Palgrave Critical Studies of Antisemitism and Racism,
https://doi.org/10.1007/978-3-319-94872-0_3

this measure is the cornerstone of List's economic policy, and, not surprisingly, it was widely cited by the national protectionist associations and national boycott movements in Central and Eastern Europe and that will be the subject of this chapter.

List's dispute with economic liberals is often reduced to simple policy differences (e.g., free trade vs. protectionism), but—as the political economist Eric Helleiner has argued—List's real dispute with Adam Smith (1723–1790), David Ricardo (1772–1823), John Stuart Mill (1806–1873), and Richard Cobden (1804–1865) was about the importance of the nation.[1] These economic liberals were, above all, cosmopolitans, and their primary frame of reference was not the nation, but rather "humanity" or "mankind." For them, free trade was not just a means for promoting economic prosperity but, in the words of John Stuart Mill, it was nothing less than "the principal guarantee of the peace of the world."[2] This may sound like a rather audacious—or even utopian—claim, but economic liberals believed that free trade could create ties of interdependence that would, in turn, foster a peaceful world community. In the words of Richard Cobden (1839), free trade "will act on the moral world as the principle of gravitation in the universe, drawing men together, thrusting aside any antagonism of race, and creed, and language, and uniting us in the bonds of eternal peace."[3]

For Friedrich List, however, such "boundless cosmopolitanism" ignored the fact that the world was divided into nations, at different and unequal stages of industrialization, each with distinctive—and often competing—national interests.[4] While free trade might be advantageous for Britain (home to the above-mentioned economic liberals), it was an impediment for "late-comers to industrialization" such as the German Confederation (where List was from).[5] And because List viewed the nation—and not humanity—as the most salient and meaningful collective community, he insisted that economic policy should not only aim to increase a nation's economic prosperity, but also to bolster a nation's

---

[1] My reading of List is largely influenced by Eric Helleiner, 'Economic Nationalism as a Challenge to Economic Liberalism? Lessons from the 19th Century,' *International Studies Quarterly*, vol. 46, (2002), 307–329.

[2] Helleiner, "Economic Nationalism," 313.

[3] Helleiner, "Economic Nationalism," 313.

[4] Helleiner, "Economic Nationalism," 311.

[5] Ivan T. Berend, *History Derailed: Central and Eastern Europe in the Long Nineteenth Century*, 140.

culture and power. For him, trade protectionism was a means to multiple ends: developing a robust national economy and, at the same time, strengthening national pride, glory, and self-sufficiency.

List's policy recommendations were developed primarily with sovereign nation-states in mind, but they found particular resonance in the multinational (and multi-confessional) Habsburg Empire, where economic life was largely stratified along national (or confessional) lines. I hesitate to use the term "nation" in this period, because many of the nations that emerged out of the ruins of the Habsburg Empire were still being imagined and constructed in the middle of the nineteenth century. And, as the Hungarian case readily demonstrates, economic nationalism was an integral part of the nation-building process. In the 1840s, Hungary was part of the Habsburg (or Austrian) Empire and nationalists such as Lajos Kossuth (1802–1894) hoped to reduce Hungary's "colonial dependence" on Austria, in part by modernizing its "backward" agricultural economy and cultivating new branches of industry. In 1846, Kossuth wrote the following:

> Anyone who interprets the term "nation" according to the criteria of the nineteenth century must be aware of the fact that those who do not possess the independent levers of civilization are only a people, or race, but cannot be treated as a nation. Among these levers, the most significant ones are trade and the manufacturing industries. Without them one can exist as a country, but not as a nation. And we Hungarians want to be considered as a nation by standards set by the present century.[6]

Kossuth was strongly influenced by List, who had visited Hungary in 1842, and whose book, *The National System of Political Economy*, had been published in Hungarian in 1843.[7] A protective tariff was not an option within the internal borders of the Habsburg Empire, so Kossuth and his associates resorted to another form of protectionism, namely a boycott of imported goods. In 1844, they established the Országos Védegylet (National Defense League), whose members pledged not to

---

[6] Quoted in Andrew Janos, *The Politics of Backwardness in Hungary, 1825–1945* (Princeton, 1982), 67.

[7] Fridrik List, *A politikai gazdálkodás nemzeti rendszere*, 2 vols., translated by Antal Sárváry (Kőszeg, 1843). See also Gottfried Fittbogen, *Friedrich List in Ungarn* (Berlin, 1942), and Eugene Wendler, *Friedrich List (1789–1846): A Visionary Economist with Social Responsibility* (Heidelberg, 2015), 233–241.

buy foreign (i.e., Austrian) manufactured goods for a period of six years. The League was introduced by one of its founders in the following terms:

> Under different conditions we would have resorted to the instrument of protective tariff for the advancement of national welfare. However, under the present conditions, our only hope lies in the tenacity of our fellow citizens. Since we cannot establish customs protection on our borders, we will have to set up ramparts at the thresholds of our own homes.[8]

In word and image, the founders of the National Defense League portrayed it as a purely defensive organization, and its slogan ("Buy Hungarian!") appealed first and foremost to a sense of affirmative national pride. Within a few months, over 100,000 people signed up and, for a while, aristocratic ladies even donned Hungarian peasant garb instead of the latest Parisian fashions.[9] The excitement did not last long, and Hungary was quite fortunate that it did not. As István Deák has noted, if Kossuth had succeeded in his protectionist campaign, "he would have ruined the nascent Hungarian economy."[10] Almost no manufactured goods were produced in Hungary in the 1840s, and Hungary's infant industries relied heavily on Austrian imports. Friedrich List admired the League's ambitions, but, at this stage, he viewed its methods as "imprudent, misguided and harmful" and its leaders as "overly sanguine."[11] The League could certainly dream about economic self-sufficiency, but in reality this goal was far away—even its "Buy Hungarian!" lapel buttons had to be manufactured in Vienna.

The significance of the National Defense League should be sought in the political rather than the economic sphere. Its economic impact was quite limited, and potentially even detrimental, but, like many boycott movements, it helped mobilize public opinion—to the tune of 100,000 supporters. It helped launch Lajos Kossuth's political career, and it gave momentum to a separatist ethos that fueled Hungary's anti-Habsburg

---

[8] Janos, *The Politics of Backwardness*, 68.

[9] Domokos Kosáry, *Kossuth és a Védegylet: A magyar nacionalizmus történetéhez* (Budapest, 1942), 59.

[10] István Deák, *The Lawful Revolution: Louis Kossuth and the Hungarians, 1848–1849* (New York, 1979), 52–53.

[11] Kosáry, *Kossuth és a Védegylet*, 83–84; Deák, *The Lawful Revolution*, 53.

revolution and war of independence in 1848–1849 and infused Hungarian nationalism until the dissolution of the Habsburg Empire in 1918.[12]

If economic liberalism was about creating ties of interdependence, then economic nationalism was about severing ties of interdependence by building separate, self-sufficient (or "autarchic") national economies. In Central and Eastern Europe, where the truncated class structure of many peasant-based nations left essential branches of the economy—such as credit and commerce—in the hands of other national or confessional groups, this meant that building a fully fledged national economy often entailed driving out members of "other" national or confessional groups.[13] One of the principal institutions in this exclusionary nation-building process was the credit or trade cooperative, a kind of community self-help association that aimed to eliminate middlemen and intermediaries from the emerging market economy. As Torsten Lorenz has observed in a recent volume on this subject, cooperatives in Eastern Europe were "tightly interwoven with the national movements and seen by their leaders as a tool for strengthening the whole, ethnically bordered nation."[14] Catherine Albrecht has shown, in the case of the Bohemian Lands, how the cooperative movement—which began there in the 1850s—"contributed to the separation of Czech and German society and to the consolidation of each group around a national principle."[15] Likewise, in Galicia, they contributed to the separation of Polish and Ruthenian society[16], and in Transylvania, to the separation of Romanian, Saxon, and Hungarian society.[17] Other, similar examples abound, especially in the multinational western borderlands of the Russian Empire.

---

[12] Janos, *The Politics of Backwardness*, 68; George Barany, 'The Age of Royal Absolutism, 1790–1848', in: *A History of Hungary*, eds. Peter Sugar et al., (Bloomington, 1990), 201.

[13] Torsten Lorenz, 'Introduction: Cooperatives in Ethnic Conflicts,' in: *Cooperatives in Ethnic Conflicts: Eastern Europe in the 19th and Early 20th Century*, (Berlin, 2006), 16–17.

[14] Lorenz, "Introduction," 9.

[15] Catherine Albrecht, 'Nationalism in the Cooperative Movement in Bohemia,' in: *Cooperatives in Ethnic Conflicts*, 227.

[16] Kai Struve, 'Peasant Emancipation and National Integration. Agrarian Circles, Village Reading Rooms, and Cooperatives in Galicia,' in: *Cooperatives in Ethnic Conflicts*, 229–250.

[17] Attila Hunyadi, 'Three Paradigms of Cooperative Movements with Nationalist Taxonomy in Transylvania,' in: *Cooperatives in Ethnic Conflicts*, 59–102; on the Saxon Raiffeisen movement in Transylvania, see Gábor Egry, 'Az erdélyi szász Raiffeisen-mozgalom kezdetei,' *AETAS*, (2004/1), 100–131.

Of course, in a region where Jews—as a typical "middle-man minority"—were highly concentrated in money-lending and trade, antisemitism came to play an outsize role in the cooperative movement, especially in the late nineteenth and early twentieth centuries. Credit cooperatives were founded, in large part, to supply secure and affordable credit to the rural poor who had no other source of credit apart from high-interest— or "usurious"—loans (to use the jargon of the day). Antisemites saw usury as "the primary evil associated with the Jews," so even non-antisemitic cooperative movements—like the Raiffeisen movement in late nineteenth-century Germany—inevitably shared affinities with openly antisemitic cooperative movements due to a shared preoccupation with the fight against "usury."[18] Friedrich Wilhelm Raiffeisen (1818–1888), father of the rural co-op movement, viewed cooperatives as a form of "institutionalized neighborly love" and discouraged attacks on Jews, but many others joined the cooperative movement with the more aggressive goal of achieving full "emancipation from the Jews."[19] This raises an important question: If antisemites and non-antisemites are motivated by different ideologies, yet use identical means to achieve an identical goal, can one make a meaningful distinction between them? Or, as David Peal put it in his article on cooperative movements in rural Germany, was the Raiffeisen movement simply an example of "antisemitism by other means"?

In the multinational Habsburg Empire, where the battlefronts were increasingly drawn along national—not confessional—lines, Jews often found themselves caught between competing nationalities: between Czechs and Germans, Slovaks and Hungarians, or Ruthenians and Poles. The Bohemian Lands serve as an illustrative case. In the first half of the nineteenth century, one could still speak of an inclusive, territorially-defined "Bohemian" identity in the Bohemian Lands, but with the sharpening of national feeling in the second half of the century, Bohemians gradually became "Czechs" and "Germans"—two mutually exclusive national groups fighting for their own political, cultural, and economic rights.[20] In mixed-language areas, the political, cultural, and economic

---

[18] David Peal, 'Antisemitism by Other Means? The Rural Cooperative Movement in Late Nineteenth-Century Germany,' *Leo Baeck Institute Yearbook*, vol. 32, (1987), 135, 148.

[19] Peal, "Antisemitism by Other Means?" 144–45, 148.

[20] Catherine Albrecht, 'The Rhetoric of Economic Nationalism in the Bohemian Boycott Campaigns of the Late Habsburg Monarchy,' *Austrian History Yearbook*, vol. 32, (2001), 47;

realms were fully intertwined, turning seemingly mundane decisions—such as which language to speak, which school to send your children to, where to do your shopping, or even which bicycle club to join—into public declarations of support for one of the competing national movements. Neutrality was rarely an option, and Jews—who were more likely to speak German than Czech—were often suspect in the eyes of Czech nationalists. So, too, were "amphibians" (*obojživelníky*)—as individuals who actively participated in both Czech and German cultural life were derisively called.[21] Indeed, with the hardening of linguistic, cultural, and political boundaries at the end of the nineteenth century, there was little tolerance—or trust—for such border-crossers.

It was in this highly charged context that boycott campaigns emerged in the Bohemian Lands in the 1890s, with the slogans *Svůj k svému* (Each to his own) in Czech and *Kauft nur bei den Deutschen* (Buy only from Germans) in German. As a rule, these slogans framed the boycott campaigns as defensive measures that drew on traditions of self-help. This was also the case in early twentieth-century Russian (Congress) Poland, where the largely antisemitic boycott movement used the slogan *Swój do swego po swoje*, a Polish variant of "Each to his own."[22]

In the case of the Bohemian Lands, the anti-Czech boycotts and anti-German boycotts had different purposes and employed different tactics.[23] Bohemian Germans were a beleaguered minority, living in towns and districts that had once been solidly German, but were now facing an onslaught of Czech-speaking newcomers who demanded the right to use the Czech language in public affairs. The anti-Czech boycott campaign aimed to "preserve demographic, cultural and economic control," and did so by employing rent and employment boycotts intended to keep the Czechs—and, by extension, the Czech cultural threat—at bay.[24] Czechs, on the

---

Jeremy King, *Budweisers into Czechs and Germans: A Local History of Bohemian Politics, 1848–1948* (Princeton, 2002).

[21] Jindřich Toman, 'Shadows of Anti-Semitism: Jan Neruda on Jews,' *Judaica Bohemiae*, vol. XLVI, (2011), 23–49.

[22] Thomas David and Elisabeth Spilman, 'Proto-Economic-Nationalism in the Early Nineteenth Century', in: *History and Culture of Economic Nationalism in East Central Europe*, eds. Helga Schultz and Eduard Kubu, (Berlin, 2006), 89–108; Konrad Zieliński, Swój do swego! O stosunkach polsko-żydowskich w przeddzień Wielkiej Wojny, *Kwartalnik Historii Żydów*, vol. 211, (2004), 325–346.

[23] Albrecht, "The Rhetoric of Economic Nationalism," 56–57.

[24] Albrecht, "The Rhetoric of Economic Nationalism," 56–57.

other hand, constituted an overwhelming majority in the Bohemian Lands, but—in the face of the German political and economic elite—they had not yet succeeded in establishing their ultimate goal of economic self-sufficiency. The anti-German boycott campaign was directed against German manufacturers and retailers in general, but its primary targets were German-Jewish retailers in the Bohemian Lands. Like the founders of the National Defense League in Hungary, the leaders of the anti-German boycott campaign called on Czechs to exercise national discipline and purchase only Czech products. Like the National Defense League, *Svůj k svému* was, in Catherine Albrecht's terms "a practical extension of Friedrich List's concept of 'national economy' to the Czech situation."[25]

Even though Jews were the primary targets of the anti-German boycott in the Bohemian Lands, not all proponents of the boycott campaign were avowed antisemites. As scholars have noted, the *Svůj k svému* catch phrase, which radical Czech nationalists popularized at the end of the nineteenth century, was originally a rallying cry for Pan-Slavic solidarity.[26] František Palacký (1798–1876), a prominent Czech historian and political leader, used the phrase in an 1871 speech to refer to the linguistic and emotional bond between Czechs and other Slavs. Albín Bráf (1851–1912), a liberal Czech political economist who employed the phrase in his works, was a committed opponent of antisemitism.[27] On the other hand, Karel Adámek (1840–1918), the anti-liberal author of *A Word about the Jews* (1899), was rather disingenuous in his disavowal of antisemitism. As Michal Frankl has pointed out, Adámek combined his anti-liberal stance with "views that one usually identifies as antisemitic."[28] He did keep some distance from the organized antisemitic movement in the Bohemian Lands, but, like

---

[25] Catherine Albrecht, 'National Economy or Economic Nationalism in the Bohemian Crownlands 1848–1914,' in: *Labyrinth of Nationalism, Complexities of Diplomacy: Essays in Honor of Charles and Barbara Jelavich*, ed. Richard Frucht, (Columbus, 1992), 70.

[26] Michal Frankl, *"Prag ist nunmehr Antisemitisch": Tschechischer Antisemitismus am Ende des 19. Jahrhunderts*, translated by Michael Wögerbauer (Berlin, 2011), 86. Originally published in Czech as *"Emancipace od židů" český antisemitismus na konci 19. století* (Prague, 2007).

[27] Albín Bráf, *České a německé "svůj k svému"* (Prague, 1911); Michal Frankl, *"Prag ist nunmehr Antisemitisch,"* 86; Karel B. Müller, *Češi, občanská společnost a evropské výzvy* (Prague, 2016), 107–129.

[28] Karel Adámek, *Slovo o židech* (Chrudim, 1899); Michael Frankl, *"Prag ist nunmehr Antisemitisch,"* 84.

many of his kindred spirits, he viewed Jewish economic power as an obstacle to Czech political and economic aspirations.

Albín Bráf notwithstanding, the *Svůj k svému* movement was rife with antisemitism, and its spokesmen constantly vilified the Jews as an obstacle to Czech national rebirth. The political economist Cyril Horáček (1862–1943) stands out in this regard.[29] In an anonymously published book, *Our Economic Failures* (1894), Horáček characterized Czechs as "a nation of beggars," and he blamed this sad reality on the economic liberalism of the Czech national movement.[30] Horáček believed that the rebirth of the Czech nation followed three chronological stages—literary, political, and economic—and that it was time to embark on the third, economic, stage.[31] The problem was that the Czechs, a predominantly agricultural nation, could never hope to compete with the Jews, whose "special racial characteristics" predisposed them to trade, commerce, and speculation. The "dangerous economic superiority" of the Jews was evident in all branches of the Bohemian economy, and it behooved the Czechs to do something about it. Under the slogan *Svůj k svému*, Horáček called for "self-help in the higher, national sense, when the nation as a social unit can only rely on its own strength." As Michal Frankl has put it, "For Horáček, antisemitism was an integral part of the economic renewal of the Czech nation and is only understandable in the context of his antiliberal social and economic ideology."[32] Indeed, for Horáček, Jews were to blame, not only for siding with Germans in the Czech-German conflict, but also for thwarting the economic development of the Czech nation. He viewed an economic boycott against Jewish retailers and manufacturers as a necessary measure to ensure the economic self-sufficiency of his own erstwhile "nation of beggars."

The anti-Czech and anti-German boycott campaigns employed tactics that have become standard practice in boycott campaigns to this day. The campaigns labeled businesses, products, and individuals as Czech or German,

---

[29] Frankl, *"Prag ist nunmehr Antisemitisch,"* 79–84.

[30] [Cyril Horáček], *Naše hospodářské nedostatky* (Chrudim, 1900). See Frankl, *"Prag ist nunmehr Antisemitisch,"* 79–84.

[31] Interestingly, Miroslav Hroch, the Czech scholar of nationalism, outlines three similar stages in his monograph, *Social Preconditions of National Revival in Europe: A Comparative Analysis of the Social Composition of Patriotic Groups among the Smaller European Nations* (Cambridge, 1985), originally published as *Die Vorkämpfer der nationalen Bewegungen bei der kleinen Völker Europas* (Prague, 1968).

[32] Frankl, *"Prag ist nunmehr Antisemitisch,"* 82–83.

often with the help of newspapers that exposed the hidden backgrounds or supposed national sympathies of proprietors, or published lists of people seen shopping at boycotted stores.[33] Nationalist associations established offices to oversee the boycott and published address books that listed Czech or German business, indicating which ones should be patronized and which ones should be boycotted. Signs were also placed in windows, declaring businesses to be "pure German" or "pure Czech," and in 1904 the Czech National Council even issued a special stamp to mark Czech goods.[34] (Two years later, in 1906, Hungarian noblewomen and students introduced a tulip-shaped insignia to mark goods produced in Hungary.)[35]

In some respects, the Czech stamp and the Hungarian tulip can be seen as early attempts at nation-branding, efforts to convince customers to purchase a product or patronize a business not because of its inherent quality or value, but because of its national origin. In fact, such nation-branding played a highly important propagandistic role. Even if the quality of a "national" product was shoddy, the consumer could still find comfort in knowing that he or she was performing a service to his or her nation by supporting the growth of domestic industry. As Rudolf Jaworski has somewhat cynically observed, "it was simply easier to claim the uniqueness of one's own national culture than to plausibly demonstrate the productivity and competitiveness of one's own national economy'."[36]

As contemporaries pointed out, it was also difficult to demonstrate the effectiveness of boycotts in achieving a long-term goal, be it cultural preservation or economic self-sufficiency.[37] A critic of boycott campaigns argued that rational market forces would always win out over irrational national sentiments. He summed it up as follows:

> In the end, the implementation of a boycott depends on material conditions that are seldom met. As a rule, when selling wares or services, the determining factor is the difference between use value and exchange value. A matter is evaluated based purely on private economic interest and reason. The boycott, in contrast, comes from a community and makes an appeal to

---

[33] Albrecht, "The Rhetoric of Economic Nationalism," 59.

[34] Albrecht, "The Rhetoric of Economic Nationalism," 59.

[35] Rudolf Jaworski, 'Zum ökonomischer Interessenvertretung und nationalkultureller Selbstbehauptung. Zum Wirtschaftsnationalismus in Ostmitteleuropa vor 1914,' *Zeitschrift für Ostmitteleuropaforschung*, vol. 53, no. 2 (2004), 267.

[36] Jaworski, "Zum ökonomischer Interessenvertretung," 267.

[37] Albrecht, "The Rhetoric of Economic Nationalism," 60.

emotion. In some individuals, an inner excitement can be sparked that goes against rational, private economic interest. This excitement, however, gradually dissipates . . .[38]

Seen from this perspective, one could argue that the primary long-term impact of economic boycott—be it the anti-Austrian *Országos Védegylet* in Hungary of the 1840s, the anti-German *Svůj k svému* campaign in late nineteenth-century Bohemia, or the anti-Jewish *Swój do swego po swoje* campaign in early twentieth-century Russian (Congress) Poland—was never going to be in the economic sphere. In fact, in the context of the Habsburg Empire (and the western borderlands of the Russian Empire), boycott campaigns were a sign of political radicalization that, to a large extent, acknowledged the failure of self-help associations, credit cooperatives, and gradual industrialization to produce separate, self-sufficient national economies in a speedy manner. To paraphrase David Peal, they constituted "nationalist politics by other means."

One can discern a palpable sense of frustration, even impatience, among the boycott activists in the multinational Habsburg Empire—frustration at the stunted growth of their putative nations, which were confined to a "prison of nations" and thereby unable to develop a fully fledged social structure, a fully fledged national economy or, to use Kossuth's felicitous term, "the independent levers of civilization." As subjected peoples, without clearly defined territorial borders, these nations-in-formation could not introduce protective tariffs, customs protection, or any of Friedrich List's policies, which were designed to help sovereign nation-states become competitive on the inter-state level. In this respect, we can understand boycotts as an adaptation of List's ideas to the conditions of a composite, multinational empire, as a tool to help putative nations "catch up" and become competitive, first on the intra-state level, and then, perhaps, on the inter-state level.

The boycott campaign was not necessarily a wholesale rejection of economic liberalism. In fact, it can be seen as an attempt to merely defer economic liberalism until the conditions were ripe for free trade—until a particular national group had obtained "the independent levers of civilization" necessary to participate in the community of nations on equal terms. In fact, this corresponds with List's stated goal of promoting a nation's

---

[38] Josef Gruntzel, "Der Boycott als handelspolitische Waffe," *Weltwirtschaftliches Archiv*, vol. 9, (1917), 241.

economic development with the ultimate goal of "prepar[ing] it for admission into the universal society of the future."[39] Indeed, one can even discern a certain cosmopolitan mindset in List's writings, but for him the nation—and not humanity—was the most salient collective community, the primary bearer of meaning. He probably would have agreed with Johann Gottlieb Fichte (1762–1814), another economic nationalist, who distinguished between patriotism and cosmopolitanism in the following terms: "Cosmopolitanism is the will that the purpose of humanity be achieved. Patriotism is the will that this purpose be fulfilled in the nation to which we ourselves belong, and that the results spread from it to the whole of humanity . . . Cosmopolitanism must necessarily become patriotism."[40]

---

[39] Helleiner, "Economic Nationalism," 314.

[40] Quoted in Michael L. Miller and Scott Ury, 'Cosmopolitanism: the End of Jewishness,' *European Review of History*, vol. 17, no. 3, (June 2010), 341. On Fichte's economic nationalism, see Isaac Nakhimovsky, *The Closed Commercial State: Perpetual Peace and Commercial Society from Rousseau to Fichte* (Princeton, 2011), and Richard T. Gray, 'Economic Romanticism: Monetary Nationalism inn Johann Gottlieb Fichte and Adam Müller,' *Eighteenth Century Studies*, vol. 36, no. 4, (Summer 2003), 535–557.

CHAPTER 4

The Enemy Within: The Anti-Jewish Boycott and Polish Right-Wing Politics in the Early Twentieth Century

Grzegorz Krzywiec

INTRODUCTION[1]

At the beginning of the twentieth century, Polish-Jewish relations in Warsaw were aggravated by concerns about 'Jewish dominance'. It was in this context that an anti-Jewish boycott developed and took meaning.

---

[1] Much has already been written about the role of the elections to the Fourth Duma in 1912 in the Kingdom of Poland, then a part of the Russian Empire, and their significance for Polish-Jewish relations in the early twentieth century. Robert Blobaum, 'The Politics of Antisemitism in the Fin-de-Siècle Warsaw', *Journal of Modern History*, vol. 73, (2001), 294–305; Pascal Tress, *Wahlen im Weichselland. Die Nationaldemokraten in Russisch-Polen und die Duma wahlen 1905–1912* (Stuttgart, 2007), 361–383; S. D. Corrsin, *Warsaw before the First World War: Poles and Jews in the Third City of the Russian Empire, 1880–1919* (Boulder, 1990), 89–104; idem, *Polish-Jewish Relations before the First World in Warsaw*, 'Gal-Ed: On the History of the Jews in Poland', vol. 11, (1989), 31–53; Paweł Korzec, *Juifs en Pologne*, (Paris, 1980), 42–45; Władysław Pobóg-Malinowski, *Narodowa Demokracja 1887–1918. Fakty i Dokumenty*, 2nd ed. (Londyn, 1998),

G. Krzywiec (✉)
Institute of History at the Polish Academy of Sciences, Warszawa, Poland

© The Author(s) 2019
D. Feldman (ed.), *Boycotts Past and Present*, Palgrave Critical Studies of Antisemitism and Racism,
https://doi.org/10.1007/978-3-319-94872-0_4

Poland as an independent state had disappeared from the European map with the partition of the Polish-Lithuanian Commonwealth into three parts by Prussia, Habsburg Austria, and the Russian Empire, between 1772 and 1795. The majority of Polish lands, and the largest number of Polish Jews (about 500,000), fell under the Tsarist rule. With its Jewish community numbering over 200,000, Warsaw was the epicentre of the Jewish population in Europe and a microcosm of the political and ethnic tensions present throughout the Congress Poland (the Kingdom of Poland, also known as Russian Poland), and to some extent in the other former Polish territories.

In 1912, arrangements for the elections to the Fourth State Duma were the catalyst for controversy over Jewish influence, which went on to trigger a nationwide storm. The Russian administration decided to require the registration of those entitled to elect representatives in the Duma. Among the 83 electors for a deputy from Warsaw, there were 46 Jews, comprising 55 per cent of the electorate. When in mid-August the government released these figures on the eligible and registered voters, this news came as a shock to Poles.[2] Most of the Polish public, whether on the political right or the centre-left, responded by forming a united front, which included Jews, to oppose any separate Jewish lists in order to ensure the election of a Polish delegate. However, the first and largest nationalist party in the Polish lands, Narodowa Demokracja (National Democracy) or Endecja (its members were called *Endeks*), insisted that there could be no alliance with Jewish voters. The nationalist press claimed that the only way to defeat 'the Jewish threat' was for all Poles to rally around National Democracy. Everyone who opposed the Endeks, it was said, was taking their cue directly from the Jews.

209–210; Mieczysław Sobczak, *Kwestia żydowska w kampanii wyborczej Romana Dmowskiego do IV Dumy Państwowej w roku 1912*, 'Prace Naukowe Akademii Ekonomicznej we Wrocławiu', no. 622, Nauki filozoficzno-historyczne (1992), 106–111; idem, *Narodowa Demokracja wobec kwestii żydowskiej na ziemiach polskich przed I wojną* (Wrocław, 2007) 185–230; Theodore R. Weeks, *From Assimilation to Antisemitism. The Jewish Question in Poland, 1850–1914* (De Kalb, 2005), 163–165. For the specific course of the campaign see G. Krzywiec, *Kampania wyborcza Romana Dmowskiego do IV Dumy Państwowej w Warszawie w 1912 roku. Przyczynek do studiów nad mobilizacją nacjonalistyczną*, 'Kwartalnik Historii Żydów', no. 1, (2015), 22–52; idem, *The Polish Intelligensia in the Face of the Jewish Question*, 'Acta Poloniae Historica', no. 100, (2009), 157–163.

[2] S. D. Corrsin, *Warsaw before the First World War*, 94.

This campaign was instigated by Roman Dmowski (1864–1939), the leading Endek politician. Ever since the Revolution of 1905, he had been the political personality most hated by the Left, and he counted on splitting Polish voices into 'national' and 'Jewish' components, which was characteristic of his binary view of the world. Jan Kucharzewski—part of the opposition, dubbed the National Concentration (Koncentracja Narodowa)—stood no chance of election without Jewish votes. Jewish electors, however, were angry at Kucharzewski's indecisive position on Jewish rights, and ultimately voted for an unknown candidate from the workers' electoral group.

In one speech, Dmowski claimed that a Polish delegate chosen with Jewish votes would represent Jewish—rather than Polish—interests, and therefore would not be acceptable.[3] During the last days of the campaign, the Endek propaganda machine waged a bitter war against their opponents, presenting the struggle with the Jews as a moral battle, a 'matter of life and death'. One of the tactics most frequently used by the Endek press was to link their opponents with Jews. The National Concentration was therefore referred to as a 'Jewish-Polish Concentration', and its members as 'Jewish' hirelings or puppets. All others were presented as 'defenders of the Jews' or representatives of 'Judeo-Polonia' and 'Judaicized Poles'.[4] As the liberal critic Józef Lange noted in 1913, 'nowadays everything in the country is Jewish, with the exception of National Democracy'.[5] At the peak of this campaign, the party began to publish the yellow daily *Gazeta Poranna 2 Grosze* (Morning Gazette Two Pennies). This announced that 'it accepted advertising only from Christians', and carried the warning 'Workers! Don't elect Jewish flunkeys!' It called for an anti-Jewish boycott, and in the end waged war against the Jews.[6]

The Endeks' aggressive campaigning was not directed specifically against the Jews, but rather against Dmowski's Polish opponents, whom he denounced as 'Szabesgoyes' or 'Jewish puppets'. Both earlier and more recent studies stress the limited influence of the economic boycott on the

---

[3] *Mowa Romana Dmowskiego wygłoszona na zebraniu prawyborców m. Warszawy dn. 1 października w sali Resursy Obywatelskiej* (Warszawa, 1912), 2.

[4] On the *Endek* rhetoric in the campaign: S D. Corrsin, *Warsaw before the First World War*, 95–97.

[5] Józef Lange, *Postęp a nacjonalizm* (Warszawa, 1913), 84.

[6] Theodore R. Weeks, *Nation and State in Late Imperial Russia. Nationalism and Russification on the Western Frontier,* 1863–1914 (De Kalb, 1996), 169.

Jewish community.[7] However, its effects went beyond purely economic ones, as the campaign was not only directed against Jewish trade and industry: it also denounced all interaction between Poles and Jews, or people considered to be 'Jewish'.

The first practical implementation of the boycott campaign was by the Society for the Development of Industry, Crafts and Trade (Towarzystwo Rozwoju Przemysłu, Rzemiosł i Handlu), whose branches spanned the whole of Russian Poland. *Rozwój* voiced its agitation against the Jews in nationalist journals, especially the *Gazeta Warszawska* and the *Gazeta Poranna 2 Grosze* (whose authors included élite nationalists of the day, such as Stanisław Kozicki, Ignacy Oksza-Grabowski, Stanisław Pieńkowski, and Władysław Jabłonowski, but not Dmowski himself, though his articles were often reprinted there), and also in specialist periodicals.[8] The boycott campaign was also widely advocated in the Catholic ecclesiastical press (for instance, *Przegląd Katolicki-Wiara, Nasz Sztandar, Polak-Katolik,* and *Posiew*), and in some popular conservative-clerical dailies, such as *Dzień, Dziennik Powszechny,* and—in Galicia—the *Kronika Powszechna.* Rozwój also issued its own publications such as *Swój do swego* (To Each His Own) and *Bojkot* (The Boycott) in Lwów (Lviv); it also supported smaller initiatives, such as *Moje pisemko,* or *Nasz Świat*—journals primarily addressed to children and adolescents.

Election results in the provinces did not differ much from previous ones; however, electoral campaigning provided a pretext for National Democracy's campaign against the Jews. The nationalist press was already full of boycott slogans, frequently referring to Irish or Czech examples from that time, justifying the fight against 'Jewish encroachment' by defending 'Polish possessions' with *Realpolitik* slogans.[9] But this kind of legitimisation (or rather, 'secondary rationalization') could not hide the

---

[7] Igancy Schiper, *Dzieje handlu żydowskiego na ziemiach polskich* (Kraków, 1990), 540; Samuel Hirszhorn, *Historja Żydów w Polsce: od Sejmu Czteroletniego do Wojny Europejskiej (1788–1914)* (Warszawa, 1935), 311–18. See also Weeks, *From Assimilation to Antisemitism,* 166–168; Konrad Zieliński, '"Swój do swego" o stosunkach polsko-żydowskich w przededniu Wielkiej Wojny', *Kwartalnik Historii Żydów,* no. 3, (2004), 335.

[8] Szymon Rudnicki, '*The* Society for the Advancement of Trade, Industry, and Crafts', *Polin,* vol. I5, (2002), 315–317.

[9] See R. Rybarski, 'Bojkoty w Irlandii', *Przegląd Narodowy,* vol. 10–11, (1913), 367–402; idem, 'Bojkoty w życiu ludów wschodnich', *Przegląd Narodowy,* vol. 12, (1913), 562–599; idem, *Bojkoty ekonomiczne w krajach obcych* (Kraków, 1916); Sobczak, *Narodowa Demokracja,* 207.

fact that the aims of the campaign against the Jews were more far-reaching. Stanisław Pieńkowski, an unofficial spokesman of the boycott campaign, declared in October 1912 that 'the boycott, or a ruthless though bloodless Polish-Jewish war, is the beginning of a new era for Poland'.[10] Jews, he said, stood behind every threat to Poland's existence—liberalism and progressivism, not to mention any kind of revolutionary movement. The columnist understood the prospect for a national revival of Polish society through militant antisemitism. During the three years just before the First World War, the language of biological racism and millenarian Judeophobia became prevalent in much of Polish public culture, but it was most extreme in the nationalist press (especially in the *Gazeta Poranna 2 Grosze*), where Jews were presented in both racial and diabolic terms. The further one leaned towards the political right, the more virulent the expressions of hatred.

Gradually, National Democracy's rhetoric also became more caustic. Their reasoning reduced 'all the affairs of this world' to the plotting and scheming of 'international Jewry', and then of the freemasons. Under the auspices of this campaign flourished more extreme forms of antisemitism, ranging from medieval accusations of ritual murder to racist disquisitions on the degenerative influence of the Jewish race on the Poles. A manifesto of this kind of thinking was provided in the publications of Dmowski, who, on the eve of the First World War, argued that a Poland without Jews was possible only in a Europe without Jews.[11]

Although the boycott was instigated by National Democracy and the Catholic press, it was supported by a large part of the progressive press, including the leading *Prawda* (Truth), *Gazeta Poranna 2 Grosze*, and *Humanista Polski* (Polish Humanist). If less overtly, the same ideas were propagated by a number of opinion-setting periodicals, such as *Tygodnik Ilustrowany* and the conservative *Świat* (World), published by the Olgerbrand family (Jewish converts to Catholicism), and even by the centre-right *Kurier Warszawski* (Warsaw Courier). Conservative journals

---

[10] Stanisław Pieńkowski, *Dwa żywioły. Głos w sprawie żydowskiej* (Warszawa, 1913), 21.

[11] (Roman Dmowski), R. J., 'Podstawy bytu narodów europejskich I', *Sprawa Polska*, no. 34, (1917); idem, 'Duch narodowy i czynniki rozkładowe I', *Sprawa Polska*, no. 10, (1917); 'Duch narodowy i czynniki rozkładowe II', *Sprawa Polska*, no. 49, (1917); 'Duch narodowy i czynniki rozkładowe III', *Sprawa Polska*, no. 50, (1917). This series of articles had been prepared before, but it was published during WWI. See as well, idem, *Upadek myśli konserwatywnej*, (Warszawa, 1914).

connected with the Party of Real Politics, such as *Kurier Polski* (Polish Courier) and *Słowo* (Word), kept their distance. The only major Warsaw daily that expressly condemned this antisemitism was the *Nowa Gazeta* (New Gazette). The independent socialist journals, whose readers were few, also opposed antisemitic agitation.

Certain individuals protested, such as the intellectuals Adam Zakrzewski and Józef Lange, both of whom left the Polish Progressive Party. More significant were the public voices condemning such antisemitic aggression: besides the Catholic feuilletonist Teresa Lubińska and the leftist activist Stefania Sempołowska, the attitude of Ludomir Grendyszyński is notable: a columnist from Erazm Piltz's school—a circle of the influential supporters who advocated reconciliation with the Tsarist Empire on political and cultural premises—and a regular contributor to the conservative press. Nothing, however, can compare with the efforts of the left-liberal intellectual and world-renowned linguist, Jan Baudouin de Courtenay, who fought doggedly against antisemitism until the outbreak of the First World War.

Such antisemitism soon turned against other 'Jewish' enterprises as well. Many nationalist dailies, such as *Gazeta Poranna 2 Grosze* and *Gazeta Warszawska*, which had led the campaign from the start, called for the boycotting of every member of the intelligentsia who was of Jewish descent. These publications became a stronghold of National Democracy's vision. Nationalist periodicals in the provinces, following in the footsteps of *Gazeta Poranna*, carried columns entitled 'Jewish Masquerade', which 'unmasked' and denounced businesses with owners or employees of Jewish descent. The boycott also extended to those who opposed the antisemitic campaign, such as the socialist sociologist Ludwik Krzywicki and Jan Baudouin de Courtenay.

The campaign initiated in 1912 was most painful for assimilated Poles of Jewish descent. The upsurge in antisemitism polarized opinion within this group. Whilst the journalists of *Nowa Gazeta* (Stanisław Kempner, Józef Wasercug, and Józef Lange among the most eminent) and the journal *Przegląd Codzienny* (Daily Review)—founded by Jewish businessmen—opposed the anti-Jewish campaign, by contrast the majority in the progressive camp—including, importantly, the Polish Progressive Union and the Polish Progressive Party of Henryk Konic— gave a degree of support to the economic boycott of Jews.[12]

---

[12] On the attitude of Polish Jews towards the boycott see Jerzy Jedlicki, 'Resisting the Wave. Intellectuals against Antisemitism in the Last Years of the "Polish Kingdom"', in: *Antisemitism and its Opponents in Modern Poland*, ed. Robert Blobaum, (Ithaca and London,

Antisemitism as a Political Tool: National Democracy, the Jewish Threat, and Polish-Jewish Relations in the Early Twentieth Century

To grasp the significance of the anti-Jewish boycott in the nationalist movement, and to understand its place in Polish society before the First World War, one must go back to the Revolution of 1905. The events of 1905 brought to light the stark division in social and political life in Russian Poland. Never before had the conservative part of Polish society been so deeply haunted by the spectre of violent revolt, allegedly fomented by a socialist-Jewish plot. Fears of the natural order being overturned, along with suspicions and anxieties over the future of the national community, were common in both the middle and higher classes (which is to say, the social establishment as a whole), and the imagined figure of the Jewish revolutionary perfectly embodied these phobias.[13]

In this regard, the vision of a disciplined society governed by a 'national organization' as defined by Roman Dmowski, seems to have offered some Poles hope of a genuine defence against the chaos of revolution, anarchy, mass strikes, and, above all, mobs on the streets. Dmowski, the principal ideologue and political leader of National Democracy, also presented his vision as the only way to preserve Polish national identity in a time of deep crisis.[14]

2004), 69–80. Specifically on the activity of Julian Unszlicht as a case of Jewish self-hatred, see Grzegorz Krzywiec, 'Antysemityzm postępowy. Przypadek Juliana Unszlichta', in: *Parlamentaryzm, konserwatyzm, nacjonalizm. Sefer Jowel. Studia ofiarowane Profesorowi Szymonowi Rudnickiemu*, ed. Jolanta Żyndul, (Warszawa, 2010), 154–170.

[13] For introductory remarks on this still-untapped theme see Agnieszka Friedrich, 'Polish Literature's Portrayal of Jewish Involvement in 1905', in: *The Revolution of 1905 and Russia's Jews* eds. Stephen Hoffman and Ezra Mendelsohn, (Philadelphia, 2008), 143–151. For a comprehensive discussion of the 1905 Revolution in Russian Poland see R. E. Blobaum, *Rewolucja. Russian Poland, 1904–1907* (Ithaca and London, 1995). Specifically on the place of the Revolution in Polish-Jewish relations, see Weeks, 'Russians, Jews, and Poles: Russification and Antisemitism 1881–1914', *Quest. Issues in Contemporary Jewish History. Journal of Fondazione CDEC*, no. 3, (July 2012) url: www.quest-cdecjournal.it/focus.php?issue=3&id=308, especially 'Revolution 1905'; '1905 as a Watershed in Polish Jewish Relations', in: *The Revolution of 1905 and Russia's Jews*, 98; ibidem, *From Assimilation to Antisemitism. The "Jewish Question" in Poland, 1850–1914*, 129–146.

[14] On Polish politics of these days in Russian Poland see Blobaum, 'The Rise of Political Parties, 1890–1914' in: *The Origins of Modern Polish Democracy*, eds. Mieczysław B. Biskupski, J. S. Pula, and Piotr J. Wróbel, (Athens, 2010), 70–87; Brian

From the very beginning radical antisemitism was central to Dmowski's ideological project and his vision of the world, and what is more interesting is how he developed and expressed it. Dmowski set out his views and ideas in a collection of essays entitled *Myśli nowoczesnego Polaka* (Thoughts of a Modern Pole) in 1903. Here racial Social Darwinism was combined with a project for the modernisation of the nation.[15] Boycotts of every 'anti-national' activity, and above all representation of Jews as parasites within the national organism and as a stumbling-blocking to Polish progress, figured several times.[16]

However, antisemitism was not key to Endek success during and immediately after the Revolution of 1905. The 'Jewish question' had only a secondary status in the party's rhetoric and political strategy at that time.[17] Nationalism attained the status of a mass movement less through the agency of the National Democracy as a political party, than through the effective leadership of a coalition of vested interests. By the end of 1905, the party had become the strongest mass political movement in Russian Poland.[18] At this time the Endek political structure was orchestrated by a handful of people, namely Dmowski and his inner circle, who paved the way for the creation of the first genuine political and propaganda

---

Porter-Szücs, *Poland in the Modern World: Beyond Martyrdom* (Chichester, 2014), 43–64.

[15] Porter, 'Who Is a Pole and Where is Poland and Nation in the Rhetoric of Polish National Democracy before 1905', *Slavic Review*, vol. 4, (Winter 1992), 639–653; idem, 'Democracy and Discipline in Late Nineteenth Century Poland', *Journal of Modern History*, vol. 2 (June 1999), 346–393; B. Toruńczyk, 'Myśl polityczna i ideologia Narodowej Demokracji', in eadem, *Narodowa Demokracja. Antologia myśli politycznej 'Przeglądu Wszechpolskiego'* (London, 1983), 26–34. In a detailed way G. Krzywiec, *Szowinizm po polsku. Przypadek Romana Dmowskiego 1886–1905* (Warszawa, 2009), 373–388.

[16] R. Dmowski, *Myśli nowoczesnego Polaka* (Lwów, 1904), 46, 50.

[17] Israel Oppenheim, 'The Radicalisation of the Endecja Anti-Jewish Line during and after the 1905 Revolution', *Shevut*, vol. 9, no. 25, (2000), 32–66; Joanna Michlic, *Poland's Threatening Other. The Image of the Jews from 1880s.to the Present* (London, 2006), 46. For greater detail see Sobczak, *Narodowa Demokracja wobec kwestii żydowskiej*, 149–162. On *Endek's* antisemitism in the nationalist political agenda of those days Janusz Jerzy Terej, *Idee, mity realia. Szkice do dziejów Narodowej Demokracji*, (Warszawa, 1971), 46.

[18] See Trees, *Wahlem im Weichselland. Die Nationaldemokraten in Russisch–Polen und die Dumawahlen 1905–1912*, 107–110; Blobaum, *Rewolucja*, 190–195; Porter-Szücs, *Poland*, 51–56.

machine in Polish lands. In the early months of 1906, this machine spread across most of the country, and won a comprehensive victory in Congress Poland's first elections to the Russian State Duma. The electoral victory of the nationalists led to a fierce confrontation between revolutionary and counter-revolutionary forces. Crucial to the Endek success at this stage was, first, its depiction of the Revolution as a case of violent anarchy from the left and an apocalyptic act against Christian order and, second, its adroit management of counter-revolutionary fears and anxieties.

The early peak of this new mass politics in Russian Poland, a mixture of anti-socialist hysteria and authoritarian rhetoric with some anti-Jewish motifs, arose in the Łódź uprising of 1906–1907. Ideological and rhetorical jousting in the press turned into local civil war in the biggest industrial city in central Congress Poland. From autumn 1906 to spring 1907, 400 people were killed in Łódź and many others were wounded in fratricidal assassinations between rightist paramilitary squads inspired by the Endek political message and leftist activists from various circles. Dmowski, as the editor-in-chief of the main nationalist daily of the time (*Gazeta Polska*), was a crucial instigator and key personality behind the anti-socialist hysteria in the nationalist press.[19] For the Endecja in the first decade of the new century, the exclusion of all 'non-Polish' groups from the national collectivity meant an uncompromising fight against them, and in extreme cases this could lead to physical elimination.

These events strengthened Dmowski's personal standing in the nationalist camp and in conservative public opinion. Endek successes in elections (one in 1906 and two in 1907) demonstrated that nationalist ideas and disciplinary visions were gaining acceptance among Polish voters and the general public. Dmowski was treated by some sections of the general public as a charismatic leader, one ready to assume responsibility

---

[19] For a general introduction see Stanisław Kalabiński, *Antynarodowa polityka endecji w rewolucji 1905–1907* (Warszawa, 1955). See also my own contributions: *Von der Massenpolitik zum (kalten) Bürgerkrieg. Der Fall der Nationaldemokratie im Königreich Polen (1905–1914) und danach*, in: *Grenzziehungen, Netzwerke: Die Teilungsgrenzen in der politischen Kultur der Zweiten Republik*, eds. Kai Stuve, Michael Műller, (Göttingen, 2017), 107–130; idem, *Z taką rewolucją musimy walczyć na noże. Rewolucja 1905 roku z perspektywy polskiej prawicy*, in: *Rewolucja 1905. Przewodnik Krytyki Politycznej*, eds. Kamil Piskała, Wiktor Marzec, (Warszawa, 2013), 326–352; On the 1905 Revolution as an actual introduction of European Civil War see also Stanley Payne, *European Civil War, 1905–1939*, (Wisconsin, 2010), 16–17.

for the whole country and the Polish cause. At the same time, a group of nationalist activists formed within his camp. These people were strictly subordinate to him, and hence dubbed 'Dmowski-ites' or the 'general staff' of the Endek army. They became the moving force behind the Endecja's later political, and above all antisemitic, propaganda, especially its press campaigns.

After 1905, the political antisemitism of National Democracy had various characteristics. First and foremost, anti-Jewish slogans had a practical value in terms of mobilizing some parts of society in Congress Poland against the Left and progressivist circles. The Endeks at this time therefore effectively used those slogans not only against the Jewish community as a whole, but also to fight the Left and the Centre, and even the conciliatory, conservative circles.[20] The most striking feature of this was how rapidly they adopted a negative attitude towards the Jews, and how far it developed. Before long, this rhetoric connected all the roles of the 'internal enemy' with the Jews. During elections to the Russian Duma in the spring of 1907, the Endeks became even more radical in their hostility to Jews, and began using political antisemitism in their fight against any opposition. The Jews began to epitomize all forms of aggression against Polishness, and National Democracy presented itself as the sole repository and defender of Polish values: the tactic was very effective.

Anti-Litwak Hysteria and the Nationalist Mastering of Moral Panic

In the long run, this development of antisemitic rhetoric should, above all, be understood in relation to the rise of the Jewish community. One phenomenon that especially affected the form and intensity of antisemitic attitudes after the Revolution of 1905 was the movement of Jews from Russia, especially Lithuania, to Congress Poland. This was reflected in the demographic growth of the Jewish population in the first decade of the twentieth century, which resulted in the greater social and cultural visibility of Polish Jewry and the development of the Yiddish, as well as, to some extent, the Hebrew press and literature, the new Yiddish theatre, the

---

[20] Oppenheimer, *The Radicalisation of the Endecja Anti-Jewish Line*, 50–54. Also, see an energetic analysis of this rhetoric in the 1906 and 1907 elections in Warsaw, in Scott Ury, *Barricades and Banners. The Revolution of 1905 and the Transformation of Warsaw Jewry* (2012), 214–263.

emergence of new Jewish political parties, and demands for cultural autonomy. 'Russian Jews', or 'Litvaks', undoubtedly played a crucial, if not a decisive, role in all these activities.[21] Resentment towards them was first voiced by the Polish Jews, and entered Polish discussion from that angle. Most Polish publications of the time viewed this Yiddish revival as either aggressive or provocative; 'Litvaks' and *'litvakism'* were blamed for the rise in Jewish visibility and confidence. Although short-lived, the Litvak myth, together with the side-effects of the Revolution of 1905, had an enormous impact upon not only Polish antisemitism, but also Polish politics.[22]

The affair which triggered the Litvak psychosis occurred in August 1909, and was fairly banal. A Czech delegation of Slavophiles visiting Warsaw was criticized by the Warsaw Yiddish dailies, *Haynt* and *Der Moment*. The popular Polish ultra-conservative daily *Dzień* (Day) denounced the criticisms as an 'arrogant intrusion of Yids into Polish matters'. In late 1909, nearly all prominent journals in the Warsaw press contributed to this strife, most of them in a hysterical and aggressive manner.[23]

From early 1910 onwards, these feelings grew in various ways. For example, the Council of Polish Progressive Union (Polskie Zjednoczenie Postępowe), the main centre-left party, claimed at a closed-door debate that the non-assimilated Jew should be treated as 'an internal enemy' of the whole Polish nation.[24] Thus Leon Wasilewski, a leading ideologue and spokesman of the Polish Socialist Party—Revolutionary Faction (Polska

---

[21] See Joanna Nalewajko-Kulikov, 'Who Has Not Wanted to Be an Editor?: The Yiddish Press in the Kingdom of Poland, 1905–1914', *Polin*, vol. 27, (2015), 279–282.

[22] On the Litvak debate see F. Guesnet, 'Wir müssen Warschau unbedingt russisch machen. Die Mythologisierung der russisch- júdischen Zuwanderung ins Königreich Polen zu Beginn unseres Jahrhunderts am Beispiel eines polnischen Trivalromans', in: *Geschichtliche Mythen in den Literaturen und Kulturen Ostmittel- und Sudosteuropas*, eds. E. Behring et alia, (Stuttgart, 1999), 99–116; F. Golczewski, *Polnisch-Jüdische Beziehungen 1881–1922. Eine Studie zur Geschichte des Antisemitismus in Osteuropa* (Wiesbaden, 1981), 97.

[23] On the affair in detail see Krzywiec, *Prasa żydowska w zwierciadle polskiej opinii publicznej*, in: *Studia z dziejów trójjęzycznej prasy żydowskiej na ziemiach polskich (XIX-XX wiek)*, ed. Nalewajko-Kulikov and others, (Warszawa, 2012), 272–275. See as T.R. Weeks, 'Fanning the flames: The Jews in the Warsaw press, 1905–1912', *East European Jewish Affairs*, vol. XXVIII, no. 2, (1998–1999), 79 on.

[24] T. Stegner, *Liberałowie Królestwa Polskiego 1904–1915* (Gdańsk, 1990), 196.

Partia Socjalistyczna—Frakcja Rewolucyjna), the independent socialist party, warned in the same manner: 'Litvakism' is an abnormal, pathological, reactionary symptom, just as pathological and reactionary as its reasons'.[25] Warnings and scaremongering against the Litvaks recurred systematically in the press of Stronnictwo Polityki Realnej (Party of Real Politics), a leading conservative party which at this time was nearly free of popular antisemitism.[26] These stirrings and currents, coming together as a mainstream moral consensus on the 'Jewish question', were the beginnings of the antisemitic tide which was to sweep twentieth-century Polish public life.

Nothing stoked patriotic feelings at this time of crisis more than uncertainty. Polish patriotic anxieties were heightened by the moves of the partitioning powers, and sought an outlet. The powerful sense of threat to the Polish cause, a feeling of the decline of Polishness shared by many Poles, was accompanied by a rise in patriotic feeling which was connected with the nationalist persecution of the Polish population in Prussia, and also with the general international unrest, which many saw as a prelude to a Europe-wide conflict. This was the atmosphere in which the celebrations of the 500th anniversary of the Battle of Grunwald were held in July 1910, with their huge masses on the streets of Galician Krakow—over 100,000 people. Side-by-side with the widespread anti-German feelings among Poles, even stronger 'anti-Litvak' fears were re-emerging.

National Consensus?

This anti-Litvak psychosis had now gone far beyond so-called progressive antisemitism, a trend usually connected with Andrzej Niemojewski, a leftist activist and noted poet who was attached to the Left around the turn of the century. Until 1905 he declared himself a friend of the Jews which, according to him, on the one hand meant that he was in favour of the complete integration of the Jewish population into Polish society, and on the other revealed his fascination with some elements of Jewish culture. Towards the end of the Revolution of 1905, his despondency about socialism went hand in hand with his deeper, independent religious studies. In 1906, he established the periodical *Myśl Niepodległa* (Independent

---

[25] L. Wasilewski, 'Litwactwo i kwestya żydowska', *Przedświt*, no. 2 (February 1910), 65–68.
[26] A. Kidzińska, *Stronnictwo Polityki Realnej* (Lublin, 2007), 156–157.

Thought), which disclosed the paradoxes and inconsistencies of faith from the viewpoint of scientism.

In the autumn of 1909, during the first wave of the Litvaks debate, antisemitic motifs slowly emerged among Niemojewski's not-quite-coherent views. The journal persistently repeated the clichés of that time, such as that Yiddish was an underdeveloped German language serviceable for everyday communication but useless for the development of culture, or that there was no literature or even serious journalism to be found in it. This charge could be seen in the attack of *Myśl Niepodległa* on the left wing of the Polish socialist movement in September 1909, the Social Democracy of the Kingdom of Poland and Lithuania (Socjaldemokracja Królestwa Polskiego i Litwy), which set off an avalanche of further accusations. As time went by, Niemojewski added new charges, using more and more aggressive metaphors. For instance, in one of his furious pamphlets in 1912, he used the phrase 'the army of the fifth partition' to define the rebirth of Jewish life. On the eve of the First World War, Niemojewski and his contributors were deeply absorbed by the racial and 'anthropological ties' that allegedly connected all Jews, as well as by the 'ethic of the Talmud', which, they claimed, prevented any assimilation.[27]

Niemojewski's attacks on the Jews were supported by another feuilletonist well-known among the progressives, Izabella (Iza) Moszczeńska. Her prolific contributions and commentaries from early 1910 onwards in *Kurier Poranny* (a daily close to the progressives, but also the unofficial tribune for the independent socialists) turned 'the Jewish question' into the chief problem for all of educated Polish opinion. Moszczeńska argued that the presence of the Jewish population hampered the modernisation of Polish society.[28]

---

[27] On Niemojewski and his impact on the Polish progresssivists, see Weeks, 'Polish "Progressive Antisemitism" 1905–1914', *East European Jewish Affairs*, vol. 25, no. 2, (1995), 49–68; D. Trześniowski, 'Biografia ideowa polskiego inteligenta: od filo- do antysemityzmu. Andrzej Niemojewski', in: *Kwestia żydowska w XIX wieku. Spory o tożsamość Polaków*, eds. Grazyna Borkowska and Małgorzata Rudkowska, (Warszawa, 2004), 319–329; Michał Śliwa, 'Antysemityzm postępowy Andrzeja Jana Niemojewskiego', in: *Obcy czy swoi. Obcy czy swoi. Z dziejów poglądów na kwestię żydowską w Polsce w XIX i XX wieku*, ed. idem, (Kraków, 1997), 96–105.

[28] Weeks, '*Polish "Progressive Antisemitism" 1905–1914*', 59–62. See also Krzywiec, "Progressiver Antisemitismus" im russischen Teil Polens von 1905 bis 1914. Ursprünge und Konzepte des polnischen politischen Antisemitismus, in: *Die 'Judenfrage' – ein Europäisches Phänomen?*, (hrsg.) M. Hettling, M. G. Müller and G. Hausmann, (Berlin, 2013), 139–141.

But what was most surprising, even to contemporaries, was that this aggressive anti-Jewish language rapidly gained ground in the socialist and leftist milieu. Leon Wasilewski, the noted linguist and an expert on minority questions, noticed that antisemitic sentiment was growing rapidly among those socialists who strove for the independence of Poland. Party propaganda now adopted antisemitic motifs and elements. For instance, terms such as a 'Levite'—an adherent of the PPS Left (PPS-Lewica), the left wing of the Polish socialist movement—and 'social-Litvakism' appeared as descriptions for 'Jewish nationalism in a socialist guise'.[29] The tension between the fighters for Poland's independence and the socialist Left had existed for years, but now ideological and political arguments were displaced by openly antisemitic generalizations.

Juljan Unszlicht was another infamous author of lengthy pamphlets on this theme.[30] His essays appeared in the progessivist *Myśl Niepodległa*, and *Kurier Poranny*, in the moderate nationalist *Goniec Poranny i Wieczorny*, and also in the socialist weekly *Przedświt* (Predawn); they were then reprinted by the main Galician socialist daily *Naprzód* (Forward) and the socialist weekly *Gazeta Robotnicza* (Workers' Gazette), which appeared among the Polish diaspora in Berlin. These were the main socialist opinion-forming periodicals of the time. Unszlicht, a former socialist, and a Pole of Jewish origin, argued openly that Socjaldemokracja Królestwa Polskiego i Litwy was simply 'an emanation of petty-bourgeois Jewish nationalism'. In his fierce attack, 'W. Sendecki' (Unszlicht's pseudonym as an author) accused the leaders of the Social Democracy of being the 'Litvak Targowica'; this referred to the Confederation of Targowica established by Polish magnates and aristocrats, notorious as traitors to Poland for their opposition, in collusion with the Russian Empress Catherine II, to the Constitution of 3 May 1791. He claimed they had provoked the violence of the partitioners, and wished to subjugate the whole Polish nation on behalf of Jewish interests. The overall atmosphere of fear of 'the Litvak swarms' reached its apogee in the early autumn of 1910, when the attacks

---

[29] L. Wasilewski, *Słowniczek gwary partyjnej w Królestwie Polskim, Nadbitka. Materiały i Prace Komisyi Umiejętności w Krakowie* (Kraków, 1912), 377, 386.

[30] On Unszlicht and his phenomenon see Krzywiec, *Antysemityzm postępowy*, 154–170; idem, *Nadwiślański Weininger? Przypadki Juliana Unszlichta (1883–1953)*, 'Zagłada Żydów. Studia i Materiały', no. 5, (2009), 243–253.

against the Socjaldemokracja Królestwa Polskiego i Litwy among Polish socialists came to the attention of the international socialist milieu.[31]

By the winter of 1909 in Congress Poland this antisemitic language, with the Jew positioned as the major threat to Poland, Poles, and all Polish affairs, suffused the language and the imagination of National Democrats completely and for good. Dmowski wanted at every turn to define the Jews as an exotic and dangerous Asiatic race. He presented them and all their doings as parasitical; 'parasitism', he proclaimed, was the genuine and exclusive ideology of Jews. He emphasized that the Jews simply could not belong to the Polish nation in any sense. In opposition to the mainstream Warsaw press, he claimed that not only the Litvaks, but the Jewish population as a whole, constituted an imminent threat to Poland. Ultimately, he strove for the unification of all anti-Jewish thinking and ideologies under the Endek banner.[32]

The nationalist camp included the two most extreme antisemitic authors of the time: Ignacy Oksza-Grabowski, a writer and contributor to many influential cultural periodicals, and Stanisław Pieńkowski, a poet, the admired translator of Nietzsche's works into Polish, and most of all an apologist for the mystic community of Aryans, who was soon to become the leading cultural critic of *Gazeta Warszawska*, the main nationalist daily in that period. Both contributed to National Democrat press with sophisticated elaborations meant to expose the 'moral corruption' of 'Polish and Aryan culture' by 'the Jewish racial element'. For these authors—and many others less prominent—the fight against the 'Jewish threat' meant more than just removing the hostile and parasitical element from the Polish national community. Getting rid of the Jews was seen as a remedy for the illnesses of 'the whole Aryan world', and as the destruction of the evil contaminating the contemporary Western world.[33]

---

[31] George Haupt, Korzec, '*Les Socialistes et la camapagne antisémite en Pologne en 1910: un épisode inédit*', 'Revue du Nord. Revue historique trimestrielle', vol. lviii, no. 225, (avril–juin 1975), 185–195.

[32] See. R. Dmowski, *Separatyzm żydowski i jego źródła*, (Warszawa, 1909), 27; idem, '*Wykształcenie praktyczne w szkole średniej*', 'Przegląd Narodowy', no. 1 (January 1910), 14; idem, '*Zagadnienie sprawy żydowskiej*', 'Przegląd Narodowy', no. 12 (December 1910), 647; idem, '*Polityka polska, kadeci i sprawa żydowska (Odpowiedź pp. Pietrunkiewiczowi)*', 'Gazeta Warszawska', no. 326 (1910), 1.

[33] See, for example, Pieńkowski's series of articles in *Gazeta Warszawska* '*Rozłam sztuki*', *Gazeta Warszawska*, no. 32, (1910), 2–4, and Wincenty Lutosławski's contribution '*Ludzie rasowi*', *Gazeta Warszawska*, no. 36, (1910), 1. This exchange of opinions (including the articles by Zygmunt Wasilewski, the editor-in-chief of the Lwów *Słowo Polskie*) had wider

In late 1911, one of the main contributors to the nationalist press, Bohdan Wasiutyński, published in the economic periodical *Ekonomista* a statistical essay on the Polish Jews, where he estimated the number of the Litvaks at over 200,000.[34] This figure was widely repeated in the Warsaw press as an ominous reminder. The Endek party and its press propaganda machine across the Polish lands were all set for a final battle against Jewry.[35] A symbolic turning point was also seen in the Catholic press, which had earlier tried to moderate excessive and racially driven anti-Jewish rantings. For instance, the Jesuit Jerzy Pawelski declared in the Kraków *Przegląd Powszechny* (Universal Review), the main Catholic opinion monthly in the Polish lands, that 'the original sense of the word *anti-Semitism* has lost its edge, for it "declares war on the Jews", while in the new situation Polish society faces a war declared by the Jews'.[36] The presence of outspoken and radical antisemites in the columns of the Catholic press throughout the Polish lands had become obvious and normal.

These trends were reflected in popular culture. In the autumn of 1909, in addition to the anti-Litvak flood, the Warsaw satirical press began to spread vile antisemitic caricatures. The imagined figure of the Jew started to take on features that were either malevolent or, in the end, downright demonic. Antisemitic *belle-lettres* and fiction was another sign of the times. The authors of these bestselling novels were generally absorbed by three problems: 'the Prussian-Jewish plot', 'the Litvaks and Litvakism', and eventually 'the boycott of the Jews'.[37]

In 1911, a tide of social tension swept across the lands of the Russian partition. This coincided with the Beilis trial in Kiev (1911–1913), involving antisemitic charges of ritual murder which reawakened medieval anti-Judaic myths. The journalist Bernard Singer recalled about his childhood in Warsaw during those days that 'boys on the streets were already shout-

---

repercussions in the nationalist periodicals. It was reported and recommended by *Przegląd Narodowy* 'Z prasy. Spór o człowieka', 'Przegląd Narodowy', no. 3 (March 1910), 371–383.

[34] B. W (Bohdan Wasiutyński), 'Rola ekonomiczna Żydów w Królestwie Polskim', *Przegląd Narodowy*, no. 10, (October 1911), 383–414.

[35] Sobczak, *Narodowa Demokracja wobec kwestii żydowskiej*, 185–192; 242–247.

[36] Ks. Jerzy Pawelski, 'Dwa światy "Krytyki" i dwa inne światy', 'Przegląd Powszechny', vol. 109 (1911), 207. On the specificities of the Catholic campaign against the Jews see Blobaum, 'Criminalizing the Other: Crime, ethnicity, and antisemitism in early twentieth-century Poland' in: *Anti-Semitism and its Opponents in Modern Poland*, ed. Idem, 88–90.

[37] Teodor Jeske-Choiński, *Żydzi w literaturze polskiej* (Warszawa, 1914), 32; Krzysztof Stępnik, 'Powieść antysemicka w ostatnich latach Kongresówki', *Krytyka*, no. 39, (1992), 79.

ing "Beilis" at bearded Jews'.³⁸ Moreover, the effects of the economic crisis of 1907–1909 were finally being felt by one of the core groups that made up the National Democrat electorate—namely, the Christian bourgeoisie and small entrepreneurs. It was then, as American historian Robert Blobaum says, that a conviction took root among the 'Christian middle class' that the presence of their Jewish competitors was the main factor hindering economic development.³⁹ Thus, by 1912, as the eminent Polish historian Jerzy Jedlicki wrote, all the positions on this front had been taken and were clearly delineated.⁴⁰ Only the catalyst was missing, and this was supplied when the elections to the Fourth Duma were announced.

Conclusion

These years witnessed a powerful revival of the Jewish community in the Polish lands, as the Jewish community began to want to appear as a legitimate society. This was a fact of enormous importance for the Polish-Jewish debate. Izhak Perez, the writer, stated at a meeting in 1907 that 'the Jews want to be themselves'. The Jewish population *en masse* no longer wanted to communicate with the Poles through middlemen—Poles of Jewish descent. The period of Polish monoculture, sustained by both sides, was no longer possible.

Most members of the Polish political class and cultural elite did not want to recognize this development, and their mono-cultural attitude was expressed in various ways. For National Democracy, it meant the exclusion of all 'non-Polish' groups from the national community, and the wish to make the fight against 'the Jewish threat' and 'the enemy within' the pivot of its entire ideological project, and part of a day-to-day political agenda. For other groups, including those referring to the tradition of the Enlightenment, it signified the factual hegemony of Polish culture and the

---

[38] Bernard Singer, *The Yiddish press* (in:) *The Jews, the left, and the Ste Duma Elections in Warsaw in 1912. Selected Sources*, trans. by Stanfley D. Corrsin, 'Polin', vol. 9, (1996), 48. On the Polish reaction to the Beilis affair J. Żyndul, *Bejlisy, czyli polska reakcja na proces kijowski*, 'Kwartalnik Historii Żydów', no. 232 (2009), 397–410.

[39] Blobaum 'The Politics of Antisemitism in the Fin-de-Siècle Warsaw', *Journal of Modern History*, vol. 73, (June 2001), 281.

[40] Jedlicki, '*The End of the Dialogue. Warsaw 1907–1912*', in: *The Jews in Poland*, ed. Sławomir Kapralski, II (Cracow, 1999), 110. See as well, idem '*Resisting the Wave: Intellectuals against Antisemitism in the Last Years of the "Polish Kingdom"*' in: *Antisemitism*, ed. Blobaum, 65.

absolute loyalty of the minorities. But only Endeks imagined a comprehensive vision of a Poland without the Jews, and only the Endeks became effective in communicating with their expanding electorate.[41] The most important side-effect of the antisemitic campaign of 1912 and the boycott call was the firm embedding of antisemitism in the political culture of Congress Poland, and later throughout the Polish lands. Indeed, with all these activities seen in a historical perspective, the increased antipathy towards Jews has to be treated as a further stage in efforts to eliminate them from Polish public life: this was first and foremost the crucial aim of the Polish nationalist agenda at that time.

Generally speaking, patriotic Poles through the long nineteenth century saw the boycott as a natural tool of self-defence against foreign oppressors.[42] In the name of the national interest, it was a common instrument of nationalist mobilization in all sectors and was used from time to time.[43] However, the anti-Jewish boycott that began in 1912 in the aftermath of the election was unique in various ways. As elsewhere, the boycott was a popular expression of protest against the integration of Jews into European society, and against their gaining equal status as citizens. Boycotts of Jews by nationalists and antisemites of various kinds opposed their social integration and targeted their economic activity (and supposed

[41] Already in the winter of 1912/1913 the Endek party either established or co-organized a nationwide network of dailies focused specifically on the boycott of the Jews; *Wiadomości Ilustrowane* (1913–) in Vilnious; *Gazeta Zagłębia* (1913–1914); *Głoslubelski* (1913–); *Goniec Częstochowski* (1913–); *Ilustrowana Gazeta Polska* (1914) in Kraków.

[42] See Sabine Grabowski, *Deutscher und polnischer Nationalismus. Der deutsche Ostmarken-Verein und die polnische Straż 1894–1914*, Marburg 1998, 209 on. William W. Hagen, *German, Poles and Jews. The Nationality Conflict in the Prussian East, 1772–1914*, (Chicago and London, 1980), 116, 158, and especially 261–265; Rudolf Jaworski, *Handel und Gewer beim Nationalitatenkampf. Studien zur Wirschaftsgesinnung der Polen in der Provinz Posen, (1871–1914)* (Göttingen, 1986), 126 on. For the phenomenon in Central and Eastern Europe more generally, see also Andreas Kappeler, *Voraussetzungen nationaler Mobilisierung*, in id., *Der schwierige Weg zur Nation. Beiträge zur neueren Geschichte der Ukraine*, Vienna–Cologne–Weimar 2003, 77–88; Miloslav Szabó, Populist Antisemitism. 'On the Theory and Methodology of Research in Modern Antisemitism', *Judaica Bohemiae*, vol. XLIX, no. 2, (2015), 76–81.

[43] Keely Stauter-Halsted, 'Nationalism and the Public Sphere: The Limits of Rational Association in the Nineteenth–Century Polish Countryside', in: *Cultures and Nations of Central and Eastern Europe. Essays in Honor of Roman Szporluk*, eds. Zvi Gitelman, Lubomyr Hajda, John Paul Himka, and Roman Solchanyk, (Cambridge, MA, 2000), 210. Eadem, *The Nation in the Village. The Genesis of Peasant National Identity in Austrian Poland, 1848–1914* (Ithaca and London, 2004), 62.

hegemony), cultural presence, and political influence. In the Polish case however, the local nationalists succeeded in mobilizing these feelings of fear and anxiety that dominated Polish politics in the years after 1905. Although the boycott campaign had begun with slogans against Jewish shops and retails stores, it was rapidly but methodically redirected against everything 'Jewish'. Endemic antisemitic initiatives in the Polish lands—such as Stanisław Stojałowski's movement in the Western Part of Galicia, the weekly *Postęp* (Progress) in Prussian Poland, or the *rolarze* movement of 'land-tillers' in Congress Poland (followers of Jan Jeleński movements)—were mostly taken under the wing of National Democracy. Antisemitism in various forms became a permanent element of the cultural code of conservative sections of Polish society.

Thus the election and boycott campaign of 1912–1914, more than any other political event of the time, was a turning point in the radicalisation of the Polish right, and the introduction of various anti-Jewish discourses into public life. Furthermore, for the majority of Poles, the Jews as a community came to constitute a separate element—if not an actively hostile one, then at best a group which did not bother with 'Polish interests'. Politically, all these changes were most harmful for progressivists and the Left. Moreover, the collapse of the Polish version of liberalism meant that the next generation of Poles—those who entered the reborn Polish state in 1918—largely echoed this xenophobic image of the Jews.

Though this antisemitic mobilization in Polish lands was a crucial, and indeed highly significant, episode in the annals of modern antisemitism in the region, it was for a long time completely neglected by Polish historiography and little known to other historians. To this day, these events are practically unknown to the Polish public and are largely missing in historical education. However, the Polish lands in that period produced an upsurge of antisemitism, and various other forms of xenophobia, that seemed to be on the one hand a wave of archaic fantasies, and on the other pure racial hatred. Popular antisemitism and the absorption of anti-Jewish xenophobia into mass popular culture also played a role in this. In that sense, the boycott campaign of 1912 and the chauvinist scaremongering afterwards had more in common with what was to come: a fusion of deep-rooted traditional anti-Jewish prejudices, an elaborate paranoid and metaphysical ideology, and deluded *raison d'état* arguments.

CHAPTER 5

Zionist "Buy National" Campaigns in Interwar Palestine

Hizky Shoham

"Buy National" Campaigns: Economic Nationalism and Boycottism

Economic nationalism was the globally dominant doctrine of the interwar era, when it partially supplanted the nineteenth-century Western belief that free trade would bring wealth and prosperity.[1] It originated before the Great War in the borderlands of Central and Eastern Europe, where nationalists championed "marketplace nationalism" and boycotted the rival ethnonational group.[2] In the heyday of modern nationalism

---

[1] Frank Trentmann, *Free Trade Nation: Commerce, Consumption and Civil Society in Modern Britain* (Oxford, 2008).

[2] David Levi-Faur, 'Economic Nationalism: From Friedrich List to Robert Reich,' *Review of International Studies,* vol. 23, (1997): 359–370 (see p. 360); Ivan T. Berend, 'The Failure of Economic Nationalism: Central and Eastern Europe before World War I,' *Revue économique,* vol. 51, no. 2, (2000), 315–22; Catherine Albrecht, 'The Rhetoric of Economic Nationalism in the Bohemian Boycott Campaigns of the Late Habsburg Monarchy,' *Austrian History Yearbook,* vol. 32, (2001), 47–67; Elizabeth A. Drummond, "'To Each His Own': Marketplace Nationalism in the German-Polish Borderland of Poznania at the Turn of the Century," a

H. Shoham (✉)
Bar-Ilan University, Ramat Gan, Israel

The Shalom Hartman Institute in Jerusalem, Jerusalem, Israel

© The Author(s) 2019
D. Feldman (ed.), *Boycotts Past and Present,* Palgrave Critical Studies of Antisemitism and Racism,
https://doi.org/10.1007/978-3-319-94872-0_5

in Europe, between the world wars, economic nationalism turned into an interventionist fiscal policy of protectionism that supported industrialization (or, in some cases, agrarianism) and favored the purchase of locally produced goods.[3] Governments imposed tariffs on imports while subsidizing local production, even when this worked to the detriment of consumers, who often paid higher prices for protected local goods. Industrialists, merchants, labor unions, journalists, consumer organizations, and in some cases governments waged intensive "buy national" campaigns that linked the mundane act of shopping with the nation's strength, associated the consumption of foreign products with national disgrace, and implored consumers to favor local products even if—or precisely when—they were more expensive or of lower quality.

Several historians who studied interwar "buy national" campaigns, whether in nation states or by anticolonial movements, argued that they often had a negligible effect on the shopping habits of consumers. Their main achievement was to attach sociocultural and political attributes to objects, money, and human labor.[4] These campaigns generated a moral pressure that created a sense of national affiliation, "expand[ing] the political field by drawing nonpolitical social groups and realms of activity into nationalist movements."[5]

---

paper presented in "boycotts—past and present" conference, London, June 2013. I would like to thank Elizabeth Drummond for sharing this unpublished work.

[3] Henryk Szlajfer, ed., *Economic Nationalism in East-Central Europe and South America, 1918–1939* (Geneva, 1990); J. Kofman, *Economic Nationalism and Development: Central and Eastern Europe between the Two World Wars* (Boulder, 1997). On interwar interventionism, see J. M. Keynes, "National Self-Sufficiency," *The Yale Review*, vol. 22, (1933), 755–769.

[4] See, in brief: Mary Douglas and Baron Isherwood, *The World of Goods: Towards an Anthropology of Consumption* (London and New York, 1996 [1979]); Arjun Appadurai, ed., *The Social Life of Things: Commodities in Cultural Perspective* (Cambridge, 1986); Roberta Sassatelli, *Consumer Culture: History, Theory and Politics* (London, 2007). See also Martin Daunton and Mathew Hilton, eds., *The Politics of Consumption: Material Culture and Citizenship in Europe and America* (Oxford and New York, 2001).

[5] Nancy Reynolds, *A City Consumed: Urban Commerce, the Cairo Fire, and the Politics of Decolonization in Egypt* (Stanford, 2012), 80. See also: Stephen Constantine, 'The Buy British Campaign of 1931,' *European Journal of Marketing*, vol. 21, no. 4, (1993), 44–59; Dana Frank, *Buy American: The Untold Story of Economic Nationalism* (Boston, 1999); Karl Gerth, *China Made: Consumer Culture and the Creation of the Nation* (Cambridge, MA, 2003).

When it comes to the construction of national identity, "There can be no 'us' without a 'them.'"⁶ On the surface, most "buy national" campaigns focus on "our" products, while the repudiated goods are "foreign," without specification of other national origins. In active national conflicts, though, as in the European borderlands, "buy national" campaigns might single out the rival ethnonational group and link "our" prosperity to the significant other's decay. In a similar vein, some interwar anticolonial movements that sought to create an economy independent of the colonial power waged "buy national" campaigns that explicitly called for a boycott of the colonial power.⁷

The questions I wish to address here are: in what conditions do "buy national" campaigns turn into boycotts? When and how does a positive campaign *for* "our" prosperity turn into a negative campaign *against* "their" prosperity, as in a zero-sum game? And if there is a significant other—what role do its products play in the construction of national identity in the sphere of consumption?

The answers to these questions are historically contingent. I pose these questions here with regard to the Zionist "buy national" campaigns in interwar Palestine. Elsewhere I have described these campaigns in detail, focusing on their institutional development and their contribution to the formation of a separate Jewish identity in Palestine.⁸ Now I will explore the villains targeted by these campaigns: the British authorities, the rival Arab-Palestinian nationalist movement, and Nazi Germany. As we shall see, Zionist "buy national" campaigns seldom called on consumers to boycott the products of a particular group. However, their intensity was directly linked to the intensity of the ethnonational conflict over Palestine and the immediate presence of a rival nationalist movement.

---

⁶ Michael Billig, *Banal Nationalism* (London, 1995), 78.

⁷ Abdelazziz EzzelArab, *European Control and Egyptian Traditional Elite—A Case Study in Elite Economic Nationalism* (Lewiston, 2002); Manali Chakrabarti, 'Why Did Indian Big Business Pursue a Policy of Economic Nationalism in the Interwar Years? A New Window to an Old Debate,' *Modern Asian Studies,* vol. 43, no. 4, (2009), 979–1038.

⁸ Hizky Shoham, "Buy Local' or 'Buy Jewish'? Separatist Consumption in Interwar Palestine,' *International Journal of Middle East Studies,* vol. 45, no. 3, (2013), 469–489.

Zionist "Buy National" Campaigns

As in most of the world, "buy local" initiatives were uncommon in the Middle East before World War I, with the exception of the 1908 Ottoman campaign against Austro-Hungarian products, which was targeted and extremely negative.[9] After the Great War, however, such campaigns emerged all across the region, reflecting the new economic nationalism that tried to assign a national identity to the territories demarcated by the borders drawn after the defeat and division of the Ottoman Empire.[10] One of these was Palestine, newly created by the British as a political and economic unit under a League of Nations mandate that affirmed the Balfour Declaration of 1917. In the wake of the European conquest, processes of urbanization and industrialization fueled the expansion of middle-class consumer societies in parts of the Middle East.[11] In Palestine, too, a Jewish urban middle class emerged, particularly in the rapidly developing Tel Aviv area.[12] Similar if slower processes took place in the Arab sector. These new middle classes emphasized self-fulfillment and self-expression through the act of consumption, which was increasingly politicized by both national movements in parallel "buy national" campaigns. In line with the doctrine of economic nationalism imported from Central and Eastern Europe, and which generally went unquestioned, the Zionist movement attempted to

---

[9] Elizabeth B. Frierson, 'Cheap and Easy: The Creation of Consumer Culture in Late Ottoman Society,' in: *Consumption Studies and the History of the Ottoman Empire, 1550–1922: An Introduction*, ed. Donald Quataert, (Albany, 2000), 246; Michelle Campos, *Ottoman Brothers: Muslims, Christians, and Jews in Early Twentieth-century Palestine* (Stanford, 2011), 100–108.

[10] Andrea Stanton, "'Palestinians Invade the Lebanon': Mandate-Era Tourism and National Branding," conference paper, MESA 2009, Boston.

[11] Elizabeth Thompson, *Colonial Citizens: Republican Rights, Paternal Privileges and Gender in French Syria and Lebanon* (New York, 2000), 175–183; Mona Russell, *Creating the New Egyptian Woman: Consumerism, Education, and National Identity, 1963–1922* (New York, 2004), 73–77; Relli Shechter, "The Cultural Economy of Development in Egypt: Economic Nationalism, Hidden Economy and the Emergence of Mass Consumer Society during Sadat's *Infitah*," *Middle Eastern Studies*, vol. 44, no. 4, (2008), 571–583; Nancy Reynolds, 'National Socks and the 'Nylon Woman': Materiality, Gender, and Nationalism in Textile Marketing in Semicolonial Egypt, 1930–1956,' *International Journal of Middle East Studies*, vol. 43, no. 1, (2011), 49–74; idem, *A City Consumed*.

[12] See esp. Anat Helman, *Young Tel Aviv: A Tale of Two Cities*, trans. Haim Watzman (Waltham, 2010).

build a Jewish economy that would be as independent of non-Jewish interests as possible. So did its Palestinian-Arab counterpart.[13]

The first documented call to protect local goods or *totseret ha-arets* ("the products of the Land") appeared in the Hebrew press in 1920 and was repeated over the next few years by local Jewish manufacturers, politicians, and educators.[14] During the course of the decade, a number of organizations, including merchants' and manufacturers' associations, chambers of commerce, workers' councils, youth groups, and political clubs promoted local products.[15] Teachers, politicians, and other cultural figures initiated and led these campaigns, which were sometimes subsidized by manufacturers and, on rare occasions, by Zionist institutions such as the Commerce and Industry Department of the Zionist Executive, directed by Nahum Tishby (1885–1952). Women's organizations and youth movements provided battalions of volunteers (whereas many of the male campaigners were paid officials).[16] In the 1920s and early 1930s, both grassroots and institutional "buy national" initiatives appeared in every sector of the Yishuv (the Jewish community in Palestine).

These Zionist "buy national" campaigns were often speaking the language of protecting the interests of Jewish workers, and therefore sometimes overlapped with concomitant struggles for "Hebrew Labor," as we will see below. Nonetheless, the latter campaigns received much more public attention in the Yishuv, as well as in the eyes of the Arabs and the British, especially during the 1930s—and for good reason. The Mandate

---

[13] Deborah Bernstein and Badi Hasisi, "'Buy and Promote the National Cause': Consumption, Class Formation and Nationalism in Mandate Palestine Society,' *Nations and Nationalism*, vol. 14, no. 1, (2008), 127–50; Sherene Seikaly, "Meatless Days: Consumption and Capitalism in Wartime Palestine 1939–1948" (Ph.D. diss., New York University, 2007); idem, 'Arab Businessmen Challenge the 1940s Status Quo,' *Mediterraneans*, vol. 14, (2010), 85–92.

[14] "Lizroʻa, lintoʻa, u-livnot" (To sow, plant, and build), *Hazefirah*, August 11, 1920, p. 2; Menahem Aldubi, 'Totseret ha-Arets' (The products of the land), *Kuntres*, vol. 139 (August 20, 1923), 19–20.

[15] Galya Hasharoni, "Shinayim totavot, shokolad ve-itriyot: ha-taʻasiyah ha-ʻivrit ba-ʻasor ha-rishon la-mandat 1919–1929—Hebetim Hevratiyim ve-Kakaliyim" (False teeth, chocolate, and noodles: Hebrew industry in the first decade of British Mandate, 1919–1929—economic and social aspects) (master's thesis, Haifa University, 2008), 109.

[16] Batsheva Margalit Stern, "Imahot ba-hazit: ha-maʻavak lemaʻan totseret ha-arets ve-ha-ʻimmut bein interesim migdariyim le-interesim le'ummiyim" (Mothers at the front: The struggle for local products and the conflict between gender and nationalist interests), *Israel*, vol. 11, (2007), 91–120.

government calculated Jewish immigration quotas on the basis of "economic absorption capacity." Hence the quotas could be reduced by Jewish unemployment, on the one hand, but also by high rates of Arab unemployment, on the other—which made the question of labor segregation a political hot potato. Moreover, the classic Zionist ideology of "productivization" highlighted the value of physical work performed by Jews and cast aspersions on Jewish capitalists (or even managers) for their "exilic" nature.[17] But labor segregation was not always compatible with the socialist tendency of the mainstream Zionist ideology, which was always fascinated by (and had a bad conscience about) the ideal of the universal brotherhood of workers.[18] Interwar Palestine witnessed several initiatives at the joint organization of Jewish and Arab workers; eventually, though, relations between Jewish and Arab workers began to focus more on "constructing boundaries" between these two ethnonational sectors.[19]

To the extent that consumption aroused ideological concerns, it symbolized the opposite of the ideal of labor. Nationalists, Jews and Arabs alike, attributed value to the "authentic" peasant (*fallah* for the Arabs, *narodnik* for Jews of Eastern European orientation) and attacked consumer culture as a moral threat to the nation. These moralizing attacks were linked to the distinction between "basic needs" and "luxuries"; they encouraged frugality, and sometimes even asceticism.[20] In the Yishuv, this discourse was influenced by the masculine nature of Zionist ideology and was often understood as a gendered division of labor, in which men

---

[17] Anita Shapira, *Ha-ma'avak Ha-nikhzav: Avoda Ivrit 1929–1939* (Futile Struggle: The Jewish Labor Controversy) (Tel Aviv, 1977).

[18] Anita Shapira, 'Kuvlanato shel shternhal' [Shternhel's complaint]. *Iyunim Bitkumat Israel*, vol. 6 (1996), 553–567; Ze'ev Shṭernhel, *The Founding Myths of Israel: Nationalism, Socialism, and the Making of the Jewish State*, trans. David Maisel (Princeton, 1998).

[19] For example, Barbara J. Smith, *The Roots of Separatism in Palestine: British Economic Policy 1920–1929* (Syracuse, 1993), 135–159; Zachary Lockman, *Comrades and Enemies: Arab and Jewish Workers in Palestine, 1906–1948* (Berkeley, 1996); Deborah S. Bernstein, 'Expanding the split labor market theory: between and within sectors of the split labor market of Mandatory Palestine,' *Comparative Studies in Society and History*, vol. 38, no. 2, (1996), 243–266; Idem., *Constructing Boundaries: Jewish and Arab Workers in Mandatory Palestine* (Albany, 2000).

[20] Oz Almog, *The Sabra: the Creation of the New Jew*, trans. Haim Watzman (Berkeley, 2000), 209–225; Seikaly, *Meatless Days*, 97–164.

produce and women consume.[21] However, it often clashed with the ethnonational productivist discourse that focused on a product's origins rather than its quality and legitimized consumption, even if excessive, as long as it contributed to the Jewish economy. The separatist campaigns indirectly legitimized the culture of consumerism and luxury (goods), which were otherwise at odds with the nationalist ethos of modest needs. The "buy national" campaigners, therefore, directed their efforts toward two groups who were notoriously irresponsible consumers: women and children. These two groups were relatively isolated from the struggle over Hebrew labor and could thus be recruited to the national cause through consumption.

Historian Anita Shapira summarized the differences between the two separatist campaigns as follows:

> The ideological cooperation between workers and employers saved the *totseret ha-arets* struggle from the bitterness and the violence that accompanied the struggle for Hebrew labor; [the former] was depicted as a struggle of the entire nation that transcended class. That was its strength as well as its weakness. The fact that there was no real opponent against whom to fight for local-Jewish products prevented the formation of a specific group that would identify with the struggle. As a result, this struggle was a mere preaching and had limited results.[22]

In other words, the *totseret ha-arets* campaign depicted buying national as the common interest of Jewish workers, capitalists, farmers, and the urban bourgeoisie, in spite of their clashes in other areas, like their counterparts the world over.[23] The campaigns for segregation in labor frequently pinpointed villains—Jewish smallholders, Arab landowners, or, in times of violence, Arab laborers themselves. The villains of the struggle for Jewish consumption, even though it was sometimes linked to the struggle

---

[21] Helman, *Young Tel Aviv*. Compare: Victoria De Grazia with Ellen Furlough (eds.), *The Sex of Things: Gender and Consumption in Historical Perspective* (Berkeley, 1996); Mary Louise Roberts, 'Gender, Consumption, and Commodity Culture,' *American Historical Review*, vol. 103, (1998), 817–844; Lisa Tiersten, *Marianne in the Market: Envisioning Consumer Society in Fin-de-Siècle France* (Berkeley, 2001); Matthew Hilton, 'The Female Consumer and the Politics of Consumption in Twentieth-Century Britain,' *The Historical Journal*, vol. 45, no. 1, (2002), 103–128.

[22] Shapira, *Ha-ma'avak Ha-nikhzav*, 232.

[23] Cf. Frank, *Buy American*, 61–64.

for Hebrew labor, as we see below, were targeted in a much vaguer and more general manner.

But the campaigns for separatism in consumption had their own complications with regard to defining Zionism's significant others. Given the unique geopolitical situation of the Yishuv, which was a settler-immigrant society building the political institutions of a "state-in-the-making" while still chafing under imperial rule, it was not clear just who or what the campaigns sought to protect.[24] Like the interwar anticolonial movements in Asia and Africa, the Jews in mandatory Palestine did not control a sovereign state with the power to levy tariffs or manage its own fiscal policy.[25] And as with the nationalist movements of those years, the campaigns were at least partly directed against the rival national movement whose members lived on the same territory. As a result, the Jewish economy that took shape, and its local products, were defined by two parameters—ethnonational ("Jewish") and territorial ("Palestine")—which were not fully aligned, and the Jewish "buy national" campaign zigzagged between "buy Jewish" and "buy local." This tension was evident in the main campaign slogan—"Buy only *totseret ha-arets*!"—whose literal meaning is "buy only local products of this land [Palestine]," in short, "buy local." In various contexts, however, it could mean "buy Jewish": reject not only imports but also non-Jewish (Arab) local products.[26] The phrase highlighted the link between the ethnic and territorial components of the new Jewish identity. For Jews of the era, *ha-arets* connoted a Jewish space that excluded the Arab inhabitants of Palestine.[27]

The blacklisted products thus fell into two main categories: imports and local non-Jewish goods. But these categories differed in their public manifestations. The crusade against imports was explicit and was on occasion joined by the British and Arabs, who were also concerned by Palestine's trade imbalance. On the other hand, explicit ethnonational separatism was not always politically expedient, and most "buy national"

---

[24] For example, Dan Horowitz and Moshe Lissak, *Origins of the Israeli Polity: Palestine under the Mandate* (Chicago, 1978).

[25] Arie Krampf, 'Reception of the Developmental Approach in the Jewish Economic Discourse of Mandatory Palestine, 1934–1938,' *Israel Studies*, vol. 15, no. 2, (2010), 80–103.

[26] Anat Helman, 'European Jews in the Levant Heat: Climate and Culture in 1920s and 1930s Tel Aviv,' *Journal of Israeli History*, vol. 22, no. 1, (2003), 71–90, esp. 79.

[27] Anita Shapira, *Land and Power: The Zionist Resort to Force, 1881–1948*, trans. William Templer (New York, 1992); Boaz Neumann, *Territory and Desire in Early Zionism* (Waltham, 2011).

organizations used territorial rather than ethnic designations when translating their names into English, such as the Council for Home Products, the Pro-Palestine Products Committee, and Palestine Home Products. Other organizations simply transliterated their Hebrew name into Latin characters.[28]

Within these two categories, were there any *specific* significant others targeted by the Zionist "buy national" campaigns? Students of Zionist culture and politics have suggested that the movement's main foil was the "exilic" Jew.[29] An analysis of the significant others in Zionist "buy national" campaigns, which aimed at demarcating sociocultural and economic borders between the emerging Jewish polity and its rivals, may clarify the question. I first investigate how the British, Arabs, and Nazis figure in these campaigns, but as we see, the possibility of a Jewish other should not be dismissed.

THE BRITISH

Between the two world wars, British economic interests were increasingly linked to exploiting the colonies as markets for British manufactures.[30] Administrators and officials throughout the empire were extremely intolerant of anti-British campaigns—and this was precisely why nationalists in places like India and Egypt openly boycotted British products as part of their struggle for independence.[31] By contrast, Zionist "buy national" campaigns were remarkably cautious about targeting British imports, even

---

[28] The Council for Domestic Products, Tel Aviv, to Tishby, the Zionist Executive, Jerusalem, December 20, 1923; the Palestine Commercial Agency to the Jewish National Fund, March 11, 1928, Central Zionist Archives (hereafter CZA) KKL5/2447; "Iggud lemaʿan totseret ha-arets: Takanon" (Union for Jewish Products: Regulations), undated, CZA S54/165.

[29] See: Yael Zerubavel, *Recovered Roots: Collective Memory and the Making of Israeli National Tradition* (Chicago, 1995), 20–28; Anita Shapira, 'The Origins of the Myth of the 'New Jew': The Zionist Variety,' *Studies in Contemporary Jewry*, vol. XIII, (1997), 253–268; Hizky Shoham, *Carnival in Tel-Aviv: Purim and the Celebration of Urban Zionism* (Boston, 2014), 122–130.

[30] Ian M. Drummond, *British Economic Policy and the Empire, 1919–1939* (London, 1972), 17–25.

[31] On the Egyptian boycott, see Shechter, "The Cultural Economy of Development"; Reynolds, "National Socks," 52; idem, *A City Consumed*, 78–113, esp. p. 84.

when relations with the authorities were at a nadir.[32] In fact, the British were never named in such campaigns until 1937; even then, a local Jerusalem initiative to boycott British products was swiftly and efficiently put down by Moshe Shertok (later Sharett), the head of the Political Department of the Jewish Agency. Shertok ordered an end to the call to boycott British goods, because he thought it inadvisable to provoke Britain but also, and no less so, because "England's position, both as the mandatory power and as the country that buys much more from Palestine than it sells to it, obligates us to [give it] special consideration."[33] In other words, aside from the political and diplomatic concerns, the commercial relationship with Great Britain was a crucial Zionist interest.

To explain this point, we must note that the Jews and Arabs in Palestine were distinguished not only by conflicting political visions but also by different economic structures, which often yielded opposing interests. The Jews were largely urban and employed in industry and services, while most Arabs were engaged in agriculture. The available statistics on patterns of consumption by the sector are inadequate, but it is clear that the purchasing power of Jews was considerably larger than that of the Arabs.[34]

In an attempt to keep the lid on the hostility between the two sectors, the British officially rejected ethnonational economic separatism and treated mandatory Palestine as a single economic unit.[35] But this position proved difficult to maintain, because British officials had to maneuver

---

[32] Barbara J. Smith, *The Roots of Separatism in Palestine: British Economic Policy 1920–1929* (Syracuse, 1993), 20–25; Hasharoni, "Shinayim totavot," 115.

[33] Shertok (Jewish Agency) to the Merkaz, February 1, 1937, CZA S54/165; see also the Merkaz to the Jewish Agency, January 3, 1936, S25/7317/2.

[34] *A Survey of Palestine*, 3 vols. (Jerusalem, 1946), 2: 373, 3: 570; Dan Giladi, *Ha-Yishuv bi-tekufat ha-ʿaliyah ha-reviʿit (1924–1929): Behinah kalkalit u-folitit* (The Yishuv during the Fourth Aliya [1924–1929]: A political-economic study) (Tel Aviv, 1973), 24–35; Smith, *The Roots of Separatism*, 167–81; Jacob Metzer, *The Divided Economy of Mandatory Palestine* (Cambridge, 1998), 117–137, 145–175, 167–168; Nahum Gross, *Lo ʿal ha-ruah levadah: ʿIyyunim ba-historiyah ha-kalkalit shel eretz yisraʾel ba-ʿet ha-hadashah* (Not by the spirit alone: studies in the economic history of modern Palestine) (Jerusalem, 2000), 383; Seikaly, *Meatless Days*; idem, "Arab Businessmen Challenge," 91; Gershon Shafir, 'Capitalist Binationalism in Mandatory Palestine,' *International Journal of Middle East Studies*, vol. 43, (2011), 611–633. See also the Iggud Lemaʿan Totseret ha-Arets to the Jewish Agency, May 7, 1940, supplement C, CZA J1/4461.

[35] *Survey of Palestine*, 3: 570. They did this, for example, when calculating the yearly quota of Jewish immigration certificates. See Aviva Halamish, 'Eretz Yisraʾel ha-mandatorit: hevrah

between the two communities' needs and demands before instituting any economic policy. The Arabs usually demanded tariffs on agricultural imports, whereas the Zionists called for heavy customs duties on imported manufactured goods but exemptions for industrial raw materials.[36] At least in the 1920s, when many British officials held that building a Jewish national home in accordance with the Balfour Declaration was not at odds with the welfare of the Palestinian Arabs, and despite their discomfort with economic separatism, they saw Jewish immigrants as allies in the drive to modernize the country. Even later, when British policy was not always favorable to the Zionist cause, it generally favored Jewish industrial development in the economic sphere.[37] The British and the Zionists did not always see eye to eye on the political future of Palestine but viewed each other as allies vis-à-vis the "non-Western" inhabitants. Bowing to British commercial interest was small price to pay, and interwar Zionist campaigners mostly understood that.

Arabs

In 1936, a British firm that was investigating the idea of establishing a factory in Palestine was astonished to discover that "when the Jews advocate for local products, they do not mean the country's products, but Jewish products."[38] For most of those involved, however, this was not much of a surprise. Indeed, the aforementioned tension between the territorial and ethnic definitions of the economic unit to be protected by Zionist economic nationalism was most apparent in the treatment of local Arab products.

In more relaxed times, the campaigners preferred not to target Arab products directly. In 1933, for example, the Palestine [Jewish] Association of Citrus Growers launched a campaign against competing Arab products, only to be rebuked by Chaim Arlosoroff, the head of the Political Department of the Jewish Agency, who warned the orchard owners not to

---

du'alit o metsi'ut koloni'alit?' (Mandatory Palestine: dual society or colonial reality?), *Zemanim*, vol. 92, (2005): 1–25.

[36] Smith, *The Roots of Separatism*, 160–181.

[37] Marcella Simoni, 'At the Roots of Division: A New Perspective on Arabs and Jews, 1930–39,' *Middle Eastern Studies*, vol. 36, no. 3 (2000), 52–92; Smith, *The Roots of Separatism*; Metzer, *The Divided Economy*, 23.

[38] Dr. Pinhas Rotenstreich to the Jewish Agency Executive, December 30, 1936, CZA S54/166.

be too blunt in their advocacy of ethnic separatism in consumption.[39] Indeed, until the ethnonational tensions escalated in the mid-1930s, foreign, rather than Arab, products were the main target of such campaigns. In those years, an all-Palestinian (Arab and Jewish) civic identity was still feasible and Jews and Arabs occasionally worked together on behalf of common territorial interests and campaigned for more stringent protection of the autarkic Palestinian economy. In the footwear industry, for example, Jewish and Arab manufacturers banded together against the flooding of the local market with cheap Syrian and European shoes. In 1930, a new Czech shoe company opened branches in Jerusalem, Tel Aviv, Nazareth, and Tiberias; it sold inexpensive products and employed innovative marketing and advertising techniques, such as advertisements screened in movie theaters. In response, more than 700 Jewish and Arab shoemakers gathered in Jerusalem (to avoid potential quarrels, an Armenian was elected chair) and demanded that the Mandate government implement a protectionist policy favoring Palestinian domestic production.[40] According to a senior Zionist official, this meeting was quietly organized by none other than Nahum Tishby.[41]

Ethnonational separatism in consumption did not take off until the mid-1930s, as the political tensions and economic competition between the Jewish and Arab sectors escalated. While the Yishuv enjoyed increased economic prosperity, thanks to the influx of new immigrants and capital from Europe (see below), many Palestinian *fellahin* lost their land and were proletarianized. In April 1936, this led to a general strike led by the Arab Higher Committee, combined with other forms of political protests. After this course of action was exhausted, a violent, peasant-led resistance movement that attacked British targets superseded it in what came to be known as the Arab Revolt, which was the most violent conflict in the annals of mandatory Palestine. Before it ended, in 1939, several thousand Arabs and hundreds of Jews and British soldiers were killed. Recent scholarship on the revolt emphasizes the contribution of the worsening

---

[39] The secretary of the Political Department of the Jewish Agency (Chaim Arlosoroff) to the Palestine Association of Citrus Growers, February 28, 1933, CZA 156/181.

[40] A report about shoes imported to Palestine, submitted to the standing committee for commerce and industry, April 21, 1929; "Tenuʿat ihud bein ha-yatzranim ha-yehudim ve-haʿaravim" (Union of Jewish and Arab manufacturers), undated [October 1930], CZA S25/7317a.

[41] Colonel Kisch to the Political Department of the Jewish Agency, December 9, 1930, CZA S25/7317/2; Tishby to the Executive, December 12, 1930, CZA S25/7317/2.

economic conflict between the two sectors over land and labor.[42] The field of consumption was also affected: in 1935, after 15 years of grassroots "buy national" activity, the various Jewish groups set up an umbrella organization, the *Merkaz Lema'an Totseret ha-Arets* (Center for the Products of the Land; hereafter "the Merkaz"), which was sponsored by the Va'ad Le'ummi (the National Council of Jews of Palestine, the Zionist "shadow government" in mandatory Palestine) and several Jewish businesses. Although this coordination increased after the 1936 quantum leap in violence, it had begun earlier.[43]

The violence of 1936–1939 disrupted manufacturers' access to markets and fueled mutual, and now more effective, calls for boycotts of Jewish and Arab products. Even the influential writer and citrus grower Moshe Smilansky, the head of the Farmers' Association and previously an opponent of economic separatism, changed his mind in the wake of the Arab Revolt.[44] Soon after it began in April 1936, the industrialist H. Frumkin, a leading member of the Merkaz, told campaign activists they "must not miss the rare opportunity to exploit the nationalist sentiment."[45] Later he informed the economic affairs committee of the Tel Aviv municipality that there had been "some improvement" in national consumption habits in May 1936.[46] This was supported by statistical data. For example, larger quantities of Jewish-grown vegetables were sold in the second quarter of 1936 than in the corresponding period the year before.[47] There continued to be trade between Jews and Arabs in Palestine but at a much reduced

---

[42] Zachary Lockman, 'Arab Workers and Arab Nationalism in Palestine: A View from Below,' in: *Rethinking Nationalism in the Arab Middle East*, ed. James Jankowski and Israel Gershoni, (Cambridge, 1997), 249–272; Mahmoud Yazbak, 'From Poverty to Revolt: Economic Factors in the Outbreak of the 1936 Rebellion in Palestine,' *Middle Eastern Studies*, vol. 36, no. 3, (2000), 93–113.

[43] Bar-Kokhba Meirovitch to Eliezer Kaplan, November 26, 1935, CZA S9/1521; Shapira, *Ha-ma'avak Ha-nikhzav*, 231–233; Yitzhak Livni, *Ha-ma'avak she-nishkah: ha-iggud lema'an totseret ha-arets: ha-mahlakah ha-hakla'it 1936–1949* (The forgotten struggle: The union for the products of the land: the agriculture department, 1936–1949) (Netanya, 1990), 5–11.

[44] Ibid., 20–22; Nahum Karlinsky, *California Dreamers: Ideology, Society and Technology in the Citrus Industry in Palestine, 1890–1939*, trans. Naftali Greenwood (Albany, 2005), 44.

[45] Minutes of the meeting of the secretaries of the Iggudim Lema'an Totseret ha-Arets with the Merkaz Lema'an Totseret ha-Arets, 31 May 1936, p. 1, CZA S9/1521.

[46] Decisions of the Economic Committee, June 1, 1936, Tel Aviv Municipal Archive (hereafter TAMA) 04-3041.

[47] Decisions of the Economic Committee, July 21, 1936, TAMA 04-3041.

pace; for the first time, the "buy national" campaigns seemed to be effective, at least to a degree.

As a result of the 1936–1939 violence, the territorial component of the "buy national" campaigns withered and the ethnic one came to fore. The Tel Aviv municipality established the aforementioned economic affairs committee, whose tasks included guaranteeing the steady flow of goods and produce to the city's markets and combating profiteering. At the same time, and paradoxically, it encouraged consumers to buy Jewish, even though this led to higher prices, because Arab products were usually cheaper. The committee even tried to encourage the consumption of flour imported from Syria rather than that produced by Arab Palestinians, so as "not to strengthen the rioters," in the words of A. Kamini, the secretary of the municipality and a prominent member of the Economic Affairs Committee.[48] In this case, the "buy national" campaign turned into an unequivocal boycott of local Arab products.

The new guise of the "buy national" campaigns as "buy Jewish" campaigns was also evident in the militancy of the agricultural department of the Tel Aviv-based *Iggud Lema'an Totseret ha-Arets* (Union for the Products of the Land).[49] The domestic Arab-Palestinian competition posed a greater threat in agriculture and construction than in industry and financial services, which were not based on the cheap Arab labor. This new separatism attracted the attention of the Mandatory government and led to several police searches of the offices of the Merkaz.[50] The British had seemed mostly indifferent to the campaigns before 1936, but the Arab Revolt made them more suspicious of separatist activities (which might occasionally turn into an anti-British campaign, as we have seen).

As the competition between the two national movements in Palestine became fiercer, the "buy national" campaigns singled out the Palestinian Arabs as "rioters" who harmed the Zionist project. Still, the new nationalist energy of the mid-1930s found another outlet in more direct attempts to make Jewish industries more competitive. New organizations conducted research on the efficiency of materials and products and increased

---

[48] Decisions of the economic committee, June 7, 1936, TAMA 04-3041.

[49] Stern, "Imahot ba-hazit," 105.

[50] Dr. Rotenstreich to the Jewish Agency Executive, December 30, 1936, and a handwritten notation by Dr. Santor there, CZA S54-165; the Merkaz to Eliezer Kaplan, January 3, 1937, CZA S25/7317a; Rotenstreich to Shertok, January 29, 1937, CZA S54/165; Shohat-Kaduri law firm, Tel Aviv, to Bernard Joseph, Jerusalem, January 31, 1937, CZA S25/7317/2.

the quality testing of products labeled as "Hebrew," that is, Jewish and local. After 1936, more and more financial and human resources of the voluntary organizations were put into economic efforts to enhance competitiveness.[51]

The outbreak of World War II produced a different economic order in Palestine: full employment and, in due course, partial austerity. The flames of the violence in Palestine were dampened. This, in turn, affected the Zionist "buy national" activity, which lowered its public profile and switched from the public campaigns and cultural work of the interwar era to greater emphasis on the standardization of products and protection of consumers, so as to improve the competitiveness of Jewish products. The boycotts of the mid-1930s and later proved efficient in demarcating the border between "our" and "their" products, thus removing the Arab-Jewish all-Palestinian identity from the agenda, to the extent it was ever there. After successfully demarcating the mental border between the Jewish and Arab economies, Zionist activists could more easily reduce the moral pressure in favor of developing "our" economy.

NAZIS AND OTHER GERMANS

When Adolf Hitler came to power in Germany in early 1933, Zionism encountered its worst foe. The Yishuv responded immediately, casting Nazism and its leader as the Jews' supreme enemy.[52] There were loud public calls to boycott German goods—in part an inversion of the Nazi boycott of German Jews.[53] All over the world, in fact, Jews boycotted German products.[54]

In the Zionist case, however, boycotting Nazi Germany turned out to be easier said than done, first because of a series of *Ha'avara* ("transfer") agreements between the Nazi regime and various Zionist organizations, signed between 1933 and 1935, and even more so from 1936, when the Jewish Agency took over the enterprise and concluded additional agreements with the Germans. The common element of these arrangements

---

[51] For example, the Economic Committee of the Tel Aviv Municipality to the Institute for the Examination of Materials, the Chemists' Association, Strauss House, September 9, 1936, TAMA, file 4-3041.

[52] Shoham, *Carnival in Tel Aviv*, 131–137.

[53] "Shema, Hitler" (Hear O Hitler), *Doar Hayom*, March 27, 1933, p. 1.

[54] On Egypt, see: "Sheikh alfaruq mashmi'a divrey hokhma vedo'eg" (Sheikh Alfaruq speaks wisely and is worried), *Doar Hayom*, April 4, 1933, p. 1.

was that they made it possible for Jews to emigrate from Germany with most of their capital, on condition that it was transferred to Palestine in the form of German industrial goods. Such bilateral arrangements were conventional in those years as a way to bypass foreign currency restrictions that applied to emigrants (the World Zionist Organization signed a similar agreement with Lithuania in 1936).[55] In the case of mandatory Palestine, it enabled the immigrants from Germany to register with the British authorities as "capitalists"; as such, they received immigration certificates automatically and were not counted against the annual immigration quota.[56] This arrangement, which operated until the eve of World War II, transferred about eight million Palestine pounds from Germany to Palestine within six years and enabled tens of thousands of German Jews to immigrate to Palestine.[57]

The *Ha'avara* arrangement became the subject of a heated public debate that split the Jewish world throughout the 1930s. In the eyes of the opponents, it weakened the moral basis of the worldwide Jewish boycott of Nazi Germany. A byproduct of the *Ha'avara*, relevant to us here, was that Palestine was flooded with German industrial goods—mostly steel and metal products such as pipes, engines, agricultural machinery, electrical devices, and pumps, along with medical equipment, lumber, cloth, paper, paints, and glass and china kitchen—and tableware.[58] To start their new life, the immigrants sold these goods at any price, which depressed prices in the entire local Palestine market. This inundation aggravated the "buy national" supporters twice over, because not only were these cheap foreign goods but those produced by the devil himself.

The *Ha'avara* Trust and Transfer Office claimed that it imported only those sorts of goods that were not produced locally in Palestine, but this was not always the case. In August 1939, for example, the *Iggud Lema'an*

---

[55] "Transfer EY-Lita" (Transfer Palestine-Lithuania), *Davar*, April 22, 1936, p. 3.

[56] Aviva Halamish, *Be-merotz kaful neged ha-zeman* (A double race against time: Zionist immigration policy during the 1930s) (Jerusalem, 2006).

[57] The literature on the *Ha'avara* agreement is vast. See: Yoav Gelber, *Moledet hadashah: Aliyat yehudey merkaz eiropa uklitatam 1933–1948* (A new homeland: The Jewish immigration from Central Europe and its absorption 1933–1948) (Jerusalem, 1990), 23–40, 78–92; Yfaat Weiss, 'The Transfer Agreement and the Boycott Movement: A Jewish Dilemma on the Eve of the Holocaust,' *Yad Vashem Studies*, vol. 26 (1998), 129–171; Hava Eshkoli-Wagman, 'Yishuv Zionism: Its Attitude to Nazism and the Third Reich Reconsidered,' *Modern Judaism*, vol. 19, no. 1, (1999), 21–40 (see 26–31).

[58] "Sakhar Eretz-Israel-Germania" [Trade between Palestine and Germany], *Davar*, March 31, 1933, p. 2.

Totseret Ha-arets demanded that it cancel a deal to import 16,000 brass faucets from Germany, inasmuch as the particular financial circumstances of the *Ha'avara* meant that they would be sold at a discount of 50% below the market price. The *Ha'avara* Office was accused of jeopardizing the livings of 50 or 60 Tel Aviv families and of undermining the local industry, with its limited ability to compete with German products that were cheaper and of better quality. The *Ha'avara* people retorted that there was no discount and that the lower price of the German faucets stemmed from regular market factors. In a further attempt to mollify public opinion and seem to support local production, they also promised to order 2000–3000 new faucets from the Tel Aviv factory.[59]

In the Yishuv, the calls to boycott Nazi Germany were voiced mostly by the right-wing opposition Revisionist Organization, led by Vladimir (Ze'ev) Jabotinsky (1880–1940), which split from the World Zionist Organization in 1935. Despite these recurring calls, that were also echoed by some within the dominant Labor Movement—the arrangement worked well until the start of World War II. Setting aside their understandable reluctance, the Zionist leaders opted for the opportunity to rescue German Jews while securing a flow of money and skilled manpower to the Yishuv, despite the political and emotional price of dealing with the Nazis. Sometimes, when the German merchandise threatened a local Jewish equivalent, the opponents of the *Ha'avara* played the "buy national" card. But from a strictly economic point of view, and in historical retrospect, the *Ha'avara* funds and human resources played a crucial role in the Jewish nation-building project in Palestine.[60] Because many agreed that the agreement coincided with Zionist interests, Zionist "buy national" campaigners did not usually single out German products as more unacceptable than other imports. (The *Ha'avara* imports did threaten British commercial interests in Palestine, but that lies beyond our present scope.)

The "buy national" movement channeled the anti-German sentiment to a boycott of a local community of Germans. The Templers were a religious sect whose settlement in Palestine in the nineteenth century preceded the mass Zionist immigrations. They were known for their diligence, dedication, and outstanding agricultural produce. During the 1930s,

---

[59] *Iggud Lema'an Totseret ha-arets* to the Haavara Office, Tel Aviv, August 6, 1939; D. Knopf (the Jewish Agency representative in the Haavara Office) to the Commerce Department of the Jewish Agency, August 14, 1939, CZA S8/385/1.

[60] For example, Eshkoli-Wagman, "Yishuv Zionism," 29.

though, their most prominent leaders identified with the Nazis.[61] In 1933, as a response to the Nazi boycott of German Jews, the Jews in Palestine instituted a boycott of the Templers. But it was not until the escalation of the "buy Jewish" campaigns in 1935–1936 that the Jewish boycott of the Templers had real effect. In the mid-1930s, for example, the Templers were selling about 4500–5000 liters of milk a day in Tel Aviv, or about one-third of the city's milk.[62] But according to a report submitted directly to Ben-Gurion in March 1936, the boycott had reduced the consumption of German milk to 2000 liters a day.[63]

It should be mentioned that the Tel Aviv branch of the Templers Bank played an important role in the *Ha'avara* arrangement.[64] Nevertheless, the *Ha'avara* Office cooperated with the campaign "for a gradual end to the sale of the German milk," as one *Ha'avara* administrator put it in an official letter.[65] "German" was indeed the adjective of contempt that was used to describe Templer products in all Zionist correspondence of the mid-decade. The Templers' unpopularity with the British rulers also made them an easy target for an economic war.

Because of the *Ha'avara* agreement, the Templers' market share was in fact minor as compared with the flow of German products into Palestine markets until the onset of World War II.[66] It was only with regard to the local Germans that the boycott was effective and enjoyed consensus support among the Zionists. Of course Germany was not popular in the Yishuv during the 1930s, but realpolitik overcame sentiment, and it was business as usual between Germany and Jewish Palestine. (It is interesting that while boycotting its own Jews, Nazi Germany continued to purchase Palestinian oranges and other products, though in somewhat lesser quantities.)[67] This was so not only among the political leadership but also

---

[61] When the war broke out, the British expelled most of them from Palestine and confiscated their land and property. See Helmut Glenk, *From Desert Sands to Golden Oranges: The History of the German Templer Settlement of Sarona in Palestine 1871–1947* (Victoria, 2005), 197–200.

[62] "Matsav shuk he-halav be-Tel Aviv" (The Tel Aviv dairy market), Yehiel Halevi to Meir Dizengoff, December 11, 1935, TAMA 04-3041.

[63] W. Santor to Ben-Gurion, March 31, 1936, CZA S54/166.

[64] Gelber, *Moledet hadashah*, 29.

[65] Ha'avara Office, Tel Aviv, to Dr. Pinhas Rotenstreich, April 3, 1936, CZA S54/166.

[66] "Ha'avara bishnat 1937" [the Haavara in 1937], *Davar*, January 5, 1938, p. 4.

[67] "Duah rishmi al export hahadarim" [Official report on citrus exports], *Davar*, July 22, 1936, p. 3; "Hapardesanut" [Citrus-growing], *Davar*, September 5, 1937, p. 17; "Sikkuyim tovim lifri hehadar" [Good prospects for citrus], *Davar*, October 13, 1938, p. 6.

among the merchant class, many of whose members were immigrants from Central and Eastern Europe who fled from there because of antisemitism but did not, in fact, boycott it.

OTHER JEWS

The picture portrayed so far is one of positive campaigns, focused on "our" prosperity, as this was understood within the Yishuv. It was only in the mid-1930s that they were ramped up and aimed at several foreign targets, but even then with only partial and temporary success, except in the case of the Templers. However, even campaigns focused on "our" products have to identify them and demarcate the borders with "theirs." This meant that interwar "buy national" campaigners had to draw up "white lists" of legitimate businesses and products that were *totseret ha-arets*, that is, local and Jewish.

The conceptual difficulty of defining "Jewish" products involved major political decisions that disclosed the sociopolitical diversity behind the apparent unity of the Yishuv.[68] One such dispute concerned whether it was Jewish capital or Jewish labor that made a product "Jewish." The Histadrut (the General Federation of Labor) and other Zionist-socialist organizations associated separatism in consumption with separatism in labor, whereas manufacturers and farmers argued that a Jewish product was one produced by Jewish capital and not necessarily Jewish labor.[69] The debate was fueled by several harsh labor disputes that fragmented the Yishuv in the 1930s, augmented by many violent incidents and mutual boycotts between the Zionist right and left (which related, among other issues, to the *Ha'avara* agreement).[70] Another issue was the organizational affiliations of "Jewish" producers; when large Jewish cooperatives that were affiliated with the Histadrut and marketed the products of Zionist-socialist settlements advertised themselves as the only sellers of Jewish products,

---

[68] Shoham, "Buy Local or Buy Jewish," 480–482.
[69] The Yitzhar factory to Dr. Rotenstreich, the Jewish Agency, December 23, 1935, CZA S54/165; minutes of the meeting of representatives of workers and industrialists regarding local products, January 27, 1927; Karlinsky, *California Dreamers*, 113–115; Shafir, "Capitalist Binationalism."
[70] Shapira, *Ha-ma'avak Ha-nikhzav*; minutes of the meeting between the Merkaz Lema'an Totseret ha-Arets and the Iggud Lema'an Totseret ha-Arets, April 2, 1936, p. 2, CZA S9/1521.

other Jewish merchants protested.[71] Some Jewish manufacturers claimed they were denied the *totseret ha-arets* label, despite meeting the ethnic standards, because they were not affiliated with the Labor Movement.[72] In several cases, the label was even granted to importers who made donations to the Merkaz. In others, Jewish growers accused the Merkaz of assisting the marketing of Arab products sold by Arab merchants who were considered to be political allies of the Zionists; the Merkaz denied all these accusations.[73]

The most difficult complication in determining the "Jewishness" of products involved the long commodity chains that made it almost impossible to identify a product's origins.[74] Thanks to the rapid industrialization of Palestine during the Mandate, production and distribution involved multiple stages, not only in financial services such as banking and insurance but also in agriculture and manufacturing. It became more and more difficult to distinguish the various sources of raw materials, packing materials, credit, and transportation. For example, "Jewish bread" was baked in Jewish bakeries, but where did the flour come from? In some cases it did come from a Jewish mill in Haifa, but this mill did not use the Jewish shipping company to import its grain.[75] And what about Jewish oranges, which were picked by Jewish workers but packed in imported boxes?[76] A subcommittee of the Merkaz deliberated these quasi-talmudic issues and reached inconsistent conclusions. There was hardly any product that was handled solely by Jews throughout the entire chain of production and distribution.[77]

In other words, the ethnic origins of products could be defined only as long as the details of the production process were not examined too closely. Consumers who insisted on buying only purely Jewish products could have kept their wallets in their pockets. Most if not all of the so-called Jewish products had non-Jewish inputs, local or foreign.

Nonetheless, once products were tagged, they were spoken of as "Jewish" or "foreign" as if those were their essential qualities. As with

---

[71] The Greengrocers' Association to the Mayor of Tel Aviv, January 8, 1930, TAMA 04-3040.

[72] Rotenstreich to the Merkaz, January 19, 1937; reply, January 21, 1937, CZA S54/165.

[73] "Zikhron devarim me-ha-pegishah she-hitkaymah ba-sokhnut ha-yehudit be-Yom 7.6.1937" (Minutes of the meeting at the Jewish Agency on June 7, 1937), CZA S54/165.

[74] Appadurai, *The Social Life of Things*, 13.

[75] Decisions of the Economic Committee, June 17, 1936, TAMA 04-3041.

[76] Minutes of the Committee to Examine Local Products, June 16, 1936, CZA S54/165.

[77] The Manufacturers' Association of Israel currently requires that at least 35% of a product's value be produced in Israel in order for it to be labeled "made in Israel." See http://www.industry.org.il/?CategoryID=1821 (accessed 13 November 2014).

most gray areas, the discourse about *purity and danger* preoccupied the public sphere.[78] Words such as "defilement" and "purification" were used quite literally in discussions of money, labor, or products in the market or at home. For example, one industrialist defined all imported products as "hametz" (unleavened bread) and asserted that they should be banished from the market just like bread during Passover according to traditional Jewish observance.[79]

The mid-1930s also witnessed an escalation in the condemnation of disloyal merchants, manufacturers, and customers. The more vigorous enforcement of the general boycott of foreign products led to violent incidents between campaign volunteers and "deviant" merchants. In one case, an "inspector" for a local Jerusalem organization was fined £P3 for enforcement activity that may have been too violent.[80] The official response of the Merkaz to such violent incidents was usually to condemn both sides.[81] The escalation of the conflict thus exposed the internal political complications of the campaign, which tried to implement the doctrine of economic nationalism by behaving like a state, without actually being one.

Much of the energy invested in the efforts to distinguish "Jewish" from "non-Jewish" products targeted Jewish manufacturers, retailers, and consumers who demonstrated "disloyal" conduct in the field of consumption. Although this was never the campaigns' explicit goal, it turned out that it was mainly Jews who were pinpointed as obstacles to Jewish economic independence.

Conclusion: The Other in Zionist Identity

The Zionist "buy national" campaigns were part of a consistent attempt, characteristic of Zionism from its outset, to construct an exclusivist Jewish identity en route to an independent Jewish polity.[82] During the Mandate

---

[78] Mary Douglas, *Purity and Danger: An Analysis of Concepts of Pollution and Taboo* (New York, 1966).

[79] Minutes of the meeting between the secretaries of the Iggudim Lemaʿan Totseret ha-Arets and the Merkaz, May 31, 1936, p. 1.

[80] "Sekirah ʿal ha-bikkur bi-Yerushalayim" (report on the visit to Jerusalem), by members Ben-David and Lipson, October 10, 1937, p. 1, CZA S54-165.

[81] Livni, *Ha-maʾavak she-nishkah*, 7–9, 17.

[82] *Shapira, Land and Power*, 83–126; Dafna Hirsch, "We Are Here to Bring the West, Not Only to Ourselves': Zionist Occidentalism and the Discourse of Hygiene in Mandate Palestine,' *International Journal of Middle East Studies,* vol. 41, (2009), 577–594; Shoham, "Buy Local or Buy Jewish."

period, Zionism employed the discourse of economic nationalism, supported by the voluntary moral power of ideology rather than sovereign power, and sought to define the economy on both ethnonational and territorial bases.

Zionist "buy national" campaigns did not, on the whole, target particular others, before the mid-1930s. The British were the colonial rulers, but in the interwar era, there was no direct economic conflict with them, if only because Britain was the main market for Palestine's products. The Palestinian Arabs were the main political rivals. Nevertheless, Arab products were not denounced with the same zeal as was Arab labor. In manufacturing they were no competition. In agriculture, where they were, a full boycott of Arab products was not a realistic option and was rarely mentioned (the Arabs, too, downplayed it), due to the geographical proximity and the economic interrelationship between the two sectors. A boycott of Nazi Germany was spoken of more often, but failed to dominate the Yishuv, particularly because of the *Ha'avara* agreement. For the Zionists, the struggle for the country was a matter of urgency, which took priority not only over the fight against colonialism but also over the effort against Nazism and European antisemitism.

The mid-1930s reshaping of the campaign into a boycott was fostered by two general conditions, one economic and the other political. Economically, those who supported boycotts felt secure enough in their own economy, whether this feeling was justified or not. Politically, the continuing violence from 1936 on stood in contrast to the limited outbreaks of violence in the past, such as the "Western Wall Uprising" of 1929, in which 133 Jews and 116 Arabs were killed and 198 Jews and 232 Arabs were injured in one week. Although this bloody week had long-range effects on Jewish and Arab separatism,[83] in the short term it had the opposite effect and produced greater caution on both sides in their everyday contacts with each other. Calls for mutual boycotts by Jews and Arabs had no effect on consumption habits and inter-ethnonational trade.[84] The aftermath of the violence even produced some unexpected (though very

---

[83] Hillel Cohen, *Year Zero of the Arab-Israeli Conflict 1929*, trans. Haim Watzman (Hannover, 2015).

[84] Metzer, *The Divided Economy*, 167–171; From Mayor Bloch to deputy mayor Israel Rokach, 29 August 1929; Anonymous memorandum to Dizengoff, 24 October 1929—TAMA 04-3040. The same held true for the Arab side. See: Bernstein and Hasisi, Buy and Promote the National Cause.

limited) Jewish-Arab economic cooperation, such as the aforementioned assembly of shoemakers in Jerusalem.[85] With the influx of Jewish capital from Europe during the 1930s, the economic tide sharpened the occupational opposition between the two competing ethnonational sectors and catalyzed the 1936–1939 Arab Revolt, which rallied both sides and intensified their "buy national" campaigns.[86] Among the Jews, this intensification included boycotts of particular sources, notably the local Germans and Arabs, but also of Jewish deviants who were not deemed sufficiently loyal to the Jewish economy. In the end, these campaigns downplayed their negative tone when the violence in Palestine declined, after 1939. In other words, the escalation of the "buy national" campaigns in the mid-1930s sometimes identified villains, but its main long-range effect was to bolster the attempt to build an independent Jewish economy, autonomous of everything non-Jewish, whether local or foreign. In that, the intensity of the second half of the 1930s played a crucial role in the separatist consciousness of the Jews of Palestine.

---

[85] See supra note 41, and Shapira, *Ha-ma'avak ha-nikhzav*, 58, and n. 27 in p. 360.
[86] Yazbak, "From Poverty to Revolt."

CHAPTER 6

Picketing Jewish-Owned Businesses in Nazi Germany: A Boycott?

Christoph Kreutzmüller

In July 1935, Selma and Georg Cohn decided they had enough. Violent blockades and threats had forced the couple to give up their families' well-established eiderdown factory in the small town of Landsberg/Warthe (now Gorzów Wielkopolski) and move to Berlin in 1933.[1] In the capital they had started a—unlicensed—fruit business that was closed down by the police on 25 July 1935 following a tip-off from a neighbour that the owners were Jewish.[2] In retaliation, the couple started picketing a baker who had been in their shop when it was closed down, rightly suspecting that this man, Fritz Wachsmuth, had reported them to the police in the first place. Wachsmuth, a member of the Nazi Party, asked his local party representative for help who in turn complained to the police that the Cohns were spreading "hostile propaganda against the [Nazi, CK]

---

[1] Sworn statement by Arno Cohn, 30 July 1957, *Compensation Office Berlin (EAB)*, 336718.
[2] Report from Police Station No 152, 26 July 1935, *State Archive Berlin (LAB)*, A Pr. Br. Rep 030, 21617.

C. Kreutzmüller (✉)
Jewish Museum Berlin/House of the Wannsee-Conference, Berlin, Germany
e-mail: c.kreutzmueller@jmberlin.de

© The Author(s) 2019
D. Feldman (ed.), *Boycotts Past and Present*, Palgrave Critical Studies of Antisemitism and Racism,
https://doi.org/10.1007/978-3-319-94872-0_6

movement and the state".[3] The couple was promptly detained for several days. After their release, Selma Cohn continued organizing public protest against Wachsmuth's bakery, asking their neighbourhood not to do business with a Nazi![4] Their action only came to an end when the couple was arrested once again on 10 August 1935.[5] If one defines a "boycott" as a nonviolent, privately organized ban or blockade, aiming to punish misconduct or asking for political or economic change, the Cohn's campaign was somehow a surprising but certainly fitting example. But does the same apply to the action against Jewish-owned businesses, law offices, and surgeries in Nazi Germany just one and a half years earlier? Was the infamous "boycott" on 1 April 1933 really a boycott? After all, even though it is generally referred to as such, it is doubtful whether it actually fulfilled the criteria we have nowadays of a boycott. Were the criteria different, then, in the 1920s and 1930s? What was the background of the picketing of Jewish-owned businesses, law offices, and surgeries? Why was it called for? Who organized it? Who picketed which shops and how did the persecution of Jewish commercial enterprises develop after April 1933? How was the process referred to at the time?

Economic Warfare

With the outbreak of the First World War, the liberal global economic system that was based on principles of free trade and most favoured nation treatment and negotiated in gold parities finally collapsed. In its place, economic regimes were installed in Central and Eastern Europe which not only jealously guarded their borders by means of customs duties and currency and transfer restrictions but also increasingly sought to reserve trade, industry, and agriculture for certain sections of the population, defined by

---

[3] Witness statement by baker Fritz Wachsmuth, 26 July 1935, ibid.
[4] Letter from the NS Group Olivia to Police Station No. 152, 9 August 1935, ibid.
[5] Police Station No. 152 Reports, 10 August 1935, ibid. The Cohns paid dearly for their brave act. Selma and Georg Cohn lost all their financial reserves, could not emigrate, and were deported to Kowno where they were murdered in November 1941: See: Federal Archive, Memorial Book, Victims of the Persecution of Jews under the National Socialist Tyranny in Germany 1933–1945, Cohn, Georg (born 25 April 1887) and Selma (nee Jacubowski born 15 May 1891). Cf. Property declaration by Georg Cohn, 13 November 1941, *Brandenburgisches Landeshauptarchiv Potsdam*, Rep. 36 A (II), 6133.

their social, religious, or ethnic identity—or by racist categories.⁶ Economic warfare—*Wirtschaftskrieg*—became the slogan of the time and boycotts one of its tools.⁷

Germany not only suffered from a rigid blockade during the "Great War" but was exempted from the most favoured nation treatment after the armistice by Great Britain and France and burdened by heavy reparations written into the peace treaty.⁸ While the Germans felt unfairly punished and saw their currency collapsing in hyperinflation, they were also reading newspaper reports on the boycott of Hungary by the International Trade Union Commission,⁹ the boycott of Japan, Shanghai, and Hong Kong by China, the boycott of Italy by Yugoslavia,¹⁰ and, of course, Gandhi's famous call for a boycott of all foreign cloths.¹¹ This in turn had a strong impact on national affairs. After all, "boycott", as the lawyer Eduard Reimer put it in 1935, "has the tendency to blossom in times of unrest"— and Germany was far from being a peaceful society after the trench fighting had stopped.¹² The newly elected German government showed just how powerful a device of economic warfare could be by suppressing a revolt by nationalist militias with a general strike in March 1920. Two years later, after the occupation of the Ruhr area by Belgian and French troops, there was a widespread call, supported by the German government, to refrain from buying any goods from these two nations.¹³

In the turmoil of revolts, reparation, and inflation, economic bans and blockades became such a widely and readily employed measure that in 1924 the State Council (*Reichsrat*) debated the introduction of a law into the *penal code* punishing illegal bans. At the same time, the inflationary use of the term "boycott" in Germany caused it to be stretched and applied to include all kinds of economic action with political aims. Hence, when in

---

⁶ Christoph Kreutzmüller, 'The Eruption of Racist Fault Lines in Central European Economy 1918–1933', in: *National Economies, Volks-Wirtschaft, Racism and Economy in Europe between the Wars (1918–1939/45)*, eds. Kreutzmüller, Christoph, Wildt, Michael, and Zimmermann, Moshe, (Newcastle, 2015), 1–17.

⁷ Cf. "Rechtsfrieden gegen Gewaltfrieden", *Vossische Zeitung*, 28.5.1919.

⁸ "Der Wirtschaftskampf", *Vossische Zeitung*, 6.8.1918.

⁹ "Der Boykott gegen Ungarn", *Vossische Zeitung*, 18.6.1920.

¹⁰ "Jugoslawischer Boykott gegen Italien", *Vossische Zeitung*, 8.8.1920.

¹¹ Cf. *Nationalökonomie auf Deutsch*, Berlin: Scherl, 1934, 11.

¹² Reimer, Eduard, *Kommentar zum Gesetz gegen den unlauteren Wettbewerb zum Zugabe und Rabattrecht*, vol. 2, Berlin: Carl Heymanns, 1935, 553.

¹³ "Kauft keine französischen und belgischen Waren", *Vossische Zeitung*, 4.2.1923, "Een algemeene boycott", *De Telegraaf*, 30.3.1923.

March 1932 the unthinkable happened and the bars and public houses of Berlin shut their taps for four whole days in a bid to force the city of Berlin to reduce its beer tax and the breweries to reduce their prices, the landlords called their action a "beer boycott", even though it was a walkout, a strike.[14]

In the wake of economic depression, amidst constant election campaigns and brutal street fighting, economic actions took an increasingly aggressive character in the early 1930s. "Country under Terror" the highly esteemed, liberal *Vossische Zeitung* headlined, reporting on the picketing practices in North Germany in March 1932. The article concluded that "SA columns, blacklists, boycott and terror are the prelude to the infernal music of the Third Reich".[15] On 12 January 1933 the Reich Minister of the Interior complained that political and "weltanschauliche" (i.e., racist) blockades and bans had reached a point that posed a serious threat to law and order. He therefore asked the police to intervene in all cases and by all means.[16] Less than three weeks later Hitler had become Reich Chancellor and the ardent Nazi Wilhelm Frick, the new Reich Minister of the Interior.

Alongside the political enemies of the various nationalists groups including the fast-growing Nazi Party, Jews suffered most from the "rusty weapon of economic boycott", as the political union of liberal Jews in Germany, the *Central Verein deutscher Staatsbürger jüdischen Glaubens* (CV), put it.[17] From his Amsterdam exile the former legal advisor of the *Central Verein*, Alfred Wiener, pointed out in 1934:

> The boycott of Jews was carried out in the country by the same nationalist organizations that furthered the rise of the National-Socialist movement throughout the years. In the years 1931 to 1933, i.e. before chancellor Hitler took his office, the boycott movement had already become a serious aggravation for self-employed trade by Jews in certain areas of Germany.[18]

---

[14] "Mißstimmung bei den Gastwirten", *Vossische Zeitung*, 1.3.1932.

[15] "Land unter Terror", Vossische Zeitung, 11.3.1932.

[16] "Gegen Boykott", *Vossische Zeitung*, 12.1.1933. Letter of the Reich Minister of the Interior to States, 27.12.1932, *Federal Archive Berlin (BArch)*, R 3101, 13859.

[17] Ahlheim, Hannah, *'Deutsche kauft nicht bei Juden!' Antisemitismus und politischer Boykott in Deutschland 1924 bis 1935*, Göttingen: Wallstein, 2011, 156.

[18] Wiener, Alfred, *Der Wirtschaftsboykott*, Amsterdam, 1934, 3.

Ostracizing Jews

In his pioneering study *Die Verdrängung der Juden aus der Wirtschaft im Dritten Reich*, Helmut Genschel argues that the "April boycott" was "only" the climax of "a whole series of terroristic attacks against Jews and others".[19] As early as 3 March 1933 the *Daily Herald* voiced fears that the new government would organize a "pogrom".[20] One week later the *Times* wrote about pickets in front of Jewish department stores, "exhorting" customers not to enter.[21] On March 24 the *New York Times* reported on more violent attacks on Jews who were "carried off to Nazi locales, maltreated and flung onto the street nearly unconscious".[22] On March 27 the *Manchester Guardian* commented that

> the anti-Semitic outrages of the last few weeks are far more horrible than could reasonably be imagined at first. Nothing like them has been known in Germany for generations. [...] And while the German Government, its press, and its ambassadors abroad deny what has been going on, what is still going on, and what is known to every inquirer who is not blind to all evidence, they do not only refrain from disparaging anti-Semitic emotion but continually whipping up afresh.[23]

Despite attempts to reign in the street violence, it did not decline and led to worried discussions within Hitler's cabinet.[24] On 25 and 26 March, Hitler met with newly appointed Minister for Propaganda, Joseph Goebbels, who as Gauleiter was also in charge of the local party administration in Berlin, and Frick in Munich to agree on concrete measures to divert antisemitic violence into channels less harmful to the image of the Nazi regime and to distract public attention from mass violence. They decided on the one hand to implement a "boycott" of Jewish businesses and on the other to lay the groundwork for excluding Jews from the civil service.[25] Even though it was initially meant to be a state-organized event,

---

[19] Genschel, Helmut, *Die Verdrängung der Juden aus der Wirtschaft im Dritten Reich* (Göttingen, 1966), 44.
[20] "Pogrom plot", *Daily Herald*, 3.3.1933.
[21] "Germany under Nazi rule", *The Times*, 10.3.1933.
[22] "Polish envoy in Reich charges 25 attacks", *New York Times*, 24.3.1933.
[23] "Facts about the Nazi terror", *Manchester Guardian*, 27.3.1933.
[24] Ahlheim, *Deutsche*, 246.
[25] Kreutzmüller, Christoph, *Final Sale in Berlin. The destruction of Jewish commercial activity 1930–1933* (New York and Oxford: Berghahn 2017), 105–110.

the German chancellor only informed the rest of his cabinet of his decision only upon his return to Berlin on 29 March 1933—the day after the call for a "boycott" had been made public.[26] In reporting about this brutal breach of etiquette the ever supportive, party-owned *Völkische Beobachter* made a point in headlining "The Reich chancellor vindicates the lie-boycott in front of the cabinet".[27] Hitler bluntly put his conservative-nationalist ministers under pressure by stating that the impending action was the last means to regain control of the situation and assuaged their reservations by a compromise whereby the event was officially organized as a Nazi Party activity.[28] Yet, since Hitler was both Chancellor and Head of the Nazi Party, a movement that aspired to represent the (new) state itself, this detail was mere hair-splitting. A clear indication how far the borders between state and party had already eroded was the fact that the Nazis' own private army, the SA and the SS, had been appointed auxiliary police in Germany's by far biggest state, Prussia, in February 1933. Unchallenged by any governing body or the police, they had set up hundreds of concentration camps throughout the county to arrest (and torture) "enemies of the state".[29] And now these storm troopers were asked to organize the "boycott" the Reich chancellor called for in the name of the German people, supported by the German newspapers that were by and large controlled by the Nazi regime.[30]

Initially, Goebbels claimed that the "boycott" was a "counter boycott" and a response to the boycott of German goods abroad. It is rather telling that this narrative was changed a day later, when it was claimed that the measure was taken to counter the unjustified negative international press reports—the so-called atrocity propaganda.[31] By so doing, as Viktor Klemperer noted in his famous diary, the Nazi Party took the Jews in Germany hostage to try to enforce more positive international press

[26] "Hitler über den Boykott", *Vossische Zeitung*, 29.3.1933.
[27] "Der Reichskanzler rechtfertigt den Lügen-Abwehrkampf vor dem Kabinett", *Völkischer Beobachter*, 29.3.1933.
[28] Friedländer, Saul, *Nazi Germany and the Jews. Vol. 1, The years of Persecution* (New York, 2005), 21f.
[29] Wachsmann, Nikolaus, *KL: A History of the Nazi Concentration Camps* (London, 2016). Cf. Wünschmann, Kim, *Before Auschwitz. Jewish prisoners in the prewar Conencentration Camps* (Cambridge and London, 2015), 17–57.
[30] Cf. for one of the rare critical reports: "Unlösbar verbunden", *Vossische Zeitung*, 29.3.1933.
[31] Fröhlich, Elke (ed.), *Die Tagebücher von Joseph Goebbels, Teil I, Aufzeichnungen 1923–1941* (Munich, 2005), vol. 2/III, 156.

coverage of the events connected to the Nazis' "Machtergreifung"—and the ongoing harassment of Jewish citizens.[32] To promote their point of view to the international press, Goebbels had bilingual posters printed in Berlin, where most of the international press agencies and newspapers had their German headquarters. A day before the event the press photographer Fritz Stepphuhn even took a series of photos to be ready for release on 1 April 1933.[33]

Photo by Fritz Stepphuhn, Berlin March 1933, Private Collection

[32] Klemperer, Viktor and Chalmers, M., *The Klemperer diaries 1933–1945: I shall bear witness to the bitter end* (London, 2000), 9.
[33] Kreutzmüller, *Final Sale in Berlin*, 105–110.

The international press, however, did not use these photos and pointed out that the defence argument was but a fig leaf:

> While presented as a counter-action to anti-German agitation inspired by Jewish interests abroad, the move is actually hailed by these adherents [of the Nazi-Party, CK] as a veritable fulfilment of the Nazi pre-election program and favored accordingly.[34]

Pressure within the ranks of the Nazi Party to take action against Jews certainly formed the background to the Nazis going ahead with their plans. Even though the international press was not reporting any new stories about human rights violations in the days leading up to the "boycott", local party officials and storm troopers continued assaulting and picketing Jews and Jewish-owned businesses in many German towns.[35]

There was certainly no way of stopping Julius Streicher, the manically antisemitic editor of the notorious weekly *Der Stürmer* (and member of the Reichstag) who had been appointed Head of the "Central committee against atrocity propaganda and boycott baiting". It seems that Hitler had chosen one of the most brutal Jew baiters to organize the campaign in order to contain the violence.[36] Yet, while the *Stürmer* reported on the alleged "Declaration of war by the all-Jewish world enemy" against non-Jewish Germans, its editor envisaged the blockade of businesses as the first step towards a veritable war against the Jews.[37] In his first statement issued on 29 March, Streicher made it clear he wanted "baptized businessmen or dissidents of the Jewish race" to be targeted, too.[38] Yet, Streicher neither explained who precisely to regard as being of "Jewish race" nor what to do with companies run by more than one owner. This was left to the discretion of the local storm troopers and the subcommittees set up in all the Nazi administrative regions, the *Gaue*. Since they only had two days to organize the "Judenaktion"—as it was termed in their files—in cities like Berlin the organizers did not have the time to thoroughly classify businesses even if they had had coherent categories to refer to. Instead they

---

[34] "German business protests boycott", *New York Times*, 31.3.1933.

[35] Kreutzmüller, *Final Sale*, 196.

[36] Roos, Daniel, *Julius Streicher und der Stürmer 1923–1945*, Paderborn et al.; Ferdinand Schönigh, 2014, 282f.

[37] "Kriegserklärung des Weltfeindes Alljuda", *Der Stürmer*, 14/1933 (April 1933). Cf. Roos, *Streicher*, 282–285.

[38] "Die Boykott-Anordnungen zur Greuelabwehr", *Der Angriff*, 31.3.1933.

reverted to the simplest method of all: checking names. Thus, businesses run under names which the local perpetrators believed to indicate a "Jewish" background were put on the blacklists hastily compiled by the local SA units.

On the morning of Saturday 1 April, at 10 PM, the storm troopers' and party officials' pickets finally moved to their assigned positions all over Germany. While some Jewish-run businesses were spared, some non-Jewish businesses were erroneously included.[39] The marking was not standardized. Some shops were marked by posters, and others were simply smeared over—with anything from badly drawn caricatures to death threats.[40] Photos show that some SA men were carrying guns.[41] This was, of course, not only a serious threat to any passer-by who might have considered walking past a picket. Since carrying weapons was (and is) a prerogative of representatives of the state in Germany, this was a clear indication that the SA—as auxiliary police—was representing state power. At 3 PM the pickets withdrew, leaving their posters and inscriptions behind. The "occasionally quite extensive cleaning" was left to the Jewish proprietors.[42]

The picketing seems to have been regarded as an event by many. All over Germany, the streets were full of people, doubling as passers-by, spectators, and audience. Although Richard Evans rightly points out that public indifference detracted from the "boycott's" success,[43] the sheer presence of an audience meant that the event, combining a power display with a blockade, was ultimately successful. If the streets had been completely empty, the pickets would have appeared ridiculous figures.

According to the official version of the events, the national blockade of Jewish businesses proceeded "with strict discipline".[44] Discipline seems to

---

[39] "Ruhiger Boykottverlauf", *Vossische Zeitung*, 1 April 1933. See also Johannes Ludwig, *Boykott, Enteignung, Mord: Die "Entjudung" der deutschen Wirtschaft* (Munich and Zürich, 1992), 312–315; Genschel, *Verdrängung*, 52.

[40] "Boykott und Auslandsmeinung", *Jüdische Rundschau*, 4 April 1933.

[41] Cf. Picture of an unknown photographer, Berlin 1 April 1933, in: United States Holocaust Memorial Museum, Photo Collection, 06007.

[42] "Nach dem Boykott", *Berliner Tageblatt*, 3 April 1933.

[43] Evans, Richard, *The Coming of the Third Reich* (London, 2004), 436. See also Ahlheim, *Deutsche*, 259f; Friedländer, *Germany*, 42f.

[44] "Boykott bei strenger Disziplin", *Berliner Börsen-Courier*, 1 April 1933. See also Buchholz, Wolfhard, *Die Ausgrenzung der Juden in der Tagespresse des Dritten Reiches, 1933–1941* (Frankfurt am Main, 2007), 63–69.

have been the watchword of the day.⁴⁵ The Foreign Ministry employed it.⁴⁶ Goebbels used it twice in his diary entry on 1 April 1933⁴⁷ and repeated it in his book *Vom Kaiserhof zur Reichskanzlei*.⁴⁸ Most German newspapers duly commented on the show of discipline, too, while the Nazi Party's own *Völkische Beobachter* even printed one of the photos from the series mentioned above.⁴⁹ The *Daily Mail*, too, remarked that the "boycott" was carried out "throughout Germany in perfect order and with cold determination".⁵⁰ Unlike the French, even the British ambassador described the event as peaceful in his report to the Foreign Ministry.⁵¹ In this situation the *Guardian* reverted to sarcasm:

> The German Jews unarmed to the teeth and numbering one in a hundred of the population were defeated by the armed Brown Shirts, supported by the police, the regular army and more than half of the total electorate.⁵²

Despite the public effort spent on the "boycott" and Nazi assurances that it would help maintain order, the violence continued throughout the day. In Kiel a veritable lynch-mob murdered a Jew.⁵³ In Berlin, where the Nazis tried to keep everything under control in order to placate the foreign press, there were a number of extremely violent assaults on both customers and Jewish proprietors who tried to keep their businesses open.⁵⁴ Street violence even found its way into the German newsreel, which captured a storm trooper aggressively lunging towards the camera filming him.⁵⁵ The

---

⁴⁵ "Disziplin: Ein neuer Aufruf des Zentralkomitees", *Deutsche Allgemeine Zeitung*, 1 April 1933.

⁴⁶ Conze, Eckart, Norbert Frei, Peter Hayes, Moshe Zimmermann, Annette Weinke, and Andrea Wiegeshoff, *Das Amt und die Vergangenheit: Deutsche Diplomaten im Dritten Reich und in der Bundesrepublik* (München, 2010), 47.

⁴⁷ Entry, 2 April 1933, *Goebbels Tagebücher*, Part 1, Vol. 2/III, 160.

⁴⁸ Goebbels, Joseph, *Vom Kaiserhof zur Reichskanzlei* (Berlin, 1933), 291.

⁴⁹ "Ganz Deutschland boykottiert die Juden", *Völkischer Beobachter*, 2./3.4.1933.

⁵⁰ "Germany's Jewish boycott", *Daily Mail*, 3.4.1933.

⁵¹ Report by H. Rumbold to J. Simon, 1.4.1933, in: *Documents on British foreign policy, 1919–1939*, Second Series, vol. V, eds. Elbert L. Woodward, Rohan Butler, (London, 1956), 16.

⁵² "The great Nazi-victory on the shop front", *Manchester Guardian*, 5.4.1933.

⁵³ Longerich, Peter, *Holocaust: The Nazi Persecution and Murder of the Jews* (Oxford, 2010), 34f.

⁵⁴ Kreutzmüller, *Final Sale*, 123.

⁵⁵ Kreutzmüller, Christoph, Simon, Hermann, and Weber, Elisabeth, *Ein Pogrom im Juni, Fotos antisemitischer Schmierereien in Berlin, 1938*, (Berlin, 2013), 14.

whole "boycott campaign" was, as Michael Wildt has rightly pointed out, "an arena of collective violence against Jews in Germany".[56]

Even for those business people who did not suffer physical violence, the experience of the racist blockade was deeply disturbing. In protest against the humiliation, Herbert Schimek, a 32-year-old war veteran and partner of the venerable used-paper dealership Josef Schimek, shot himself in Berlin.[57] Listing the outrages against Jews in Germany in 1933, the *Comité des Délégations Juives* made a point of mentioning their psychological effects: "The damage is immeasurably large when Jew hatred [...] is legitimated in orders and speeches by the political leadership and supported by propaganda, so that even the most apolitical, withdrawn and dull-witted people are unable to overlook it".[58]

The historian Avraham Barkai, whose father had run a small business in Berlin, stresses that the gravest result of the so-called boycott was that it "legitimized anti-Jewish measures in the economic field".[59] Of course, it also marked which companies were regarded as Jewish and consequently to be ousted. All over Germany, town and city councils cut their ties with companies owned by Jews and tried to force their officials to do the same. The consequences were so severe that the *New York Times* described them as a "cold pogrom".[60] The picketing in front of shops did not stop either, even though the "boycott" was officially called off after just one day. To name but one example, the owner of a shop in the town of Belgrad in Pommerania (today Białogard) complained in late April 1933 to the Reich Ministry of Economics that local Nazis were writing down the names of his customers and telling them "that they would be in trouble". This threat had caused his business to come to a standstill.[61] A few weeks later the district court in Landsberg/Warthe—where the Cohns had fled from—ruled that a company even had the right to lay off Jewish employees to prevent an impending blockade.[62] Especially in small towns and

---

[56] Michael Wildt, 'The boycott campaign as an arena of collective violence against Jews in Germany', in: *Nazi Europe and the Final Solution*, eds. David Bankier/Israel Gutman, (Jerusalem, 2003), 53–72.
[57] World Alliance for Combating Anti-Semitism, *J'accuse*, London, 1933, 5.
[58] Comité des Délégations Juives (ed.), *Das Schwarzbuch. Tatsachen und Dokumente. Die Lage der Juden in Deutschland* (Paris, 1934), 312.
[59] Barkai, *Boycott*, 23.
[60] "3,000,000 in Reich feel 'cold pogrom'", *New York Times*, 16.4.1933.
[61] Letter P. Leiser to Reich Ministry of Economics, 26.4.1933, BArch, R. 3101, 13859.
[62] Ruling District Court, 16.5.1933, HM 2/8778 RGVA 721/1/2678.

rural areas the situation soon became unbearable. This in turn led to a major influx of Jews from smaller towns and rural areas to the large cities, where picketing was not so easy and where there were far greater opportunities for economic survival.[63]

In winter 1934 a new wave of violence spread throughout Germany.[64] Against the background of economic depression and rising prices for food, antisemitic convictions and frustration at the pace of anti-Jewish persecution triggered renewed violence.[65] The capital, whose economic recovery lagged behind that of the Reich as a whole, quickly became a centre of unrest. On New Year's Eve 1934 a gang of marauding men attacked various shops and their customers yelling, "We don't buy from Jews".[66] In January 1935, blacklists and placards appeared in the Spandau district,[67] and in early February, "massive numbers" of stickers appeared all over the district of Pankow reading, "He who buys from Jews is a traitor to his people".[68] These stickers, whose design recalled that of *Der Stürmer*, were professionally made and mass-produced.[69] By mid-June, there was agitation and violence across the city of Berlin, and the campaign had begun to agitate for a concrete goal. The *Central Verein* noted:

> For approximately 14 days, people have been assembling in front of ice-cream parlours all over the city. At the command of certain individuals, these

---

[63] Christoph Kreutzmüller, Ingo Loose, and Benno Nietzel, 'Persecution and Strategies of Survival. Jewish Entrepreneurs in Berlin, Frankfurt/Main/Breslau 1933–1942', *Yad Vashem Studies*, vol. 39, (2011), 31–70.

[64] Nietzel, Benno, *Handeln und Überleben. Jüdische Unternehmer aus Frankfurt am Main von den 1920er bis in die 1960er Jahre* (Göttingen, 2013), 87f; Ahlheim, *Deutsche*, 360–379.

[65] Tooze, Adam, *The Wages of Destruction. The Making and Breaking of the Nazi Economy* (London, 2007), 61–65, 186.

[66] Letter from the General Prosecutor at the Prussian Regional Court to Reich Minister of Justice via General Prosecutor at Berlin Superior Court, 18 April 1935, *Political Archive of the Foreign Ministry (PArch AA)*, R. 100249.

[67] Letter from Heimannsohn to Simonis, 24.1.1935; File note Rubinstein, 8.2.1935, both *Central Archiv of the History of the Jewish People (CAHJP)*, HM2 8806 (RGVA 721/3161).

[68] File note Rubinstein 18.2.1935, *CAHJP*, HM2 8806 (RGVA 721/3161). Letter Otto Hirsch to Julius Lippert, 8.3.1935, *Warburg Archive Foundation, Hamburg (SWA)*, I, 3-5-5. See also Ahlheim, *Deutsche*, 379–390.

[69] Christoph Kreutzmüller, 'Sticker und Stigmata: Antisemitische Kampagnen in der Wirtschaft 1900–1938', in: *Alltagskultur des Antisemitismus im Kleinformat: Vignetten der Sammlung Wolfgang Haney ab 1880*, eds. Isabel Enzenbach and Wolfgang Haney, (Berlin, 2011), 123–135, here 129.

people prevent customers from entering these places of business. Customers are threatened and occasionally punched, ice cream cones are knocked from people's hands, and shop windows are shattered. In the majority of cases, shop owners are forced by people in civilian clothing to shut their businesses, or risk having them completely destroyed. At night, shop windows and fronts are smeared with graffiti, covered with SA pamphlets or have the word 'Jew' painted on them.[70]

When the disturbances reached the inner city, international newspapers started reporting on it.[71] As this was grist to the mill of the growing movement to boycott the 1936 Olympic Games in Germany, the Nazi regime tried to suppress the assaults. This, however, turned out to be rather difficult as the following police report shows:

In the past few days, it has emerged that the source of the unwanted anti-Jewish demonstrations…was the numerous sellers of *Der Stürmer* (almost exclusively Hitler Youth). These sellers act illegally. Working together with two or three helpers, they affix provocative pages of *Stürmer* and posters, some of which depict naked Jews, to trees and walls. The papers are sold while the sellers call out anti-Jewish slogans. As soon as the sellers have sold all of their wares, they and their helpers join others and form the core of a demonstration that marauds through the streets.[72]

The picketing went on. In the wake of the Nuremberg Laws, the Reich Association of Retail and Wholesale Traders had to admonish their members in September 1935 that any kind of "Jew boycott" including the marking of shops as "non-Aryan" was strictly forbidden.[73] Yet, when the violence had finally subsided, the economic expert Cora Berliner concluded in a report on the economic situation of Jews in October 1935 that "this summer's wave of boycotts claimed far more numerous and serious victims than any previous wave of boycotts".[74]

Still, due to the influx of new companies and the success of various economic survival strategies, the number of businesses in Berlin shrank

[70] CV file note, 2 July 1935, ibid.
[71] Kreutzmüller/Simon/Weber, Pogrom im Juni, 16f.
[72] Report 133rd Police Precinct to Gestapo, 22 July 1935, *LAB*, A Pr. Br. Rep. 030, 21638.
[73] Secret circular by the Reich-Association of Retail- and Wholesale Traders, Sept. 1935, *CAHJP*, HM 2/8787 RGVA 721/2880.
[74] Report Cora Berliner, 1.10.1935, *Leo Baeck Institute*, AR 1578.

only negligibly between 1933 and the summer of 1938, when the regional party economic commissioner (Gauwirtschaftsberater) stated that there were still more than 46,000 "Jewish" companies in the German capital.[75] To increase pressure, Goebbels ordered his storm troopers to systematically smear shop windows. On 20 June 1938 the *New York Times* reported once again on street violence against Jews in Berlin—and compared it to the incidents in April 1933:

> A daylight ride down Berlin's main shopping streets today revealed a thousand or more crudely decorated Jewish-owned shops and stores that had been victims of one of the most sinister but also one of the most clumsily executed anti-Jewish demonstrations undertaken in the German metropolis since the advent of the National-Socialist regime.[76]

In her bestselling *Blood and banquets. A Berlin social diary*, the journalist Bella Fromm recalled an incident she had witnessed in June 1938 off the main shopping streets, in an unfashionable quarter near Alexanderplatz:

> We were just about to enter a tiny jewellery shop when a gang of youngsters in Hitler Youth Uniforms smashed the shop window and stormed into the shop, brandishing butchers knives, yelling: 'To hell with Jewish rabble!' [...] The smallest boy of the mob climbed inside the window and started his work of destruction by flinging everything he could grab into the street. Inside, the other boys broke glass shelves and counters, hurling alarm clocks, cheap silverware to their accomplices outside. A tiny shrimp of a boy crouched in a corner of the window, putting dozens of rings on his fingers and stuffing his pockets with wristwatches and bracelets. His uniform bulging with loot, he turned around, spat squarely into the shopkeeper's face, and dashed off.[77]

While the *New York Times* reported that the attitude of the spectators was "distinctly" one of "unexpressed disapproval",[78] the SS stated that some non-Jewish Berliners asked whether the "government in its sixth year really needed to fall back on the propaganda methods used in the

---

[75] Kreutzmüller, *Final Sale*, 234.
[76] "Berliners frown on drive on Jews", *New York Times*, 20.6.1938.
[77] Fromm, Bella, *Blood and banquets. A Berlin social diary* (New York, 1990), 274.
[78] "Berliners frown on drive on Jews", *New York Times*, 20.6.1938.

'Judenboykott' on April 1 1933".[79] The SS also pointed out that even some "Aryan shops had been identified as Jewish and consequently boycotted".[80] Thus, by 1938 the social practice of what the Nazis called "boycott" had come to include enforced closures and even the looting of shops!

The plunder of shops in the pogroms in November 1938 could not fall under the term "boycott", as the violence had been too disturbingly visible. Instead the pogrom was referred to as "expressions of discontent" or November action and was eventually called "Crystal Night".[81] Yet, even after the official closure of Jewish-owned retail businesses in Germany, decreed by Hermann Goering on 12 November 1938, there were still occasional blockades. Thus, when Jakob Derbfleisch, owner of a menswear shop in Erfurt who was allowed to reopen for business because he was a Polish citizen, tried to organize a final sale in April 1939, more than 150 people gathered in front of his shop and forced it to close.[82]

As it was, the events the Nazis referred to as a boycott were counterproductive. They aimed to drive the Jews out of Germany by destroying their livelihood. In the process, however, many Jewish families were stripped of the necessary means to emigrate.[83] In the end, the vicious circle of plunder and emigration led to enforced emigration, the founding of the *Zentralstelle fuer jüdische Auswanderung,* and the rise of a former Standard Oil representative called Adolf Eichmann. But that is a different story.[84]

BOYCOTT?

How to label the frequent actions against Jewish-owned businesses was an uneasy question in Germany at the time. Certainly, all German papers used the term "boycott" in April 1933. But they were no longer independent

---

[79] Eilbericht des SD-Oberabschnitt Ost an die Sicherheitspolizei, 24.6.1938, RGVA, 500, 1, 645.

[80] Mitteilung des Oberabschnitts Ost an Stabskanzlei des SD, 22.6.1938, RGVA, Fond 500, 1, 645; emphasis added.

[81] Court Verdict, 4 Sept. 1939, in: *LAB*, A Rep 358-02, 118422; Sworn statement Magdalena Reddehase, 4 Aug. 1949, in LAB, B Rep. 058, 14101.

[82] Kreutzmüller, Christoph, and Schörle, Eckhard, *Stadtluft macht frei? Jüdische Gewerbebetriebe in Erfurt 1919–1939* (Berlin, 2013), 46.

[83] Kreutzmüller, Final Sale, 326f.

[84] Stangneth, Bettina and Otto Adolf Eichmann, 'Reich Main Security Office. The RSHA's "Jewish Expert"', in: *The Participants. The men of the Wannsee-Conference,* eds. Jasch, Hans Christian and Kreutzmüller Christoph, (New York and Oxford, 2017), 40–56.

ventures and claimed—against their better knowledge—that the whole campaign had been peaceful. The SS—as we have seen—tried to enforce the use of the word, but would sometimes write "Judenaktion" in internal reports. The Foreign Ministry's press department amassed seven volumes of files on the matter, but only reported on "Atrocity Propaganda and Boycotts against Germany and Our Countermeasures".[85] The political union of liberal Jews in Germany, the *Central Verein*, would sometime use the term "boycott" in their files but more often complained about the disturbance of public order or plainly referred to assaults on Jewish-owned businesses. In his study on the laws of competition, the lawyer Eduard Reimer[86] stated in 1935 that "economic boycotts were a cancerous growth" and that the antisemitic "boycott" was "unethical" because it asked for something impossible: "a change of race".[87] The *Schwarze Korps* fiercely attacked Reimer's book which was taken off the shelves and pulped shortly afterwards.[88] Only a few copies of the 1935 edition survive in public libraries. In his dissertation on *Boycott and collective boycott in international law*, published in 1935, Gerhart Runte was more conformist and somehow managed to avoid the question of whether the blockades of Jewish-owned businesses were a "boycott".[89] So did the well-known *Meyers Enzyclopedia*, published in 1937. The editorial board merely defined boycott as a political or economic "means of enforcement" (Zwangsmittel) and mentioned Charles Boycott, the English labelling system, and the boycott of Germany by "world Jewry" but not the picketing of Jewish-owned businesses in or after April 1933.[90]

Outside Germany the line was seemingly drawn between violent and less violent action taken. Thus, on 17 June 1938, when reporting on the third amendment of the Reich citizenship law defining Jewish businesses, the *New York Times* headlined "Boycott of Jews". One day later, when

[85] Letter from the Foreign Office to the Chief of Police, 12 April 1933, PArch AA, R 121211.
[86] On the fate of Reimer, see: Simone Ladwig Winters, *Anwalt ohne Recht, Das Schicksal jüdischer Rechtsanwälte in Berlin nach 1933*, Berlin 2007, S. 244.
[87] Reimer, *Kommentar*, 559. See: "Boykott zunächst einen Tag", *Frankfurter Zeitung*, 1.4.1933.
[88] "Der sittenwidrige Antisemitismus", *Das Schwarze Korps*, 16.4.1936. See: Gerhart Runte, *Boykott und Kollektiv-Boykott im Völkerrecht* (Emsdetten, 1935), 16.
[89] Ibid.
[90] Bibliographisches Institut (eds.), *Meyers Lexikon* (Leipzig, 1936ff), vol. 2, 58.

focussing on the ongoing violence, it ran the headline "Anti-Jewish raids". In 1933 the *New York Times* had already analysed the blockade of Jewish businesses as a "maelstrom of ultranationalist frenzy"[91] while in Belgium *Het laatste Nieuws* headlined "Declaration of War against the German Jews".[92] The *Washington Post* called the event the "April-Fool's-Day-purge of 1933" in retrospect.[93]

Apart from the violence, the other important aspect is the involvement of the state. The barrister Jakob Ball Kaduri who witnessed the "boycott" interpreted the incidents to be "the first trial of the German government to organize a pogrom".[94] David Bankier agreed that it was "de facto a state action".[95] States can, of course, boycott states but a ban on a certain group of individuals within a state by public bodies involves an unfair imbalance of players and power and might better be called a blockade. In this light, calling the racist blockade of Jewish-owned businesses, law offices, and surgeries a "boycott" seems to have been another of Goebbels' clever public relations tricks, selling the start of the systematic persecution of Jews in Germany to the world as a not unusual measure in a normal political struggle. This was made easy by the fact that the word "boycott" was on everyone's lips in the early 1930s and used as a synonym for economic warfare. Like so many other words from contemporary discourse taken up by the Nazis, be they "Final Solution" or "Aryanization", "boycott" masks the violence that came as part and parcel of the persecution of Jews and the destruction of Jewish commercial activities in Germany. In retrospect Alfred Wiener rightly pointed out in 1958 that the "April boycott" 1933 was merely a "boycott of law" and thus "the writing on the wall".[96]

---

[91] "Hitlerites limit boycott to a day", *New York Times*, 1.4.1933.
[92] De Oorlogsverklaring aan de Duitsche Joden, Het Laatste Nieuws, 1.4.1933.
[93] "Nazis arrest 1000 Jews in fresh purge", *Washington Post*, 16.6.1938.
[94] Kurt Jakob Ball-Kaduri, *Das Leben der Juden in Deutschland 1933. Ein Zeitbericht* (Frankfurt, 1963), 83.
[95] Bankier, David, *Die öffentliche Meinung im Hitler-Staat. Die "Endlösung" und die Deutschen. Eine Berichtigung* (Berlin, 1994), 94.
[96] "Vom Judenboykott zum Boykott des Rechts", *Die Zeit*, 3.4.1958.

CHAPTER 7

Boycott Campaigns of the Radical Left in Cold-War West Germany

Alexander Sedlmaier

Although not all boycotts take place in the commercial sphere, most prominent campaigns affect commerce with the boycotted party in one way or another, and many have been consciously conceived as a form of consumer activism. The author of a book on consumer boycotts in the United States defines a consumer boycott as "an attempt by one or more parties to achieve certain objectives by urging individual consumers to refrain from making selected purchases in the market place."[1] This focus on individual purchase decisions as the only means of "urging" may cast the practice of boycott too narrowly, since there are two levels of urging: that between the initiator of a boycott and the public and, in a second step, that between those following the boycott and the targeted party. An important characteristic of boycott campaigns that is implicit in Friedman's definition is the fact that the process of "urging" has usually been an organised and public affair that goes well beyond abstention by individuals.

---

[1] Monroe Friedman, *Consumer Boycotts: Effecting Change through the Marketplace and the Media* (New York, 1999), 4.

A. Sedlmaier (✉)
Bangor University, Bangor, UK
e-mail: a.sedlmaier@bangor.ac.uk

© The Author(s) 2019
D. Feldman (ed.), *Boycotts Past and Present*, Palgrave Critical Studies of Antisemitism and Racism,
https://doi.org/10.1007/978-3-319-94872-0_7

Definitions that highlight the "act of voluntarily abstaining" (*Wikipedia*) or "withdrawal from social or commercial interaction" (*OED*) miss the important dimension of public coercion or pressure and tend to put the focus on individual economic acts, which are usually just one means among others, while the defining characteristic is the aim of excluding the targeted party from regular (commercial) intercourse.

Boycott campaigns have not only sought to coordinate consumer choices and to trigger economic consequences but also, by means of political communication, to cause critical discourse and popular protest in order to discipline, delegitimise, ostracise, weaken, or overcome what the boycotters saw as morally reprehensible aspects of regimes of provision. The regime-of-provision perspective that is applied in the following analysis addresses a "network of activities that attaches consumption to the power relations that make it possible and at the same time hinders other forms of consumption and production."[2] This points to the political arena as the space where different social, economic, and moral concepts compete for influence, recognition, and legitimacy.

The first part of this chapter provides a general overview of boycott activity in West Germany in the 1950s and 1960s, when comparisons with the antisemitic boycotts of the Nazis were omnipresent among contemporary observers. An analysis of the legal debate concerning boycotts will provide categories and criteria that will be useful in the comparative assessment of the boycott campaigns treated subsequently. The second part examines various boycotts of the radical left that emerged in the context of the "new" social movements of the 1960s, 1970s, and 1980. The third and final part discusses anti-Israel or anti-Zionist boycotts as a particular example that highlights the moral and political explosiveness inherent in boycott campaigns.

Boycott Activity in the 1950s and 1960s and Its Legal Repercussions

Boycotts—which had been an important tool in the arsenal of the workers' movement before the period of National Socialism—were largely discredited and dormant in West Germany up to the 1950s due to their association with the Nazi boycott of shops owned by Jews. When boycotts did appear in West Germany, they were mostly directed against East

---

[2] Alexander Sedlmaier, *Consumption and Violence: Radical Protest in Cold-War West Germany* (Ann Arbor), 10–11.

Germany and communism—especially before the banning of the Communist Party of Germany (KPD) by West Germany's Federal Constitutional Court in 1956 and after the erection of the Berlin Wall in August 1961—and occasionally against individuals and groups associated with the Nazi past. This constellation led to boycotts that triggered landmark cases of constitutional law. The resulting judgements provided the framework for subsequent conflicts over boycott campaigns, and a deeper understanding of this precedence is necessary for the subsequent treatment of boycotts by the radical left.

In September 1950, Erich Lüth, Director of the Press Office of the federal state of Hamburg, called for a boycott against the film *Unsterbliche Geliebte* (*Immortal Beloved*) by Veith Harlan. This was the first post-war production of the film director who had made a name for himself as one of the leading propaganda directors for the Nazi regime, most notoriously with his strongly antisemitic film *Jud Süß* (1940). In an open letter to Harlan's distributor, Lüth argued that it was not only "the right of decent Germans" but even their duty to "go beyond protest in this fight against this unworthy representative of German film by holding ready for a boycott." This took place against the backdrop of Harlan being cleared in his denazification trial. Lüth was not alone. In an address to the Bundestag, prominent Social Democratic politician Carlo Schmid called it a disgrace to show "Harlan's concoctions" since the director had contributed to "creating the mass psychological conditions for the gas chambers at Auschwitz." When his denazification case was first heard, Harlan had been acquitted of the charge of having been an accessory to the commission of crimes against humanity. The court argued that no causality of any criminal relevance could be established between film and genocide. However, the Supreme Court of the British Zone of occupation nullified the acquittal pointing out that *Jud Süß* had been a significant tool of antisemitic propaganda. In a final trial at Hamburg Regional Court, Harlan made the dubious claim that the Nazis had misused his art and forced him to be the director of *Jud Süß*. Presiding Judge Walter Tyrolf—who had been a member of the National Socialist German Workers' Party (NSDAP) and a prosecutor at the *Sondergericht* Hamburg where he had been responsible for a number of death sentences for petty crimes—followed Harlan's reasoning and acquitted him in late April 1950.[3] In 1951, Harlan

---

[3] Peter Reichel and Harald Schmid, *Von der Katastrophe zum Stolperstein: Hamburg und der Nationalsozialismus nach 1945* (Hamburg, 2005), 32–34.

succeeded in obtaining an injunction against Lüth that ordered him to refrain from public calls for boycott. The judges pointed to Harlan's denazification record and deemed Lüth's call for boycott immoral.

It took eight years before the Federal Constitutional Court overturned the lower court decision confirming Lüth's right to freedom of expression including the call for a boycott. In the opinion of the court, Lüth had been publicly known as an advocate of a "re-establishment of a genuine peace with the Jewish people." In this context, the court reaffirmed Lüth's argument that "it was of high importance that a shared understanding developed abroad that the German people had turned away from National Socialist attitudes and denounced these, not for reasons of political opportunity, but as a result of mental change and of the subsequent insight into the reprehensibility of such attitudes." Moreover, Lüth had had no means of coercion at his disposal to reinforce his demand. He could only appeal to the moral position of those he addressed. This verdict became a landmark decision, and it served as a precedent in the legal treatment of the blockades carried out by the radical left in the late 1960s.

The second boycott that triggered a groundbreaking decision was the 1961 campaign of the publisher Axel Springer against the Hamburg weekly *Blinkfüer*. This campaign revived a pattern of boycotts that had been pioneered by the federal government in March 1950 when it forbade the public sector to award contracts to firms that simultaneously maintained business relations with organisations deemed anti-constitutional, such as the KPD, the East German youth organisation Free German Youth, and a few National Socialist successor organisations.[4] After the erection of the Berlin Wall, a number of anti-communist boycott campaigns emerged. West Berlin's Mayor Willy Brandt (SPD) and the Confederation of German Trade Unions rather successfully called for a boycott of the East German-run Berlin S-Bahn. The East German railway company lost hundreds of thousands of customers, demonstrators picketed entrances to stations, and a number of sabotage acts were committed against trains and railway installations.[5]

---

[4] Cabinet minutes (132, 6): "Maßnahmen gegen wirtschaftliche Unterstützung verfassungsfeindlicher Bestrebungen, BMI," February 27, 1951, Bundesarchiv, accessed October 13, 2017, http://www.bundesarchiv.de/cocoon/barch/001/k/k1951k/kap1_2/kap2_18/para3_6.html#d8e39_rueck

[5] "S-Bahn Boykott: Zu teuer," *Der Spiegel*, March 25, 1964, 37.

Springer publishing supported the S-Bahn boycott and further intensified its massive campaign against the East German regime. In a circular to newspaper wholesale dealers, dated September 2, 1961, Springer threatened to terminate business relations with wholesalers who failed to abandon the distribution of press products carrying the East German television programme. At first, the leftist weekly *Blinkfüer* succeeded in obtaining an injunction against Springer from the Hamburg Regional Court, prohibiting the publisher's boycott. The court stated that the termination of supply agreements was politically motivated and constituted an inadmissible interference with a commercial enterprise. At the same time, *Blinkfüer* sued Springer for compensation. Springer appealed to the Federal Court of Justice (BGH), which issued a ruling that was exceedingly advantageous for the publishing giant. This 1963 decision held that Axel Springer had not pursued his subjective economic interest, but a civic concern. Springer's conduct, the judges ruled, was covered by freedom of expression. This led to a constitutional complaint that urged the judges to take into account Springer's economic power and the fact that freedom of opinion also applied to *Blinkfüer*. The decision was not announced until May 1969. In the meantime, Springer's papers had resumed printing the East German television programme, *Blinkfüer* had gone bankrupt, and Springer publishing had itself become the target of a major boycott campaign in the context of the protest movements of 1968. Eight years after the erection of the Berlin Wall, the Federal Constitutional Court overturned the BGH's judgment. The judges underlined that calls for boycott were covered by freedom of expression and explicitly referred to the Lüth case. This also applied to the economically powerful who would otherwise be excluded from public debate. However, such calls for boycott were not protected by the law if they were accompanied by economic pressure, as was the case when Springer threatened the wholesalers, which, the judges decreed, was not conducive to the free competition of opinion. The BGH's judgment had amounted to an interference with the freedom of the press. The press had to be protected against attempts to eliminate competition of opinion by means of economic pressure.[6] In other words, had Springer contented himself

---

[6] Bundesverfassungsgericht, "Entscheidung vom 26.2.1969—1BvR 619/63" (Blinkfüer-Urteil), BVerfGE 25,256, 1969; Kurt Groenewold, 'Das Urteil des Bundesgerichtshofes in der Blinkfüer-Affäre: Ein Kommentar,' in: *Kapitalismus und Pressefreiheit am Beispiel Springer*, ed. Peter Brokmeier, (Frankfurt, 1969), 142–56; Donald P. Kommers, *The*

with calling for a boycott of East German television and those who printed its programme, he would have been covered by freedom of expression just like Lüth. It was the economic pressure that went beyond individual purchase decisions that made this type of boycott illegal.

Boycotts of the Radical Left in the Context of the "New" Social Movements

The "new" social movements only embraced boycotts, coupled with direct action, in the late 1960s.[7] The West German radical left engaged in a wide range of boycott activities that paralleled its political agenda. The boycott campaign against Springer publishing was a corner stone of what is commonly remembered as the student protests of "1968," but prior to this and lasting throughout the 1970s, there were a series of understudied transportation boycotts protesting fare increases in many German cities. Boycotts of electricity companies in the context of anti-nuclear protest were less prominent, but provide an additional insight into the role of violence in campaign formation. The West German varieties of boycotts against entire countries—Chile, South Africa, Israel—were not necessarily seen in connection with the former, which were much more domestically rooted. The various campaigns against multinational companies that emerged had overlapped with some of the boycotts mentioned above but campaigns against individual companies had their own momentum. Overall, there is no strict causal relationship between the various campaigns treated in this section. The different boycotts reinforced each other, serving as model and inspiration; especially the anti-apartheid campaign with its international scope and strong claim to moral legitimacy influenced activities in other fields. It is safe to assume that most activists of the radical left were involved in several but not necessarily all of these campaigns. Moreover, it will become clear that all operated against the evolving backdrop of the legal treatment of boycotts.

The West German extra-parliamentary opposition initiated its anti-Springer campaign in the autumn of 1967. The *Sozialistische Deutsche Studentenbund* (SDS) called for a boycott of Springer—which they blamed for inciting violence against the students and their leaders—targeting the

Constitutional Jurisprudence of the Federal Republic of Germany, 2nd ed. (Durham, 1997), 372–75.

[7] Sedlmaier, *Consumption and Violence*, 146–204.

stall operated by the Springer-owned publisher Ullstein at the 1967 Frankfurt Book Fair, an effort that led to tumult and police involvement. A boycott resolution "against the monopoly of Axel Springer" was signed by 71 members of the renowned literary association Gruppe 47 and 7 major publishers.[8] The anti-Springer campaign is well known for its violent escalation at Easter 1968 after the attempted assassination of student leader Rudi Dutschke. All over Germany protesters engaged in large-scale protest rallies and blockades that tried to prevent delivery of Springer tabloid papers. Confrontations between protesters and police involved 21,000 policemen across the Federal Republic. Two protesters were severely injured when delivery vans sped through a crowd, and a photojournalist and a student died as a result of the skirmishes in Munich, with police and demonstrators accusing each other of responsibility for the deaths.[9] However, long before these violent developments, the anti-Springer campaign was compared to terror. For example, in a defence of Springer published in the company's *Die Welt* and written by the Austrian-American author and publisher Hans Habe, Springer's critics were denied any intellectual or political merit: "Even in Berlin I was not able to discover any Springer terror organisation that would flog your papers – but rather terror organisations that use violence to prevent their sale and seek to intimidate the reading public with threats."[10] The main point of moral and legal controversy was whether boycotts were to be viewed as illicit or even criminal offences or, rather, as political articulations protected by constitutional basic rights, especially freedom of expression and freedom of assembly. This question applied not only to performative and physical articulations (e.g., in the case of a boycott enforced by a blockade) but also to mere speech acts (e.g., a call for boycott made in a public speech or printed in a flyer). Many campaigns combined both aspects, such as the protests against public transport fare increases that peaked with Hannover's

---

[8] "Gruppe 47: Dichter, Dichter," *Der Spiegel*, October 16, 1967, 178–82; 'Gegen das Monopol von Axel Springer,' in: *Vaterland, Muttersprache: Deutsche Schriftsteller und ihr Staat seit 1945*, eds. Michael Krüger, Susanne Schüssler, Winfried Stephan, and Klaus Wagenbach, (Berlin, 1979), 251.

[9] Stefan Hemler, 'Von Kurt Faltlhauser zu Rolf Pohle: Die Entwicklung der studentischen Unruhe an der Ludwig-Maximilians-Universität München in der zweiten Hälfte der sechziger Jahre,' in: *1968: 30 Jahre danach*, ed. Hans-Günther Hockerts, (St. Ottilien), 231–33.

[10] Hans Habe, "Die Parforcejagd auf Axel Springer: Ein offener Brief an den Verleger," *Die Welt*, December 27, 1967, 6.

spectacular 1969 Red Spot campaign, when protests caused the collapse of the city's entire public transport system and eventually forced the transport company and the municipality to rescind the increases.

Public transport boycotts affected many West German cities from 1966 to the early 1980s. Specific groups radicalised the protests by introducing more militant means, which had the effect of reducing the mass appeal of the campaign. The *Spontis*—a group of political activists that sought to continue the traditions of the 1968 movement by invoking the spontaneity of the masses—gained momentum in Frankfurt, where their most prominent members, Joschka Fischer and Daniel Cohn-Bendit, invested the fare increase issue with revolutionary hopes. Beginning in May 1974, they agitated in factories and urban areas trying to drum up support for a boycott of the trams and demanding free fares and paid travel time to and from work, a demand that exceeded those of earlier protests against fare increases. Although the term boycott was frequently used during such campaigns, it was not the only label applied. Protest ranged from individual forms of fare boycott, such as fare dodging, to the effective enforcement of a boycott by means of sit-down strikes on tramway tracks. Just like more conventional consumer boycotts, the latter were a form of economic, social, and political pressure to exclude a company from regular commercial intercourse.

In June 1969, the red spot came to symbolise a well-organised system of hitching lifts in private cars that replaced the paralysed public transport system of Hannover. It grew especially after the public transport service company ceased operations due to blockades. Thousands of motorists displayed the red spot behind their windscreens, while those in need of rides held up spots at converted tramway stops. An SDS flyer explained: "Only decisive action and utilisation of our instruments of power (economic pressure through boycott or blockade) will bring the operator and the government to their senses."[11]

This leads us to the third momentous legal case that governed the treatment of boycott campaigns in West Germany. The association of sit-in blockades with violence entered German legal history in the verdict against Klaus Laepple, a rather moderate student functionary, who was charged

---

[11] "ÜSTRA-Boykott – Aktion ROTER PUNKT," flyer, SDS-Hannover, June 12, 1969, Materialien zur Analyse von Opposition (MAO), "Fahrpreiserhöhungen in Hannover: Die Proteste des Jahres 1969," accessed 13 October, 2017, http://www.mao-projekt.de/BRD/NS/HAN/003/Hannover_MIE_UESTRA_1969.shtml

with "mental coercion" (*geistige Nötigung*). Laepple, a member of the conservative party Christian Democratic Union (CDU) and chair of the student union *Arbeitskreis Kölner Hochschulen*, had signed a call for a demonstration and for sit-in blockades of tramways against drastic fare increases by the Cologne public transport services (KVG) in October 1966. While the demonstration at first proceeded peacefully, in its aftermath confrontations culminated in the use of mounted police and water cannon against protesters.[12] The KVG took civil action against Laepple who was initially sentenced to reimburse the company for two-fifths of the loss of income caused by the blockade—roughly 89,000 deutsche marks—because of his "illegal and culpable interference" with a business enterprise.[13] A parallel criminal case against him went all the way up to the Federal Court of Justice, which in 1969 rescinded an earlier acquittal and sentenced Laepple on the charge of "mental coercion." Chief Judge Paulheinz Baldus, who had been a high-ranking jurist during the Nazi period, freely invoked the notion of terror in the reasons given for the judgment: "The students who sat or stood on the tram tracks to thus blockade the tram traffic used violence to coerce the tram drivers to stop their vehicles. [...] An acknowledgment of a right to demonstrate [...] would come down to the legalisation of a terror exercised by militant minorities, which is absolutely incompatible with a [...] constitution based on the principles of democracy and liberty."[14] This wide concept of violence with respect to coercion established a precedent for a number of controversial rulings against sit-in blockades in the 1970s and 1980s in the face of the peace movement and anti-nuclear protests.[15] The Federal Constitutional Court did not reverse this equation of passive resistance with violence until 1995.[16]

---

[12] Ferdinand Ranft, "'Schreien sie ruhig nach Demokratie …': Studentenführer Laepple und die Grenzen des Demonstrationsrechts," *Die Zeit*, October 25, 1968.
[13] Eva Schmidt-Häuer, "Der 'Provo' von der CDU," *Die Zeit*, January 6, 1967, 3.
[14] Bundesgerichtshof, "Entscheidung vom 8.8.1969—2StR 171/69" (Laepple-Urteil), BGHSt 23, 46; Kerstin Freudiger, *Die juristische Aufarbeitung von NS-Verbrechen* (Tübingen: Mohr Siebeck, 2002), 415–16.
[15] Jürgen Baumann and Hans-Dieter Schwind, *Ursachen, Prävention, und Kontrolle von Gewalt: Analysen und Vorschläge der unabhängigen Regierungskommission zur Verhinderung und Bekämpfung von Gewalt* (Berlin, 1990), vol. 1, 39.
[16] Freia Anders, 'Die Gewaltfrage an der Startbahn West,' in: *Gewalt im politischen Raum: Fallanalysen vom Spätmittelalter bis ins 20. Jahrhundert*, eds. Neithart Bulst, Ingrid Gilcher-Holtey, and Heinz-Gerhard Haupt, (Frankfurt, 2008), 285.

As a consequence, the various boycott campaigns against multinational companies, and also against entire countries, that emerged from 1973 onwards were legally required to refrain from measures of passive resistance or else face criminalisation. These protests reached a peak during the 1988 meeting of the International Monetary Fund and World Bank in West Berlin. Some 150 ideologically diverse groups including environmental, autonomist, and Third World activists organised multiple counter-events in West Berlin and other German cities, a demonstration drew 80,000 people. Calls for boycotts of the regimes in South Africa, Chile, and El Salvador were accompanied by a significant number of attacks against shops and branch offices of international businesses. Many of these were carried out by the *Autonomen* (autonomists), a social movement that emerged in West Germany in the early 1980s, chiefly in the context of the squatter movement.[17] Their concept of militancy combined an emphasis on the everyday dimension of resistance, a subjective concept of the politics of the first person, and a refusal of hierarchies.

The campaign against Chilean export products during the military dictatorship of General Augusto Pinochet did not unfold immediately after the coup in September 1973.[18] Chilean fruit exports only took off in the late 1970s, and then more decisively in the 1980s as a result of the free-market reforms embraced by the dictatorship's Chicago-school economists. In various West European countries, flyers and posters sought to establish a connection between the fruits on European shelves and the dictatorship's human rights abuses. A West German placard showed half an apple with a skull for its core beneath the slogan: "Don't buy fruit from Chile."[19]

However, the idea of boycotting the Chilean government was older. It originated with US-sponsored efforts to topple the Allende government

---

[17] See Freia Anders, 'Wohnraum, Freiraum, Widerstand: Die Formierung der Autonomen in den Konflikten um Hausbesetzungen Anfang der achtziger Jahre,' in: *Das alternative Milieu: Antibürgerlicher Lebensstil und linke Politik in der Bundesrepublik Deutschland und Europa, 1968–1983*, eds. Sven Reichardt and Detlef Siegfried, (Göttingen, 2010), 473–98.

[18] Urs Müller-Plantenberg, 'Historische Grundlagen: Der Putsch in Chile und die Solidaritätsbewegung in Europa,' in: *Links von Nord und Süd: Chilenisch-deutsche Ortsbestimmungen im Neoliberalismus*, eds. Olaf Kaltmeier and Michael Ramminger, (Münster, 1999), 27–37.

[19] Karoline Boehm, 'Warenboykott! Vom Arbeitskampf zum Angriff auf das Image,' in: *Kommt herunter, reiht euch ein: Eine kleine Geschichte der Protestformen sozialer Bewegungen*, eds. Klaus Schönberger and Ove Sutter, (Berlin, 2009), 216.

by means of undermining and sabotaging its regime of provision at a time when Chile's export portfolio was still overwhelmingly dominated by copper. Fourteen western countries imposed a copper boycott on Chile in 1971, when a constitutional amendment for complete nationalisation was proposed by Allende and agreed unanimously by Congress. The American copper company Kennecott—which owned one of the three main copper mines—retaliated with a large-scale international legal campaign against anyone buying Chilean copper. This brought the copper war between the United States and Chile to West Germany, which was the largest importer of Chilean copper.[20] In some ways, protesters in Germany and other countries reappropriated the boycott as a form of protest. However, in contrast to the Nixon administration's rather effective trade war, boycott activities by German consumers remained marginal to the left's campaigning for solidarity with the Chilean people. Initially, the West German Chile-solidarity-committees were firmly anti-imperialist and socialist, locating the Pinochet regime in a tradition of fascism. Later on, campaigns were also supported by groups subscribing to a humanist or Christian ethos of justice, which facilitated the adoption of the boycott idea on the model of the anti-apartheid campaign.

The most prominent campaign of systematic boycotting developed in the context of the international anti-apartheid movement. However, the German anti-apartheid movement emerged comparatively late. Although there had been some critical focus on South Africa in 1960s student politics,[21] a more popular German anti-apartheid movement was only inaugurated in the 1970s.[22] Following the suggestion of South African women's groups, in 1978, a German women's organisation, the *Evangelische Frauenarbeit in Deutschland*, started issuing brochures entitled "Don't buy fruit from South Africa." This was five years after the extensive boycott of South African oranges in the Netherlands. The German booklet took as a point of departure the words of South African Prime Minister J.B. Vorster in 1972, "Every time a South African product is bought, it is another brick in the wall of our continued existence."[23]

---

[20] "Chile-Kupfer: Wie eine Zitrone," *Der Spiegel*, January 15, 1973, 72.

[21] Quinn Slobodian, *Foreign Front: Third World Politics in Sixties West Germany* (Durham, 2012), 21–25.

[22] Jürgen Bacia and Dorothée Leidig, *'Kauft keine Früchte aus Südafrika!': Geschichte der Anti-Apartheid-Bewegung* (Frankfurt am Main, 2008), 46–55.

[23] Evangelische Frauenarbeit in Deutschland (ed.), *Kauft keine Früchte aus Südafrika! Baut nicht mit an der Mauer der Apartheid* (Frankfurt, 1978); Edda Stelck, *Politik mit*

Although the women's organisation did not gain full support from their superiors in the Evangelical Church of Germany, their material reached print runs above 10,000 and considerable resonance among the liberal bourgeoisie. For countless women the practical activity of politicising issues of their daily shopping by putting up information stands in front of local supermarkets became an emancipatory experience.[24]

A boycott campaign that gained partial support from trade unions and political parties only emerged in the second half of the 1980s when German companies, especially banks, became crucial commercial partners for South Africa after the progressive withdrawal of investors from Britain and the United States. With Marxist militancy on the decline, boycotting South Africa offered a project of emancipation that could be realised on a local scale. It also had a performative element, allowing people to mark their commitment to an issue of moral politics through individual consumption choices. The fruit boycott was eventually effective enough that South African producers adopted a costly packaging system which systematically veiled the origin of their produce.[25] After the World Council of Churches called on private customers to cancel their accounts with banks that provided South Africa with loans, the German anti-apartheid movement embraced the banking campaign, and in 1987, the Evangelical Church Congress, yielding to pressure from grassroots action groups, closed its accounts with Deutsche Bank, Dresdner Bank, and Commerzbank. Activists declared May 27, 1988, a nationwide "day of action against banks." Mobilising for the event, the journal *Consum Critik* highlighted that white South Africans enjoyed one of the highest living standards in the world.[26] A decade earlier, South African activist Brigalia Bam had already emphasised in her preface to the first German fruit-boycott brochure that white South Africans were "bathing in luxury" while hundreds of black children died of malnutrition and thousands of innocent people were thrown into jail. She saw the economic boycott as a final resort to avert "a terrible race war."[27]

dem Einkaufskorb: Die Boykott-Aktion der evangelischen Frauen gegen Apartheid (Wuppertal, 1980).

[24] Institut für Friedenspädagogik Tübingen, "Kauft keine Früchte aus Südafrika – Erfahrungen mit einer Boykott-Aktion" (1981), accessed 13 October 2017, http://87.106.4.207/themen/gewaltfr/aktionen/aktio_10.htm

[25] "Verbraucher: Kap der guten Früchte," *Der Spiegel*, November 30, 1987, 89–95.

[26] "27. Mai 1988: Bankenaktionstag gegen Apartheid," *Consum Critik,* vol. 6, no. 2, (1988), 4.

[27] Evangelische Frauenarbeit in Deutschland (ed.), *Kauft keine Früchte aus Südafrika*, 3–4.

The mainstream anti-apartheid movement in West Germany with its strong roots in church organisations embraced a decidedly non-violent outlook that emphasised the moral contrast between peaceful boycott and the South African regime's reliance on violence. However, during the second half of the 1980s a militant branch of the movement emerged, chiefly represented by the autonomists and the *Revolutionäre Zellen* (Revolutionary Cells (RZ)), a decentralised network of militant activists that emerged in the early 1970s in parallel with the Red Army Faction. The RZ sought to combine anti-imperialist and social-revolutionary ideas, frequently leading to ideological divisions among individual cells. In the autumn of 1985, an RZ committed bomb attacks against *Zahnradfabrik Friedrichshafen*, a German company that exported parachutes and parts for armoured vehicles, and two branches of *Daimler-Benz*, which sold trucks and cross-country vehicles to the South African army. Their claim of responsibility for the bombings started with the tried and tested battle cry of the Watts Riots "Burn, baby, burn" and pointed to those injured, interned, and executed by South African police forces. Applauding raids on white residential neighbourhoods, the militants hoped that the youth resistance movement would not content itself with fighting for leftovers from the tables of the white masters but would combine criminal appropriation with militant politics.[28] Since German companies continued to supply crucial parts to the South African apparatus of oppression "in defiance of all chatter of boycott [and] sanctions,"[29] the RZ made clear that it wanted to go beyond mere solidarity campaigns and any "pseudo-ethical cosmetics" such as making South African gold coins an illegal import:

> Our topic is not disinvestment, minimum wages, an anti-racist code of conduct, or hiding the Krugerrand in the back drawers: we don't want to urge fair business policies on the almost 150 German multinationals linking the South African sub-continent to the exploitation and capital flows of the metropoles. As part of a worldwide imperialist structure of exploitation they are to be attacked here as well as there. [...] This must [...] produce conflagrations in their production halls and under their consumer shit.[30]

---

[28] 'Anschlag gegen Brüggemann & Brandt, Hagen und Mercedes Lueg, Bochum,' in: *Früchte des Zorns: Texte und Materialien zur Geschichte der Revolutionären Zellen und der Roten Zora*, 2nd ed., vol. 2, ed. ID-Archiv im IISG, (Amsterdam, December 1985), 532.
[29] Ibid., 531–532.
[30] Ibid., 533.

It is clear that the RZ wanted to go beyond the concept of a consumerist boycott advocated by more moderate activists, but the aim of their militant acts remained that of a boycott in the wider sense: to exert pressure to exclude South African companies and a polity based on apartheid from regular commercial intercourse.

Two years later, the RZ launched a bomb attack against the food store chain *REWE* as part of a campaign against racism and sexism, destroying 17 trucks and trailers in the North Rhine-Westphalian city of Wesel in November 1987.[31] An RZ statement claiming responsibility accused *REWE* of making profits from the oppression of African women by "bartering away" South African fruits, vegetables, and canned goods in more than 7000 stores. The statement likened the exploitation in multinational factories and plantations to early capitalism, with female agricultural labourers working 60–70 hours per week, often forced to take their children along, and at much lower rates of pay than male workers:

> The fruit offered in our supermarket chains [...] is the product of women's work under conditions that represent the entire spectrum of capitalist and sexist oppression: the mechanisation of cultivation methods and subsequent reductions in labour requirements have reduced most female workers to the status of seasonal or day labourers; at the same time they have to bear the health consequences of capitalised farming operating with pesticides and artificial fertilisers that cause diseases.

Moreover, the RZ pointed out, these women were subject to the everyday violence of white overseers; according to the RZ, South Africa had the highest incidence of rape worldwide. In an attempt to imitate and transfer the social and political struggles of South Africa to West Germany, the RZ applauded women's roles in these struggles, in the strikes at Daimler-Benz's South African plants, and when organising resistance against rent increases, boycotts, and raids on wholesalers. In contrast to their earlier statement, the feminist branch of the RZ explicitly commended the German women's church groups who had been propagating the boycott for years. The stated goal of the attack against *REWE* was simple: "We want the goods to disappear from the shelves."[32]

---

[31] "Verbraucher: Kap der guten Früchte," *Der Spiegel*, November 30, 1987, 89–95.

[32] 'Aktion gegen Firma REWE,' in: *Früchte des Zorns*, vol. 2, ed. ID-Archiv im IISG, (November 1987), 536–37.

Autonomists interpreted apartheid as war. Protests against banks were widespread.[33] Commodity boycott, however, was marginal to such direct action against multinationals carried out in the spirit of solidarity with South African workers' liberation struggle.[34] There is little evidence that autonomists got involved in the fruit boycott campaigns, though a rare placard from West Berlin shows a drawing of a crowd demolishing goods in a supermarket. More prominent on their agenda were the relations between German and South African companies in the field of nuclear and military technology. In comparison with earlier anti-imperialist campaigns, which had been more clearly driven by socialist or communist ideals, the heightened emphasis on consumer markets in both the more moderate consumer-boycott and fair-trade campaigns and the campaigns of the radical left mirrored the growing sense of individualism propagated by contemporary neo-liberalism. Such boycotts, particularly that against apartheid but also the campaign against Nestlé, were important steps in a popularisation of "moral economies" via purchase decisions based on ethical criteria. They prepared the way for a new type of consumer capitalism in which the image of politically and ecologically responsible production became ever more important.[35]

The boycott campaigns of the radical left considered so far called attention to the destruction and violence that went hand in hand with the production of consumer goods in faraway countries. Violence against objects emerged as a militant variation of this type of protest. At this point, we should take into account another protest scenario—with many bridges to the protests against the global economic order—where the trajectory went the opposite way and consumer boycott was only adopted in response to violence which threatened to make protest impossible. Initially antinuclear energy protests hardly adopted the viewpoint of the consumer. By the early 1970s, energy lobbyists had largely succeeded in claiming the consumers' perspective in the debates over nuclear energy. Shortages and rising prices in the wake of the so-called oil crisis allowed them to present nuclear energy as the cleaner and cheaper alternative, which seemed entirely in the interest of the consumer. This position was challenged fol-

[33] HKS 13, *vorwärts bis zum nieder mit – 30 jahre plakate unkontrollierter bewegungen* (Berlin, 1990).
[34] Arbeitskreis Internationale Solidarität, *Shell raus aus Südafrika: Materialien zur Anti-Shell Kampagne* (Amsterdam, 1990).
[35] See *The Ethical Consumer*, eds. Rob Harrison, Terry Newholm, and Deirdre Shaw (London, 2005).

lowing the major violent confrontations between police and protesters at the construction site of Brokdorf nuclear power plant in November 1976.

The plan to boycott electricity companies was developed by moderate protesters with the explicit aim of finding alternative means of resistance so as to continue non-violent protest after the failure of violent confrontation. The main goal, however, was public visibility rather than economic pressure.[36] A protest group that was largely led by Protestant clergy declared that "given the massive violence of the state," it was necessary to "imaginatively exercise and utilise the non-violent arsenal of resistance [...]. Boycott measures against the companies making profits from nuclear energy are to be considered."[37] This was explicitly tied to the idea that the authorities' campaign in favour of nuclear energy benefitted from luring anti-nuclear energy protesters into militant conflict. In February 1977, the first flyers calling for electricity boycotts were passed out at an anti-Brokdorf rally in the nearby town of Itzehoe.[38] However, calls for boycott were only admitted into the wider programme of the Association of Environmental Citizen Initiatives (BBU) in 1978, when they began to take a distance from what increasingly seemed futile skirmishes at construction sites.

A nationwide boycott was part of a more decentralised approach to protest that was embraced in the context of resistance against the planned reprocessing plant and repository for nuclear waste at Gorleben. Electricity boycotters aimed for a nationwide platform at the first major demonstration against Gorleben, which took place in Hannover in March 1979. The form of boycott they envisioned was a partial withholding of payment: protesters would only pay 90 per cent of their electricity bill and transfer the remaining 10 per cent into a custodial account until the demands of the campaign—the abandonment of nuclear projects—were met. The federal government deplored the initiative, but the campaign was eventually strengthened by some courts. A Hamburg district court acknowledged

---

[36] Alexander Rossnagel, 'Stromboykott,' in: *Energie: Krise oder Geschäft: Materialien zur Auseinandersetzung der Bürgerinitiativen mit der Energiewirtschaft*, ed. Bundesverband Bürgerinitiativen Umweltschutz, (Freiburg, 1980), 60–61.

[37] Ulfrid Kleinert, *Gewaltfrei Widerstehen: Brokdorf-Protokolle gegen Schlagstöcke und Steine* (Reinbek, 1981), 142; Roger Karapin, *Protest Politics in Germany: Movements on the Left and Right since the 1960s* (University Park, 2007), 136.

[38] Kleinert, *Gewaltfrei Widerstehen*, 144, 170–180.

that the respective positions of electricity companies and electricity boycotters represented two different sets of cultural assumptions and values concerning human life and the potential for human development on this planet.[39] A Stuttgart district court went a step further in declaring that the partial withholding of electricity payments was legal because nuclear power plants did indeed create a potential threat to the general public. To substantiate their reasoning, the judges pointed to the recent Three Mile Island accident and to the yet unsolved problem of ultimate waste disposal. Due to the fact that in cases of contested electricity bills the amount in dispute was small and thus below a certain threshold, the Stuttgart decision had no binding effect for cases at other courts, which usually supported the energy companies' claims against boycotters.[40]

The militantly anti-nuclear RZ lamented that the electricity "boycott" initiative had not been radicalised. Now the Green Party had successfully embraced the boycotting position and—in the eyes of their radical critics—was trying to tie the movement to the state and to legality. Nodding to Adorno and Horkheimer, the RZ countered that "enlightenment in late-capitalist societies" easily became consumption: "Economic violence and other relations of violence are internalised as lawful; and this violence must be made visible again via breaching legality."[41] From this militant interpretation of structural violence, the RZ sought to place the boycott within a broad portfolio of protest measures designed to prevent the construction of nuclear power stations. A statement seeking to justify explosive devices deployed against the offices of two companies involved in the development of nuclear power stations and against a power pole in November 1982 issued a call to action over the coming "years when we will have time to boycott, to sabotage, to occupy, to blockade, to blast." The example of the partial boycotting of energy companies shows that in some cases effective consumer protest was difficult given the semi-monopolistic structure of the energy sector that left consumers literally without a choice. Consumers were bound to their local provider, one of

---

[39] Theo Hengesbach and Wiltrud Rühle, 'Eine Lawine nimmt Gestalt an: Zum aktuellen Stand der Stromgeldverweigerung in der Bundesrepublik,' *Gewaltfreie Aktion*, vol. 39/40, (1979).

[40] Rossnagel, "Stromboykott," 60–61.

[41] "Subversiver Kampf in der Anti-AKW-Bewegung," in: *Früchte des Zorns*, ed. ID-Archiv im IISG, vol. 1, (1980), 350–51.

the eight oligopolistic consortia of the West German energy industry which enjoyed comfortable market conditions leaning on the Energy Industry Act of 1935, which, in the interest of "common welfare," sought "to prevent the economic impact of competition."[42] In the long run, the liberalisation of the energy market made it possible for consumers to simply subscribe to delivery packages from companies without nuclear power generation. Boycotts had a share in making market structures more flexible.

Before proceeding to the final part of this chapter, a preliminary conclusion can be drawn: politically motivated boycott campaigns were first embraced and staged by strong players in the political contest (the state, large corporations, and sizable parts of the population) before the extra-parliamentary opposition and the "new" social movements seized the method and, in an effort to articulate and mobilise critical minority views, harnessed it to political ends that were often diametrically opposed to those pursued by boycott campaigns from above. Springer used boycott flanked by economic pressure against *Blinkfüer* and the German Democratic Republic (GDR) long before the students boycotted Springer; Willy Brandt and the Confederation of German Trade Unions called for a boycott of the East German-run Berlin S-Bahn prior to students protesting public transport fare increases; the US government and large American companies boycotted the Chilean government under Allende a decade before students embraced fruit boycotts in a fight against the Pinochet government; and the CIA-sponsored *Kampfgruppe gegen Unmenschlichkeit* (Combat Group against Inhumanity) committed stink bomb and incendiary attacks against East German department stores long before any left-wing protesters launched limited arson attacks.[43] Some of the boycott campaigns from below, especially the more militant ones, were perceived as inappropriate or tasteless and gave immediate rise to critical comparisons with Nazi boycotts, whereas Cold-War boycott campaigns from above usually did not trigger this analogy. When comparing these different boycott campaigns, it is important to keep in mind the power relations between boycotters and boycotted as well as the nature of the targets of boycotts, whether these are commodities, people, companies, or states.

[42] "Strom: 'Es wird bewußt diskriminiert'," *Der Spiegel*, March 14, 1977, 90–98.
[43] Enrico Heitzer, *"Affäre Walter": Die vergessene Verhaftungswelle* (Berlin, 2008), 191–93.

The Moral and Political Explosiveness of Anti-Zionist Boycotts

Only a small minority of German left-wing radicals were prepared to go so far as to put Israel on a level with South Africa and to subscribe to analogous calls to boycott Israeli products. When leftists embraced anti-Zionist boycotts in the 1970s, they entered a field of political communication that, for historical reasons, was particularly difficult in Germany; their calculations usually backfired.

The RZ used both boycott and incendiary attacks against targets associated with Israel in West Germany. The strategy of militant boycott campaigns represented a move away from large-scale terrorist acts on the international stage following the public-relations disaster effected by the international wing of the RZ (closely allied to the Popular Front for the Liberation of Palestine) with the Entebbe hijack in July 1976.[44] From then on, the RZ concentrated on the global process of economic restructuring. The Israeli economy remained a target for the RZ, but as just one of many targets. According to the federal prosecutor's office, the RZ confessed to 186 militant attacks against a variety of targets between 1973 and 1993.[45] Less than 5 per cent of these were directed against Israel.

In 1978, an RZ attacked the Frankfurt branch of Agrexco, a company owned by the state of Israel and Europe's largest importer of Israeli fruit, causing damage to the building but no casualties. A statement linked the attack to cases of Arab workers allegedly injecting mercury into Israeli oranges. Oranges injected with mercury had indeed been found in Europe in January and February 1978, but it is doubtful that any Palestinian organisations were involved in these acts of poisoning. Evidence presented by the Israeli International Institute for Counter-Terrorism suggests that radical European solidarity groups—perhaps the RZ or similar Dutch groups—invented this form of protest. Letters sent from Stuttgart, threatening to poison Israeli agricultural products in the name of an otherwise obscure Arab Revolutionary Army, were received in several European capitals. The Palestine Liberation Organisation (PLO) and the Popular

---

[44] See Alexander Sedlmaier and Freia Anders. "Unternehmen Entebbe' 1976: Widerstreitende Perspektiven auf eine Flugzeugentführung.' *Jahrbuch für Antisemitismusforschung,* vol. 22, (2013), 267–89.

[45] Der Generalbundesanwalt, "Anklage gegen ein Mitglied der 'Revolutionären Zellen (RZ),'" November 12, 2000, accessed October 13, 2017, http://www.generalbundesanwalt.de/txt/showpress.php?newsid=23

Front for the Liberation of Palestine (PFLP) were initially not impressed with boycott as a new form of struggle because they believed it had the potential to discredit the perpetrators; they embraced it only later and on a limited scale.[46]

The RZ attack and June 1978 statement appear to address public discourse in the aftermath of a wave of copycat citrus fruit poisonings throughout Europe that also affected non-Israeli oranges. The RZ pointed out that such attempts were sabotage rather than poisoning, since the goal was to make the oranges unusable rather than to kill people. Elemental mercury is in fact poorly absorbed by ingestion, and toxicity from swallowing is rare. None of the 50 oranges found contaminated with mercury in various European cities threatened anyone's life. Although the actual danger posed by mercury in citrus fruits was small, the incidents provoked a climate of fear and had detrimental effects on sales of fruit, the original intention of the perpetrators.

The RZ suggested that only lack of solidarity on the left and media smears had raised suspicions of antisemitism against their campaign. No one had suffered any serious harm from their actions while, it alleged, the "imperialist state" of Israel financed its army to no small degree from the export of citrus fruits. The RZ would no longer "idly watch" the "war of extermination against the Palestinians"; instead, the attack was meant as only the prelude to further measures in the commercial sphere: "boycott campaigns against Israeli goods, discussions with people doing their shopping, but also stink bombs and acid attacks against Israeli products, destroying the stocks of Israeli fruit displayed in every department store." The RZ could not resist comparing what they perceived as the "expulsion, persecution, and extermination of an entire people" to the "blood and soil" politics of the Nazis. At the same time, they explicitly declared that their opposition to Zionism was also a resolute fight against antisemitism in any form.[47]

Another attack, in 1979, targeted the fruit import and wholesale trade company *Hameico*, again in Frankfurt. The demand was that companies withdraw Israeli produce and that "anti-fascist" activists provoke boycotts

---

[46] Ehud Sprinzak and Ely Karmon, "Why So Little? The Palestinian Terrorist Organizations and Unconventional Terrorism," June 17, 2007, accessed October 13, 2017, https://www.ict.org.il/Article.aspx?ID=978#gsc.tab=0

[47] 'Aktion gegen die Israelische Import-Gesellschaft Agrexco, Frankfurt,' in: *Früchte des Zorns*, vol. 1, ed. ID-Archiv im IISG, (June 1978), 131–32.

by injecting butyric acid into "Zionist fruits." The charging of commodities with ideological projections went so far that the authors of the statement seem to have overlooked the almost comical notion that a grapefruit might be Zionist. The RZ were among the pioneers of militant boycott campaigns that targeted Israel. The British Palestine Solidarity Campaign did not embrace the Boycott Israeli Goods Campaign until 1982.[48] In 1988, in the context of the First Intifada, squatters from Hamburg's Hafenstraße painted a mural on the exterior wall of a tenement building dominated by the slogan: "Boycott 'Israel'! Goods, kibbutzim and beaches."[49] Above the words was the outline of a machine gun against the background of a giant Palestinian flag. To underline the allegedly illegitimate nature of the Zionist state, the word Israel appeared in quotation marks, the same way the Springer press referred to the "DDR." This message triggered controversies within and beyond the radical left about the extent to which the slogan was antisemitic.[50] A discussion meeting at Hafenstraße sought to establish the right to criticise the state of Israel without immediately being accused of antisemitism. A key speaker was Israeli civil rights activist and Fatah member Uri Davis, the author of a book arguing that Israel's policies towards Palestinians were comparable to South Africa's apartheid policies.

Despite immediate and vehement criticism, both from within and beyond radical circles, autonomist activists unleashed a campaign against Israeli goods in Hamburg and other German cities. Orange crates were knocked over in supermarkets, while at an open-air market blood and red paint were poured over Israeli goods—actions understandably perceived as distasteful in light of the Nazis' boycott campaigns.[51] The boycott campaign triggered by the Hafenstraße mural undoubtedly played a prominent part in German autonomist groups' political repertoire, but a perusal

---

[48] Ehud Rosen, *Mapping the Organizational Sources of the Global Delegitimization Campaign against Israel in the UK* (Jerusalem, 2011), 30.

[49] Monika Sigmund and Marily Stroux, *Zu bunt: Wandbilder in der Hafenstraße* (Hamburg, 1996), 27–31.

[50] Jan Philipp Reemtsma, 'Die andere Wand – Über die Parole 'Boykottiert "Israel"!' an einem der Häuser der Hamburger Hafenstraße,' in: *u.a. Falun: Reden & Aufsätze* (Berlin, 1992), 147–53.

[51] "'Das Gut-Böse-Raster': Zur Auseinandersetzung um das Wandbild in der Hamburger Hafenstraße," *calcül* 6 (1999), accessed 23 October 2017, http://www.conne-island.de/nf/72/24.html#t01; *Materialien zur Kampagne boykottiert "Israel" – Waren, Kibbuzim, und Strände. Palästina – Das Volk wird sich befreien* (Freiburg, 1988).

of their journals and posters shows that more conventional protests against aspects of Israeli policy—for example, the 1982 Lebanon War—were more frequent.

Conclusion

The landmark decisions of the Federal Constitutional Court provide a useful analytical framework for the comparative historical assessment of boycott campaigns: they should be covered by freedom of expression, and they appear to be a legitimate means of political communication as long as the boycotters resort to no means of coercion other than an appeal to the moral position of those addressed. It is debatable how far such communicative appeals might be stretched into the realm of symbolic violence against objects, but the crucial point is that boycott campaigns forfeit this fundamental rights protection once they eliminate the competition of opinion by means of economic or other coercive pressure that goes beyond the mobilisation of public opinion and individual purchase decisions. Historically, such extended boycott campaigns were still able to mobilise other sources of legitimisation, for example, by supporting state-sponsored economic sanctions as in the case of the anti-apartheid campaign. More generally, legitimate boycott campaigns try to alter the regime of provision they are attacking by means of political communication in the public and commercial sphere, but they do not seek to eliminate the boycotted party.

This also helps to address the controversial tension between claims to the high moral ground by anti-Zionist and other boycotters and the frequent accusations that they were effectively iterating an antisemitic tradition. In this analysis of boycotts in Cold-War West Germany, boycotting has emerged as a communicative strategy of favouring and/or discrediting particular interests that, as such, can be used by adherents of any political persuasion. Many boycott campaigns, especially those directed against Israel, were perceived as inappropriate or distasteful and gave rise to immediate comparisons with Nazi boycotts. Frequently, a lack of political and perhaps moral judgement led them to ignore the dangers of adopting political symbols and means of agitation that not only invited detrimental comparisons with Nazi campaigns but might also prove compatible with antisemitic discourse. However, there are important differences between their attempts to mount a communicative position of self-proclaimed moral strength and the conduct of Nazi storm troopers in German shopping streets of the 1930s; and these go beyond the obvious contrast in the dimension of the injustice done. From a position of relative political weakness and motivated by ideas of international solidarity, left-wing boycotters committed symbolic attacks against goods of Israeli origin, but they did not physically attack Jewish vendors, nor were they backed up by state-sponsored and paramilitary violence. Despite sympathies and alliances with Palestinian organisations that were involved in military struggle with the state of Israel, such acts were not expressions of a pervasive eliminatory ideology. The targets were the military politics of Israel's government and large corporations with close connections to the Israeli state, not individuals, let alone non-Israeli Jews. The aim was the inclusion of the Palestinian people into the international state system and corresponding regimes of provision, while the Nazis' *völkisch* regime of provision was thoroughly based on exclusion.

These apparent contrasts do not yet answer the crucial question whether anti-Zionist and anti-Israeli boycotts differed fundamentally from other boycotts in Cold-War West Germany. Were boycotters operating double standards when Israel was targeted? And if so, did these double standards contain the seeds of antisemitism that, if unchecked, could feed another trajectory of violence against Jews? It may be the case that some activists were stimulated by a variant of a secondary antisemitism motivated by a deflection of guilt for the Holocaust, but this is very difficult to prove. Concerning the radical left, this is frequently alleged rather than empirically demonstrated.[52] The comparative perspective on different boycott campaigns does not exactly support such allegations because it is difficult to argue that radical or militant boycotts were the outgrowth of secondary antisemitism since activists were involved in several interrelated boycott campaigns that pursued rather similar patterns of agitation, with Israel just one among several targets. Judging from my research on boycotts in particular and on the radical left in Cold-War West Germany more broadly, I am tempted to adapt a famous quip by Isaiah Berlin: anti-Israeli boycotts were just like other boycotts, only more so.[53] On balance, they were nei-

---

[52] For example, Wolfgang Kraushaar, 'Antizionismus als Trojanisches Pferd: zur antisemitischen Dimension in den Kooperationen von Tupamaros West-Berlin, RAF und RZ mit den Palästinensern,' in: *Die RAF und der linke Terrorismus*, vol. 1, ed. W. Kraushaar, (Hamburg, 2006), 676–95; Wolfgang Kraushaar, *"Wann endlich beginnt bei Euch der Kampf gegen die heilige Kuh Israel?" – München 1970: über die antisemitischen Wurzeln des deutschen Terrorismus* (Reinbek, 2013).

[53] Shlomo Avineri and Alan Ryan, 'Isaiah the Jew,' in: *The Book of Isaiah: Personal Impressions of Isaiah Berlin*, ed. Henry Hardy, (Woodbridge, 2009), 159.

ther more prominent in the protest spectrum of the left, nor fundamentally different from the many other boycott scenarios on the radical left. However, they were perceived more intensely and thus developed a momentum of their own.

An essential part of the communicative strategy of boycotting is to bridge distance (both spatially and historically) in order to connect political contexts seemingly far removed. Past or present injustices and violence associated with the boycotted party are joined together as activists justified the specific forms of boycott and protest that they held to be legitimate. Conversely, their opponents tried to delegitimise certain forms of boycott and protest by pointing to past or present crimes. Given the unique weight of the Holocaust in Germany and its historical relationship with the Arab-Israeli conflict, in the case of boycotts against Israel, there was a surfeit of discursively explosive matter available on both sides of the debate. Every so often, antisemitic statements—and accusations of antisemitism—were the outcome of this process, but among the vast majority of radical left-wing boycott activists in Cold-War West Germany, antisemitism was not a precondition, let alone a motivation, of their activism, an important difference compared to the self-avowed and pervasive antisemitism of Nazis and neo-Nazis.

CHAPTER 8

"The Onward March of a People Who Desire to Be Totally Free": The 1953 Baton Rouge Bus Boycott

Derek Charles Catsam

In 1953, black citizens of Baton Rouge undertook a bus protest that merged the issues of race and class in a challenge that would not only bring together issues of subsistence and civil rights, it would provide a template two years later for the famed Montgomery bus boycott in Alabama.[1] As in any city in the South, segregation on the buses represented

---

[1] Much of what follows owes a great debt to the following: *The Louisiana Weekly*, an African-American newspaper published in New Orleans, particularly issues from June–August 1953; LSU Library Special Exhibit, "The Baton Rouge Bus Boycott of 1953 … A Recaptured Past," available at http://www.lib.lsu.edu/special/exhibits/e-exhibits/boycott/ (accessed 3 October 2011); Louisiana Public Television, *Signpost to Freedom: The 1953 Baton Rouge Bus Boycott*, (2009); Theodore Judson Jemison, Sr., *The T. J. Jemison Story*, (Nashville, 1994); Aldon D. Morris, *The Origins of the Civil Rights Movement: Black Communities Organizing for Change* (New York, 1984), 17–25; Shannon Frystak, *Our Minds on Freedom: Women and the Struggle for Black Equality in Louisiana, 1924–1967* (Baton Rouge, 2009), 62–69; Christina Melton, "We'll Keep Walking!': The Baton Rouge Civil Rights Boycott of 1953,' *Louisiana Endowment for the Humanities*, (Spring 2007), 62–71; August Meier and Elliott Rudwick, *Along the Color Line: Explorations in the Black*

D. C. Catsam (✉)
University of Texas of the Permian Basin, Odessa, TX, USA

© The Author(s) 2019
D. Feldman (ed.), *Boycotts Past and Present*, Palgrave Critical Studies of Antisemitism and Racism,
https://doi.org/10.1007/978-3-319-94872-0_8

a daily reminder of the second-class status that black people faced daily. Memories abounded of those who challenged that segregation and faced the consequences. For example, Black Baton Rouge residents long told of a young man who had challenged bus segregation in the early 1940s. He had refused to give up his seat to white people, who then attacked him, chased him when he tried to get away, and beat him. Willis Reed, an important leader in the black community, believed that a driving force for African American resistance was "the policies, the attitudes of the policemen and the attitudes of the bus drivers. They were very un-courteous to people, they talked to them as if they were inhuman ... and I would think that about eighty percent of the riders at that time were black people!"[2]

The Baton Rouge bus boycott represents several important elements of the long civil rights movement. It took place prior to events such as *Brown v. Board of Education*, the landmark case that overturned the doctrine of "Separate but Equal" in public education and signaled the death knell to *de jure* segregation, and the Montgomery Bus Boycott, both of which forced civil rights into the public consciousness. And it did so largely invisible beyond the local context. The Baton Rouge boycott consisted of local black leadership responding to local social and political circumstances that nonetheless were typical of confrontations with segregation across the region and indeed frequently outside of the South. And the events in Baton Rouge, as with so many events in the civil rights movement, also revealed and in some cases exacerbated schisms within the black community, for these were, after all real people with real egos and differences of opinion for how to proceed in confronting white supremacy.

* * *

In January 1953, the Baton Rouge City-Parish Council voted to raise the fares on municipal buses by 50%, from 10 cents to 15 cents per trip. As a City-Parish councilman from those years later explained, "The bus com-

---

Experience (Urbana, 1976), 365–366. For a historiographical perspective on the African American experience in Louisiana, see Charles Vincent, "Of Such Historical Importance ...': The African American Experience in Louisiana,' *Louisiana History*, vol. 50, (Spring 2009), 138–158. See also Michael G. Wade, 'Does Louisiana's Past Have a Future?: The Challenge of the Present,' *Louisiana History*, vol. 50, (Spring 2009), 389–406.

[2] Louisiana State University Libraries, Special Exhibits, "Baton Rouge Bus Boycott: The People," http://www.lib.lsu.edu/special/exhibits/boycott/thepeople.html, accessed July 23, 2009.

pany was always struggling, and the city couldn't afford to take it over."³ The bus company held a City-Parish-sanctioned monopoly, as in 1950 the bus company had requested an exclusive contract for bus services in Baton Rouge. The Council acceded to the financially struggling bus company's request for privileged status and revoked the licenses of more than three dozen independent black-owned buses with evocative names like "The Blue Goose Bus" and "Jelly Bean." The fare hike was an onerous one for many of the working-class black Baton Rouge residents who relied upon the buses to get them to and from their jobs, including masses of women who worked in the homes of Baton Rouge's middle-class white families.

As was customary throughout the South, the buses in Baton Rouge had both black and white passengers and were segregated by race. Black passengers would pay the same to ride the buses as whites, but they filled the buses from the back while whites rode in the front half of the vehicle with the front ten seats reserved exclusively for whites. When the buses were crowded, passengers stood, but if the white section was sparsely filled and the black section full, black passengers still had to stand in their crowded area.

Reverend Theodore Judson Jemison, Sr. served as pastor of the Mt. Zion Baptist Church, the largest black church in Louisiana and a venue that would later be called "a building block for the Southern struggle for civil rights."⁴ Jemison arrived in Baton Rouge with a bachelor's degree from Alabama State University and a master's degree from Virginia Union, both historically black schools, and he had done graduate work at New York University.⁵ When he originally arrived in town, Mt. Zion was housed in a dilapidated wooden building. In 1953, the erection of a new church building had begun under Jemison's watch. He arrived to take over the church in 1949, and if he was still relatively new to the city and its politics, he was no wallflower. His father had been president of the National Baptist Convention, the largest African American organization in the world. On February 11 at a meeting of the City-Parish Council, Reverend T. J. Jemison stood up and denounced both the fare hike and the policy of segregated reserved seating. He would later write:

> On numerous occasions, as I stood on East Boulevard watching the builders erect our church, the buses would pass by going into South Baton Rouge with hardly any whites on the bus. The Negro passengers would be standing

[3] Melton, "'We'll Keep Walking'," p. 65.
[4] Frank Etheridge, "Bus Stop," *Gambit Weekly*, June 17, 2003.
[5] Morris, *The Origins of the Civil Rights Movement*, 19.

up over empty seats which had to be reserved for whites by company policy. Many of the woman passengers on the buses were maids and cooks coming home from a hard day's labor. I thought this was wrong and unchristian and felt something had to be done about it. The Whites who rode the buses were those who had stores in the Negro community, or who worked there, and were therefore making a living from the black passengers who were riding the buses, exhausted from their day's work. This was a wrong that had to be corrected and I felt God had placed this responsibility on me.[6]

Jemison noted a further irony. "The blacks going down into South Baton Rouge were forced to stand up over empty seats. They could put their bags, their bundles, in the seats, but they couldn't put their bodies."[7]

Jemison's protest to the Council did not fall on deaf ears. Lewis Doherty had been elected to that body in 1952 when he was just 26 years old, and he recognized that there were "unequal facilities for black people as compared to white people and I was aware of that. At the time the law, the history and the culture were one of segregation. It was just something that was understood, not questioned."[8] Apparently, Doherty was not alone in his relatively enlightened views on the Council and the members of that body passed Ordinance 222, which mandated that blacks fill the bus from the back, whites from the front, all based on a first-come, first-served basis. The line of segregation would thus remain but would be flexible and based upon the composition of the ridership at any given time. The Council passed the ordinance unanimously and it would go into effect on March 19. Doherty believed that most of the Council agreed with his views about the buses. "I felt it was only fair where people had paid their fare and there were seats available, that they could sit down and take those seats."[9] The African American newspaper *Louisiana Weekly* deemphasized the challenge to segregation, instead pointing out that the ordinance "was to prevent busses from being uneconomically loaded with reserved seats vacant and paying fares deprived of seating accommodations."[10]

---

[6] Jemison, *The T. J. Jemison Story*, 37.
[7] Louisiana State University Libraries, Special Exhibits, "Baton Rouge Bus Boycott: The People," http://www.lib.lsu.edu/special/exhibits/boycott/thepeople.html, accessed July 23, 2009.
[8] Melton, "'We'll Keep Walking'," p. 65.
[9] Melton, "'We'll Keep Walking'," p. 68.
[10] *Louisiana Weekly*, June 27, 1953.

The fare hike would remain in place, as the Council agreed with the bus company that the costs of operation mandated a rise in fares. The segregation policy was clearly a racial issue. The fare hike was more complicated as it theoretically affected all passengers equally even though for the bulk of black passengers the five cents likely cut more deeply.

This softer and gentler if more expensive form of segregation may well have prevailed. But whatever the letter of the law, the white bus drivers by and large ignored it after the City-Parish Council issued a directive to the bus company and its drivers. After three months, black leaders met with city officials to argue that the bus company must adhere to the new policy. They left that meeting believing that drivers would be compelled to adhere to the laws. Reverend Jemison and B. J. Stanley, the head of the local branch of the National Association for the Advancement of Colored People (NAACP), prepared and distributed fliers that explained the rights of black riders and told them how to address intransigent bus drivers and police officers.[11]

Martha White, a 23-year-old housekeeper, walked so many miles to the bus stop, stood so often on the bus, and was on her feet for so many hours for her job that, as she later remembered, she "never knew what a chair looked like." On June 13, "I was just wore out." Although black passengers were standing, there were "white" seats available toward the front of the bus, and she took one of them. She explained to the driver that she would give up her seat if a white person boarded. The driver told her to get out of the seat, at which point another woman, whom White identified only as "Pearl," sat down beside her and announced to the other passengers and to the driver, "Everybody's gonna stick together this morning. No one's gonna get off the bus and we're gonna stick together."[12] Initially even some of the black passengers had "laughed and made a mockery of White" before realizing that a serious challenge was under way.[13]

At this point, the ever-vigilant Reverend Jemison, whom the *Louisiana Weekly* declared to be "this dauntless leader," became involved.[14] He had been preparing to test the enforcement of the ordinance himself when he happened upon the incident on Martha White's bus. Police were there in

---

[11] Melton, "'We'll Keep Walking'," p. 68; LPB *Signpost to Freedom*.
[12] Melton, "'We'll Keep Walking'," pp. 68–69.
[13] Alexis Alexander, "Baton Rouge bus boycott," *The Southern Digest*, online edition, February 25, 2005; See also Louisiana Public Broadcasting, *Signpost to Freedom*.
[14] *Louisiana Weekly*, June 27, 1953.

response to the driver's summons and Jemison tapped a policeman on the shoulder. According to White, Jemison said, "Now officer, you know you can't do that," and while the police officer relented, the driver removed Jemison from the bus. "I'll never forget," Jemison later recounted. "The bus company manager, H. D. Cauthen, came to the scene and told the driver, 'Get back and drive the bus because the City Council passed an ordinance that said they could sit down there. I agree. Let them sit'."[15]

A day later the company suspended two drivers for ignoring the city ordinance. It seemed that Baton Rouge was prepared to go gently into compliance with something representing equality under a policy of separation on the city's buses.

In response to the suspensions and incidents such as Jemison's, 95 bus drivers in Baton Rouge went on a strike on June 15 that lasted for four days. The *Louisiana Weekly* asserted, "This erstwhile placid and harmonious city where the status quo has never been challenged by mass action, was shocked by the sudden and unprecedented strike by bus drivers of the Baton Rouge Bus Company."[16] Drivers claimed to be looking out for the interests of white passengers, but they ended up facing considerable public backlash. An editorial in the Baton Rouge *State Times* argued, "The City Ordinance is an important step toward the betterment of race relations among the citizens of this community and should be given a fair chance to work." Letters to the editor overwhelmingly agreed. One reader worried, "This silly strike is sending Louisiana back to the days of King Cotton. This is a progressive state and I hope the company fires all the drivers who won't comply with the laws of the people." Another opined, "All Baton Rougeans who favor increased social fair play for Negroes will let it be known and back them up."[17] The bus drivers countered through their wives and children, many of whom marched on the parish courthouse on Wednesday, June 17, announcing that their families "were suffering because of the strike and urged the council to rescind the seating ordinance."[18]

On June 19, the Louisiana Attorney General Fred Leblanc declared Baton Rouge's new city ordinance illegal as it flew in the face of segrega-

---

[15] Melton, "'We'll Keep Walking'," p. 69.
[16] *Louisiana Weekly*, June 27, 1953.
[17] *State Times*, June 17, 1953. Also quoted in Melton, "'We'll Keep Walking'," p. 69.
[18] *State Times*, June 17, 1953. See also Frystak, *Our Minds on Freedom*, 64–65.

tion laws.[19] The bus drivers ended their strike, but bus company authorities and city officials received no respite. A new organization of black city denizens, the United Defense League (UDL), met and organized a bus boycott. Jemison served as the new organization's president. Although the UDL was heavily male-dominated, one woman, Fannie Washburn, a housewife active in the Voter's League, was the sole woman on the UDL executive board.[20]

The UDL served to coordinate and direct the events of the boycott, but it did so within the context of the many churches and other organizations that saw themselves as being involved in the movement as well. The black churches served as the most important institutions in the city for conveying information, providing re-enforcement for the boycotters and funds for the larger effort. But the UDL could both coordinate and draw in considerable secular support that was beyond the reach of the churches. In the words of historian Aldon Morris, the UDL thus "became an organization of organizations."[21]

Jemison and a local tailor, Raymond Scott, went on radio station WLCS at 11:30 on Thursday night to announce the bus boycott, asking blacks to avoid the buses and announcing a "Free ride" system of car pools and taxi services, which they called "Operation Free Car Lift," to ensure as little hardship as possible on those many blacks for whom using the buses was not a luxury but rather a necessity to allow them to go to work and otherwise live their lives. Jemison's church donated US$ 2000, early on in anticipation that the funds would support a potential boycott.[22] Jemison and Scott also asserted that the boycott would continue either until drivers recognized the recent ordinance or until "a franchise could be obtained for a Negro corporation to operate a bus system."[23] The boycott organizers managed to corral approximately 125 cars and trucks "and everything that would roll" to assist in the Free Ride program, festooning the vehicles with signs to indicate their role in the city's new transportation infrastructure.[24]

Hazel Freeman, one of the boycott participants, noted about Jemison's leadership, "We had a lot of powerful black people, but the others had not

[19] *Louisiana* Weekly, June 27, 1953; New *York Times*, June 21, 1953.
[20] Frystak, *Our Minds on Freedom*, 65.
[21] Morris, *The Origins of the Civil Rights Movement*, 21–22.
[22] Jemison, *The T. J. Jemison Story*, 38.
[23] *Louisiana Weekly*, June 27, 1953.
[24] LPB, *Signpost to Freedom*.

had the courage and the guts to come forward. Reverend Jemison came here a young man, very bold, and others joined him."[25] Jemison had some freedom because of his role as leader of the largest and most economically stable church in the black community. He therefore was not dependent on whites for his or his church's economic well-being. Prior to the boycott, he had taken chances to advocate for members of his community. He took on the white proprietor of a candy store in the black community who was accused of "fondling" young black girls who entered his store. Jemison apparently threatened the store's owner with bodily violence from "young tough blacks," which served to be enough to get the man to close his store. On another occasion, Jemison came to the aid of a black family that crowded a mother, father, and nine children into one small room by helping to provide them with land and a spacious home. Some within the community believed that Jemison must have had ulterior motives, including alleging that he must have kept the title to the home for his own future benefit, but when Jemison and his followers took out a full-page newspaper advertisement showing the title in the family's name it curbed the criticism. "From that point," Jemison recalled, the black community "had confidence" in his leadership and motives. "There were other incidents. Several of them. It was incidents like this that made people know that I was more or less for other people rather than for myself, and that I could be followed and that I could be trusted."[26]

It also helped rather than hurt Jemison that he was a relative newcomer to the city. Much as with Martin Luther King, Jr. in Montgomery a couple of years later, Jemison benefited from being unsullied by local factional rivalries.[27]

In the words of Aldon Morris, "The lateness of Jemison's arrival thus enhanced his ability to unite the diverse segments of the community for sustained protest," as did the fact that he "became well integrated into community activities and belonged to a number of organizations."[28]

But if Jemison was by and large recognized as the movement's leader, he did not act alone. The many prominent figures in local churches provided considerable guidance and leadership. Without their ongoing support, the boycott likely would have failed. The UDL augmented and

---

[25] Melton, "'We'll Keep Walking'," p. 68.
[26] Morris, *The Origins of the Civil Rights Movement*, 20.
[27] Ibid., 20–21.
[28] Ibid., 21.

coordinated the work of the churches and "promoted creativity, discouraged jealousies and rivalries, eliminated needless duplication of effort, and maximized group cohesiveness." In the words of Jemison, "No matter how the power structure and splinter white groups tried to tear us apart, we were able to maintain a united front ... We were united."[29]

Above all, the thousands of boycott participants did the real work, made significant sacrifices, and ran substantial risks. Dupuy Anderson, one of the Free Ride volunteer drivers, recognized that he was putting himself at risk by working with the boycotters. "You don't prepare to go to jail," [but] "when you are fighting for right and justice, you accept what ever goes along with it."[30] Furthermore, some white women picked up their maids and others whom they saw walking. Isadore Tansil, President of the Usher Board at Mt. Zion Baptist Church, and a postal worker who therefore could not directly be involved with politics—though he did make donations—noted that this sort of support from some white community members "brought a lot of camaraderie for a lot of us."[31]

There was also a mass meeting that night, and as Martha White recalled, "The place was full, and they end up saying that nobody ride the next morning, and everybody leave that place that night knock on somebody's door all night if it takes you. Don't go home, knock on the people's door and let 'em know that no black people's riding that bus next morning. And that's what we done."[32]

The boycott began the next day and although early on there were a few black passengers who had not heard about the strike, by the day's end black ridership of city buses was zero.[33] That night Jemison's Mt. Zion Baptist Church, which had earlier in the day seen the boycott's first mass meeting to mobilize the community, received that least subtle of messages: burning crosses on the church lawn. Boycott participants knew that there were hardships ahead. Willie Spooner, Jr., a boycott supporter, noted years later, "It was a tremendous sacrifice for me because I was married, I was working on Terrace and Highland Road, so bus transportation was

---

[29] Ibid., p. 22.
[30] Louisiana State University Libraries, Special Exhibits, "Baton Rouge Bus Boycott: The People," accessed at http://www.lib.lsu.edu/special/exhibits/boycott/thepeople.html, accessed July 23, 2009.
[31] Ibid.
[32] Melton, "'We'll Keep Walking'," p. 70.
[33] Jemison, *The T. J. Jemison Story*, 39.

the only transportation that I had at that time. But we gave it up, my wife and I. We gave it up to try to make the bus boycott work."[34]

Substantial support for the boycott was based largely just north of central Baton Rouge in the African American community of Scotlandville. Scotlandville included Southern University, a historically black school that provided an intellectual and economic epicenter for local civil rights protest and contributed to statewide civil rights leadership and provided not only education but also social awareness. The area included a fairly substantial black middle class from which it drew much of its leadership, with a host of educated professionals, skilled tradesmen, teachers, ministers, professors and other university employers, and industrial workers, many of whom had union protections or worked for national corporations that provided more protection than did local employers. Esso-Standard Oil, based in New Jersey but providing "the backbone of the local economy" both employed and did business with many within the black community. Among these was Horatio Thompson, a prominent local businessman who owned several service stations and who was the first African American in the South to operate an Esso service station.[35]

In subsequent days boycotters collected gas money for those operating car pools and held mass meetings at the Mt. Zion Baptist Church, McKinley High School and, in a sign of the expanding popular appeal of the boycott, at Memorial Stadium.[36] Horatio Thompson sold gasoline at cost to those who maintained the car pools. "I couldn't attend all the rallies and marches," Thompson noted many years later, "But I wanted to support them. It was a heck of a sacrifice for me at the time."[37] Mrs. Almenia Freeman drove one of the cars for the Free Ride system and would later remember, "I was available to get out and drive up and down

---

[34] Louisiana State University Libraries, Special Exhibits, "Baton Rouge Bus Boycott: The People," accessed at http://www.lib.lsu.edu/special/exhibits/boycott/thepeople.html, accessed July 23, 2009.

[35] Melton, "'We'll Keep Walking'," pp. 65–66; LPB *Signpost to Freedom*.

[36] Aldon Moris points out that Jemison's church could only hold about 1000 people and that at the high school, "which normally seated about 1200 ... on those hot June nights, 2500–3000 people would wedge themselves into the auditorium, and according to Jemison they stood around the walls, sat on window sills, and occupied all available space." Furthermore, "Bumper-to-bumper traffic en route to the mass meetings tied up the town of Baton Rouge." Morris, *The Origins of the Civil Rights Movement*, 18.

[37] Lottie L. Joiner, "Baton Rouge Bus Boycott Paved Way for King's Montgomery Effort," *The Crisis*, (July/August 2003), 7.

the road, take people wherever they needed to go. It was like a daily job."[38] Women, who disproportionately relied on the buses to get to jobs as domestic workers, played vital roles throughout the course of the Baton Rouge boycott, providing the initial challenge, serving as drivers, attending meetings, and of course participating in the boycott through its duration.[39]

According to Jemison, the leadership of the boycott also "closed all bars in the Negro community. In other words we patrolled all our sections in the city to ensure order."[40] But even the hard-core drinkers "didn't seem to mind too much because their new role was to open up the car doors of movement participants as they arrived."[41] This sense of comprehensive involvement in the boycott, even among those who may not have otherwise been politically inclined, proved essential.

Although the boycott was overwhelmingly peaceful, it was not an explicitly nonviolent protest. Jemison had armed bodyguards. One of these bodyguards, Chester Laborde, told of his role many years after the events in 1953. "Jemison, he gave us some guns, told us to guard the house" while Jemison went about dealing with some of the business related to the boycott. "So we stayed there. Two policemen came by in a car and they saw us with the guns. I had the gun cocked on him. He told me to lower it. I didn't hear him say that! Well, the policeman said, 'I'll have to take you uptown.' So I went up" to the police station "with him. We was out there to shoot or be shot, too." Jemison went to the police station to get Laborde, who had been held but not arrested. Bodyguards rode with Jemison on several occasions and kept watch over Jemison's home and the church. Another bodyguard, Freddie Greene, who also served as Jemison's driver, remembered that he would go into various businesses with Jemison and the proprietors or employees would slip envelopes full of money under the counter because the storekeepers and

---

[38] Louisiana State University Libraries, Special Exhibits, "Baton Rouge Bus Boycott: The People," accessed at http://www.lib.lsu.edu/special/exhibits/boycott/thepeople.html, accessed July 23, 2009.

[39] For the best treatment on the role of women in the Baton Rouge boycott, see Frystak, *Our Minds Set on Freedom*, 62–69, *passim*. See also Frystak, 'Louisiana Women and the Black Struggle for Equality, 1924–1968,' in: *Louisiana Beyond Black & White: New Interpretations of Twentieth-Century Race and Race Relations*, ed. Michael S. Martin, (Lafayette, 2011), 125–144.

[40] Jemison, *The T. J. Jemison Story*, 39.

[41] Quoted in Morris, *The Origins of the Civil Rights Movement*, 19.

workers wanted to support the boycott but did not want to be seen visibly doing so.[42] In the wake of the Montgomery bus boycott and King's rise to prominence, it is easy to paint the civil rights movement as wholly committed to nonviolent protest, but as Baton Rouge shows, such was never wholly the case.[43]

On the morning of Saturday, June 19, there was a meeting between Baton Rouge's Mayor President, Jesse Webb, Jr., union representatives, the City Council, and representatives of the UDL, including Jemison. The Parish Attorney had called the meeting. But the union attorneys were out of town and therefore that group did not feel as if they were officially represented. That night the UDL held another mass meeting, which drew more than 1000 attendees. Jemison explained the lack of traction from that morning's summit meeting. The boycott would thus continue. Jemison explained that even with wholesale prices from Thompson and other black service station owners, gas was costing the boycott US$ 250 daily and so he called for an offering, which netted US$1189.69. Officials decided that the free ride program would continue until the Bus Drivers Union capitulated or else the bus company hired black drivers to replace them, or else the city allowed a franchise for a black-owned and operated bus system. The next day, reports came in that churches raised another US$ 2000.[44]

Within four days, the bus company manager reported that the boycott was 100% effective. "A continuation of this loss will ultimately mean we will have to cease operations."[45] The company was losing US$ 1600 a day,

---

[42] Louisiana State University Libraries, Special Exhibits, "Baton Rouge Bus Boycott: The People," accessed at http://www.lib.lsu.edu/special/exhibits/boycott/thepeople.html, accessed July 23, 2009.

[43] There is a growing literature on self-defense in the Civil Rights Movement. See, for example, Christopher B. Strain, *Pure Fire: Self-Defense as Activism in the Civil Rights Era* (Athens, 2005) and Lance Hill, *The Deacons for Defense: Armed Resistance and the Civil Rights Movement* (Chapel Hill, 2006); Timothy B. Tyson, *Radio Free Dixie: Robert F. Williams and the Roots of Black Power* (Chapel Hill, 1999); Akinyele Omowale Umoja, *We Will Shoot Back: Armed Resistance in the Mississippi Freedom Struggle* (New York, 2013); and Charles E. Cobb, Jr. *This Nonviolent Stuff'll Get You Killed: How Guns Made the Civil Rights Movement Possible* (New York, 2014).

[44] *Louisiana Weekly*, June 27, 1953. On fundraising for the boycott see Morris, *The Origins of the Civil Rights Movement*, 23–24.

[45] Melton, "'We'll Keep Walking'," p. 70.

and soon the company was on the verge of collapse.[46] Word of the protest spread nationally too. In the words of historian Adam Fairclough, "The shear [sic] fact that they could boycott the buses for a week and do this in a very disciplined way was an example, and it showed that white supremacy was something that was simply not going to be accepted by black people in the South. Change was in the air. A revelation in consciousness was evolving."[47]

The boycott promoted backlash beyond the striking bus drivers. Both city council members and boycott leaders received death threats. Johnnie Jones, who had been serving as the lawyer for the boycotters, was driving across railroad tracks when two cars tried to trap him when a train was approaching.[48] The situation may have become more volatile had the boycott continued much longer.

Within days, on June 23, Reverend Jemison called off the boycott and ended the free ride program after long negotiations between city leaders and the boycott organizers, though divisions within the black community meant that many were outraged and some even continued to avoid the buses. The UDL executive voted 5-3 to end the boycott.[49] At a meeting at the city's Municipal Stadium, more than 7000 African Americans gathered in hot and humid conditions. A vote of the rank and file supported the decision to end the boycott, but it was far from unanimous. Many of them wanted to continue with the boycott, shouting: "We don't have to ride the buses!"; "There is nothing wrong with our feet!"; and "We'll keep walking!" Some wanted to protest against Reverend Jemison because, in the words of Hazel Freeman, they were "ready for change [...] could see a change coming and this was the beginning of it."[50]

In the end, as part of the compromise, the City-Parish Council passed Ordinance 251 declaring that with the exception of the front and back rows of the buses, still reserved for white and black passengers, respectively, open seating would prevail in between. Though the City-Parish Council's new law represented a modest victory for the boycotters, the maintenance of token Jim Crow revealed that for many white southerners the symbolism of Jim Crow still mattered even if its realities were fading.

---

[46] LPB *Signpost to Freedom*.
[47] Melton, "'We'll Keep Walking'," p. 70.
[48] Ibid., p. 70.
[49] Morris, *The Origins of the Civil Rights Movement*, 24.
[50] Melton, "'We'll Keep Walking'," p. 63.

As the *Louisiana Weekly* surmised, "Apparently the compromise law was enough to end the strike, but it does not end the Negroes' desire for the right to sit where they please on the buses."[51] Jemison promised that the UDL would file suit over any form of segregation on the city's buses, and he kept that promise later that summer.[52]

Jemison's largely unilateral decision came as a shock even to many members of the UDL leadership, but it was not an arbitrary one. In the words of one writer who has studied the boycott, "It would seem that Jemison and the United Defense League had the upper hand. But, what was the next step? At the time the boycott's leaders had no roadmap laid out before them and no way to judge the white community's response to a full-fledged challenge to segregation."[53]

Still, many in the black community were angry and frustrated and feared that Jemison had sold them out. Willis Reed believed that there was great promise in continuing the boycott and he especially did not like the way Jemison simply went forward with a compromise. "They should have at least consulted us before stopping the boycott. That's what they should have done but didn't."[54]

Over the years Reed, who would go on to serve as editor, owner, and sole proprietor of the free weekly African American the *Baton Rouge Post*, has developed some bitterness about the way the boycott played out and about Jemison's outsized role in the telling of the tale. "People often attempt to position themselves as leaders in the black community, but they're not real leaders." As the fiftieth anniversary of the boycott approached, Reed would insist that he had in fact been the driving force behind the boycott in his position as head of the First Ward Voters League, which he had founded in 1952, "months and months" before the establishment of Jemison's UDL. Reed argues that the Voters League held the first mass meeting to protest segregated bus seating and that the first meeting took place illegally at all-black Capital High School, a gathering that the school principal forbade. At the fiftieth anniversary events in 2003, the First Ward Voters League held several events to try to "set the record straight."[55]

[51] *Louisiana Weekly*, June 27, 1953.
[52] *Louisiana Weekly*, August 15, 1953.
[53] Melton, "'We'll Keep Walking'," p. 70.
[54] Ibid., p. 70.
[55] Etheridge, "Bus Stop."

Jemison graciously refused to enter the fray about Reed's assertions. "I'm not going to comment on what he said about me and the bus boycott. It's too late in my life now to be contradictory. Willis Reed was a member of my church. He's a good man, and did a lot of good for the people, and I won't say anything to take that all away from him now."[56] Boycott lawyer Johnnie Jones, however, would not be so reticent. "Willis Reed's contention is wrong. He's tried to convince me of his side for years, and it's simply not true. The concept of the boycott may have originated with the First Ward Voters League. But talk didn't start it. The boycott started when Reverend Jemison decided to ride the bus in the face of segregation. He did the same thing Rosa Parks did, and like her, he started the boycott."[57]

Whatever the truths of the origins of the Baton Rouge Bus Boycott—and it seems pretty clear that Jones is right in defending Jemison, but that Reed may well have a point in wanting to remind people of the role of the First Ward Voters League in the larger struggle for civil rights in Baton Rouge—the boycott's conclusion has continued to be a point of controversy as the years have passed. Horatio Thompson, who would continue to build on his business holdings by becoming a significant force in North Baton Rouge real estate, tempered his frustrations. While he believed that the boycott "wasn't what it should have been," he also acknowledged, "but during that time that was about all you could get."[58]

Jemison certainly recognized the criticisms and even would later acknowledge that maybe his own professional ambitions played a role. "I didn't go to the end in desegregation. I stayed on the side where I could become president of the National Baptist Convention," which he later did, following in his father's footsteps. "I wasn't trying to end segregation. We started the boycott simply to get seats for the people, and once we accomplished that what else was there for us to get?"[59] Contrasting his decision with that of Martin Luther King, Jr. and the boycotters in Montgomery a few years later, Jemison would say, "King accomplished so much for people; as his good friend, I supported and backed him the whole way. But I chose to stay focused on the church, not the whole country."[60]

[56] Ibid.
[57] Ibid.
[58] Melton, "'We'll Keep Walking'," p. 70.
[59] Ibid.
[60] Etheridge, "Bus Stop."

Historian Douglas Brinkley has looked at Baton Rouge through the lens of what later took place in Montgomery after Rosa Parks set that epochal event in motion. "I think" Jemison "capitulated too soon."

> But look, Jemison did try to get a group of people with different attitudes all together to take on the authorities. That's not an easy task. Are people right to be frustrated and feel more could have been done? Of course. But let's not lose sight of his role in history. He was somebody who had the courage to stand up, and don't kid yourself, he was putting his life on the line and he deserves to be treated as one of the great heroes of the Civil Rights Movement, not somebody who failed, but somebody who won because he was willing to try.[61]

A further reality is that nearly all of the criticism of Jemison has appeared in the last decade or so, decades after the original boycott, and only after the successes of the Civil Rights Movement have in the light of hindsight come to seem inevitable. In reality, the events in Baton Rouge were nearly unprecedented. It seems unfair to criticize Jemison too harshly for not doing more when he went farther than anyone else had ever gone.

The situation on the buses would occasionally still flare up. In October, 1953, Joe Howard was arrested when he sat next to a white man on one of the front seats. The arrest did not lead to a new boycott but rather revealed that the buses continued to represent a source of racial tension as long as any form of segregation prevailed. Because of the passage of Ordinance 251, District Court Judge Charley Holcombe dismissed a case that Jemison's organization had brought challenging the segregation laws. And for some blacks that symbolic segregation still grated. But even the UDL lawyer, Johnnie Jones, who had just been admitted to the Louisiana bar, knew that the legal case was a virtual non-starter. Jemison wanted to pursue the case in state rather than federal court because, according to Jones, "he didn't want to alienate the powers that be." But the reality was that, "The state court could not deal with what the federal court did, because state law was based on Plessy v. Ferguson, and the state's interpretation of that ruling was Jim Crow." Therefore, when Holcombe "ruled against us on no right of cause of action" it "was the correct decision. We could have won in federal court on my arguments, but not in state court." When Jones admitted that it was the right decision for that court to make,

---

[61] Melton, "'We'll Keep Walking'," p. 70.

he received a great deal of grief. "The black community was outraged with me. They called me a sell-out and said stuff like 'don't let the hungry dog guard the bones,' meaning I was too young and inexperienced to handle it. But later on, in the later cases, when they found out I was right, everybody loved me." In telling this story, the octogenarian Jones punctuated his comments with a laugh.[62] The Baton Rouge Bus Boycott thus represents a clear (if incomplete) victory over segregation in public transportation. The boycott over racial separation took precedence over the fare hikes. In cities like Baton Rouge, segregation was incomplete. Blacks and whites rode the same city buses and occupied the same public spaces despite what might have been the ultimate fantasies of some segregationists. Hazel Freeman, looking back on the boycott from the vantage point of several decades, believed that the boycott had tremendous impact on the psyche of the city's black community, the members of which could:

> See themselves organizing and bringing about things that they had held within them and were afraid to say. And they felt free and open to be able to express themselves. Just imagine people, when they see a change coming and knowing, 'we are part of bringing it about,' and that felt good! Can you imagine that? Can you imagine that?[63]

The editors of the *Louisiana Weekly* were in a celebratory mood in the days after the boycott ended. "The courageous and united stand by the citizens of Baton Rouge in the recent bus dispute was indeed inspirational and heart warming to all with fighting hearts throughout the state." The paper tied the growing political consciousness of black Baton Rouge to its economic empowerment. "We now have bigger incomes and are now a factor to be considered in the political life of any community." With regard to the buses, blacks in Baton Rouge "are paying for service that they are not getting. It just doesn't make sense to be the largest group riding the bus not to be treated fairly, especially when [it's] their money that is largely responsible for the successful operation of the bus company." This economic power was crucial. "We have come of age now. We have money to spend, invest and expect to be treated as human beings. Certainly we don't expect to be pushed around any longer as second class citizens." And the lesson should not have applied just to the capital city. "The sooner

---

[62] Etheridge, "Bus Stop."
[63] Melton, "'We'll Keep Walking'," p. 71.

more communities in Louisiana learn the lesson of unity that was displayed in Baton Rouge by its stalwart citizenry the quicker we will get the respect of those who previously have saw [sic] fit to ignore us as human beings and deny our group first-class citizenship."[64]

There was victory in Baton Rouge and that victory did not prove ephemeral. Not only did an erosion of segregation take place, but the Baton Rouge boycott also helped to reveal the power of mass meetings in black churches, it helped to reveal the capacity for religious leaders to shape opposition to white supremacy, and it showed that the black community would put their money and time into desegregation efforts. Martin Luther King, Jr. would contact Reverend Jemison in 1955 to try to pick his brain about how Baton Rouge had approached their boycott. Indeed, Jemison would be one of the founding officers of the Southern Christian Leadership Conference that emerged as the result of the Montgomery Bus Boycott.[65] King was not the only impressed observer in Montgomery and across the country. Rosa Parks told her biographer Douglass Brinkley that "she was completely captivated by what happened in Baton Rouge. She was part of the underground civil rights circuit in the South. They were all in awe" of the bus boycott in Baton Rouge.[66]

But King's phone call to Jemison would come in the future. During the strike, Jemison had referred to the struggle in Baton Rouge as part of an "onward march of a people who desire to be totally free."[67] For the time being, Baton Rouge stood as something of a lone symbol about what might be accomplished, but not necessarily of what must come to pass.

[64] *Louisiana Weekly*, June 27, 1953.
[65] Jemison, *The T. J. Jemison Story*, 39–41.
[66] Melton, "'We'll Keep Walking'," p. 63.
[67] LPB *Signpost to Freedom*.

CHAPTER 9

The United Farm Workers Union and the Use of the Boycott Against American Agribusiness

Lori A. Flores

When one thinks of the use of the boycott during the civil rights movement in the United States, one might think first of the Baton Rouge or Montgomery bus boycotts led by African Americans in the 1950s to protest policies of racial segregation and discrimination on public transportation. Shifting the analytic lens from the US South to the US West, however, reveals a parallel struggle taking place for Mexican- and Filipino-origin farmworkers' rights and the use of the boycott in a different way. This chapter addresses how workers in the civil rights-era United States, particularly agricultural laborers, turned to the tactic of the consumer boycott to augment the effectiveness of their labor strikes in the fields. The United Farm Workers Organizing Committee (UFWOC) was the first union in US history to successfully employ a national consumer boycott—first against grapes and wine, and then against lettuce—to achieve gains in farmworkers' labor rights and conditions. Led by Mexican-American community organizers Cesar Chavez and Dolores Huerta, the UFWOC capitalized on

---

L. A. Flores (✉)
Stony Brook University (State University of New York), Stony Brook, NY, USA
e-mail: lori.flores@stonybrook.edu

© The Author(s) 2019
D. Feldman (ed.), *Boycotts Past and Present*, Palgrave Critical Studies of Antisemitism and Racism,
https://doi.org/10.1007/978-3-319-94872-0_9

a civil rights ethos in the 1960s (and a national media already primed to pay attention to boycotts) to employ multiple organizing tactics including pilgrimages, fasts, and grocery store demonstrations that galvanized supporters in rural and urban areas of the country.

Consumer boycotts of food and drink had happened before in the United States—abolitionists in the eighteenth and nineteenth centuries had engaged in the free produce movement and boycotted goods produced by slave labor such as sugar and rice, and Jewish communities had boycotted consumer goods imported from Nazi Germany. In its use of the boycott, the UFWOC combined racial and class discourses to send a message to the American public that the (mostly Mexican and Mexican American) farmworkers who fed and nourished the nation were not being adequately fed or nourished themselves because of the lack of a living wage in the agricultural industry. The union framed the varied produce that consumers saw in their supermarkets as reminders of choice and plentitude and argued that impoverished farmworkers lacked that same agency and abundance in their lives. In its first campaign to boycott grapes from 1966 to 1970, the UFWOC planted pickets outside of popular chain grocery stores in cities like Los Angeles, San Francisco, Chicago, Detroit, New York, Philadelphia, Atlanta, Baltimore, and Washington DC. In addition, it sent organizers to conduct boycott campaigns in Canada, focusing on the cities of Toronto and Montreal, and reached out to allies who could publicize the boycott in Europe. Through this international boycott, the UFWOC's goal was to persuade shoppers to only buy grapes emblazoned with the union's black Aztec eagle symbol, and to turn their business away from stores that carried non-union grapes. This drop in sales would hopefully push grower-employers to come to the bargaining table and negotiate worker contracts. The subsequent lettuce boycott in 1970 had similar objectives, but in that case Cesar Chavez would threaten an entire web of boycotts against other products sold by corporations tied to the agricultural industry.

There are many reasons why the UFWOC food boycotts are still heralded as clever and successful in American history. First, the union tapped into the desire for empowerment, not just from its farmworker constituency but also from the consumers it targeted at grocery stores. Through just one simple purchasing decision, food shoppers could feel like they were helping the farmworker no matter how distant their identity felt from that of a poor farmworker or how far away they lived from the fields of California. This was a time period characterized not only by ethnic "power" movements but the consumer rights movement that encouraged Americans to express their moral and political views through what they did and did not consume. Not buying grapes became a particularly attractive, and not arduous, way of expressing one's politics. The UFWOC reached out across racial lines to include consumers of all backgrounds in a moral economy, and in this way gained the support of people who otherwise might not have cared about the struggles of Latino and Asian farmworkers. Second, the UFWOC (particularly its female organizers) recognized how effective a gendered or family-centered discourse could be in reaching shoppers who tended to be women—mothers, daughters, and housewives—and who were in charge of making their household's food purchases. The union banked on the power of the purse and encouraged women (especially middle-class white women) to stand up with them against the mostly male leaders of agribusinesses and managers of grocery stores by threatening to take their dollars elsewhere. Finally, because the boycotts occurred in multiple locations under different organizers' styles, they retained a capaciousness and flexibility that enabled them to embrace supporters across many lines of difference including race, class, gender, and geography. These diverse allies, and the broader "rights" agenda and climate of the time, helped the UFWOC gain visibility, strength, and support. In pairing boycotts with strikes, and in connecting food items to consumers' ethics and sympathy for downtrodden laborers, the UFWOC brought the agricultural industry to its knees in a way that Americans had never seen before, and have not seen since.

By the 1930s, California agriculture could genuinely be characterized as agribusiness—more land and wealth had consolidated in the hands of fewer people, and employers were using increasingly industrialized and corporatized systems of farm production and taking advantage of successive waves of low-wage workers. Native Americans, Asians, and Asian Americans (Chinese, Japanese, Filipino, Indian), Anglo American migrants from the Dust Bowl, and Mexicans and Mexican Americans all took their turns toiling in various segments of the state's agricultural industry. During the 1930s, coalitions of field, cannery, and packing house workers joined labor unions and staged strikes in crops such as cotton, lettuce, and cantaloupe, but the results of these moments of labor militancy were mixed. While some workers won higher wages and better conditions, others experienced physical violence such as tear-gassing and beatings in the streets, or fires set to their labor camps (oftentimes, this violence was the direct result of their employers' collusion with local and state law enforcement officials). What exacerbated agricultural workers' vulnerability was absolute neglect by US federal law. Protective New Deal legislation including the National Labor Relations Act (NLRA or Wagner Act), which permitted workers to join collective bargaining units, and the Fair Labor Standards Act, which established a 44-hour workweek, established a national minimum wage, guaranteed "time-and-a-half" for overtime work, and prohibited child labor, was applied to industrial workers but excluded domestic workers and farmworkers. Exploited and economically desperate, farmworkers traveled the migrant labor circuit all over California and the entire country, and this peripatetic lifestyle further hindered any stable political mobilization.

World War II ushered in another massive obstacle to agricultural workers' unionization. The Bracero Program, a guestworker program negotiated between the US and Mexican governments in the summer of 1942 to relieve the wartime labor shortage, imported thousands of Mexican men to work on US farms and railroads. With a cheaper, non-unionized reservoir of foreign labor at their disposal, agricultural employers lobbied for Congress' renewal of the program until 1964. Meanwhile, they depressed wages for US citizen farmworkers (who were mostly Mexican or Filipino American by this time) or, if these citizens protested, replaced them altogether with braceros who worked 10–14-hour days for an average of one dollar a day. The Bracero Program fundamentally altered the labor landscape of the United States and, along with taking away US farmworkers' bargaining power, kept them in migratory conditions that made them ineligible for health insurance, welfare, or voting rights. In the fields, all farmworkers, regardless of nationality, continued to suffer from inadequate water, rest, and shade, as well as overexposure to pesticides. Many women farmworkers experienced sexual harassment on the job, and migrant farmworker children remained the nation's "most educationally deprived" population.[1] By the early 1960s, California agribusiness had become a 4-billion-dollar-a-year industry, but the wealth was not trickling down to laborers who still dreamed of a successful and centralized farmworkers' union. In 1964, Congress finally terminated the Bracero Program due to various protests against its lack of regulation and monitoring of guestworkers' laboring conditions and personal safety. This opened a precious window of opportunity for Cesar Chavez's and Dolores Huerta's

---

[1] Lori Flores, *Grounds for Dreaming: Mexican Americans, Mexican Immigrants, and the California Farmworker Movement* (New Haven, 2016), 163.

burgeoning National Farm Workers Association (NFWA). When Filipino labor activist Larry Itliong asked the NFWA to join his Agricultural Workers Organizing Committee (AWOC) in a grape workers' strike in Delano, California, the three organizers identified two main targets—Schenley Industries and the DiGiorgio Corporation—that represented some of the most powerful California agribusiness interests.

Very quickly, Chavez became the figurehead for the Delano grape strikers' movement. He presented as humble yet charismatic, and due to his own experiences as a migrant laborer, he was a relatable figure to Mexican-American and Filipino-American farmworkers. A devout Catholic who likened his philosophy of non-violence to contemporary civil rights leaders such as Martin Luther King, Jr. and Mahatma Gandhi, Chavez captivated the US political mainstream and media by imbuing the farmworker cause with religious overtones and moments that involved food. He publicly fasted on numerous occasions, once for 25 consecutive days, to highlight the deprivation and suffering of poor farm laborers (one of the biggest media moments for the farmworker struggle took place when Robert Kennedy flew in to California to help Chavez break his fast by sharing a Communion tortilla). In March 1966, Chavez led thousands of farmworkers in a 300-mile pilgrimage from Delano to California's capitol of Sacramento. The march fascinated many watching along the route and on television—onlookers handed out food to the marchers and sometimes even joined them—and by the time the march ended on Easter Sunday on the steps of the California capitol building, it had grown to 10,000 people. News photos and videos of the limping and bleeding Chavez, along with the crowd roaring "Viva Cesar!" and "Viva Huelga!" (Long Live Cesar! And Long Live the Strike!) showed Americans that a farmworker movement was taking shape. After the media attention in Sacramento, Schenley Industries recognized the NFWA as a union. In August 1966, the NFWA merged with the AWOC to form the UFWOC, with Chavez serving as president and Huerta as vice president. Negotiations with DiGiorgio were prolonged and more difficult, and when the UFWOC sought to negotiate with a third entity, Giumarra Vineyards (California's largest table grape grower), it encountered even more resistance. Giumarra refused to recognize the union and hired a mostly foreign labor force to replace its striking workers. When the UFWOC called for a boycott against Giumarra's products, the company simply packaged and distributed its goods under other growers' labels.

Pushed to take more drastic action, the UFWOC called for a national boycott of all California table grapes in January 1968. The union now argued that the entire grape industry, not just a few growers, was corrupt and exploitative. In their appeals to consumers, the union declared non-union grapes were toxic—not only because of pesticides but because they had been cultivated under unethical labor conditions and farmworkers' suffering. While it was true that the NLRA prohibited workers from engaging in secondary boycotts, farmworkers' notorious exclusion from this act meant that they had found a loophole, and the secondary boycott remained a viable organizing tool for them. The UFWOC sent organizers to conduct the grape boycott in almost 50 cities around the country and in Canada.[2] In all of these places, boycott organizers were responsible for contacting and mobilizing potential allies—labor unions, political activists and community organizations, religious supporters, women's clubs, peace groups, student protesters, and concerned consumers—who could stand behind the union as it boycotted grocery stores selling non-UFWOC grapes. The union knew it had to make its demand on consumers simple; all one had to do was commit to not buying grapes or shopping at stores that sold grapes. This task did not cause much disruption to people's routines, but allowed them to feel that they had contributed to the farmworker movement and expressed their opposition to labor abuses.

Women quickly distinguished themselves as leading figures among the boycott's organizers. Some women made the decision to lead the campaigns in unfamiliar cities alongside their spouses—Mary Elena and Albert Rojas directed together in Pittsburgh, Alfredo and Juanita Herrera managed the boycott in Denver, Julio and Fina Hernández coordinated in Cleveland, and Marcia and Manuel Sánchez organized in Miami.[3] Other women took on the job solo. UFWOC Vice President Dolores Huerta directed the boycott in New York City, the largest grape distribution center in the United States, and later served as East Coast boycott coordinator in 1968 and 1969. Jessica Govea, who had worked in the fields since she was nine years old and joined the UFWOC as a teenager, led boycott operations in Montreal. Maria Saudado ran the Indianapolis office, Peggy

---

[2] Sarah Stern, "'We Cast Our Lot With the Farm Workers': Organization, Mobilization and Meaning in the United Farm Workers' Grape Boycott in New York City, 1967–70" (Thesis, New York University, 2013), 23.

[3] Margaret Rose, "Woman Power Will Stop Those Grapes': Chicana Organizers and Middle-Class Female Supporters in the Farm Workers' Grape Boycott in Philadelphia, 1969–1970,' *Journal of Women's History*, vol. 7, no. 4 (Winter 1995), 6–7.

McGivern coordinated the boycott in Buffalo, and Hope Lopez directed the campaign in Philadelphia.[4] Oftentimes, women organizers were the ones who recognized the effectiveness of gendered discourse and strategy in the boycott. Knowing that women tended to be the food shoppers for their households, UFWOC boycotters used a maternalist and family-centered rhetoric that appealed to housewives' and mothers' morality. Leaflets with images of starving farmworker children accompanied demonstrators' verbal pleas for women shoppers to boycott supermarkets that sold grapes.

Other groups of women workers in US history—from laundresses to garment workers to miners—had strategically framed their labor struggles around the preservation and well-being of family to gain more public support. The women boycotters of the UFWOC continued this legacy by arguing that although farmworkers nourished Americans by putting food on their tables, they were not making a living wage that allowed them to nourish themselves and properly feed their children. The grape boycott campaign led by Hope Lopez in Philadelphia was particularly illustrative of this maternalist, woman-centered strategy. A 41-year-old widowed, college-educated farmworker from California, Lopez arrived in Philadelphia in February 1969 with two of her five children and assistants Antonia Saludado and Carolina Franco, who were all farmworkers as well. Saludado had previously worked on boycotts in Los Angeles and New York, and Franco had been an original marcher to Sacramento and worked on boycotts in Los Angeles, New York, and Boston. Lopez and her staff conducted their campaign out of a house in Philadelphia affectionately called the "Grape House," which served as both their residence and office and sheltered other boycott leaders and participants for a year and a half. The Philadelphia contingent collected endorsements for the boycott from the city's mayor, various labor unions (including the Meatcutters Union, American Federation of Teachers, and the United Auto Workers), college students, and the Catholic Archdiocese. They also welcomed assistance from women from other racial, ethnic, and class backgrounds. Middle-class white housewives volunteered their administrative services at the boycott headquarters. Maria Lina Bonet, the president and founder of the *Fraternidad Puertoriquena*, publicized the boycott and encouraged people to join and extend the boycott to Puerto Rican bodegas. Mary Rouse, head of the Kensington Council on Black Affairs and editor of *The*

---

[4] Rose, "Woman Power," 7.

Informer, gave the UFWOC plenty of space to print information about the boycott in Spanish and English in the publication.[5]

In targeting the large supermarket chains of Philadelphia—Acme, A&P, Food Fair, Penn Fruit, and Great Scott—Hope Lopez made sure to highlight the power of the woman consumer. "May I remind you," she wrote to one store manager, "that 99% of your customers are women. The ladies put you in the position of strength that you now hold and these same ladies can knock you right off that pedestal." When managers refused to budge and take grapes off their shelves, Lopez put herself in a very visible position and began a fast in late May 1969 in front of one branch of the A&P Market. Unlike Cesar Chavez's famed fast the year before, Lopez's fast had the added valence of her being a suffering mother with suffering children. To further publicize the event, an interdenominational candlelight service was planned for supporters to rally around the weakened Lopez, adding a religious aura to elicit more consumers' sympathy.[6] Other women, Latina and white, fasted as the boycott continued. The UFWOC very consciously communicated the message that women—across lines of race and class—needed to support each other in protecting and improving the lives of their children and families. To that end, women shoppers were encouraged to collaborate in denouncing the (mostly male) store managers who were evading their responsibility to choose ethically produced food. A&P eventually authorized its managers to remove non-union grapes but only if customers personally registered an objection. Women did just that, meeting with managers in delegations (sometimes with their children and babysitters in tow) until they caved to their demands. After an intense two-month campaign planned and carried out by Latina, black, and white women, all the major market chains in the city of Philadelphia were free of grapes.[7]

As Lopez and other UFWOC organizers knew, boycott strategies needed to remain flexible enough to welcome diverse supporters from all ages, races, classes, genders, and geographies. This meant that in every city, the boycott looked somewhat different. While the Philadelphia campaign capitalized on women consumers' power, for example, the discourse

---

[5] Margaret Rose, "'Woman Power Will Stop Those Grapes': Chicana Organizers and Middle-Class Female Supporters in the Farm Workers' Grape Boycott in Philadelphia, 1969–1970,' *Journal of Women's History*, vol. 7, no. 4, (Winter 1995), 6, 10–16.

[6] Rose, "Woman Power," 17–18.

[7] Rose, "Woman Power," 18–19.

of the New York boycott seemed to center on the figure of the exploited worker struggling against the wealthy and corrupt grower-businessman.[8] Young people were particularly fierce allies of the cause. The organization Students for the Grape Boycott picketed multiple supermarkets and planned numerous rallies and demonstrations, one of which was held outside the Federal Office Building in Manhattan to protest the US government being the third largest purchaser of California growers' grapes.[9] In the Columbia University area, the "Friends of the Farm Workers"—a coalition of labor representatives, clergy members, students, and political organizations—formed picket lines and distributed flyers with slogans such as "Put the grapists up against the wall!" that communicated how agribusiness' greed and violation of workers' rights were acts of socioeconomic violence.[10] Other tactics used in boycott cities included "shop-ins" (where dozens of activists entered a grocery store simultaneously, filled the bottoms of their shopping carts with grapes and stacked heavy canned products on top, and abandoned the carts at the checkout line) and "pray-ins" staged by Protestant, Catholic, and Jewish clergy who led groups in kneeling in supermarket aisles and praying for social peace and labor justice.[11] As more Americans joined in waving the UFWOC flag, shouting "Huelga!," or wearing "Don't Buy Grapes" pins, people living and working outside of US borders offered their aid as well. When President Richard Nixon tried to help growers circumvent the boycott by shipping their grapes to US armed forces in Vietnam and to Europe, Mexican-American sailors threw boxes of grapes into the Gulf of Tonkin and activists across the Atlantic made sure that grapes rotted on the docks of London and Hamburg. Meanwhile, a blockade on non-union grapes extended to multiple ports in Scandinavia.[12]

The cumulative effects of the boycott began to take a toll on grape sales and shipments, particularly in large urban markets. Grape shipments fell by 34 percent in New York, 41 percent in Chicago, 32 percent in Detroit,

[8] Stern, "We Cast Our Lot," 32.
[9] Stern, "We Cast Our Lot," 39–40.
[10] Stern, "We Cast Our Lot," 40.
[11] Heidi Tinsman, *Buying Into the Regime: Grapes and Consumption in Cold War Chile and the United States* (Durham, 2014), 153.
[12] Frank Bardacke, *Trampling Out the Vintage: Cesar Chavez and the Two Souls of the United Farm Workers* (London, 2011), 326; Matt Garcia, "Remembering Cesar Chavez and the Farm Workers Movement" panel remarks, Organization of American Historians Conference, San Francisco, California, 13 April 2013.

42 percent in Boston, 53 percent in Baltimore, 23 percent in Philadelphia, and 16 percent in Los Angeles.[13] Dismayed by these numbers, the grape industry finally approached the negotiating table to begin collective bargaining talks with the UFWOC. Several companies signed union contracts during the spring of 1970. Then, in July, 27 grape growers in Delano, California, signed UFWOC contracts, finally bringing an end to a five-year strike. Giumarra Vineyards was one of these growers, and its contract ensured raises from US$ 1.65 an hour to US$ 2.05 an hour for 8000 grape workers as well as a health and welfare fund and restrictions on harmful pesticide use.[14] These concessions were the most comprehensive that any unionized group of US farmworkers had ever won, and by the end of the 1970 harvest season, the UFWOC had signed 150 table grape contracts covering 30,000 workers. The rural farmworkers' strike and the urban grape boycott campaign had worked in tandem with each other, with the latter being essential to the former's success.

Celebrations would not last long, however, as the UFWOC learned that north of Delano, in the Salinas and Santa Maria Valleys, more than 170 *lettuce* growers had surreptitiously signed "sweetheart" contracts with the Teamsters Union without the knowledge or consent of their workers in order to preempt the UFWOC moving into the region. The Teamsters, which had a national membership of nearly 1.5 million, covered various types of workers including field, cannery, clerical, transportation, and warehouse workers. Their leadership was largely white, making them more racially familiar to white agribusiness leaders, and their contracts often allowed grower-employers to continue using harmful chemical pesticides and importing foreign laborers if US citizen farmworkers did not agree to work under certain conditions. For these reasons, Cesar Chavez felt he had no choice but to move UFWOC headquarters to the Salinas Valley and begin a new boycott against the lettuce industry.

The UFWOC lettuce strike and boycott of 1970 has not been studied as extensively as its grape counterpart, but it was arguably larger, more violent, and involved a greater diversity of participants across lines of race, class, and citizenship. The wide array of people who made up the Salinas Valley's agricultural workforce—US-born Mexican Americans, former braceros who had overstayed their contracts or naturalized as citizens, undocumented Mexican immigrants, and a small number of white, African

---

[13] Rose, "Woman Power," 22; Stern, "We Cast Our Lot," 23.
[14] "Farm Union Reaps First California Victory," *Business Week*, 16 April 1966, 159.

American, and Filipino farmworkers—had been following the Delano grape strike closely, and were ready to break from their imposed Teamsters contracts and join the UFWOC. Meanwhile, grower-employers doubted that their farmworkers had the political unity or capacity to carry out a successful strike. After all, they told themselves, three powerful corporations dominated the region's agriculture. The valley's largest lettuce grower was InterHarvest, a group of agricultural firms under the United Fruit Company, which was dubbed "the octopus" in Latin America for its extensive control of plantations, transportation monopolies, and dictatorships. United Fruit owned InterHarvest's 20,000 acres of lettuce in Arizona and California. The Purex Corporation's farming operation Freshpict covered 42,000 acres in California, Arizona, Colorado, and New Mexico. Finally, S.S. Pierce and Company of Boston bought out several strawberry operations in California and named this conglomerate Pic-N-Pac.[15] Growers believed that these three behemoths would not acquiesce to the demands of Chavez and a heavily Mexican-origin UFWOC membership.

These preconceived notions were shattered as thousands of Salinas Valley farmworkers signed UFWOC membership cards in the summer of 1970. Union organizer Marshall Ganz, who had organized black voters during the "Freedom Summer" campaign in Mississippi, recalled, "It blew me away because we had really struggled to organize workers in the grape industry...[in Delano] the workers were hopeless and terrified...In Salinas, all of that was different...the people were ready for us."[16] Fellow organizer Jessica Govea agreed. "The Salinas workers were so much more confident than the Delano workers....There was an electricity, a vibrancy that was different."[17] In part, the organization of the lettuce economy aided in this level of worker efficiency and solidarity. Lettuce workers (or *lechugueros*) structured themselves differently from grape workers in that they organized themselves into crews—often made up of family or friends—even before being hired by an employer. Now these crews were making the collective decision to all join the UFWOC together. Along with *lechugueros*, crews of *freseros, apieros* and *brocoleros* (strawberry, celery, and broccoli workers) began bringing stacks of signed membership cards to union

---

[15] Bardacke, *Trampling Out the Vintage*, 350.
[16] Marshall Ganz, interview with the author, Los Altos, California, 5 September 2009.
[17] Miriam J. Wells, *Strawberry Fields: Politics, Class, and Work in California Agriculture* (Ithaca, 1996), 81.

headquarters.[18] Chavez, Huerta, and their organizers believed that if they could lead hundreds of workers in walking off their jobs, this would persuade the Teamsters to informally turn over all of their farmworker contracts (representing 70,000 workers) to the UFWOC. In meetings mediated by the US Catholic Bishops Committee on Farm Labor, the UFWOC succeeded in convincing the Teamsters to do so. When these plans were presented to grower-employers, however, they refused to honor the outcomes of these mediated meetings. They argued their unionization under the Teamsters was a done deal, and ignored the UFWOC's insistence that workers never gave their consent to such representation.

In response, the UFWOC staged one of the largest agricultural strikes in American history. By August 27, 1970, 7000 farmworkers were striking against 40 Salinas Valley farming operations. Some growers went to county courts to stop the UFWOC from picketing near their fields and convinced Judge Anthony Brazil to issue a temporary restraining order against the UFWOC that kept the union from picketing at 22 farms. Citing the California Jurisdictional Strike Act, Brazil ruled that since growers technically had their workers under a union contract, the battle was between the UFWOC and Teamsters over worker jurisdiction, not between the UFWOC and the growers. Initially discouraged by these injunctions, strikers were soon heartened by the tangible economic effects of their walkout. The State and Federal Marketing Service estimated that less than half the Salinas Valley's lettuce was flowing to market, and over the next three weeks, the central coastal berry industry of California suffered an estimated US$ 2.2 million loss due to the *freseros* who went out on strike alongside their *lechuguero* comrades.[19]

To put power behind its picket lines in the Salinas Valley, the UFWOC revived its successful national consumer boycott strategy in supermarkets, reappearing in cities such as Los Angeles, San Francisco, New York, Philadelphia, and Montreal. It continued to rely on its diverse group of allies—which had grown to include The American Federation of Labor and Congress of Industrial Organizations (AFL-CIO) unions, students,

---

[18] Bardacke, *Trampling*, 342–46, 351.

[19] Doug Willis, "Calif. Lettuce Rots as Farm Unions Clash," *Washington Post*, 28 August 1970, A6; Miriam J. Wells, 'Legal Conflict and Class Structure: The Independent Contractor-Employee Controversy in California Agriculture,' *Law & Society Review*, vol. 21, no. 1, (1987), 55; Harry Bernstein, "Growers Losing $500,000 A Day," *Los Angeles Times*, 27 August 1970, 1 and "Chavez-Grower Contract Talks Stalled by Suit," *Los Angeles Times*, 29 August 1970, A1.

civil rights organizations including the Student Nonviolent Coordinating Committee (SNCC) and Congress of Racial Equality (CORE), wealthy liberal East Coast donors, anti-pesticide environmentalists, and religious leaders—to help with leafleting and demonstrating in front of stores.[20] An additional tactic that Cesar Chavez deployed, which distinguished the lettuce struggle from that of the grape, was to threaten additional boycotts of other products tied to corporations that controlled the lettuce industry. Chavez threatened United Fruit's CEO Eli Black, for instance, with a worldwide boycott against all United Fruit brand products including popular Chiquita bananas, Baskin Robbins ice cream, and A&W root beer. One boycott had turned into the specter of many boycotts, and United Fruit did not want to experience a multilayered boycott of their varied food and drink products. Thus, on August 31, InterHarvest signed a UFWOC contract. The two-year agreement, which covered approximately 1000 field workers in the Salinas Valley and other parts of California and Arizona, raised hourly wages from US$ 1.85 to US$ 2.10 and piece rates from 36 cents to 40.5 cents per carton of lettuce, a huge jump compared to what workers were making under the Teamsters pact. It also contained unprecedented prohibitions against five harmful pesticides, enforced a week of paid vacations, instituted grievance procedures and a hiring hall in the place of labor contractors, and provided workers and their families with a medical insurance plan.[21] After this victory, the UFWOC won a contract with Freshpict after threatening an additional boycott against its parent company Purex, which produced bleach and other household cleaners widely used by Americans. Pic-N-Pac fell soon after, and the D'Arrigo company agreed to sign a UFWOC contract by the end of November.[22] All the while, the UFWOC maintained its picket lines at farms still holding out from negotiations, and Chavez decided to expand the strike and boycott to even more Salinas Valley growers including prominent lettuce grower Bud Antle.

[20] Bernstein, "Growers Losing $500,000," 1; Jacques Levy, *Cesar Chavez: Autobiography of La Causa* (New York, 1975), 196.

[21] Bardacke, *Trampling*, 361; "Chavez Union Signs Pact With Major Vegetable Grower," *Los Angeles Times*, 31 August 1970, 3; "UFWOC Signs with Valley's Largest Lettuce Grower," *El Malcriado*, 1 September 1970, 7.

[22] "Chavez May Face Jail or Fine in Court Contempt Action," *Los Angeles Times*, 25 November 1970, A3; Levy, *Cesar Chavez*, 417; Harry Bernstein, "Another Grower Signs Contract With Chavez Union," *Los Angeles Times*, 9 October 1970, 3; Jim Stingley, "Chavez Signs 3rd Big Salinas Grower," *Los Angeles Times*, 10 October 1970, A1; "Chavez, Salinas Lettuce Grower Agree to Pact," *Los Angeles Times*, 21 November 1970, C5.

Furious at Chavez's disregard for court orders to stop picketing growers with Teamsters contracts, Monterey County Superior Court Judge Gordon Campbell called Chavez to appear before him on December 4, 1970. Declaring Chavez guilty of contempt of court, Campbell sentenced him to a fine of 1000 dollars and imprisonment until he ended the lettuce boycott. Chavez, who had strategized and hoped for such a sentence to bring more attention to the UFWOC, was going to jail for the first time in his organizing career. Before being led away, Chavez shouted to his followers and the press, "Boycott Bud Antle! Boycott Dow! And boycott the hell out of them! Viva!" Dow Chemical, which had saved a financially struggling Antle in 1969 by buying 17,000 acres of farmland for a fraction of its value and then reselling it to Antle, produced dangerous pesticides as well as napalm used by the United States during the Vietnam War. By verbally connecting the two, and reiterating the threat of continued and additional boycotts, Chavez reminded the American public of agribusiness' connection to corporations that caused global suffering. In turn, he also reminded Americans that the boycott was still a tactic they could use to weaken any corporate entity that was taking away the labor and civil rights of vulnerable and marginalized people.[23] The UFWOC lettuce strike and boycott continued to emphasize their ties to other rights movements and well-known allies. Ethel Kennedy and Coretta Scott King, both widows of leaders associated with the civil rights movement, paid separate visits to the Salinas Valley to see Chavez in his jail cell and speak to UFWOC members. Three weeks into Chavez's jail time, the California Supreme Court ordered his release and removed the bans on the UFWOC strike and boycott. The lettuce strike and boycott continued until late March 1971, when the UFWOC and the Teamsters signed a three-year agreement allowing the former to take over all farmworker contracts in the region.

Throughout the early 1970s, the UFWOC (renamed the United Farm Workers in 1972) continued to earn impressive wage raises, pesticide bans, and medical plans for its members. These gains, however, needed constant maintenance. After union contracts won in 1970 expired in 1973, several grape and lettuce growers resisted renegotiation with the UFWOC and signed contracts with the Teamsters again without elections or their employees' consent. Some firms shut down or reopened under new names to stop or stall the unionization process. Other grower-employers turned

---

[23] "Cesar Jailed, Boycott Goes On," *El Malcriado*, 15 December 1970, 3.

back to labor contractors as middlemen figures who could hire their employees for them, which would permit them to evade dealing with union representatives altogether. The United Farm Workers (UFW) boycotts began again, now against the grape, wine, and lettuce industries combined. As scholar Heidi Tinsman has noted, these 1973 boycotts took place against the backdrop of another relevant boycott. A Chile solidarity movement alliance of leftists, academics, religious institutions, labor unions, and Chilean refugees in the United States began a boycott of Chilean imports (including grapes and wine) in 1973 to protest Allende's overthrow and Pinochet's military dictatorship. Unfortunately, the UFW and Chile boycott organizers did not collaborate as much as they could have, given the connections between their two movements. Both protested injustices against Spanish-speaking people, and New York and California agribusiness interests were actually investors, importers, and promoters of Chilean grapes throughout the decade.[24]

And although young people had always been a part of the UFW's struggle, other historians have remarked on children's participation in the 1973 boycotts. Wearing T-shirts emblazoned with the UFW's black eagle symbol and standing by their parents, children passed out leaflets at grocery stores selling non-union produce and Gallo wines (Gallo being a major grape grower) and pleaded with customers to shop elsewhere. Their young faces and voices turned dozens of sympathetic people away each day they demonstrated.[25] The UFW did not let the power of their youngest members go unnoticed, and began offering "resource kits" to teachers in primary schools that explained the union's and boycott's objectives. Teachers then instructed students to write letters or send drawings to Cesar Chavez himself or the UFW's newspaper *El Malcriado*. Students even boycotted their own school cafeterias if they discovered non-union produce being served there. After completing these exercises in their schools, these children often went home and told their parents and grandparents about the boycott, doing the intergenerational publicity work that the UFW hoped they would.[26] Entire families, particularly Mexican-American families, continued the legacy of traveling for the union and coordinating boycott campaigns. In 1968, Maria Luisa Rangel had moved her family of nine to Detroit, Michigan, for the grape boycott. In 1970, Juanita Valdez convinced her

[24] Tinsman, *Buying Into the Regime*, 8, 134.
[25] Jennifer Robin Terry, "Niños por la Causa: Children and the United Farm Workers in the 1970s," Paper, Western Association of Women Historians, San Diego, 28 April 2017, 1.
[26] Terry, "Niños por la Causa," 5–6.

husband and seven children to come with her to Cincinnati, Ohio, for the lettuce campaign. In 1973, Herminia Rodriguez relocated her family of six to Washington, DC, for the grape, lettuce, and wine boycotts.[27] The farmworker struggle had always been about families' work, and UFW members knew that a successful strike and boycott required families' work as well.

As much as UFW leaders cared about the boycott, they made sure to stay active in the legislative sphere and fought for the passage of the Agricultural Labor Relations Act in June 1975 that gave California farmworkers the right to choose their union representatives through elections. When UFW contracts with lettuce growers expired again in 1979, the strike-boycott combination was resuscitated once more and resulted in 125 new contracts for 30,000 workers that raised starting wages for farmworkers by 40 percent to US$ 5.25 an hour and instituted an improved medical plan, paid vacations, pesticide restrictions, and employer-paid union representatives to monitor workers' conditions locally.[28] These 1979 victories, however, were the final peak in the UFW's organizing history. Soon after, Chavez's plaguing paranoia about losing his total authority over the union drove him to purge some of the union's most valuable leaders and the paid union representatives in the fields. By the early 1980s, many alienated UFW members had left the organization.[29] Moreover, the UFW failed to adapt to the demographic shifts in the United States during the 1980s—particularly, an influx of new migrants and refugees from southern Mexico and Central America—which meant a lost opportunity to organize the foreign-born workers who replaced Mexican Americans as the dominant agricultural workforce. Undocumented immigrants, who made up a sizeable portion of this new laboring population, were very reluctant to protest their wages and conditions or join a union.

---

[27] Margaret Rose, 'Traditional and Nontraditional Patterns of Female Activism in the United Farm Workers of America, 1962 to 1980,' *Frontiers*, vol. 11, (1990), 29; Barbara L. Baer and Glenna Matthews, "The Women of the Boycott," *The Nation*, 23 February 1974, 234; Margaret Rose, 'From the Fields to the Picket Line: Huelga Women and the Boycott, 1965–1975,' *Labor History*, vol. 31, no. 3, (1990), 273, 276.

[28] Tinsman, *Buying Into the Regime*, 162; Flores, *Grounds for Dreaming*, 209–10.

[29] For more on tensions within the UFW see Miriam Pawel, *The Union of Their Dreams: Power, Hope, and Struggle in Cesar Chavez's United Farm Worker Movement* (New York, 2009) and Matt Garcia, *From the Jaws of Victory: The Triumph and Tragedy of Cesar Chavez and the Farm Worker Movement* (Berkeley, 2014).

The UFW launched a third boycott against California grapes in the mid-1980s that focused on pesticide use. In 1986, it distributed a video called *The Wrath of Grapes* that spliced images of Latino children born without limbs (birth defects thought to result from the mother's exposure to pesticides) with footage of field and vineyard workers being sprayed with chemicals from low-flying planes. This boycott campaign asked consumers to stop buying California grapes until growers agreed to ban five widely used pesticides and herbicides and allow fair union elections.[30] The boycott did not succeed in gaining any contracts—rather, the number of farmworkers covered by UFW contracts fell over the rest of the decade due to the aforementioned demographic shifts and internal union strife, as well as a changed political climate under the presidency of Ronald Reagan and the ever-deepening pockets of agribusiness (the California Table Grape Commission devoted a whopping US$ 250,000 annually to advertising against the UFW boycott). In dramatic contrast to the UFW's first grape boycott in the 1960s, which lowered national sales of grapes by 20 percent, the average American was convinced by slick advertising to go from consuming an average of four pounds of grapes in 1980 to almost eight pounds in 1990.[31] Chavez's unexpected death in 1993 suspended the boycott, and the UFW turned over to his son-in-law Arturo Rodriguez. Recently a new president, Teresa Romero, has taken over the union's reigns, and she will continue to face the challenge of reviving the UFW's influence as it represents only a fraction of the farmworkers that it used to.

Some have critiqued the UFW's strike-and-boycott strategy for having limited objectives and impact. While boycotts in cities did drum up enough consumer support to bring growers to the negotiating table for union contracts, these short-term agreements only gave farmworkers power for a few years at a time and not permanently. The great public response to supermarket boycotts in the 1960s and 1970s was never harnessed into legislative change at the federal level, and laws were not created that bestowed agricultural laborers with more rights or curtailed the power and freedom of agribusiness. The American agricultural industry has continued to evade the institution of a minimum wage, overtime pay, and collective bargaining rights for farmworkers, and field work is still characterized by a lack of rest breaks, water, and sanitary facilities. Sexual harassment is prevalent, complaining workers are threatened with firing or deportation,

---

[30] Tinsman, *Buying Into the Regime*, 146.
[31] Tinsman, *Buying Into the Regime*, 148, 169.

and hundreds of thousands of US farmworkers suffer from pesticide poisoning each year. Individual states have passed minimum wage and safety laws for farmworkers, but the federal neglect of these laborers that began in the New Deal era persists to the present day.

That being said, the UFW food and drink boycotts remain historically significant in US Latino and labor history and the history of global boycotts. The broader civil rights context in which the union's boycotts took place resulted in the farmworker rights cause being more popular, supported, and successful than it would have been before or after such an ethos pervaded American political culture. Recognizing that the tactic of the boycott was particularly apposite in this climate, the UFW paired it with the conventional labor strike to galvanize national participation and affect agribusiness in a more direct financial manner. Today, the organic, free-range, sustainable, farm-to-table, and local "foodie" movements have thoroughly permeated many consumers' daily lives in the United States. Some activists and scholars are working to bridge the gap. The Coalition of Immokalee Workers (CIW), for instance, has succeeded in organizing Florida's tomato industry and persuaded employers and stores to participate in a Fair Food Program that informs shoppers if the food they choose is the product of fairly-treated labor. Generally, however, discourses about eating desirable food are still frequently disconnected from interrogations of the conditions experienced by the laborers (mostly Latino and immigrant) who harvest that desirable food. Would a national food boycott connected to laborers' rights ever succeed in the United States again? The history of the UFW boycotts provokes us to ask what we might need in the twenty-first century—a civil and human rights-centered political ethos that overpowers racism and xenophobia, a charismatic figurehead like Chavez, or a coalition of diverse activists willing to take on the powerful agribusiness lobby together—to finally set in place the protections that farmworkers have always deserved.

CHAPTER 10

Sanctions Against South Africa: Myths, Debates, and Consequences

Yehonatan Alsheh

INTRODUCTION

Students of the fall of apartheid and the negotiated transition to majority rule tend to agree that the international campaign for boycott and divestment sanctions against minority rule in South Africa had only a limited and highly contextual effect on eventual democratization there. However, the prevailing view among the wider public has been very different, parading the international mobilization against apartheid South Africa as the luminous—albeit single—success story of a global community conscience. The network of international organizations and activists involved in that campaign have understandably enough tended to overstate their contribution and its effects. Yet, as this chapter suggests, this image was promoted for instrumental reasons, especially by Thabo Mbeki, in the context of a foreign policy based on exporting the South African miracle. This was at the expense of giving due recognition to the internal processes and activism in 1980s South Africa, as well as to the armed struggle, led by Mbeki's opponent as Mandela's heir, Chris Hani. As the South African case

Y. Alsheh (✉)
Balsillie School of International Affairs, Wilfrid Laurier University, Waterloo, ON, Canada

© The Author(s) 2019
D. Feldman (ed.), *Boycotts Past and Present*, Palgrave Critical Studies of Antisemitism and Racism,
https://doi.org/10.1007/978-3-319-94872-0_10

becomes a beacon of hope for other struggles, popular misconception propagates a false image of how struggles are actually won as well as obscuring the real forces behind the crystallization of an international *cause celebre* and the actual effects it has on the unfolding of the suffering of people in some remote disprivileged part of the world.

Exporting the South African Miracle

Replacing Nelson Mandela in 1999 as the second democratically elected president of South Africa, Thabo Mbeki was determined not to allow South Africa to lose its position at the center of international attention, held for decades, and fall back to the place normal for states of its size and economic importance. Mbeki envisioned South Africa as a global power of some sort and himself as a world-class statesman. Unable to draw on the symbolic resources already exhausted by Mandela, Mbeki set out to craft new globally inspiring dreams. First and foremost, he advocated an African Renaissance which the new South Africa would lead.[1] Beyond that, Mbeki announced the rise of the Global South, contesting the existing biases of the international agenda.[2] These aims were given institutional expression in Mbeki's efforts to rejuvenate the Organization of African Unity, re-established as the African Union and proudly launched in Durban in 2002 with Mbeki as its first president, as well as in his insistence on breathing new life into the non-aligned movement in the United Nations (UN).

Mbeki advocated a grand and open-ended narrative of liberation on a global scale, with the new South Africa as champion of an ongoing (non-violent) crusade against racism on the international level and against what he denounced as a global apartheid regime. This crusade was to take many forms. They included a demand for international reparations for colonialism

---

[1] Thabo Mbeki, *African Renaissance: The New Struggle* (Capetown, 1999); see also: Fantu Cheru, *African Renaissance: Roadmaps to the Challenges of Globalization* (London, 2002); for a critical analysis of Mbeki's ideology of the African Renaissance see: Peter Vale and Sipho Maseko, 'Thabo Mbeki, South Africa and the idea of an African Renaissance', in: *Thabo Mbeki's World: The Politics and Ideology of the South African President*, eds. Sean Jacobs and Richard Calland, (London, 2013); for the African Renaissance in the context of the African Union see: Mammo Muchie, Phindil Lukhele-Olorunju, and Oghenerobor Akpor (eds.), *The African Union Ten Years After. Solving African Problems with Pan-Africanism and the African Renaissance* (Capetown, 2013).

[2] Johnson Richard W. *South Africa's brave new world: the beloved country since the end of apartheid* (New York, 2009).

and slavery,[3] but also an international campaign against other regimes in which forms of apartheid were still practiced, for example, the caste system in India[4] and the ethnocratic regime in Israel-Palestine.[5,6]

As euphoric as African nations were about the democratization of South Africa at last—as Africa's first liberation movement, the African National Congress (ANC), also became the last to achieve its goal—they did not share Mbeki's belief that the new South Africa was the preordained and long expected leader and savior of Africa. Given the promethean nature of the internal challenges facing South Africa, many wondered if Mbeki should be investing so much time and resources in globalizing South Africa's triumph over apartheid—exporting the South African miracle instead of actually making sure the miracle actually took root in South Africa itself.

One of Mbeki's key initiatives in his efforts to place South Africa on the global stage was to host and sponsor the UN World Conference Against Racism (UNWCAR) between 31 August and 8 September 2001 in Durban. The conference brought together state delegates and also an unprecedented number of representatives and delegations of indigenous populations and disprivileged minority groups from all over the world, as well as countless representatives of NGOs, the latter two categories permitted to be more closely connected to a world conference than ever before.[7] This signified the ever greater importance given to global civil society, but also asserted the historical role of internal and global civil society organizations in the democratization of South Africa, an explicit inspiration for the conference.

---

[3] Suhas Chakma Susha, 'The Issue of Compensation for Colonialism and Slavery at the World Conference Against Racism'. in: *Human Rights in Development Yearbook 2001: Reparations Redressing Past Wrongs*, eds. George Ulrich and Louise Krabbe Boserup, (New York, 2003); Rhoda Howard-Hassmann, *Reparations to Africa* (Philadelphia, 2008).

[4] Deepa Reddy, 'The Ethnicity of Caste', *Anthropological Quarterly*, vol. 78, no. 3, (2005), 543–584.

[5] Ran Greenstein. 'Israel/Palestine and the Aparteid Analogy: Critics, Apologists and the Strategic Lessons', in: *The Case for Sanctions Against Israel*, ed. Audrea Lim, (London, 2012), 149–158.

[6] Na'eem Na'eem. *Pretending Democracy: Israel, an Ethnocratic State* (Johannesburg, 2014).

[7] Bayefsky Anne. 'The UN World Conference Against Racism A Racist Anti-racism Conference', *Proceedings of the Annual Meeting (American Society of International Law)*, vol. 96, (2002), 65–74.

The UNWCAR conference in Durban had in fact been preceded by two similar conferences in 1978 and 1983, both held in Geneva. But these, boycotted by the US, received far less international attention or historical recognition. Mbeki intended the 2001 conference to equal, if not surpass, such events as the 1955 Bandung conference and the 1968 Teheran conference.[8] Things did not turn out that way.

The framing of the conference—in terms of colonialism, of the Atlantic slave trade, of slavery as a crime against humanity requiring reparations—raised sensitive and volatile issues. So too did discussion of the systematic (albeit informal) discrimination against Dalits (the untouchables) in India's caste system, the persecution of Roma people (gypsies) in Europe, and other injustices against indigenous and other disempowered minorities around the world. Many governments, not least that of the US, were hoping to minimize the importance and impact of the conference. Such hopes were met, probably more effectively than any opponents of the political objectives of the conference could have anticipated, when the respectability and legitimacy of the whole conference was effectively tarnished by blunt expressions of antisemitism and the strategically imprudent refusal to allow antisemitism equal status as another form of racism. Even before the attack on the World Trade Center in New York three days later reshuffled the global agenda and international readiness to entertain radical criticism of American hegemony, the UNWCAR in Durban had effectively self-destructed.

To the extent that the conference was meant to launch Mbeki's proffered leadership of the disempowered South against the hegemonic North Atlantic, it is not surprising that he wished to disassociate himself and South Africa from the unruly fiasco that unfolded. As an attempt to export the South African miracle, the conference was a complete failure, most of all in

---

[8] Roland Burke, *Decolonization and the Evolution of International Human Rights* (Philadelphia, 2010). Between 18 and 24 April 1955 in Bandung, Indonesia, 29 mostly Asian and a few African newly independent states convened. The conference's stated aims were to promote Afro-Asian economic and cultural cooperation and to oppose colonialism. The conference was an important step toward the Non-Aligned Movement. Between 22 April and 13 May 1968 in Teheran, Iran, a UN conference commemorating the twentieth anniversary of the universal declaration of Human Rights incorporated many of the principles and values of the Bandung conference into the UN's Human Rights agenda, further consolidating the so called anti-imperialist bloc in international affairs.

its misunderstanding of the political prudence, insightful diplomacy, and cultivation of appearances and images which underwrote that miracle.

My aim here, however, is to point out how a self-congratulatory and inaccurate representation of the efficacy of the international sanctions against apartheid South Africa came to be used as a premise grounding a similar campaign against Israel.

At the 2001 Durban conference, the lengthy (474 paragraphs) statement, composed by the NGOs forum, which included more than 7000 representatives from all across the global civil society, made the following demands:

> 418. Call for the immediate enforcement of international humanitarian law, specifically the Fourth Geneva Convention 1949, in the Occupied Palestinian Territories through the adoption of all measures to ensure its enforcement including all measures employed against the South African Apartheid regime. Call for the immediate convening of the High Contracting Parties to implement this process in fulfillment of their obligation to ensure respect for the Convention in all circumstances. Also call for the immediate deployment of an independent, effective international protection force for Palestinian civilians and the dismantlement of the illegal Jewish Israeli colonies (settlements) and a complete withdrawal of the colonial military occupation.
>
> 424. Call for the launch of an international anti Israeli Apartheid movement as implemented against South African Apartheid through a global solidarity campaign network of international civil society, UN bodies and agencies, business communities and to end the conspiracy of silence among states, particularly the European Union and the United States.
>
> 425. Call upon the international community to impose a policy of complete and total isolation of Israel as an apartheid state as in the case of South Africa which means the imposition of mandatory and comprehensive sanctions and embargoes, the full cessation of all links (diplomatic, economic, social, aid, military cooperation and training) between all states and Israel. Call upon the Government of South Africa to take the lead in this policy of isolation, bearing in mind its own historical success in countering the undermining policy of "constructive engagement" with its own past Apartheid regime.

Opponents of the movement for Boycott, Divestment and Sanctions (BDS) against Israel are fond of pointing out that the paragraphs about Israel in the NGOs forum declaration provide the secret—and denied—origin of the BDS movement, officially founded only on 5 July 2005. In fact, those paragraphs in the 2001 declaration are originated in a preconference meeting of NGOs held in February 2001 in Teheran.[9,10] The exact incriminatory value of unearthing these allegedly denied and secret origins is not entirely clear, except for the fact that it ties the BDS with the antisemitic aura of the 2001 UNWCAR in Durban and the inimical Iranian regime. In any case, the 9 July 2005 BDS movement call—its foundational document—undoubtedly refers to the anti-apartheid precedent:

> In view of the fact that people of conscience in the international community have historically shouldered the moral responsibility to fight injustice, as exemplified in the struggle to abolish apartheid in South Africa thorough diverse forms of boycott, divestment and sanction and
> Inspired by the struggle of South Africans against Apartheid and in the spirit of international solidarity, moral consistency and resistance to injustice and oppression[11]

Scornful reactions to the BDS campaign published by NGOs such as the Simon Wiesenthal Center,[12] and NGO Monitor,[13] angrily reject the analogy between Israel-Palestine and apartheid South Africa and come close to vilifying anyone who proposes it. However, they never question the basic premise that the sanctions against apartheid South Africa was a highly effective and successful campaign and that in principle should another apartheid regime come to be, such a campaign ought to be repeated as the best possible way to rid the world of such a crime against humanity. Their point is only to deny that apartheid is in any way an applicable or even relevant paradigm for analyzing the situation in Israel-Palestine.

In other words, both those advocating BDS against Israel and those opposing it and even delegitimizing those who support it, share an underlying agreement about the uncontestable efficacy of the international sanctions against apartheid South Africa.

---

[9] Tom Lantos, 'The Durban Debacle: An Insider's View of the UN World Conference Against Racism'. *The Fletcher Forum of World Affairs,* vol. 31, (2002).

[10] Herbert London and Jed Babbin. The BDS War against Israel (London, 2014).

[11] http://www.bdsmovement.net/call. The call was also reproduced in Audrea Lim, *The Case for Sanctions against Israel* (London, 2012).

[12] http://www.wiesenthal.com/atf/cf/%7B54d385e6-f1b9-4e9f-8e94-890c3e6dd277%7D/REPORT_313.PDF

[13] http://www.ngo-monitor.org/article/ngo_leadership_in_boycott_and_divestment_campaigns

The apparent achievements of the unprecedented wide and dense network of international organizations and activists involved in that campaign, though arguably overstated,[14] have understandably enough motivated and inspired other international struggles. Given the current trend toward human rights skepticism[15,16] and critical reassessments of that "last utopia",[17] such nostalgia toward humanity's community of conscience in its finest hour is quite understandable. However, other sanctions campaigns, such as the one against Iraq since 1990 (which was not at all rooted in civil society activism and advocacy, but originated from the Security Council and American foreign policy), though very different in outcome and disturbingly costly in terms of the suffering afflicted on the Iraqi population,[18] have not discounted the rosy image of the sanctions against South Africa. The longing for a unity of good intentions overcomes the grim forecasts of unexpected consequences.

Criticism of the image of the international sanctions that "unseated" apartheid is often misunderstood as denial that these sanctions had any effects, or any deserving attention, or as assertion that their effects were overwhelmingly more adverse than beneficial. My point however is quite different. As was always the consensus among scholars of the subject,[19] I argue that the impact of the international sanctions on the democratization of South Africa was above all highly contextual—a particular factor within a complex constellation of circumstances and actors with multiple motivations, interests, and beliefs. No one in fact contests that the single most important factor, if one must be isolated, was the end of the Cold War.[20]

Mbeki, as we see, well understood the exact limits of the leverage the sanctions provided for the ANC in a very specific window of opportunity.

---

[14] Hakan Thorn, *Anti-Apartheid and the Emergence of a Global Civil Society* (London, 2006).
[15] David Rieff. *A Bed for the Night: Humanitarianism at Crisis* (New York, 2002).
[16] Stephen Hopgood. *The End Times of Human Rights* (Ithaca, 2013).
[17] Samuel Moyn, *The Last Utopia* (Cambridge, MA, 2010).
[18] Geoff Simons, *Imposing Economic Sanctions* (London, 1999).
[19] David Welsh, *The Rise and Fall of Apartheid* (Charlottesville, 2009); Herman Giliomee, *The Afrikaners* (Capetown, 2003); Herman Giliomee, *The Last Afrikaner Leaders* (Capetown, 2012); Guelke Adrien, *Rethinking the Rise and Fall of Apartheid South Africa* (London, 2006).
[20] Herman Giliomee, *The Afrikaners* (Capetown, 2003).

The avalanche of sanctions on South Africa during the 1980s, especially in the second half of the decade, carried the risk of intoxicating the movement—tempting it to misjudge the real balance of power. The sanctions made the apartheid regime appear weaker than it was and the international community more supportive than it was. Because of its public nature, the campaign against South Africa was always weaker than it seemed to be—its image greater than its substance. Unfortunately, the current popular understanding of the sanctions against South Africa (to no small degree because of Mbeki's own marketing of this exportable version of the South African miracle as part of his failed foreign policy) contains very little of this complexity.

The Contested Efficacy of the Sanctions

In his autobiography, *The Last Trek*, South Africa's last white president, Wilhelm De Klerk, argued that while the boycotts, sanctions, and divestment campaign did damage the South African economy (by lowering its growth rate, preventing its integration into the globalizing economy, and holding it back in terms of technology), they nevertheless did not bring down apartheid—in fact they did more to delay the process of transformation than to advance it.[21] This view stands in contrast to the opinion of Joe Slovo, at the time leader of the South African Communist Party (SACP),[22] who publically expressed in 1988 complete faith in the efficacy of the sanctions.[23]

Slovo's faith in the efficacy of international sanctions was to some degree merely propagandist, aimed at encouraging both those imposing them and still more South Africa's disenfranchised masses struggling under the repression of the state of emergency. How far he and other leaders of the struggle making similar claims over the years really believed in the power of international sanctions, or the relative value of sanctions among other measures—above all the armed struggle—cannot be easily judged. For example, Mbeki declared in 1985 that the time had come for

---

[21] De Klerk Wilhelm, *The Last Trek – A New Beginning* (London, 1999), 70.

[22] About Joe Slovo, *Slovo: The Unfinished Autobiography of ANC Leader Joe Slovo* (Cape Town, 1997); see also the biographical sketch in http://www.sahistory.org.za/people/joe-slovo

[23] P. Davis Stephen, 'Economic Pressure on South Africa: Does It Work?', in: *Effective Sanctions on South Africa: The Cutting Edge of Economic Intervention*, ed. George Shepherd (Westport, 1991), 66.

the armed struggle to move beyond what was up until then merely "armed propaganda" (quoted in Welsh[24]). Were the sanctions ever assumed to be more than another means of propaganda? Given the ideological framework within which members of the SACP understood their actions, one might even wonder where exactly did international non-violent action fit within revolutionary doctrine.

The radical left opposition to the ANC, the Azanian People's organization (AZAPO), preached absolute self-reliance and hence opposed foreign investment or any other sort of involvement in South Africa. They explicitly opposed the boycott, disinvestment, and sanctions campaign as a form of international collective action, believing that:

> The liberation movement must be indigenous in genesis and autonomous in operation [...] intervention by a foreign country in our favor is a misplaced and dangerous delusion [...] those who believe that the black oppressed and exploited have a stake in the present system of colonialism and imperialist pursuits are placing irrational hope in the rising indignation of international imperialists on developments in this country. They forget that imperialists and their agents know no other interests but their own.[25]

The SACP and the ANC, on the other hand, were resolutely in favor of concerted international action against South Africa, rejecting the view that such external interventions necessarily remain within the imperialist logic. To some extent, promotion of economic sanctions was understood in relation to the classic liberal opposition to such measures. The liberal view was grounded in the assumption that economic development and the prosperity it brings, would necessarily have an eroding effect on apartheid. For example, Merle Lipton, one of the most prominent liberal critics of apartheid (Lipton 1985[26]; see also about the liberal vs. other interpretations of South African history: Lipton 2007[27]) argued in 1988 that:

---

[24] David Welsh, *The Rise and Fall of Apartheid* (Charlottesville, 2009), 273.
[25] Quoted in Jack B. Bloom, *Black South Africa and the Disinvestment Dilemma* (Johannesburg, 1986), 88–89.
[26] Merle Lipton, *Capitalism and Apartheid* (London, 1985).
[27] Merle Lipton, *Liberals, Marxists and Nationalists: Competing Interpretations of South African History* (London, 2007).

> If the sanctions have their intended effects, economic decline could erode those economic bonds that have drawn together the divers people of [what became] South Africa, and strengthen the fissiparous tendencies, thus making more possible partition, against a background of growing violence throughout the region.[28]

The right-wing opposition to the ANC, the Inkatha Freedom Party, disapproved of the economic sanctions, but on the grounds that they would mean extra suffering for the disenfranchised of South Africa. Opinion polls of black South Africans during the 1980s suggested that this concern was indeed the major reason for black opposition to the sanctions. It was somewhat unreliably estimated at the time that at least 35% (and possibly up to 50%) of the blacks opposed the sanctions; however, the opposition declined toward the end of the 1980s, when some 80% of blacks supported the sanctions. But given the violent nature of the times, the degree to which participants truly expressed their opinion is doubtful.[29] The Inkatha position in any case was that blacks, as the weakest part of the work force, would suffer most from the disinvestment and sanctions, while the government would be unlikely to assist them. Inkatha's leader, Chief Mangosuthu Buthelezi, then Chief Minister of the Kawazulu homeland, declared in 1984:

> How can I give approval to pressures regardless of the suffering they will entail for my people? I cannot bring myself to tell the poor of this country that I am working for the cessation of foreign investment in South Africa, investment which means jobs for the unemployed, clothes for the naked and food for the hungry.

Desmond Tutu, at the time the Anglican archbishop of Cape Town and the 1984 Nobel Peace prize laureate, answered Buthelezi. Speaking in Washington in December 1984, he stated that, "we don't want our chains made comfortable, we want our chains removed":

---

[28] Merle Lipton, *Sanctions and South Africa: The Dynamics of Economic Isolation* (London, 1988), 122.

[29] Jack B. Bloom, *Black South Africa and the Disinvestment Dilemma* (Johannesburg, 1986), 58–73; David Welsh, *The Rise and Fall of Apartheid* (Charlottesville, 2009), 257–258.

> Well-meaning people say blacks will be the first to suffer if economic pressure is applied. Truly they would be the first to lose their jobs. But blacks are suffering now. They would much rather suffer, even gladly, if it is going to end this oppressive system rather than go on endlessly suffering with no prospect of an end to their suffering. (Quoted in Bloom[30])

Tutu advocated sanctions as the only hope for a peaceful change repeatedly throughout the second half of the 1980s. But how exactly were sanctions supposed to achieve that?

Already in 1967, Johan Galtung, acclaimed founder of the discipline of conflict resolution, cautioned against what he termed "the naïve theory of sanction", in which a simple and proportional relation was assumed between the punitive economic measures imposed by the international community and the political disintegration of the targeted regime. As Galtung suggested, this naïve theory fails to take into consideration the resilience of besieged economies, their capacity to adapt and compensate. Such concerted international non-violent attacks: "may initially lead to political integration and only later – perhaps much later, or even never – to political disintegration".[31]

And indeed the South African economy adapted to the growing punitive implications of international hostility to apartheid and the threat of embargo, not least by expanding arms and fuel production. The UN arms embargo on South Africa (voluntary from 1963, then mandatory from 1977) resulted in the creation of Armscor in 1968 which, with government support, became a massive armament manufacturing and procurement enterprise. Similarly, international calls for an oil embargo gathered force, despite repeated vetos in the Security Council. Strategic prudence encouraged the South African state to secure energy supplies through state-owned enterprises Sasol and Mossgas as well as the creation of national stockpiles of oil that would have enabled the country to survive for three years without imports.[32]

---

[30] Jack B. Bloom, *Black South Africa and the Disinvestment Dilemma* (Johannesburg, 1986), 82.

[31] Johan Galtung, "On the effects of international Economic Sanctions", *World Politics*, vol. 19, no. 3, (1967), 389.

[32] Neta C. Crawford, 'How arms Embargoes work', in: *How Sanctions Work: Lessons from South Africa*, eds. Neta C. Crawford and Audie Klotz, (London, 1999); Neta C. Crawford, 'Oil Sanctions against Apartheid', in: *How Sanctions Work: Lessons from South Africa*, eds. Neta C. Crawford and Audie Klotz, (London, 1999); G. Simpson, 'The Politics and Economics of the Armaments Industry in South Africa', in: *War and Society*, eds. J. Cock and L. Nathan, (Cape Town and Johannesburg, 1989).

Between 1984 and 1990, no less than 33% of all foreign companies, especially those based in the US, officially left South Africa. This however resulted in substantial gains for certain South African conglomerates, as they bought out the departing companies or assets at well below their actual market value. At the same time, in many instances, sophisticated arrangements around licensing, franchising, and trademark agreements enabled foreign companies to present themselves as adhering to the boycott while in fact continuing to profit from various indirect activities.[33]

In other words, the sanctions led to the creation of local substitutes, to local investment replacing foreign capital, and to the devising of ways to exit without really exiting. While adaptation to the conditions created by sanctions demanded resources that could have been allocated differently under other circumstances, the South African economy was far from collapse. In fact, as far as its white populations were concerned at the time, the problem was not imminent economic ruin but the disturbing notion that they were not doing as well as they theoretically could have, or as well as they did—which was very well—until the mid-1970s. However, and this appears to be a highly important point, most of the whites still feared—as their government kept telling them—that abdicating their monopoly over the state would have catastrophic consequences.

The sanctions also (fulfilling Galtung's[34] prediction) led to political concentration as white populations became more entrenched in their support of apartheid. Opinion polls among whites from across the political spectrum over the second half of the 1980s showed a hardening of attitudes in response to what they perceived as illegitimate meddling in South Africa's internal affairs.[35] From the perspective of the National Party (NP) and as far as the polls of voter opinion can be trusted, the sanctions on South Africa had a negative impact on the willingness of whites of south Africa to compromise.

At the time, the great majority of whites in South Africa, even those supporting the Progressive Federal Party (PFP) (let alone the NP or the

---

[33] Neta C. Crawford and Audie Klotz (eds.), *How Sanctions Work: Lessons from South Africa* (London, 1999).

[34] Johan Galtung. 'On the effects of international Economic Sanctions', *World Politics*, vol. 19, no. 3 (1967).

[35] David Welsh, *The Rise and Fall of Apartheid* (Charlottesville, 2009), 256.

Conservative Party (CP)), saw the international ostracization and vilification of South Africa as expressing a complete double standard. In view of human rights abuses throughout Africa and the eastern bloc (which government propaganda persistently stressed), the majority of whites in South Africa felt that however wrong and unacceptable apartheid might be, its depiction as the single worst political regime since 1945 and the unprecedented international mobilization against it was (in their view) hypocritical and even contemptible. In fact, the white public was generally under the impression that the more South Africa was willing to reform—and the Botha government had indeed reformed apartheid in ways unthinkable before the 1980s—the greater the international pressure became.

In 1987, the CP for the first time won more seats than the PFP, hence replacing it as the formal opposition. For the first time since 1948, the NP's opposition came from the right. The CP continued to grow stronger, wining 31% of the vote in 1989 and realistically forecast to become the biggest party in the next elections.

Neville Stultz, an American political scientist specializing in Afrikaner politics, suggested in 1982 that three distinct models link sanctions to actual political change.[36] The first, which he termed the revolutionary model, predicts the rightward turn of growing numbers of white voters in response to tightening sanctions. According to Stultz, the revolutionary model is premised on the essential incapacity of the South African regime to democratize from within—the privileged populations cannot be persuaded in a non-violent way to end apartheid. Fundamental change would thus only come after a violent overthrow of the regime itself. The role of sanctions in this regard (and in contradiction to Tutu's vision of sanctions as the only non-violent way to end apartheid) was only to weaken the regime so as to enable the revolutionary forces to defeat it more easily.

According to this model, the rise in unemployment among the blacks in the townships, which reached 68.7% by 1988,[37] and especially the unemployment of young blacks who in fact never had a chance of entering

---

[36] Neville M. Stulz, 'Sanctions, models of change and South Africa', *South Africa International*, vol. 13, no. 2, (1982); see also Audie Klotz, 'Making sanctions work: comparative lessons', in: *How Sanctions Work: Lessons from South Africa*, eds. Neta C. Crawford and Audie Klotz, (London, 1999); Gary C. Hufbauer, Jeffrey J. Schott, Kimberly Ann Elliot, and Barbara Oegg, *Economic Sanctions Reconsidered* (Washington, DC, 2007).

[37] David Welsh, *The Rise and Fall of Apartheid* (Charlottesville, 2009), 252.

the work force, was one of the key desired outcomes. Though no revolution erupted in the end, the politically volatile township youth did play a significant role by rendering townships practically ungovernable in the 1980s. Having said that, by the time the Berlin Wall fell in November 1989, the South African state was in no real danger of being overthrown. The sanctions did not close the enormous gap between the military capacities of the South African state and the freedom movement. At the same time, the sanctions did provoke in the regime a sense of siege and insecurity and hence made it more willing to invest resources in security and to tolerate a limited decline in the standard of living for the sake of security.

Stultz's second model, termed "the thumb-screw approach", is premised on a classic rational-choice understanding of politics. Here sanctions were aimed at making the continuation of apartheid more and more expensive so as to counter its benefits for the privileged populations. According to this model, there would be a threshold beyond which apartheid would simply be too expensive while the democratization of South Africa would become too attractive to resist.

In many ways, this model suffers from the same problem as what Galtung called the naïve theory of sanctions. It forgets to take into account the friction, the stickiness of political reality. Populations may prove surprisingly irrational in their willingness to pay prices for preserving their independence in the face of what they regard as illegitimate—and irresponsibly smug—external interference. More so in this case since the benefits of a democratic South Africa were not an already existing reality but a projected vision, people might prove unwilling to trust this vision. Since the white populations of South Africa had been exposed to the less than successful drama of African decolonization since the late 1950s, which the apartheid state never failed to present as undeniable proof of the folly of seeking the dismantling of apartheid, how costly must apartheid become before the whites would seriously consider trading it for a speculative vision of a democratic South Africa? And indeed as late as August 1989, 62% of all whites (78% of the Afrikaners) opposed negotiations with the ANC, only 4% less than in 1986.[38] Even by the time of the referendum in 1992 which sought the whites' support in negotiating a constitution for the new South Africa, most whites were certain that this constitution would establish a power-sharing, consociational democracy, not a simple centralist one.[39]

---

[38] Herman Giliomee, *The Last Afrikaner Leaders* (Capetown, 2012), 297.
[39] Herman Giliomee, *The Last Afrikaner Leaders* (Capetown, 2012), 343.

The question of the economic cost of apartheid (as distinct from the moral and political costs) had troubled South Africans since the South African economy ran into difficulties in the second half of the 1970s.[40] However, attempts to calculate the cost of apartheid in the 1970s and 1980s tended to overestimate what the growth rate of the South African economy would have been without apartheid and the punitive costs imposed by the international community. For example, the economist Stephen R. Lewis argued in a book published in 1990 that but for apartheid and policies aimed at the preservation of white supremacy and domination, South Africa would have been able to enjoy growth rates between 1975 and 1987 like those between 1946 and 1975, and the 1987 real GDP would consequently have been 45% higher than it actually was (Lewis;[41] see also Welsh[42]). This seems unlikely: by the mid-1970s neither Western Europe nor North America were seeing anything like the growth rates of the miraculous postwar decades.[43] While the South African economy was declining from the mid-1970s onward (reaching zero growth in 1987), so were many western economies—South Africa was not doing well but it was not doing exceptionally badly.

Apartheid and the international punitive measures it incurred did however greatly limit South Africa's capacity to liberalize its economy and dramatically reduce the state's involvement in it, as most other countries were doing. At the time, and given the almost unchallenged new economic orthodoxy preached by the International Monetary Fund (IMF), the World Bank, and the entire profession of economics, few doubted that this was very bad for the economic future of South Africa. It is significant in this regard that the IMF explained its refusal to grant additional funds to South Africa in 1983 by arguing that apartheid was an economic impediment, greatly disrupting labor mobility as well as creating severe shortages in skilled labor, thus in the medium-term constraining potential growth.[44]

Integration into the globalizing economy and its financial markets came to be conditional on the obedient restructuring of the economy along neo-liberal principles. Apartheid had to be restructured away, not because

---

[40] C. H. Feinstein, *An Economic history of South Africa* (Cambridge, 2005).
[41] Stephen R. Lewis. *The Economics of Apartheid* (Washington, DC, 1990), 127.
[42] David Welsh, *The Rise and Fall of Apartheid* (Charlottesville, 2009), 253.
[43] Thomas Piketty. *Capital in the 21st Century* (Cambridge, 2014).
[44] Xavier Carim, Audie Klotz, and Olivier Lebleu. 'The Political Economy of Financial Sanctions', in: *How Sanctions Work: Lessons from South Africa,* eds. Neta C. Crawford and Audie Klotz, (London, 1999), 163 and fn 16.

it was morally rotten and unjust, but because it was economically inefficient and unviable. Apartheid gravely disrupted the labor market and the real estate market, and limited South Africa's internal consumer market, because of its own internal logic. While the prevention of non-white workers from unionizing made apartheid a highly effective instrument for exploiting black labor in the first decades after 1948, by the mid-1970s apartheid had become more a problem than a solution in this regard.

Faced with violent unruly strikes (starting in Durban in 1973) without a legitimate representative organization to negotiate with, industry and mine owners demanded that the government allow non-white workers to unionize, which reluctantly it did in 1979.[45] The black trade unions, united as the Congress of South African Trade Unions (COSATU) in 1985, became the ANC's strongest power base. Negotiating with black trade-union leaders eased the South African business elite's concerns about the radical—revolutionary—aspirations of black politics. Sanctions had coerced the South African government into a trajectory which threatened to be more dangerous to the interests of the South African business elite than trusting in the ANC's willingness to abandon its redistributive vision and to pledge allegiance to the market economy.

Revolution Deferred?

The South African business elite has never of course been a homogenous entity with unified interests and political outlook. The social reality of apartheid has affected different sectors in different ways. Some industries found the intensification of the struggle in the 1980s beneficial as it enabled them to enjoy monopoly profits and windfall gains when departing foreign companies sold their assets and holdings below market value. However, it is possible to generalize and argue that by the mid-1980s, captains of industry and other heads of the private sector became convinced that apartheid could not last in the long run and that de-radicalizing the ANC might prove a more attainable and sustainable strategy than maintaining their alliance to apartheid.

---

[45] Don Ncube, *The Influence of Apartheid and Capitalism on the Development of Black Trade Unions in South Africa* (Johannesburg, 1985).

The NP government under P.W Botha, whose two last friends in the world (setting aside for moment the regime's special relationship with Israel) were Margaret Thatcher and Ronald Reagan, was no enemy of private enterprise or pro-business structural reforms. However, the need to counter the growing international sanctions and pressure constrained Botha's capacity to promote the interests of the private sector. It became more and more apparent that the NP attempted to cater to the needs of the business elite, proving that the NP was the capital's best ally, and at the same time, to maintain apartheid against an ever more hostile world was simply not feasible. While the sanctions did not ruin the South African economy, they did make it increasingly hard for the NP government to keep the business elite on its side.

In September 1985, Gavin Relly, at the time the chairman of Anglo-American, led a delegation of senior businessmen to a meeting in Zambia with the (still banned) ANC.[46] At the meeting, attended by most of the ANC leading figures not imprisoned on Robben Island (in particular Oliver Tambo, Chris Hani, and Thabo Mbeki), the businessmen were more than pleased to discover that the ANC leadership had abandoned most of its dreams of nationalization and uninhibited redistribution. Young, worldly and sophisticated, lent credibility by his senior comrades from the movement, Mbeki above all succeeded in impressing the businessmen with his commitment to market economy, renouncing traditional Marxist-Leninist jargon and dogma. On the flight back, Relly went so far as to say: "I would be happy to have that guy as my president" (Quoted in Gevisser[47]).

P.W Botha had given a very different impression in his notorious Rubicon speech in Durban on 15 August 1985, which was broadcast live worldwide. It had been expected—not least because of comments from the foreign minister Pik Botha that he would follow the reformist line, heralding an end to apartheid, prepared by an earlier Cabinet meeting of the NP.[48] Instead however an angry old man appeared in a suit and a hat, unaccustomed to television politics (television had only been introduced to South Africa 9 years earlier), wagging his finger as he warned the world: "don't push us too far". Although the speech was actually packed with significant reforms which in a sense did spell out the end of major aspects

---

[46] David Welsh, *The Rise and Fall of Apartheid* (Charlottesville, 2009), 261–262.

[47] Mark Gevisser, *A Legacy of Liberation: Thabo Mbeki and the Future of the South African Dream* (New York, 2007); Mark Gevisser, *Thabo Mbeki the Dream Deferred* (Johannesburg, 2007).

[48] Herman Giliomee, *The Last Afrikaner Leaders* (Capetown, 2012), 199–203.

of apartheid, its content was completely lost in a performance that validated the world stereotype about apartheid's ruling elite: ugly, racist men imprisoned in a never ending 1950s, living relics of a reality the world has long left behind.[49]

From his exile in Lusaka, Oliver Tambo, then still president of the ANC, responded next day to Botha's speech, saying that the world now saw "A ruling group who could not help but show itself for what it is":

> a clique of diehard racists, hidebound reactionaries and bloodthirsty, fascist braggarts who will heed nobody but themselves [...] Posturing like a pathetic dictator in the mould of his predecessor and mentor, whose fascist rule was brought to an end 40 years ago, P.W. Botha stood last night pretending that he can withstand and defeat all the forces at home and abroad that are engaged in struggle to end the system of white minority domination [...]Those among our own people who have pinned their hopes on Botha changing heart and conceding that there is an urgent need for change must abandon all their illusions. They have to act against the Botha regime to realise the objectives which they have enunciated and which this regime has now rejected with utter contempt. I refer here to the business community of our country, the professionals and the intellectuals, the religious community and others. To these we say, your own interests demand that you join in the struggle to destroy the monstrous apartheid Frankenstein. [...]The time has come that the Western world should abandon all pretenses that it has any way of influencing change in South Africa other than through the imposition of sanctions.[50]

To be sure, it was the angelic Mandela whom the ANC presented as the overwhelming opposite of Botha. Mbeki however, yuppie-looking (catering for the aesthetic sensibilities of the late1980s), well versed in the principles and ideas of the emerging "end of history" globalizing new world order, was no less important. Beyond images, Mbeki was crucial in convincing the ANC to abandon their lifelong commitment to communism as an integral part of the true liberation of South Africa. As late as 1985, most of the high-ranking members of the ANC, including its president Tambo, were still considering the soviet model as a real option for the new democratic South Africa. If not only because of ideological conviction,

---

[49] The text of the speech: http://www.nelsonmandela.org/omalley/index.php/site/q/03lv01538/04lv01600/05lv01638/06lv01639.htm

[50] ANC PRESS STATEMENT PRESENTED BY OLIVER TAMBO LUSAKA, AUGUST 16, 1985 http://www.anc.org.za/ancdocs/pr/1980s/pr850816.html

then also because the USSR was still the ANC's greatest supporter in terms of funding and a network of allies. Mbeki, though originating from this communist background, had become convinced by the early 1980s that the ANC might benefit far more from prudently and clandestinely dissolving its loyalty to the Eastern side of the Cold War. The end of the Cold War therefore found the ANC well prepared.

In the early 1980s, the ANC was not prepared to negotiate with the NP government even if Botha would have been willing from his side. The main reason was that the ANC understood that, given the existing power balance, any initial framework for negotiation would require the ANC to agree on respect for property rights and the autonomy of a free market economy. Mbeki, on the other hand, understood that the power balance would not shift in the ANC's favor unless the ANC could win the backing of the South African business elite as well as the global one. The sanctions could never weaken the South African state—which was in those days approaching nuclear capability—enough for it to be vulnerable to whatever military force the freedom movement might gather. Mbeki understood that the sanctions could only truly benefit the ANC by discrediting the apartheid regime's claim to be the capital's best existing option. While many may currently find this way of conceptualizing politics simplistic (who is capital? How does it decide things?), it was just the way that someone of Mbeki's upbringing and political education saw the world.

The partnership created in 1985 between Mbeki and Frederik van Zyl Slabbert, the leader of opposition to the NP (until his resignation from official politics in February 1986) and the classic unsung hero of the democratization of South Africa, proved crucial at this stage. Van Zyl Slabbert convinced Mbeki to meet with a group of left-leaning Afrikaner intellectuals in Dakar, Senegal, in July 1987,[51] opening the door for a serious consideration of a pact between elites. This would enable South Africa to democratize without harming the interests of the existing elites while at the same time it enabled the establishment of new non-white elites, not only political but also economic and professional. The boycott and sanctions against South Africa, harming the interest of the economic, academic, and cultural white elite, gave ANC the leverage by which enabled they could buy their entrance into such circles in the new South Africa.

---

[51] Herman Giliomee, *The Last Afrikaner Leaders* (Capetown, 2012), 229–33.

Mbeki was able to convince the SACP (he was one of the six members of its politburo) at their conference in Havana in 1989 to accept this major deferring of the revolution, persuading them to accept a new manifesto titled: *the Path to Power*.[52] The logic of this decision, which opened the way to the implementation in 1996 of an extremely conservative package of neo-liberal macro-economic policies, was grounded in the classic two-phase approach of a national democratic revolution leading to a second socialist revolution in a later stage (for the process leading to the 1996 entrenchment of neo-liberalism in South Africa and its effects in the past 20 years, see: Hart[53]; Habib[54]; for a detailed analysis of the process in the 1990s, see: Allan[55]; Bond[56]).

Conclusion

There is an undeniable gap between the image suggested by the term the South African miracle—itself part of the theological language applied during the first years of democracy under the leadership of Archbishop Tutu and the Truth and Reconciliation Process—and the realities of the transformation of apartheid South Africa into the new democratic South Africa. Bloody civil war of the Angolan or Mozambican kind was avoided not by divine intervention, but because the ANC and other movements were always too weak to risk it. While very aware of its military impotence, the ANC was prudent enough to identify other potential sources of power, namely, its international public image and making a credible commitment to a neo-liberal restructuring of the South African state. The international sanction against South Africa influenced the specific context in which the ANC could suggest itself to the economic (but also academic and cultural) elites as a better option than the apartheid regime. The sanctions in themselves were only one specific factor, although the one most visible to the

---

[52] South African Communist Party, The Path to Power, program of the SACP adopted 1989: www.SACP.org.za

[53] Gillian Hart. *Rethinking the South African Crisis: Nationalism, Populism, Hegemony* (Athens, 2013).

[54] Adam Habib, *South Africa's Suspended Revolution: Hopes and Prospects* (Athens, 2013).

[55] Mitchel H. Allan, *Globalization, Negotiation, and the Failure of Transformation in South Africa* (London, 2006).

[56] Patrick Bond. *The Elite Transition: From Apartheid to Neoliberalism in South Africa* (London, 2000).

external world. They were never the crucial element. If one such single primary factor must be identified, the end of the Cold War would probably be the best and obvious candidate.

The South African miracle has been and still is a required myth in the laborious and far from achieved South African nation-building project. In the same way, the myth about the international community of conscience forging a collective will and the power of non-violent action to unseat the unabashedly racist, exploitative, and cruel apartheid regime is also quite understandable. While one may speculate about what exact political entity was actually constituted by this foundational myth or the kind of political projects that this grand movement was unreflectingly carrying on its back, in itself the vision of a global civil society caring about the misfortunes of others is undoubtedly a blessed one.

However, once these myths are displaced into a prescriptive blueprint—a model to reapply on other situations and within a very different context—these myths may prove more damaging than beneficial. This chapter has shown how the sanctions against South Africa are currently being used as a blueprint for a BDS campaign against Israel. The voices opposing this campaign, even those motivated by ideals that share very little with universal and humanistic values, tend to concentrate on what they perceive as a false and wicked accusation that Israel is an apartheid state. They do not however contest the myth that it was the sanctions that unseated apartheid and that in the South African case the sanctions and boycott were completely justified (rather than also an example of the hypocrisy and double standard of the international community).Of course, admitting that apartheid South Africa was also singled out by the international community at the time would imply that strategic rather than purely normative calculations were—and still are—at stake. Orchestrating the sanctions and boycott against South Africa was made possible and desirable by a concrete political bloc composed of different stakeholders (such as but not limited to certain segments of the white elite in South Africa and the ANC) operating in a given context.

At the moment, a comparable bloc does not appear to exist in the Israeli-Palestinian case and the overall context (both in terms of international political economy and an international ideological consensus of the kind emerging in the late 1980s) is also significantly different. However, international contexts change as do political blocs and what appear strategically wrong at a given moment may prove the right way forward sooner than one may expect. In other words, if a proper comparison with the

South African precedent tells us something about the BDS campaign against Israel, it is that the question was, is, and always will be purely strategic. Apartheid South Africa was never more deserving of an international campaign of sanctions and boycott than Israel (as well as quite a few other ugly regimes in the world) currently is. South Africa was simply at one crucial point significantly and contextually vulnerable to one.

CHAPTER 11

Sanctioning Apartheid: Comparing the South African and Palestinian Campaigns for Boycotts, Disinvestment, and Sanctions

Lee Jones

INTRODUCTION[1]

In 2005, Palestinian civil society activists called for boycotts, disinvestment, and sanctions (BDS) against Israel, stating they were 'inspired by the struggle of South Africans against apartheid'.[2] Indeed, the South African experience and analogy is central to their campaign. It provides a framework for a moral critique of Israel as an 'apartheid state', creating an imperative for outsiders to support Palestinians as they did black South Africans, in the name of 'moral consistency'. More problematically, the South African anti-apartheid movement's (AAM) use of BDS provide a

---

[1] Research for this chapter was funded by an Economic and Social Research Council (ESRC) grant (RES-061-25-0500). I am grateful for research assistance from Sahar Rad, Zaw Nay Aung, Kyaw Thu Mya Han and Aula Hariri.

[2] Omar Barghouti, *Boycott, Disinvestment, Sanctions: The Global Struggle for Palestinian Rights* (Chicago, 2011), 240.

L. Jones (✉)
Queen Mary University of London, London, UK
e-mail: l.c.jones@qmul.ac.uk

© The Author(s) 2019
D. Feldman (ed.), *Boycotts Past and Present*, Palgrave Critical Studies of Antisemitism and Racism,
https://doi.org/10.1007/978-3-319-94872-0_11

new strategy to fight Israeli oppression following the failure of other approaches, including armed struggle and the Oslo peace process. BDS is 'the South Africa strategy for Palestine'.[3]

Framing current struggles using historical analogies is a well-worn practice. Marx, observing the 1848 Paris Commune, noted that revolutionaries 'anxiously conjure up the spirits of the past to their service, borrowing from them names, battle slogans, and costumes in order to present this new scene in world history in time-honoured disguise and borrowed language'.[4] Later, US foreign policymakers repeatedly invoked the Munich debacle to justify militarily confronting, rather than 'appeasing' communism during the Cold War.[5] And many other advocates of international sanctions have used the South Africa analogy. US Senator Mitch McConnell, for example, justified sanctions against Myanmar (Burma) by claiming that 'sanctions worked in South Africa, and they will in Burma too', while Archbishop Desmond Tutu branded Myanmar the 'South Africa of Southeast Asia', urging the world to 'do for Burma what it did for South Africa'.[6] The Free Burma Campaign explicitly sought to 'recreate what went on during the AAM', employing its methods and even its now-redundant activists.[7]

Such framing, while potentially useful, carries significant risks. Marx argued that the 'awakening of the dead' from earlier revolutions was justified only insofar as it 'served the purpose of glorifying the new struggles, not of parodying the old; of magnifying the given task in the imagination, not recoiling from its solution in reality; of finding once more the spirit of revolution, not making its ghost walk again'. As this implies, historical analogies can distract from contemporary realities and priorities, preventing genuine progress. This, Marx argued, was the case in the upheavals of 1848–1851, when, 'only the ghost of the old revolution circulated'.[8]

---

[3] Ibid., 63.
[4] Karl Marx, "The Eighteenth Brumaire of Louis Bonaparte," *Die Revolution* (1852), ch. 1, http://www.marxists.org/archive/marx/works/1852/18th-brumaire/ch01.htm
[5] Yuen Foong Khong, *Analogies at War: Korea, Munich, Dien Bien Phu, and the Vietnam Decisions of 1965* (Princeton, 1992).
[6] Morten B. Pedersen, *Promoting Human Rights in Burma: A Critique of Western Sanctions Policy* (Lanham, 2008), 33, 49–50.
[7] Free Burma Coalition (FBC), *The Free Burma Coalition Manual: How You Can Help Burma's Struggle for Freedom* (Madison, 1997).
[8] Marx, "18th Brumaire".

This chapter argues that this is also true of the BDS movement's use of the South African analogy, where easy rhetoric distracts from the hard task of meaningful strategising and popular mobilisation. Focusing on domestic political economy and social conflict in the target state, rather than international dynamics, I argue that the analogy masks critical differences between these two cases. Crucially, in South Africa, BDS was a *supplementary* tool used by a powerful, strategically led and mass-mobilised liberation struggle. In Palestine, BDS is partly intended to *create* such a movement, following the liberation struggle's ruination. This asks too much: BDS did not serve this function in South Africa, and its prospects for doing so in contemporary Israel/Palestine are weak. Furthermore, the absence of mass struggle in Israel/Palestine makes it unlikely that BDS will be effective; it was only such struggle that allowed BDS to 'bite' in South Africa. Finally, lacking the ANC's clarity on goals and strategy, the Palestinian BDS campaign is politically incoherent, lacking consensus on the end goals and the mechanisms by which BDS is meant to achieve them. Consequently, it neither focuses on activating these mechanisms, nor does it evaluate 'success' sensibly.

My purpose in highlighting these problems is not to dismiss the BDS campaign or the Palestinians' plight. Rather, it is to stimulate critical, sympathetic reflection on political strategies for those seeking liberation. As Marx argued, a genuinely radical movement 'cannot take its poetry from the past but only from the future. It cannot begin with itself before it has stripped away all superstition about the past'. Its agents must

> constantly criticise themselves, constantly interrupt themselves in their own course, return to the apparently accomplished, in order to begin anew; they deride with cruel thoroughness the half-measures, weaknesses, and paltriness of their first attempts… until a situation is created which makes all turning back impossible.[9]

The chapter comprises four parts. The first briefly outlines the African National Congress's (ANC) view of BDS. The second highlights the critical difference between the ANC's use of BDS and the Palestinian movement's position. The third argues that the absence of Palestinian mass struggle will constrain the efficacy of BDS. The fourth highlights the BDS campaign's strategic incoherence.

[9] Ibid.

The ANC's View of BDS

The ANC's perspective on BDS reflected its sophisticated analysis of South African society and its associated strategy to hasten apartheid's demise. Its analysis was grounded in a Marxist reading of South Africa's political economy and the social forces underpinning the apartheid regime. Based on this, the ANC adopted a revolutionary strategy based on 'four pillars': mass struggle, underground organisation, armed resistance, and international solidarity. BDS measures formed part of the fourth 'pillar' and were always supplemental to the primary 'pillar', mass mobilisation. BDS were intended to help alter the balance of forces struggling for power in South Africa: to fragment the ruling bloc and to bolster anti-apartheid forces, thereby forcing the regime to negotiate. Mass struggle was thus indispensable for BDS to have meaningful impact.

The ANC viewed apartheid as functional for a 'colonial' form of capitalist development, and saw the regime as rooted in a coalition of class forces benefiting from this arrangement.[10] Following classical Marxist theories of revolution, they argued that regime change would occur when this ruling coalition—English and Afrikaner capitalists, the white middle and working classes, and subordinate, non-white elites running the Bantustans and other apartheid institutions—was overwhelmed by mass, non-white opposition, through civil disobedience, strikes, and sabotage aimed at rendering society 'ungovernable', compelling the regime to negotiate a transition to multiracial democracy.[11] The ANC's 1955 Freedom Charter specified clear, democratic-socialist end goals, subsequently adopted by most anti-apartheid forces, including the trade unions and the United Democratic Front (UDF).

BDS fit coherently into this overall strategy. They were seen as useful in 'restraining the regime's capacity [to suppress opposition], dividing the alliance of forces behind the apartheid state, [and] uniting and broadening the anti-apartheid support base'.[12] The first two—destructive—mechanisms were particularly emphasised, as a means to help weaken the ruling coalition vis-à-vis the rising power of the mass opposition constructed by the

---

[10] ANC, "The Nature of the South African Ruling Class," Document of the National Preparatory Committee, ANC National Consultative Conference, Kabwe, Zambia, June 1985, http://www.marxists.org/subject/africa/anc/1985/nature-ruling-class.htm

[11] ANC, "Strategy and Tactics of the ANC," Morogoro Conference, Tanzania, April 25–May 1, 1969; http://www.marxists.org/subject/africa/anc/1969/strategy-tactics.htm

[12] Mac Maharaj, ANC senior official, interview with author, September 8, 2011.

other 'pillars'. ANC President Oliver Tambo argued that external flows of trade, investment, technology, and military cooperation bolstered the state's repressive capacity. By severing these flows, sanctions would 'weaken the system and making it less capable of resisting our struggle'.[13] Thabo Mbeki argued that undermining white prosperity would support the 'breaking up of the power structure... out of this you will get a realignment of forces'.[14] In particular, since the ANC's Marxist analysis indicated that big business exerted predominant influence over the state, 'the real target', a senior trade union leader states, 'was internal capital'. Harming its interests would encourage it to defect from the ruling coalition, engage in 'civil disobedience' and 'put pressure on' the regime. Sanctions were thus 'designed to turn as many significant forces within this society as possible against apartheid'.[15] BDS played only a minor role in constituting the rising mass opposition that would exploit this growing regime weakness. The BDS campaign, being nonviolent, included groups like churches that were squeamish about other ANC tactics.[16] However, it was the campaign itself, not the effects of BDS measures, that had this mild effect, and the primary factor mobilising opposition was obviously apartheid rule itself.

By the 1980s, the AAM sought BDS targets that reflected this strategy. Early boycott campaigns, launched in 1960, did not do so, focusing instead on symbolic South African products like fruit, and sporting and cultural boycotts. ANC strategists did not expect these measures to coerce pro-apartheid forces; they were instead intended to mobilise Western publics, to build support for more meaningful sanctions later on, which would harm key groups inside South Africa.[17] Consequently, despite fantastical claims about the sports boycotts' efficacy, the primary means by which BDS were intended to work was material not, as liberals often suggest, psychological. As one analyst argued: 'sanctions are not intended primarily to influence the

---

[13] Starnberger Institute, *The Impact of Economic Sanctions Against South Africa* (Harare, 1989), 49–50; Joseph Hanlon and Roger Omond, *The Sanctions Handbook* (Harmondsworth, 1987), 26.

[14] Tom Lodge, 'State of Exile: The African National Congress of South Africa, 1976–86', in: *State, Resistance and Change in South Africa*, eds. Philip Frankel, Noam Pines, and Mark Swilling, (London, 1988), 250–251.

[15] Alec Erwin, former Congress of South African Trade Unions senior official, interview with author, September 12, 2011.

[16] Allan Boesak, former United Democratic Front (UDF) patron, interview with author, September 12, 2011.

[17] Maharaj, interview.

subjective intentions of the existing power holders… Rather, they are seen as contributing, in conjunction with other forms of struggle, towards creating objective conditions in which… a transfer of power is placed on the agenda'.[18] Thus, in the 1980s, as internal opposition mounted, the ANC advocated sanctions that would inflict maximal damage on South Africa's economy, hoping to damage large-scale business interests perceived as central to the ruling bloc.[19]

Crucially, BDS were only ever a supplement to the primary 'pillar' of ANC strategy: mass mobilisation. ANC leaders repeatedly emphasised that BDS alone 'will not bring results'.[20] The AAM's Abdul Minty stated: 'victory will come through the struggle of the people… sanctions must be regarded as a complement to that struggle and not as an alternative'.[21] The ANC's political analysis told them that, since objectionable regimes are always underpinned by powerful societal interests, they cannot be 'persuaded' to change, including by BDS; they must be forced to do so by mass struggle. This analysis was proven correct since, without mass struggle, BDS failed to compel political change. Sanctions were imposed on South Africa for decades, including oil embargoes from the 1960s and an arms embargo in 1977. However, the regime evaded these by creating import-substituting industries, enriching many loyal businesses and individuals. The exorbitant cost—over US\$ 50bn—was borne as the price of white domination and was affordable so long as the non-white labour that generated South Africa's wealth remained quiescent. Because sanctions were imposed following defeats of the internal opposition (the 1960 Sharpeville massacre and the 1976 Soweto uprising), the regime was able to deflect their costs onto the oppressed population.[22]

Only mass resistance rendered this strategy defunct. By the mid-1980s, black urban unrest was so intense and sustained that the regime could no longer repress it by force. Crucial here was the strategic centrality of the

---

[18] Davies, cited in Koos van Wyck, 'State Elites and South Africa's International Isolation: A Longitudinal Comparison of Perception,' *Politikon*, vol. 15, no. 1, (1988), 64–65.

[19] Erwin, interview.

[20] Tom Lodge, 'Sanctions and Black Political Organisations', in: *Sanctions Against Apartheid*, ed. Mark Orkin, (New York, 1989), 38–39.

[21] Grassroots Palestinian Anti-Apartheid Wall Campaign (GPAAWC), "Towards a Global Movement: A Framework A For Today's Anti-Apartheid Activism," June 2007, 129, http://bdsmovement.net/files/bds%20report%20small.pdf

[22] Lee Jones, *Societies Under Siege: Exploring How International Economic Sanctions (Do Not) Work* (Oxford, 2015), ch.2.

black working class: while the UDF was temporarily neutralised by police crackdowns, the regime could not quash the unions without crippling the economy; consequently, labour militancy actually rose. Accordingly, the regime was forced to try to undercut the rebellion by increasing welfare spending. However, as the then finance minister recalls, because sanctions—in combination with an unrelated, deep, and structural economic crisis—constrained overall resources, the regime struggled to finance sanctions busting, coercion, and welfare simultaneously. Consequently, the government 'saw a revolutionary type of situation developing, where we would not [even] have been able to deal with conflict control'.[23] Absent mass mobilisation, this dilemma would simply not have existed. Mass struggle also disabled the regime's attempt to draw non-white elites into neo-apartheid political structures: Bantustan governments, coloured and Indian legislatures, and black local authorities. Rent and service-charge payment strikes, street protests, and attacks on collaborators paralysed these institutions, causing this strategy of co-optation to fail. The white ruling elite thus faced a choice between spiralling unrest or negotiations. Powerful and wealthy groups increasingly realised that their interests could no longer be served by apartheid, and began demanding change. The rest is history.[24]

In South Africa, then, BDS were part of a coherent strategy aimed at clearly defined goals. They were expected to modestly assist the overall strategy of fragmenting the ruling power bloc, which, in combination with rising mass opposition, would compel the regime to negotiate a settlement. Crucially, they harmed the ruling coalition only in combination with mass struggle.

CRITICAL DIFFERENCES: THE WEAKNESS OF THE PALESTINIAN LIBERATION MOVEMENT

While in South Africa BDS supported a mass liberation struggle, Palestinian activists want BDS to construct one. Here, there is no burgeoning, strategically led, mass-mobilised movement seeking an additional means to coerce its enemies, but a legacy of defeat, fragmentation, and despair. BDS activists lack clear goals, hoping instead that their campaign might generate

---

[23] Barend Du Plessis, former South African Finance Minister, interview with author, September 5, 2011.
[24] Jones, *Societies Under Siege*, ch.2.

political consensus and revive collective struggle. There is no analysis of power relations in Israel/Palestine, nor any strategy for shifting these into which BDS fits; BDS is simply grasped at because 'nothing else has worked'.[25] Accordingly, the suggested mechanisms through which BDS might 'work' are often contradictory or copied unreflectively from the South African experience, without asking whether they are replicable in Israel/Palestine—and they typically are not. This strategic incoherence leads activists to confuse means and ends, making spurious claims of 'success' despite negligible results on the ground.

The Weakness of the Palestinian Liberation Movement

While it is rarely stated explicitly, the 2005 BDS Call was clearly a response to the dramatic decline of the Palestinian struggle for national self-determination. The Palestinian Liberation Organisation (PLO) was once in the vanguard of a worldwide anti-imperialist movement, modelled on the Vietnamese struggle and receiving extensive transnational support. However, following the defeat of progressive forces in Arabia and beyond, the PLO was cut adrift and fell into decay.[26] Although hopes were raised by the 1993 Oslo Peace Accords, many Palestinians now view the 'peace process' as a sham that co-opted their leaders and demobilised their movement.[27]

Through the creation of the Palestinian National Authority (PNA), 'a small clique of leaders who were mostly detached from the struggling Palestinians on the ground hijacked... decision-making power'.[28] The PNA's circumscribed mandate left it *'inherently incapable* of supporting any effective resistance strategy... Indeed... [it] has actually been detrimental'.[29] As a de facto gendarme of the Israeli state, the PNA assumed the worst aspects of authoritarian Arab regimes, demobilising the masses and repressing dissent, often violently. It became absorbed with municipal

---

[25] Neve Gordon, 'Boycott Israel', in: *The Case for Sanctions Against Israel*, ed. Audrea Lim, (London, 2012), 191.

[26] Paul T. Chamberlin, *The Global Offensive: The United States, the Palestinian Liberation Organization, and the Making of the Post-Cold War Order* (Oxford, 2012).

[27] Edward W. Said, *The End of the Peace Process: Oslo and After*, 2nd ed. (London, 2002). See also Tariq Dana, "The Prolonged Decay of the Palestinian National Movement," *National Identities,* early online (2017).

[28] Ramzy Baroud, 'Palestine's Global Battle that Must be Won', in: *Generation Palestine: Voices from the Boycott, Disinvestment and Sanctions Movement*, ed. Rich Wiles, (London, 2013), 11.

[29] Barghouti, *BDS*, 56.

administration and state-led 'development', backed by the international financial institutions, which created vested interests in the status quo and further undermined political resistance. The Authority became 'a kind of mafia', dispensing monopolies, contracts, and special deals to build patronage networks.[30] These measures, including joint ventures with Israeli firms, led to the 'systematic… corruption and co-optation of a whole class of Palestinian politicians, businessmen, and intellectuals, [such that] the Palestinian culture of resistance and heritage of struggle has been distorted and undermined'.[31] By 2002, the Authority employed around 140,000 people, making up to one million Palestinians indirectly dependent upon PNA patronage and thus unlikely to challenge its rule.[32] Others formed numerous NGOs, dependent on foreign funding and constrained to pursue only technocratic agendas, thereby 'mirroring [the loss of credibility] experienced by the political leadership'.[33] Thereby, as a leading BDS activist observes, many 'sectors of Palestinian society have become so dependent upon interim arrangements and foreign aid… as to put paid to the possibility their contributing to the fight for real change'.[34]

By the early 2000s, then, the Palestinian resistance was in ruins. As Edward Said lamented, under the PNA's

> large, corrupt, bureaucratic and repressive apparatus… people are cowed into silence and apathy… [they] seem to have given up all hope and all will to resist the extraordinary disasters visited on them by their leadership, which cares not a whit for anything except its own survival… [it] has simply abandoned them… We are an unmobilised people. We are unled. We are unmotivated… It is as if we have been anaesthetised as a people, unable to move, unable to act.[35]

The situation worsened after Said's death, with the Fatah-Hamas split. One former PLO official observed:

> every institution or overarching structure that once united Palestinians has now crumbled and been swept away… no single body… [can] claim legiti-

---

[30] Said, *Peace Process*, 22.
[31] Omar Barghouti, 'Palestine's South Africa Moment has Finally Arrived', in: *Generation Palestine*, ed. Wiles, 217.
[32] Said, *Peace Process*, 344.
[33] GPAAWC, "Towards a Global Movement", 133–134.
[34] Mustafa Barghouthi, 'Freedom in Our Lifetime', in: *The Case for Sanctions*, ed. Lim, 10.
[35] Said, *Peace Process*, 18–19, 291.

mately to represent all Palestinians; no body [is] able to set out a collective policy or national programme of liberation. There is no plan… we are at a nadir in our history of resistance.[36]

Accordingly, the contemporary BDS campaign is not intended to bolster a powerful, well-led and mobilised liberation struggle, as in 1980s South Africa, but rather to try to produce such a struggle. BDS activists state this explicitly. Said himself stumbled towards calling for an international BDS campaign as a means of 'reactivat[ing] o[ur] will' and 'mobilis[ing] ourselves and our friends'.[37] Others state that the BDS Call was needed merely to 'affirm that our national liberation movement is still alive' and to 'revive our culture of collective activism'.[38] Activists deliberately adopted very minimalist goals as a 'basis… to campaign upon and a means to limit sectarianism' for 'organisations unable to present a stronger platform', hoping to 'recreate the sense of unity and purpose' lost since the 1980s.[39] BDS would, it was hoped, serve as a 'political catalyst and moral anchor for a strengthened, reinvigorated international social movement'.[40]

Understandable and necessary as these goals are, BDS are unlikely to help achieve them. Despite deliberately appealing to the lowest common denominator, the BDS Call still does not command universal support. It specifies three demands: (1) an end to the Israeli occupation of Palestinian territories and the dismantling of the West Bank Barrier, (2) recognition of the rights of Arab citizens of Israel to full equality, and (3) respect for Palestinian refugees' right to return. Beyond this, unlike the ANC's detailed Freedom Charter, the movement eschews substantive goals and programmes. As one leading figure notes: 'individual BDS activists and advocates may support diverse political solutions', so the 'movement… does not adopt any specific political formula'.[41] The BDS Call thus expresses rather than surmounts Palestinians' disorganisation and division, compelling the avoidance of substantive political goals. Although one might argue that this is merely a starting point to rebuild consensus, in practice, even this minimalist platform has not unified Palestinians.

[36] Karma Nabulsi, 'Lament for the Revolution,' *London Review of Books*, vol. 32, no. 20, (2010), 34–35.
[37] Said, *Peace Process*, 194–195.
[38] Barghouthi, "Freedom in Our Lifetime", 6.
[39] GPAAWC, "Towards a Global Movement", 159, 162.
[40] Barghouti, *BDS*, 193.
[41] Ibid., 51–52, 218.

Several NGOs opposed BDS as a 'blow to the P[N]A and a subversion of the strategic direction of the Palestinian national movement'.[42] The comprador Palestinian business elite opposes BDS,[43] as did the PNA for five years, before timidly endorsing only a minimal boycott of products from illegal Israeli settlements.[44] Thus, BDS seems not to be facilitating political reunification.

Nor is it clear how BDS can revive collective activism. Some BDS advocates apparently recognise that 'the "South African treatment" [involves] global boycotts from outside supporting mass struggle inside'.[45] Yet they do not explain how this mass struggle is to be produced. BDS did *not* create this struggle in South Africa; ANC leaders explicitly denied that sanctions were required to spur the masses into action, insisting they would only supplement an already-mobilised mass movement. Key to this was the emergence of a well-organised black working class, whose labour was essential to South African capitalism, and of Charterist civic organisations through decades of grassroots organising. Contemporary conditions in Israel/Palestine are markedly different. The Palestinian working class is poorly organised and led and entirely lacks a strategic position in the Israeli economy. Although Israeli capitalism became dependent on Palestinian labour after 1967, following the First Intifada (1987), Israeli businesses deliberately reduced their Palestinian workforces, turning instead to migrant workers and new Jewish immigrants from the former Soviet bloc. Accordingly, economic dependency has been reversed: Palestinians now rely on Israeli firms to provide them with livelihoods,[46] even being compelled to help build illegal Israeli settlements.[47] As for civic organisations, while the BDS Call may provide a platform for some collaboration, unlike UDF groups, many NGOs are beholden to foreign donors and the PNA, constraining their political freedom. It is unclear how BDS can transform this structural constraint.

Moreover, BDS are generally better at creating division than unity. Notwithstanding the simplistic myths peddled about South Africa by BDS campaigners, sanctions were extremely divisive there, being opposed by

---

[42] Noura Erakat, 'BDS in the USA, 2001–2010', in: *The Case for Sanctions*, ed. Lim, 88.
[43] GPAAWC, "Towards a Global Movement", 135.
[44] Barghouti, *BDS*, 56–57; Erakat, "BDS", 89.
[45] Barghouti, *BDS*, 64.
[46] GPAAWC, "Towards a Global Movement", 119, 123–124, 132.
[47] Jihan Abdalla, "A Palestinian Contradiction: Working in Israeli Settlements," *Al-Monitor*, February 18, 2014.

the anti-apartheid white opposition party, some non-white unions, and non-ANC black leaders like the Zulu chief Mangosuthu Buthelezi, who all argued that they harmed non-whites and provoked white intransigence. It took active political mobilisation to win the majority over to the ANC/ UDF position, including a violent struggle against Buthelezi's Inkatha organisation. Similarly, in the 1990s, Iraqi opposition groups initially rallied around sanctions, but as soon as sanctions began to bite, they caused fatal divisions.[48] In Myanmar, Aung San Suu Kyi's call for sanctions alienated middle class urbanites, unemployed workers, other opposition parties, and ethnic minority groups desperate for economic development.[49]

Given the Palestinian opposition's parlous state, if an analogy must be drawn to South Africa it should be to the 1960s, not the 1980s. In 1960, rising social unrest was quashed by the Sharpeville massacre, and the ANC was banned and its leaders jailed or exiled. Serious mass resistance did not resurface until 1976, when it was again suppressed by force. Sanctions, imposed after each crackdown, did not 'bite' until *sustained* mass unrest re-emerged in the mid-1980s, alongside a profound economic crisis. Palestine remains remote from this scenario.

Contradictions and Incoherence in Goals and Tactics

Reflecting the overall lack of political direction, the BDS campaign exhibits significant confusion over its goals and methods.

Disagreement over the *goals* of BDS is fundamental. As noted, BDS campaigners cannot specify even the bare outlines of a political solution to the Israeli-Palestinian conflict. Thus, for example, while Barghouti claims that most BDS advocates support a two-state solution,[50] Erakat suggests that the BDS Call is 'an implicit endorsement of the one-state solution'[51]— possibly because only this seems compatible with the right of return for all Palestinian refugees. Without a collective political vision, it is difficult to build a substantive consensus, or to make or measure progress towards its realisation.

Accordingly, there is also considerable confusion over the mechanisms by which BDS are meant to contribute to Palestinians' struggle. Writing on

---

[48] Jones, *Societies Under Siege*, ch.4.
[49] Ibid., ch.3.
[50] Barghouti, *BDS*, 51–52.
[51] Erakat, "BDS", 89.

South Africa, Crawford and Klotz suggest four basic mechanisms by which sanctions might 'work':

1. 'Compellance': BDS increases the cost of objectionable policies over their benefits, causing targets to change course.
2. 'Normative communication': BDS signals moral condemnation, 'persuading' targets to change their policies.
3. 'Resource denial': BDS denies the target the resources required to sustain its objectionable policies.
4. 'Political fracture': BDS stimulates a domestic legitimacy crisis, leading to a change of government and policy.[52]

As noted, the ANC saw sanctions working primarily through 'political fracture'. The 'resource denial' and 'compellance' mechanisms were only *co-constituted by* 'political fracture', since the costs of maintaining apartheid were affordable until mass unrest created new demands on state finances; consequently, these mechanisms did not work independently of mass mobilisation. The ANC had little faith in 'normative communication', rightly believing that oppressive regimes cannot be 'persuaded' to relinquish power.

Unlike the ANC, however, Palestinian BDS campaigners lack a coherent analysis of social power relations in Israel and a strategy for shifting these in which BDS is situated. Instead, they grasp at diverse, contradictory possibilities. Many propose that BDS can help in 'raising awareness' of Palestinians' plight, harming Israel's 'image' and diminishing its legitimacy—that is, 'normative communication'.[53] Exactly how this will generate political change, however, is never specified. As Falk observes, 'winning the "legitimacy war" may not be enough. It has not... [been for] the people of Tibet or Chechnya'.[54] Even in the far more favourable historical conditions of the mid-1970s, 'the PLO could point to a range of international supporters... but it was no closer to its goal of creating a

---

[52] Neta C. Crawford and Audie Klotz, 'How Sanctions Work: A Framework for Analysis', in: *How Sanctions Work: Lessons from South Africa*, eds. *idem*, (London, 1999).

[53] Erakat, "BDS", 95; Barghouti, *BDS*, 15–16; Global Exchange, *Divesting from Israel: A Handbook* (San Francisco, 2003), 6; GPAAWC, "Towards a Global Movement", 4–5, 62.

[54] Richard Falk, 'International Law, Apartheid and Israeli Responses to BDS', in: *Generation Palestine*, ed. Wiles, 97.

Palestinian homeland'.⁵⁵ To make strategic sense, one must specify a plausible causal sequence whereby delegitimising Israeli behaviour through BDS produces *some other change* which, *in turn*, leads to concrete political transformation. For example, the goal could be, as with early South African boycotts, to build Western public support for terminating US aid or more meaningful sanctions that would materially diminish Israel's repressive capabilities, or foster domestic political realignments.⁵⁶ On this view, the initial target of 'normative communication' is not actually Israel, but rather Western publics and governments, with a view to enabling later sanctions that would be aimed at Israel, to produce 'resource denial' or 'political fracture'.

However, not only is this two-stage strategy not articulated, but other activists openly reject the idea of an intermediate step, insisting that BDS will directly create change in Israel/ Palestine. Furthermore, this group is divided over how this might work. Some favour 'normative communication', suggesting that BDS 'relies on persuasion', seeks to 'convince Israel of its moral degradation and ethical isolation', and promotes 're-education in Israel'.⁵⁷ More common, however, is an ANC-esque perspective that 'the basic logic of BDS is... pressure – not diplomacy, persuasion, or dialogue'.⁵⁸ Yet exactly how this 'pressure' can generate change is, again, not clearly specified.

Some imply a 'compellance' logic, suggesting that BDS should 'raise the cost of the occupation'.⁵⁹ The problem with 'compellance', however, is that sanctioned governments are frequently willing to pay handsomely to pursue cherished political ends—over US$ 50bn in South Africa, for instance. The Israeli occupation's cost is already increasing without sanctions: after yielding net profits from 1967 to 1987, it now costs an estimated US$ 9bn yearly, of which military costs (US$ 6bn) are rising by 7

⁵⁵ Chamberlin, *Global Offensive*, 262.

⁵⁶ See US Campaign to End the Israeli Occupation (USCEIO), "Divest Now! A Handbook for Student Disinvestment Campaigns," September 16, 2010, 9, http://www.bdsmovement.net/2009/divest-now-handbook-5144; GPAWWC, "Towards a Global Movement", 54–55; Erakat, "BDS", 96.

⁵⁷ Falk, "International Law", 88; Banks, cited in Barghouti, *BDS*, 212; Ilan Pappe, 'Colonialism, the Peace Process and the Academic Boycott', in: *Generation Palestine*, ed. Wiles, 136.

⁵⁸ Lisa Taraki and Mark LeVine, 'Why Boycott Israel?', in: *The Case for Sanctions*, ed. Lim, 165.

⁵⁹ Dalit Baum and Merav Amir, 'Economic Activism Against the Occupation: Working From Within', in: *The Case for Sanctions*, ed. Lim, 41; see also Barghouti, *BDS*, 18, 25, 207.

per cent annually.⁶⁰ Yet, there is no prospect of the occupation ending. The key challenge, then, is not simply to raise Israel's costs, but to create conditions where Israel can no longer absorb rising costs. In South Africa, this took sustained mass mobilisation. In Palestine, there is no prospect of this.

Other activists suggest a 'resource denial' logic, similar to the second part of the two-step strategy suggested above. Disinvestment, it is suggested, can 'cut-off the funding used to sustain the occupation'; tourism boycotts can deny Israel 'vital investments and foreign currency'⁶¹; academic boycotts can weaken Israeli universities that supply 'the ideology and tools of occupation'⁶²; and an arms embargo would make Israel 'unable to continue its war crimes'.⁶³ Whether 'resource denial' makes strategic sense ultimately depends on the importance of these external flows in sustaining Israeli dominance. This is asserted by many BDS advocates, but never actually demonstrated.⁶⁴

Consider just the suggested arms embargo. Israel has received about US$ 3bn of US aid annually since the 1980s, much of which finances arms imports. However, Israel has also developed a large domestic armaments industry, which exports around three-quarters of its output, yielding US$ 6.5bn in 2016.⁶⁵ Because this industry probably relies heavily on international technical collaboration, components supplies, and so on, it would likely suffer if these links were severed. However, the South African experience shows that even embargoed states without an arms industry can develop one and produce sophisticated conventional, chemical, and even nuclear weapons. Sanctions never deprived South Africa's security forces of their coercive capacity; rather, sustained unrest made coercion an impractical means of maintaining long-term social order. Even if Israel's arms industry suffered relative decline under BDS, its existence and adaptive capacity makes it extremely unlikely that the Israeli state would be

---

⁶⁰ Shir Hever, 'BDS: Perspectives of an Israeli Economist', in: *Generation Palestine*, ed. Wiles, 115–116.

⁶¹ GPAWWC, "Towards a Global Movement", 70–73.

⁶² Nadia Ella, 'The Brain of the Monster', in: *The Case for Sanctions*, ed. Lim, 53–55.

⁶³ GPAWWC, "Towards a Global Movement", 53–54.

⁶⁴ For example, Barghouti, *BDS*, 50, 209, 232; Taraki and LeVine, "Why Boycott Israel?", 169; GPAWWC, "Towards a Global Movement", 42, 52.

⁶⁵ Anna Ahronheim, "Israeli Military Exports Rise to $6.5 Billion," *Jerusalem Post*, March 30, 2017.

starved of the equipment necessary to repress the Palestinians. And, again, without mass mobilisation, coercion will remain a viable option.

A final group of BDS activists invoke 'political fracture' logics. Barghouti envisages that under BDS pressure, initially Israel's 'colonial society bands together' but later, this

> unity starts to crack... the natural human quest for normalcy... will lead many... Israelis to withdraw their support for Israeli apartheid and occupation. Many may even join movements that aim to end both. Collapse of the multitiered system of oppression then becomes a matter of time... we've seen it all before in South Africa.[66]

Others likewise suggest that BDS will 'catalyse an anti-Zionist movement in Israeli society', 'create a critical mass of minority dissidents' and 'prompt the Israeli public to reconsider'.[67]

There are two problems here. First, again reflecting the lack of clear strategic leadership, activists disagree over whether BDS actually targets Israeli society and, if so, how. As Said had earlier insisted,[68] Warschawski asserts that 'the Palestinian national movement needs as many Israeli allies as possible... [consequently] BDS is addressed to the Israeli public'.[69] But Taraki and LeVine flatly assert: 'the BDS movement does not address the Israeli public directly in order to persuade it or to appeal to its sense of justice', despite having identified 'mov[ing] the Israeli body politic' as 'the logic of BDS' just four pages earlier.[70] Similarly, while Falk maintains that 'Israeli participation is valued highly'[71] and Pappe asserts 'it is vital to keep in touch with the progressive and radical Jewish dissidents' as a 'bridge to the wider public in Israel',[72] Barghouti is openly suspicious of 'soft Zionists' and the 'Zionist left' hijacking BDS to 'save Israel' as an apartheid state.[73] Unsurprisingly, despite the BDS committee's official invitation to

---

[66] Barghouti, BDS, 222–223.

[67] GPAWWC, "Towards a Global Movement", 53; Greenstein, cited in Atallah Hanna, 'Towards a Just and Lasting Peace: Kairos Palestine and the Lead of the Palestinian Church', in: *Generation Palestine*, ed. Wiles, 103; USCEIO, "Divest Now!", 10.

[68] Said, *Peace Process*, 284, 329, 296–297.

[69] Michael Warschawski, 'Yes to BDS! An Answer to Uri Avnery', in: *The Case for Sanctions*, ed. Lim, 195–197.

[70] Taraki and LeVine, "Why Boycott Israel?", 174, 170.

[71] Falk, "International Law", 87.

[72] Pappe, "Colonialism", 133.

[73] Barghouti, BDS, 32, 60.

'conscientious Israelis to support [their] call', even sympathetic Israelis perceive that 'Palestinian society does not welcome Israeli solidarity anymore'.[74]

A second problem concerns the simplistic South African analogy: it is simply inaccurate to suggest that BDS spurred a politically significant AAM among whites. When sanctioned, historically more liberal, English-speaking South Africans typically rallied around the incumbent government.[75] Afrikaners, meanwhile, expressed little guilt over their treatment of non-whites, even by the 1980s.[76] A late-1980s survey of Afrikaner elites found moderate to strong racism, hostility to majoritarian democracy, and fear of a 'communist' takeover.[77] Despite their growing sense of isolation, white elites overwhelmingly adopted a defiant attitude to BDS.[78] A 1989 poll found that, despite widespread falling living standards, only 24 per cent of whites favoured negotiations with the ANC and just 2 per cent a transfer of power to the black majority, while 59 per cent believed that those imposing sanctions were making 'extreme' demands and favoured making no concessions.[79] Rather than changing attitudes, popular responses to BDS were filtered through party affiliations, thereby confirming people's pre-existing beliefs.[80] Insofar as attitudes changed, they hardened: the right-wing Conservative Party increased its share of the vote from 17 to 29 per cent from 1981 to 1987, displacing the anti-apartheid Progressive Federal Party as the official parliamentary opposition.[81] Thus, there was no simple connection between BDS-induced economic pain and progressive changes in white opinion. As mentioned earlier, the really decisive shift

---

[74] Ra'anan Alexandrowicz and Rebecca Vilkomerson, 'An Effective Way of Supporting the Struggle', in: *The Case for Sanctions*, ed. Lim, 205.

[75] L. Schlemmer, 'External Pressures and Local Attitudes and Interests', in: *International Pressures and Political Change in South Africa*, ed. F. McA. Clifford-Vaughan, (Cape Town, 1978).

[76] Robin Cohen, *Endgame in South Africa? The Changing Structures and Ideology of Apartheid* (London, 1986), 10–13.

[77] Kate Manzo and Pat McGowan, 'Afrikaner Fears and the Politics of Despair: Understanding Change in South Africa,' *International Studies Quarterly*, vol. 36, no. 1, (1992).

[78] Van Wyck, "State Elites."

[79] Investor Responsibility Research Centre (IRRC), *The Impact of Sanctions on South Africa: Part II, Whites' Political Attitudes* (Washington, DC, 1990), 11, 14, 17.

[80] Ibid., 12, 14.

[81] Merle Lipton, "The Challenge of Sanctions," Discussion Paper 1, Centre for the Study of the South African Economy and International Finance, London School of Economics, 1990, 38.

was in the orientation of large-scale capital—not the wider public. As the ANC had perceived, big business leaders exercised profound structural influence over the state, and they played a significant role in lobbying for change and preparing the wider population for a negotiated settlement.[82]

From this perspective, targeting sanctions at particularly powerful social groups could be an important element of BDS strategy. However, reflecting its lack of coherent strategic vision, the Palestinian BDS National Committee has apparently undertaken no sustained analysis of the key forces and alliances underpinning the Israeli regime. The only individual who has apparently begun this vital analysis is the Israeli economist Shir Hever. He identifies large-scale conglomerates as the key linchpin of the Israeli state: their 'taxes fund Israel's military budget, and the owners… exert extensive political power over the Israeli political sphere'. Consequently, he suggests, BDS should target them to 'pressure… them to create positive change', inflicting maximal damage on companies' markets, investment flows, and stock prices, since only a 'painful impact' will force their hand.[83]

However, because the BDS movement lacks a centralised leadership and strategy, individual activists are instead left to decide how they think BDS might work and, accordingly, who to target. Barghouti insists that 'tactics and the choice of BDS targets at the local level must be governed by the context particularities, political conditions, and the readiness in will and capacity of the BDS activists… BDS can be adapted to according to the specific context in each country'.[84] 'Your preferences', one campaign tells activists, should dictate the choice of target.[85] A 'narrow focus', for example, on settlement products is 'perfectly fine'.[86] But this may simply be false. If the movement adopts the two-stage strategy suggested earlier, then initially focusing on firms in the Occupied Territories which 'epitomise the most oppressive aspects of the occupation'[87] may be sensible, insofar as no significant economic or political consequences within Israel are anticipated at this stage. However, if the intention is to immediately damage the Israeli economy, this focus is completely pointless. These firms are 'marginal… [they] do not contribute substantially to the

[82] Jones, *Societies Under Siege*, 81–90.
[83] Hever, "BDS", 112–115.
[84] Barghouti, *BDS*, 61, 217.
[85] Global Exchange, *Divesting*, 7.
[86] Barghouti, *BDS*, 219.
[87] USCEIO, "Divest Now!", 16.

settlements' economic sustainability',[88] they do not 'play the most significant role in shoring up Israel's occupation', and nor do they exercise significant political leverage.[89] Instead of adapting BDS to the context where activists are located, it would make far more sense to adapt them to the context in Israel/Palestine.

Means-Ends Confusion and Spurious 'Success' Claims

As some BDS activists recognise, '*BDS is not a goal in itself.* Rather, it is a means by which to pressure the Israeli government'.[90] Logically, therefore, success should be measured by the political effects BDS measures produce on the ground, and whether/how these advance the overall liberation strategy towards its final goal. However, because the campaign lacks both clear end goals and a strategy, this is impossible. Instead, the relationship between ends and means becomes muddled and spurious claims of 'success' are made despite no improvement in Palestinians' situation.

The US Campaign to End the Israeli Occupation, for instance, defines the *achievement of BDS measures* as the end goal, with BDS campaigns as the means to achieve them.[91] Activists report 'success' and 'achievements' merely when the volume of boycotts and disinvestment increases.[92] 'Success' is implicitly defined circularly: the 'immediate noteworthy outcomes' of one cultural boycott are further cultural boycotts.[93] This may make sense as part of the two-stage strategy hypothesised earlier, but even then we would still want to distinguish and evaluate: (1) the achievement of the initial boycott or disinvestment, (2) whether this generates political support for tougher sanctions, and then, for stage two, (3) the imposition of those sanctions, and (4) the consequential impact on the situation in Israel/Palestine. Given the extreme distance between (1) and (4), declar-

---

[88] Baum and Amir, "Economic Activism", 43.
[89] Hever, "BDS", 112.
[90] Hanna, "Towards a Just and Lasting Peace", 102.
[91] "Divest Now!", 16.
[92] For example, Hind Awwad, 'Six Years of BDS: Success!', in: *The Case for Sanctions*, ed. Lim, 180–184; Rafeef Ziadah, 'Worker-to-Worker Solidarity: BDS in the Trade Union Movement', in: *Generation Palestine*, ed. Wiles, 180–184; Australians for Palestine, *BDS: Boycott, Disinvestment, Sanctions – A Global Campaign to End Israeli Apartheid* (Melbourne, 2010), 41–46.
[93] Omar Barghouti, 'The Cultural Boycott: Israel vs. South Africa', in: *The Case for Sanctions*, ed. Lim, 30.

ing 'success!' at (1) is obviously premature. While it may boost campaigners' morale, it is nonetheless essential to maintain a clear means-end distinction, within an overall strategy, with clearly defined goals, to avoid hasty, romantic self-congratulation and to stimulate continual reflection on the efficacy of individual tactics.

This is doubly important because BDS has so far made no appreciable difference to Palestinians' situation. Sourani asks: 'what has been the impact on Israel's policies and practices? In short, we are living through the worst period in the history of the occupation'.[94] Economically, 'BDS has not had a significant impact on companies' outside of the Occupied Territories.[95] Indeed, 'the Israeli economy is stronger than ever'.[96] Politically, the Israeli left has been completely 'marginalised', with growing 'public sympathy for police and army violence against protestors'.[97] Even among those directly targeted by BDS, like academics, 'not much has changed'.[98] Peace talks, resumed in July 2013, collapsed in May 2014, with almost 70 per cent of Israelis backing their government's decision to walk away.[99]

Conclusion

Comparing the Palestinian BDS movement to its chosen analogue, South Africa, reveals several interrelated shortcomings. Unlike the ANC, the BDS movement lacks political leadership, clearly defined political goals, a coherent economic and political analysis of Israel/Palestine, and a strategy for transforming that situation. Instead, Palestinians have grasped at BDS out of desperation, seeking to reincarnate a meaningful liberation movement. Yet BDS has not catalysed greater Palestinian unity, nor is it realistic to hope that external solidarity can rebuild the Palestinian resistance. Reflecting Palestine's socio-political divisions, the BDS campaign exhibits strategic incoherence, generating muddled activist thinking and practices that are disconnected from the situation on the ground. The South African analogy distracts activists from confronting and surmounting these reali-

---

[94] Raji Sourani, 'Why Palestinians Called for BDS', in: *Generation Palestine*, ed. Wiles, 66.
[95] Hever, "BDS", 119.
[96] GPAWWC, "Towards a Global Movement", 137.
[97] Baum and Amir, "Economic Activism", 39.
[98] Pappe, "Colonialism", 134.
[99] Yifa Yaakov, "Most Israelis Support Peace Talks Freeze, Poll Shows," *Times of Israel*, May 7, 2014.

ties, permitting the comforting but ultimately delusional fantasy that victory is just around the corner.

This analysis suggests several priorities. The most urgent task remains the rejuvenation of the Palestinian liberation movement. BDS can play little meaningful role until Palestinians' divisions, disarray, and demobilisation are overcome and the masses are re-engaged in a sustained struggle for their own liberation. Many activists clearly recognise this, but are misled—partly by misrepresentations of the South African case—into thinking that BDS can catalyse this renewal. Actually, South Africa shows that, at best, BDS can supplement an active struggle, not create one. Second, the BDS National Committee must exert more forceful leadership, defining clear goals and a plausible strategy for achieving them. The current disarray—mindlessly celebrated by some as 'horizontalism'—must be supplanted by clear analysis of Israel/Palestine and appropriate strategic planning. Sympathetic scholars can contribute by studying the mechanisms used to maintain Israeli oppression and identifying weak points where external pressure could induce change. However, Palestinian activists remain responsible for building these evaluations into an overall strategy and supporting tactics and winning mass support.

Finally, the South African analogy must be used appropriately. Its main force is moral, equating the regimes to demand an equivalent international response. However, the alleged moral similarities of two targets tell us absolutely nothing about their relative vulnerability to BDS. Marked differences in social power relations, the degree and extent of opposition mobilisation, the mechanisms of rule, the political economy, and so on, mean that even identical sanctions produce divergent outcomes in different times and places. Invoking South Africa may help to reinspire the struggle for Palestinian freedom. However, as Marx warned, we must avoid 'parodying the old' or risk failing to confront present-day realities and priorities. The conditions that allowed South Africans to succeed do not exist in Israel/Palestine. They must be made anew.

CHAPTER 12

A Collision of Frames: The BDS Movement and Its Opponents in the United States

Sina Arnold

In the United States, the "Boycott, Divestment and Sanctions" (BDS) movement can claim increasing success in arenas as diverse as churches, food co-ops, and financial investments.[1,2] The first American boycott activities against Israel started after the UN conference on racism in Durban in 2001, where the South African NGO committee SANGOCO suggested taking action against Israel modeled on what had been done

---

[1] Mahmoud Kassem, "Soros Fund Drops Shares in Israel's SodaStream," *The National*, 2 August 2014. http://www.thenational.ae/business/industry-insights/economics/soros-fund-drops-shares-in-israels-sodastream#full

[2] Cp. Boycott, Divestment, Sanctions, "Palestinian Civil Society Call for BDS," last modified July 9, 2005, https://bdsmovement.net/call. The three main goals of the movement are made clear here: "(1) Ending the occupation and colonization of all Arab lands and dismantling the Wall; (2) Recognizing the fundamental rights of the Arab-Palestinian citizens of Israel to full equality; and (3) Respecting, protecting, and promoting the rights of Palestinian refugees to return to their homes and properties as stipulated in UN Resolution 194" (accessed September 29, 2017).

S. Arnold (✉)
Center for Research on Antisemitism (Zentrum für Antisemitismusforschung – ZfA), Berlin, Germany
e-mail: arnold@tu-berlin.de

© The Author(s) 2019
D. Feldman (ed.), *Boycotts Past and Present*, Palgrave Critical Studies of Antisemitism and Racism,
https://doi.org/10.1007/978-3-319-94872-0_12

against apartheid South Africa.[3] In the United States, this suggestion particularly found resonance on the campus, and petitions for divestment were submitted at approximately 50 American universities by both students and professors.[4] In 2005, Palestinian civil society actors issued a call for BDS and an international campaign began which also found support in the United States. Since then, boycotts against Israel have been a central field of action for various strands of the American left, and the movement gained even more prominence after the Israeli military operation "Cast Lead" 2009 in the Gaza strip. While BDS is supported by very different groups—for example, the thematically unrelated Occupy Wall Street encampment in Oakland voted almost unanimously for support of BDS[5]—the campaign currently is most prominent on college campuses and among pro-Palestinian student groups. Here, the issue is mostly about divestment, that is, withdrawing college funds from Israeli companies in general or targeting companies that profit from the occupation more specifically. Between 2012 and 2016, over 100 divestment resolutions were launched in US colleges and universities, out of which about half were successful.[6] BDS campaigns were launched among others at the universities of Berkeley, San Diego, Boston, and Irvine. Successes range from boycotting Israeli humus in the dining hall to student governments approving resolutions calling for divestment of university funds from Israel. Student groups are supportive of BDS on several hundred campuses. Moreover, over 1300 faculty members publicly endorse the "US Campaign for the Academic and Cultural Boycott of Israel" (USACBI).[7] And in recent years, several academic associations have passed resolutions endorsing the boycott. These include the American Studies Association, the Association for Asian American Studies, the Native American and Indigenous Association, the

---

[3] Manfred Gerstenfeld (ed.), *Academics Against Israel and the Jews* (Jerusalem, 2007).

[4] Kenneth S. Stern, *Antisemitism Today. How It Is the Same, How It Is Different, and How to Fight It* (New York, 2006), 119.

[5] Emma Silvers, "Occupy Oakland Votes 135-1 to Support BDS," *The Jewish News of Northern California*, 9 February 2012. http://www.jweekly.com/article/full/64224/occupy-oakland-votes-135-1-to-support-bds/

[6] Cp. "Scorecard on U.S. Campuses 2012–2016", AMCHA Initiative, https://amchainitiative.org/israel-divestment-vote-scorecard/ (accessed September 29, 2017).

[7] Cp. US Campaign for the Academic and Cultural Boycott of Israel, http://www.usacbi.org/endorsers/#org (accessed September 29, 2017).

Critical Ethnic Studies Association, the African Literature Association, and the National Women's Studies Association.[8]

BDS has caused heated debates off- and on-campus. Amongst other aspects, the campaign has been accused of furthering antisemitic positions or of being explicitly antisemitic. Under the catchphrase of "Campus Antisemitism," student BDS activities in particular have triggered lively discussions.[9] The background to these concerns is a parallel increase in documented antisemitic activity on college campuses.[10] And according to a survey by the Institute for Jewish and Community Research from 2011, 43% of all Jewish students perceived antisemitism on campus.[11] College campuses remain one of the first and most central places where young people are exposed to and enter into political activism, and one of the few American institutions that has significant influence on extraparliamentary political life.[12] Debates around BDS and "Campus Antisemitism" therefore also touch upon questions raised by the paradigm of the "New Antisemitism",[13] which focuses on the political left as one of the key contemporary actors and the relationship between antisemitism and critiques of Israel as one of the central topoi.

---

[8] Cp. "Academic Associations Endorsing Boycott and Resolutions", US Campaign for the Academic and Cultural Boycott of Israel, http://www.usacbi.org/academic-associations-endorsing-boycott/ and "Academic Boycott", UC Campaign for Palestinian Rights, https://uscpr.org/campaign/bds/bdswins/#1499798328669-154c6be3-635c (accessed September 29, 2017).

[9] Kenneth L. Marcus, 'The Resurgence of Anti-Semitism on American College Campuses,' *Current Psychology*, vol. 26, no. 3/4, (2007), 206–212; Eunice G. Pollack (ed.), *Antisemitism on the Campus: Past&Present* (Boston, 2011); Jeffrey A. Ross and Melanie L. Schneider, 'Antisemitism on the Campus. Challenge and Response', in: *Antisemitism in America Today: Outspoken Experts Explore the Myths*, ed. Jerome A. Chanes, (New York, 1995); Gary A. Tobin, Aryeh K. Weinberg, and Jenna Ferer, *The Uncivil University* (San Francisco, 2005).

[10] Deborah E. Lipstadt, 'Strategic Responses to Anti-Israelism and Anti-Semitism on the North American Campus', in: *American Jewry and the College Campus. Best of Times or Worst of Tmes?*, eds. Deborah E. Lipstadt, Samuel G. Freedman, and Chaim Seidler-Feller, (New York City, 2005), 5–26.

[11] Aryeh Weinberg, *Alone on the Quad: Understanding Jewish Student Isolation on Campus* (San Francisco, 2011), 3.

[12] Kenneth S. Stern, *Antisemitism Today. How It Is the Same, How It Is Different, and How to Fight It* (New York, 2006), 118.

[13] Doron Rabinovici, Ulrich Speck, and Natan Sznaider (ed.), *Neuer Antisemitismus? Eine globale Debatte* (Frankfurt am Main, 2004).

Therefore debates around BDS on US college campuses represent a microcosm of debates around antisemitism from and within the left. This chapter aims to explore this microcosm by focusing on the two sides of the debate: BDS advocates and BDS opponents. Certainly, BDS is a diverse social movement with different players and positions. However, most BDS advocates in one way or another identify as progressives, radicals or leftists. Its critics are very diverse—while most of them are on the political right, they also include prominent leftists and supporters of the Palestinian cause such as Noam Chomsky and Norman Finkelstein. In order to stress the opposing points of view, this chapter analyzes the opposing ends of the spectrum, remaining necessarily schematic. Rather than exploring BDS and whether or not it is antisemitic, this essay seeks to understand the discourse surrounding BDS. Its data is based on qualitative interviews with Jewish and non-Jewish pro-Palestinian and anti-war activists[14] and on participant observation at events and conferences as well as analysis of movement literature. After describing the problems posed by these divergent analytical frames, this chapter points to possible political consequences, both for the BDS movement and its critics.

CASE STUDY: BUTLER/BARGHOUTI AT BROOKLYN COLLEGE

The following event provides a useful case study for the aforementioned dynamics. On February 7, 2013, a panel discussion entitled "BDS Movement for Palestinian rights" took place at Brooklyn College in New York City, featuring Omar Barghouti and Judith Butler. Barghouti is the founding committee member of the "Palestinian Campaign for the Academic and Cultural Boycott of Israel," one of the leaders of the BDS movement and an active public speaker, whereas Butler is a prominent philosopher, literary theorist, and outspoken Jewish critic of Israel. The event was initiated by "Students for Justice in Palestine" (SJP), an umbrella organization founded in 2001 for Palestinian advocacy work that has

---

[14] The 30 interview partners come from five interrelated currents of the extraparliamentary far left: the anti-war movement, Palestine solidarity groups, Occupy Wall Street and Jewish-identified groups. Moreover, three individuals active in the queer and anarchist scenes were part of the sample. Many of these groups are also part of the BDS movement. The activists interviewed were between 19 and 73 years old and residents of New York City or the San Francisco Bay Area. Sixteen identified as Jewish, most others as atheists with a Christian background, two as Muslim and one as Mormon—although almost all perceived themselves as non-religious.

become, according to the Anti-Defamation League,[15] "the fastest growing and most active anti-Israel group in the U.S." and "the primary organizer of anti-Israel activity on American college campuses." SJP has around 190 chapters and affinity groups, organizing activities such as lectures, actions, university divestment campaigns as well as national conferences.[16]

The political science department at Brooklyn College, part of the City University of New York (CUNY), co-sponsored the event with other groups. Weeks before the event a sharp public debate broke out which attracted national media attention. Opponents criticized the department for co-sponsoring and called for it to cancel the event or withdraw the sponsorship. Among them were the Anti-Defamation League, mayoral candidate William Thompson Jr., several assemblymen, ten members of the City Council who wrote an open letter to the college's president, and the lawyer and right-wing political commentator Alan Dershowitz[17] who had called the event an "anti-Israel hatefest."[18] Anti-BDS students circulated a petition[19] and City Council members threatened to withhold funding to all of Brooklyn College unless the conference was canceled.[20] New York mayor Bloomberg got involved, criticizing BDS but supporting free speech and by extension the right for the event to happen.[21] In the

---

[15] Anti-Defamation League, "The 2013 Top Ten Anti-Israel Groups in the U.S." Accessed October 22, 2013. http://www.adl.org/assets/pdf/israel-international/israel%2D%2Dmiddle-east/Top-Ten-2013-Report.pdf, p. 19.

[16] Cp. Students for Justice in Palestine, http://nationalsjp.org/ (accessed September 29, 2017).

[17] Alan Dershowitz, "Brooklyn College's Anti-Israel Hatefest," *New York Daily News*, 30 January 2013. http://www.nydailynews.com/opinion/brooklyn-college-anti-israel-hatefest-article-1.1250553

[18] Cp. Lewis A. Fiddler, "The Council of the City of New York," published 29 January 2013. http://coreyrobin.files.wordpress.com/2013/02/letter-from-lew-fidler.pdf

[19] Steve Lipman, "Brooklyn College BDS Brouhaha," *The New York Jewish Week*, 30 January 2013. http://www.thejewishweek.com/news/new-york-news/brooklyn-college-bds-brouhaha

[20] Cp. Baher Azmy and Heidi Boghosian, "Letter to City Council Members Who Threatened to Withhold Funding to Brooklyn College over BDS Student Event," published 11 February 2013. http://ccrjustice.org/files/CityCouncilLetter_2%208%2013_PAL%20%282%29.pdf

[21] Kate Taylor, "Mayor Backs College's Plan to Welcome Critics of Israel," *The New York Times*, 6 February 2013. http://www.nytimes.com/2013/02/07/nyregion/bloomberg-defends-brooklyn-colleges-right-to-bds-talk.html?_r=1&

end, the panel took place with police outside checking bags of the 200 attendees whose names were on an approved list, as 150 anti-BDS protesters gathered in front of the building. During Butler's speech, four Jewish students were removed from the event for holding literature and flyers with anti-BDS positions in their hands.[22] This caused the controversy to continue, as the organizers were accused of antisemitism on account of their decision to eject these students, and for stifling critical debate during the question and answer period.[23] Four months later, the Zionist Organization of America (ZOA) filed a student-backed legal complaint against the college using Title VI of the Civil Rights Act to allege anti-Jewish discrimination against the four students.[24,25] With the help of an outside law firm, the university subsequently launched an investigation that interviewed 40 witnesses and released a detailed 40-page report two months later, during which time the student group sought legal aid from the Center for Constitutional Rights. Finally, the report stated that while many things were not well planned, during the event there was no evident intent to discriminate based on the religion of the removed students or other attendees. However, it also stated that the removal was motivated by a "political viewpoint."[26] The college eventually reached a negotiated settlement with ZOA over the Title VI complaint.[24] In March 2014,

---

[22] Natalie Schachar, "Pro-Israel Students Ousted from BDS Event," *Tablet*, 8 February 2013. http://www.tabletmag.com/scroll/123792/pro-israel-students-ousted-from-bds-event; Ari Ziegler, "Silenced by Brooklyn College. A Graduate Student Describes How He Was Kicked Out of a Pro-Palestinian Event," *The New York Daily News*, 12 February 2013. http://www.nydailynews.com/opinion/silenced-brooklyn-college-article-1.1261287

[23] Reuven Blau, "Pro-Palestine Student Group at Brooklyn College Defends Booting Four Jewish Students, Despite Audio Recording," *The New York Daily News*, 14 February 2013. http://www.nydailynews.com/new-york/brooklyn/brooklyn-college-student-group-defends-booting-jewish-students-controversial-forum-article-1.1264648

[24] Susan Tuchman, "ZOA Negotiates Important Victory for Jewish Community at Brooklyn College." Last modified March 12, 2014. http://zoa.org/2014/03/10235694-zoa-negotiates-important-victory-for-jewish-community-at-brooklyn-college/

[25] Title VI of the Civil Rights Act of 1964 prohibits discrimination based on race, color or national origin. Since 2010, it also covers members of religious groups, therefore allowing the addressing of antisemitism.

[26] Cp. "Report on BDS Forum held at Brooklyn College on February 7, 2013," Brooklyn College, accessed September 29, 2017, http://de.scribd.com/doc/135651806/REPORT-ON-BDS-FORUM-HELD-AT-BROOKLYN-COLLEGE-ON-FEBRUARY-7-2013

Brooklyn College President Karen Gould apologized for how the school handled the event and has since institutionalized new guidelines for the management of public events hosted by student clubs.[27]

This short descriptive background to the event illustrates how heated these debates are and how they take on a wider social relevance which extends into the political arena. Moreover, this example shows there is typically little room for actual exchange of views. These dynamics can be understood by way of frame analysis, an approach from Social Movement studies developed by Erving Goffmann[28] that in the past 20 years has become one of the central paradigms for research on movements. Frames are "schemata of interpretation" that allow actors to identify and categorize events and experience. Such a scheme of interpretation "simplifies and condenses the 'world out there' by selectively punctuating and encoding objects, situations, events, experiences, and sequences of actions within one's present or past environment," as David Snow and Robert Benford[29] put it. Framing functions in much the same way as a frame around a picture: The attention is focused on those issues that are supposed to be highlighted and away from those that can be ignored, on what is important and away from irrelevant items in the field of view.[30] This also helps movements explain their actions and motivate their members. So far, there has been only limited connection between Social Movement studies and research on antisemitism, which is surprising given that antisemitic mobilization has most often been a collective effort. Analyzing collective action frames in the given case allows us to answer the two following questions: Firstly, what counts as a political problem for the BDS movement, and by extension

---

[27] Cp. "Statement of President Gould regarding the February 7, 2013 BDS event," Louis D. Brandeis Center, last modified March 10, 2014, http://brandeiscenter.com/index.php?/news/news_full/brandeis_center_welcomes_brooklyn_college_administrations_apology_for_its_h

[28] Erving Goffman, *Frame Analysis: An Essay on the Organization of Experience* (New York, 1974).

[29] Robert D. Benford and David A. Snow, 'Master Frames and Cycles of Protest', in: *Frontiers in Social Movement Theory*, eds. Aldon D. Morris and Carol McClurg Mueller, (New Haven, 1992), 133–55.

[30] Hank Johnston and John A. Noakes, 'Frames of Protest: A Road Map to a Perspective', in: *Frames of Protest. Social Movements and the Framing Perspective*, eds. Hank Johnston and John A. Noakes, (Lanham, 2005), 1–32.

what does not?[31] Secondly, how do BDS opponents present competing interpretations by way of "counter-frames"?

Boycott, Divestment, and Sanctions Frames

BDS arguments are always closely linked to an analysis of the Middle East conflict and rely upon a handful of central frames.

Firstly, the interpretation of BDS actions within an "Antiracism" frame is dominant. The "International Jewish Anti-Zionist Network" (IJAN) provides a typical characterization: "BDS is an anti-racist movement against the daily, brutal occupation of Palestine and military threat to the region by the State of Israel."[32] In this frame, Israel is portrayed as either an inherently racist state or a state with specific racist policies. Therefore, BDS activism by extension understands itself at a fundamental level as an antiracist movement. This frame is especially powerful and attractive in the United States given that antiracism has been a central paradigm for the American Left since the Abolitionists and later the Civil Rights movement and New Left.[33] The consequences of this frame are analyzed below.

This frame is strongly linked to an "Anti-colonialism/Anti-imperialism" frame. In his central book *Boycott, Divestment, Sanctions: The Global Struggle for Palestinian Rights,* Omar Barghouti claims that BDS calls are "directed strictly against Israel as a colonial power that violates Palestinian rights and international law".[34] In her CUNY presentation, Butler spoke of BDS as an "opposition to oppression, to the multi-faceted dimensions

---

[31] This question is particularly relevant against the background of insight from the sociology of social problems (Michael Schetsche, *Empirische Analyse sozialer Probleme. Das wissenssoziologische Programm* (Wiesbaden, 2013)): It is not objective factors that lead to the perception of a given situation as a "problem", much rather it is processes of social definition that allow it to be perceived as a "problem" by individuals or movements in the first place.

[32] Cp. "Statement by Jewish Activists and Organizations active in BDS against Israel," accessed August 2, 2014. http://www.akteure.palaestina-heute.de/Religiose_Organisationen/Judische_Organisationen/International_Jewish_Anti-Zion/body_international_jewish_anti-zion.html

[33] Eli Zaretsky, *Why America Needs a Left: A Historical Argument* (Cambridge, 2012).

[34] Omar Barghouti, *Boycott, Divestment, Sanctions: The Global Struggle for Palestinian Rights* (Chicago, 2011), 149.

of a militarized form of settler colonialism",[35] while on other occasions she has characterized Israel as "a pernicious colonialism that calls itself democracy".[36] These semantic frames in turn open the way for comparisons with apartheid, as Barghouti makes clear in an article in *The Nation*: "Our South Africa moment has arrived".[37] The "Anti-colonialism" frame is often used together or interchangeably with an "Anti-imperialism" frame, one of the dominant schemes of political interpretation on the US left.[38] Moishe Postone speaks of a general "neo-anti-imperialism" on the left, particularly since the 9/11 attacks.[39] In this view, the United States and Israel are perceived as the centers of global imperialism. Taking their cues explicitly from the BDS movement, the editors of the left-intellectual *Jacobin Magazine* consequently portray the Middle East conflict as "a focal point of anti-imperialist struggle, where peasants and slum-dwellers are now fighting a desperate struggle against tanks and F-16 s".[40]

Another argument is to frame calls for boycott and divestment from Israel as an issue of human rights. Butler's Brooklyn College speech portrayed BDS as primarily a "movement to achieve basic political rights for Palestinians".[35] The *Handbook for Student Divestment Campaigns*, published by the "US Campaign to End the Israeli Occupation," points specifically to the *strategic* use of this frame when dealing with political opponents. It reads: "Be sure you can set terms for the debate so you are not cornered into a defensive position that you can't get out of. Don't let your main points drown in a sea of details about past peace deals or

---

[35] Judith Butler, "Judith Butler's Remarks to Brooklyn College on BDS," *The Nation*, 7 February 2013. www.thenation.com/article/172752/judith-butlers-remarks-brooklyn-college-bds

[36] Judith Butler, *Parting Ways. Jewishness and the Critique of Zionism* (New York, 2012), 24.

[37] Omar Barghouti, "BDS for Palestinian Rights: 'Equality or Nothing!'" *The Nation*, 3 May 2012. http://www.thenation.com/blog/167708/opinionnation-forum-boycott-divestment-sanctions-bds#; Omar Barghouti and Lisa Taraki, "Academic freedom in context." *Al-Ahram*, no. 747, 16–22 June 2005. http://weekly.ahram.org.eg/Archive/2005/747/op13.htm

[38] Chris Dixon and Barbara Epstein, 'A Politics and a Sensibility: The Anarchist Current on the U.S. Left', in: *Toward a New Socialism*, eds. Anatole Anton and Richard Schmitt, (Lanham, 2007), 455.

[39] Moishe Postone, 'History and Helplessness. Mass Mobilization and Contemporary Forms of Anticapitalism,' *Public Culture*, vol. 18, no. 1, (2006), 93–110, 96.

[40] Editors. "Palestine and the Left," *Jacobin Magazine*, no. 10, 21 April 2013. http://jacobinmag.com/2013/04/palestine-and-the-left/

2000 years of anti-Semitism. Stick to your main point that human rights are being violated (…)".[41] "Human rights" is a frame that finds wide resonance in large segments of the American public and therefore gets applied both in practice and strategically.

Finally, Jewish identity claims are often applied in BDS debates as counter-frames: To refute accusations of antisemitism, Jewish activists often use a form of strategic essentialism[42] to make themselves visible, or they are likewise made visible by others. For example, in criticizing BDS opponents, Omar Barghouti writes: "The growing support among progressive European and American Jews for effective pressure on Israel is one counter-argument that is not well publicized".[43] Thus the very presence of Jewish BDS supporters is turned into an "argument" against BDS critics. This strategic use of the "Jewish identity" frame has to be understood against the background of current general debates over representation and identity within the American-Jewish community—conflicts referred to by some as a "crisis"[44] or even a "growing civil war".[45] Since World War II, American-Jewish identity has been strongly centered on the Holocaust and support of the state of Israel. This identification, however, is increasingly challenged by Jewish leftists who struggle for alternative definitions of ethnic-religious identity, who refer instead to the prophetic tradition, the principle of "tikkun olam," and to the tradition of Jewish involvement in the socialist, communist, and Civil Rights movements. In turn they criticize Israel as well as mainstream Jewish advocacy organizations in the United States for claiming to represent all American Jews. In the words of Judith Butler, this strategy is about "affirming a different Jewishness than the one in whose name the Israeli state claims to speak".[46]

Finally, "Freedom of speech/Academic Freedom" is another important frame. The national organization "Jewish Voice for Peace" (JVP),

---

[41] US Campaign to End the Israeli Occupation, "Divest Now! A Handbook for Student Divestment Campaigns." Accessed September 21, 2017. https://bdsmovement.net/files/2011/02/divestguide.pdf, p. 30.

[42] Gayatri C. Spivak, 'Can the Subaltern Speak?', in: *Marxism and the Interpretation of Culture*, eds. Cary Nelson and Lawrence Grossberg, (Chicago, 1988), 271–314.

[43] Omar Barghouti, "The Boycott and Palestinian Groups," *Counterpunch*, 21 October 2008. http://www.counterpunch.org/2008/10/21/the-boycott-and-palestinian-groups/

[44] Peter Beinart, *The Crisis of Zionism* (New York: Times Books, 2012), 60.

[45] Ruth Rosen, "American Jews and the Fate of Israel," *Dissent Magazine*, 12 May 2011. http://www.dissentmagazine.org/online_articles/americans-jews-and-the-fate-of-israel

[46] Judith Butler, *Parting Ways. Jewishness and the Critique of Zionism* (New York, 2012), 2.

which co-sponsored the CUNY event, collected signatures with a petition titled "Support Free Speech and Open Debate at Brooklyn College."[47] Donna Nevel of JVP and of the group "Jews Say No" made similar free speech arguments at a press conference, advocating for the "right to engage in critical examination and inquiry of important political ideas".[48] But for BDS advocates, freedom of speech means more than being able to conduct events, it also means having a university that is free of the influence by pro-Israel organizations like the "American Israel Public Affairs Committee" (AIPAC). Their activities supposedly influence the curriculum and the general atmosphere on campus in ways that lead to the impossibility of critically addressing Israel's politics and role in the Middle East conflict. Thereby, the frame "Freedom of speech/Academic Freedom" touches upon very fundamental questions of discursive hegemony in the United States. But the application of this frame is not limited to the US context: It also addresses an alleged lack of effective academic freedom for Palestinian students in the occupied territories due to Israeli military control. In 2005, Omar Barghouti noted that for BDS critics.[49]

> [f]reedom to produce and exchange knowledge and ideas was deemed sacrosanct regardless of the prevailing conditions. There are two key faults in this argument. It is inherently biased – regarding as worthy only the academic freedom of Israelis. The fact that Palestinians are denied basic rights as well as academic freedom due to Israel's military occupation is lost on those parroting it. And its privileging of academic freedom as a value above all other freedoms is antithetical to the very foundation of human rights. The right to live, and freedom from subjugation and colonial rule, to name a few, must be of more import than academic freedom. If the latter contributes in any way to suppression of the former, more fundamental rights, it must give way. If the struggle to attain the former necessitates a level of restraint on the latter, then so be it.

By applying the frame of "Academic Freedom" not only does Barghouti call for broadening questions of academic freedom internationally and

---

[47] Cp. Jewish Voice for Peace, "Support Free Speech and Open Debate at Brooklyn College." accessed June 9, 2013. http://salsa.democracyinaction.org/o/301/p/dia/action/public/?action_KEY=12412

[48] Donna Nevel, "Supporting Free Speech at Brooklyn College." Last modified February 5, 2013. http://www.muzzlewatch.com/2013/02/05/supporting-free-speech-at-brooklyn-college/?utm_source=feedburner&utm_medium=feed&utm_campaign=Feed%3A+MuzzleWatch+%28MuzzleWatch%29

[49] Omar Barghouti and Lisa Taraki, "Academic Freedom in Context," *Al-Ahram*, no. 747, 16–22 June 2005. http://weekly.ahram.org.eg/Archive/2005/747/op13.htm

boycotting a country that in his eyes practically negates academic freedom for Palestinians, he also debates academic freedom in the context of human rights, which he sees as more fundamental and primary. Butler[50] agrees, noting that "academic freedom is essentially linked to other kinds of freedoms and entitlements and comes to make sense as a doctrine only in the context where these other broader freedoms are actively articulated and secured." According to Barghouti, this might also serve as a kind of wake-up call for Israeli society, opening up discussions in the country and its universities. Thus he claims that "[f]rom this angle the boycott is seen as generating true academic freedom".[51]

To summarize then, BDS advocates mostly argue their cause in the frames "Antiracism," "Anti-colonialism"/"Anti-imperialism," "Human rights," "Jewish identity," and "Freedom of speech/Academic Freedom." The next section analyzes the forms of argumentation used by BDS opponents.

Anti-BDS Frames

BDS campaigns mostly take place on college campuses, and many critics are located here as well, often not only targeting BDS but anti-Israel activities in general. These opponents of BDS draw attention to conferences and events, collect signatures against divestment efforts, lobby universities and politicians, and put out anti-BDS resources for events and workshops. Groups involved include "Scholars for Peace in the Middle East," "StandWithUs," AIPAC, and "The Israel on Campus Coalition," a network of national organizations that collaborate to promote education and advocacy regarding Israel on campuses across the United States.[3] Heated debates have also taken place in "Hillel," the largest global Jewish student organization, around acceptable positions on Israel, and by extension, what groups are permitted within its ranks.[52]

---

[50] Judith Butler, 'Israel/Palestine and the Paradoxes of Academic Freedom,' *Radical Philosophy*, vol. 135, (2006), 8–17.

[51] Omar Barghouti and Lisa Taraki, "Academic Freedom in Context," *Al-Ahram*, no. 747, 16–22 June 2005. http://weekly.ahram.org.eg/Archive/2005/747/op13.htm

[52] The current "Hillel" guidelines on Israel state that the organization will not "partner with, house, or host organizations, groups, or speakers that as a matter of policy or practice: [...] Support boycott of, divestment from, or sanctions against the State of Israel" (cp. "Hillel Israel Guidelines," Hillel, accessed September 21, 2017, http://www.hillel.org/jewish/hillel-israel/hillel-israel-guidelines). Some chapters, however, have declared themselves "Open Hillels" and openly welcomed anti-zionist groups (cp. Philip Weiss, "Meet the Jewish

For opponents, the main frame for portraying BDS is "Antisemitism." Commenting on the Butler/Barghouti debate, a trustee at CUNY said, "These BDS advocates single out Israel as a cover for rank anti-Semitism",[53] and a Brooklyn assemblyman warned: "We are talking about the danger of a second Holocaust here".[54] An anti-BDS student activist involved in this conflict was quoted as saying that "[t]he political science department is known to be anti-Semitic",[55] while the ZOA spoke 11 times of "the anti-Semitic BDS event" in a single press release.[24] In the course of the event, the editor-in-chief of the Jewish publication *Algemeiner* said on a public panel that "The BDS movement is an 'anti-Semitic movement'".[56] This line of argumentation holds true more generally within anti-BDS discourse, for example, the "Simon Wiesenthal Center" entitled one of its information brochures "BDS: An Anti-Semitic, Anti-Israel Pill".[57] In a similar vein, Israel's Prime Minister Benjamin Netanyahu in an address to AIPAC stated that "[a]ttempts to boycott, divest and sanction Israel, the most threatened democracy on Earth, are simply the latest chapter in the long and dark history of anti-Semitism. Those who wear [...] the BDS label should be treated exactly as we treat any anti-Semite or bigot".[58] Framing pro-Palestinian activities, and left-wing politics in general, as antisemitic is a recurring response by critics and opponents of these movements. The most recent visible movement of the extraparliamentary left, Occupy Wall Street (OWS), experienced this several times. Although there

students who are taking on the Jewish establishment," *Mondoweiss*, February 24, 2014, http://mondoweiss.net/2014/02/jewish-students-establishment.html

[53] Jeffrey S. Wiesenfeld, "Taxpayer Funded BDS at CUNY Is Illegitimate, Racist and Anti-Semitic," *The Algemeiner*, 29 January 2013. http://www.algemeiner.com/2013/01/29/taxpayer-funded-bds-at-cuny-is-illegitimate-racist-and-anti-semitic/

[54] Amy Schiller, "NYC Politicos Rally Against Brooklyn College BDS Panel," *The Daily Beast*, 2 January 2013. http://www.thedailybeast.com/articles/2013/02/01/nyc-politicos-rally-against-brooklyn-college-bds-panel.html

[55] Ibid.

[56] Alex Kane, "Israel Boosters Threaten Civil Rights Claim Against Brooklyn College and Suggest Barring Student Activists from Campus," *Mondoweiss*, 14 February 2013. http://mondoweiss.net/2013/02/threaten-brooklyn-activists.html

[57] Harold Brackman, "Boycott Divestment Sanctions (BDS) Against Israel: An Anti-Semitic, Anti-Peace Poison Pill." Accessed September 21, 2017. http://www.wiesenthal.com/atf/cf/%7B54d385e6-f1b9-4e9f-8e94-890c3e6dd277%7D/REPORT_313.PDF

[58] Benjamin Netanyahu, "Full Transcript of Netanyahu's 2014 AIPAC Address," *The Times of Israel*, 4 March 2014. http://www.timesofisrael.com/full-transcript-of-netanyahus-aipac-address/#ixzz39t0Eg3YT

indeed were singular instances of open antisemitism within OWS,⁵⁹ they were in no way representative of the movement generally and were often disavowed by activists. Some US and Israeli commentators, however, have accused the entire Occupy movement of "naked antisemitism," to quote Phyllis Chesler,⁶⁰ or imagined a situation comparable to pre-World War II Germany, as in an article in Israel Today.⁶¹

Secondly, BDS critics have a concept which is intended to repudiate the "Jewish identity" frame of their BDS opponents: "Jewish self-hatred." This accusation is a response to the strategic essentialism of Jewish supporters of BDS and is mostly applied by Jewish critics. In the debate at hand, some Jewish commentators called Judith Butler a "'self-hating Jew' by any standard,"⁶² a charge she had experienced before.⁶³ Jewish activists report being called "Nazis" by other members of the Jewish community during pro-Palestinian demonstrations, being accused of self-hatred by family members, labeled as collaborators like the *Judenräte*,⁶⁴ or finding their names on collections like the "Jewish S.H.I.T. List – Self-Hating and/or Israel-Threatening" on the internet.⁶⁵ Debates from within the American-Jewish community are at the heart of many of these accusations.

---

⁵⁹ Sina Arnold, "'Bad for the Jews?' Antisemitismus und die 'Occupy'-Bewegung in den USA', in: *Jahrbuch für Antisemitismusforschung 21*, ed. Stefanie Schüler-Springorum, (Berlin, 2012), 370–91.

⁶⁰ Phyllis Chesler, "Occupy Wall Street's Anti-Semitism Should Scare You," *Arutz Sheva*, 20 October 2011. http://www.israelnationalnews.com/Articles/Article.aspx/10737#.U-YA3BkQ8Xy

⁶¹ Cp. *Israel Today*, 16 October 2011. http://www.israeltoday.co.il/News/tabid/178/nid/22978/language/en-U.S./Default.aspx

⁶² Cp. Olivier Melnick "American Campuses: A New Breeding Ground for a New Judeophobia!" 9 February 2013, accessed September 29, 2017. http://www.newantisemitism.com/israel/american-campuses-a-new-breeding-ground-for-a-new-judeophobia

⁶³ Raphael Ahren, "Frankfurt Under Fire for Giving €50,000 Prize to 'Virulent Israel Critic'", *The Times of Israel*, 4 September 2012. http://www.timesofisrael.com/frankfurt-giving-prize-named-after-passionate-israel-supporter-to-us-jewish-academic-who-critics-say-demonizes-israel/; Benjamin Weinthal, "German Jewish Leader: Rescind Israel Hater's Prize," *The Jerusalem Post*, 27 August 2012. http://www.jpost.com/International/German-Jewish-leader-Rescind-Israel-haters-prize

⁶⁴ This accusation was made by right-wing publicist Pamela Gellner, cp. "Chilling: Nazi Party Representatives Attend 1933 Berlin Jewish Community Charity Drive Gathering," last modified December 18, 2011, http://pamelageller.com/2011/12/chilling-nazi-party-representatives-attend-1933-berlin-jewish-community-charity-drive-gathering.html/

⁶⁵ Cp. Masada2000 accessed September 8, 2013. http://www.masada2000.org/list-A.html

Butler[66] hints at this dynamic when she writes: "When one set of Jews labels another set of Jews 'anti-Semitic', they are trying to monopolize the right to speak in the name of the Jews. So the allegation of anti-Semitism is actually a cover for an intra-Jewish quarrel."

Finally, the frame of "Academic Freedom" is not only used by BDS advocates, but also by BDS critics. Yet it takes a slightly different form: As shown above, in their application of this frame, BDS advocates demand the right to bring up specific issues and to have a critical discussion. This does not necessarily mean a politically neutral debate. Much rather, the bottom line of the argument is to keep academia free of political influence from pro-Israel lobby groups trying to push an agenda. BDS critics take a similarly structural approach in their take on "academic freedom." However, in their perception, academic freedom suffers from a liberal bias, particularly in the humanities and social sciences. This fact allegedly causes faculties to endorse events like the Barghouti/Butler panel and makes for an anti-Israel bias in classrooms. Concerning the CUNY event, Alan Dershowitz stated: "Shame on the Brooklyn College political science department for falsely invoking academic freedom and freedom of speech to deny equal freedoms to those who disagree with its extremist politics".[67] And according to Manfred Gerstenfeld, board member of the pro-Israel research organization "Jerusalem Center for Public Affairs," "BDS is also an expression of the specific problems of various Western universities where major antisocietal forces have developed over the decades. The boycott actions against Israel have brought further proof that 'tenured radicals' have permeated a number of faculties and campuses, where they try to undermine society rather than objectively pursue knowledge".[68] Judith Butler, in return, criticizes the consequences of this idea of academic freedom which aims for a regulated balance of opinions, claiming that "[u]nder the name of academic freedom, this conservative seizure of academic freedom explicitly calls for increased surveillance of faculty viewpoints and activities".[50] Butler sees a danger of heightened surveillance based on political viewpoints. Ironically, BDS critics mirror her argumentation: As some earlier boycott resolutions have suggested excluding

---

[66] Judith Butler, "Judith Butler Responds to Attack: 'I Affirm a Judaism That Is Not Associated with State Violence'," *Mondoweiss*, 27 August 2012. http://mondoweiss.net/2012/08/judith-butler-responds-to-attack-i-affirm-a-judaism-that-is-not-associated-with-state-violence.html

[67] Alan Dershowitz, "Brooklyn College Political Science Department's Israel Problem," *The Huffington Post Blog*, 30 January 2013. http://www.huffingtonpost.com/alan-dershowitz/brooklyn-college-politica_b_2582561.html

[68] Manfred Gerstenfeld (ed.), *Academics Against Israel and the Jews* (Jerusalem, 2007), 53.

critical Israeli academics and intellectuals from BDS campaigns, they fear that boycotts would suspend or grant academic rights based on political viewpoints or even national identity and would thereby stifle the freedom to hold divergent political opinions.

Different Frames of Mind

Having laid out the central frames of BDS advocates and opponents, the following paragraphs briefly sum up why the dominant divergent frames on both sides are bound to collide, why these different frames are mostly irreconcilable, and moreover, why they often stand in the way of truth seeking on account of their analytical shortcomings.

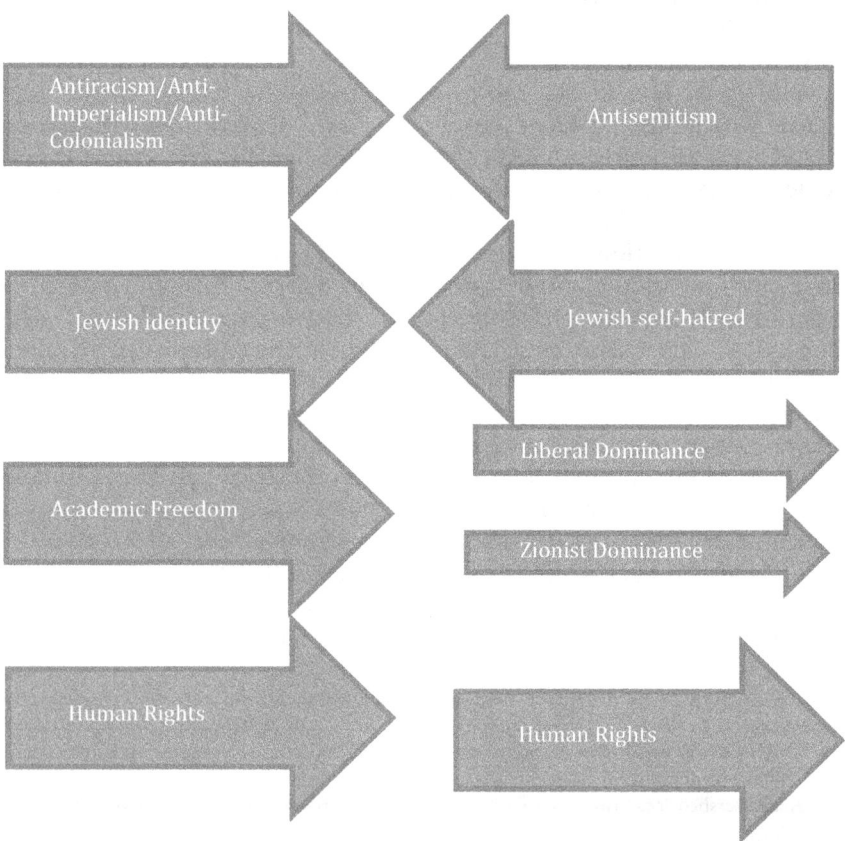

The biggest clash is between BDS' "Antiracism" frame and closely linked with it, the "Anti-colonialism/Anti-imperialism" frame on the one hand, and the "Antisemitism" frame on the other. The dominance of the "Antiracism" frame has a significant influence because it leaves no analytic space for talking about the situation of Jews: Due to a process of upward mobility, Jews since World War II have undergone a process of "whitening" in the United States.[69] In a country strongly shaped by the black/white racial divide, by what DuBois[70] famously called the "color-line," this perception has political consequences, as being perceived as "white" automatically puts one on the "wrong" side of power in the eyes of a large part of the radical left. The notion of "Jewish privilege" encourages the left to perceive Jews as perpetrators and not victims.[71] It has been inspired by the concept of "white privilege," which is central to Critical Whiteness studies, a dominant paradigm of antiracism in both activism and academia since the 1990s.[72] This offshoot of critical race theory puts the black/white binary at the center of the analysis of contemporary racism and critically examines the historical construction of white identity and its implications of power and privilege. In the perception of the left, white privilege for American Jews means social recognition and representation, personal security against attacks due to the possibility of "passing," economic security, and an exclusive victim status because of the experience of the Holocaust.

This view can in turn also involuntarily echo and reinforce antisemitic stereotypes about disproportionate Jewish power and influence. Thus the dominance of an antiracist frame inspired by Critical Whiteness studies often has the effect of rendering antisemitism invisible, leading to "antisemitism trivialization." Antisemitism trivialization includes belittling the real dangers of antisemitism, ignoring and refusing to address the reality

---

[69] Karen Brodkin, *How Jews Became White Folks and What That Says About Race in America* (New Brunswick and London, 1998).

[70] W.E.B. Du Bois, *The Souls of Black Folk* (Mineola, 1994 [1903]).

[71] Sina Arnold, *Antisemitismusdiskurse in der US-amerikanischen Linken nach 9/11* (Hamburg, 2016).

[72] Blair Taylor, 'Long Shadows of the New Left: From Students for a Democratic Society to Occupy Wall Street', in: *The Sixties: Interdisciplinary Perspectives on America's Longest Decade*, eds. Laura Bieger and Christian Lammert, (Berlin, 2013), 77–94; Adolph Reed Jr., 'Marx, Race, and Neoliberalism,' *New Labor Forum*, vol. 22, no. 1, (2013), 49–57.

and continuity of antisemitism worldwide, actively derailing conversations about antisemitism, and the marginalization of antisemitism on a spectrum of power relations (sexism, racism, homophobia etc.). In the course of heated disinvestment debates at the UC Berkeley, the local chapter of "Students for Justice in Palestine" tweeted "The ZiZis are literally white people crying about their privilege, lol."[73] This tweet illustrates how the specific content of the "Antiracism" frame can cause blindness toward Jewish issues. In another instance, the pro-BDS "Revolutionary Communist Party" wrote in their magazine "Revolution": "Jewish people who resent being resented for Israel's crimes (like white people who resent being blamed for white racism and the history of the oppression of Black people in this country) need to loudly and unequivocally speak out against Israel's crimes".[74] This quote not only draws a direct connection between individual US Jews and Israel's politics but also places blame for antisemitism on Jews themselves. It also demonstrates that this frame can have actual effects on individuals, causing Jews to feel like their feelings do not matter, and causing Jews of Color specifically to feel alienated.[75]

This perception of Jews as privileged whites also causes opponents of BDS to fail when trying to link their "Antisemitism" frame to the "Antiracism" frame of the left. Manfred Gerstenfeld attempted this when he offered this suggestion on how to deal with BDS: "The more extreme boycotters should be systematically exposed as racists who discriminate against scholars on the basis of their nationality or ethnicity".[76] However, for pro-Palestinian groups and others on the left, antisemitism ranks low on a list of racisms: Anti-Black racism has always been more prominent in the United States, and anti-Muslim racism has been increasingly visible since 9/11.[77] By contrast, Jews are not perceived as a vulnerable group

---

[73] "ZiZi" is an abbreviation for both Zionists or "Zio-Nazis," "lol" is an internet term for "laughing out loud." For a retweet see Allen L (@Leibochips), "More racism from SJP: @BerkeleySJP: The ZiZis are literally white people crying about their privilege lol @turrrminator," https://twitter.com/hashtag/UCBDivest?src=hash, Twitter, April 18, 2013, https://twitter.com/Amerimuslima/status/324789784079921153

[74] Alan Goodman, "Behind the Silencing of Helen Thomas: Covering Up and Carrying Out Great Crimes," *Revolution*, No. 203, 13 June 2010. http://revcom.us/a/203/Helen_Thomas-en.html

[75] Aryella Moreh, "Keeping Prejudice Under Control," *The Daily Californian*, 6 May 2013. http://www.dailycal.org/2013/05/06/checking-our-prejudices/

[76] Manfred Gerstenfeld (ed.), *Academics Against Israel and the Jews* (Jerusalem, 2007), 71.

[77] Costas Panagopoulos, 'Arab and Muslim Americans and Islam in the Aftermath of 9/11,' *Public Opinion Quarterly*, vol. 70, no. 4, (2006), 608–624.

affected by racism; therefore trying to appeal to the antiracist conscience by speaking about possible antisemitic consequences of BDS actions is a strategy that is generally bound to fail.

Anti-imperialism/Anti-colonialism → ← Antisemitism

BDS advocates' association of Israel and Jews with imperialism causes a similar collision of frames. "Jews are the epitome of white imperialism" is how one interview partner critically summed up what according to her is a common left view. However, when the Middle East conflict is only perceived in the frame of imperialism or colonialism—and by extension as apartheid—then there is no room in which to acknowledge agency on the Palestinian side: Hamas' Islamist politics, Palestinian antisemitism, Israeli security concerns about rocket attacks—none of these factors can be addressed within a Manichean anti-imperialist world view. Instead, one can observe a "double standard of self-determination": any political methods used by the Palestinian side are endorsed as resistance, whereas the Israeli side is criticized because of the structural inequality of the current situation. To quote from Judith Butler's presentation at the CUNY event: "Resistance movements do not discriminate against oppressors, though sometimes the language of the movement can use discriminatory language, and that has to be opposed".[35] Not only does the term "discriminatory language" understate the deadly effects the antisemitic politics of groups like Hamas can have but also, just like the "Antiracism" frame, the focus on "Anti-imperialism"/"Anti-colonialism" has the effect of making the legitimate grievances of the Jewish-Israeli civil population in the Middle East conflict secondary, and does not take into account antisemitism as *one* of the factors driving the Middle East conflict. This frame therefore is not only bound to clash with BDS critics' "Antisemitism" frame, it also contributes to the "antisemitic trivialization" described above.

Indeed, it is remarkable and symptomatic for BDS and the US left more generally that "Antisemitism" appears to have no relevance as a frame for the Middle East conflict. This reflects analytical shortcomings: Specific theoretical traditions within the political left—amongst them an antiracist analysis informed by Critical Whiteness studies and a schematic anti-imperialism—have resulted in ignorance, if not rejection, of antisemitism as a relevant political issue.[71] When the subject of antisemitism is raised, US leftists generally react with denial, blame-shifting, or relativization. It is symptomatic that accusations of antisemitism are never taken at face value, something to be scrutinized and accepted or rejected on the grounds of careful analysis. The signature drive by "Jewish Voice for Peace," mentioned above, claimed that BDS "in no way can [.] be construed as anti-Semitic." BDS activists seldom take into account that antisemitism *can* in fact be one motivation to boycott Israel,[78] or *can* be found openly among some BDS supporters, as examples have shown.[79] Robert Fine has called this dynamic "antisemitism denial," meaning "the reluctance or refusal to take seriously the charge of antisemitism, in relation to criticism of Israel [...]".[80] Rather, concern over antisemitism is typically seen as mere camouflage designed to invalidate criticism of Israel. The uniqueness of this left response to allegations of antisemitism is remarkable: Whereas charges of racism brought forth by Blacks, or accusations of sexism by women are most likely to be taken seriously and closely scrutinized in activist circles, Jewish claims of antisemitism are simply seen as a mere derailing of the conversation, a cynical Zionist plot. This is such a common trope in BDS circles that such allegations are typically dismissed as nothing more than "Hasbara"—Israeli propaganda.

Yet on the other side, BDS critics also sometimes apply the "Antisemitism" frame with overhasty accusations based on too limited an analysis. Considering the movement to be necessarily antisemitic, as in some of the examples above, all of its demands and politics are delegitimized because they fall into the category of hate speech. Consequently, it is not only analytical shortcomings that cause antisemitism to be a near-invisible topic in left or pro-BDS circles. Partly, this blindness is a reaction: Hasty accusations of antisemitism result in an unwillingness by activists to take criticism seriously and leads them to stigmatize concern about antisemitism as an inherently right-wing topic. To quote Butler's talk once more[35]: "We may not exploit and re-ignite the traumatic dimension of

---

[78] Heiko Beyer and Ulf Liebe, 'Three Experimental Approaches to Measure the Social Context Dependence of Prejudice Communication and Discriminatory Behavior,' *Social Science Research,* vol. 49, (2015), 343–355.

[79] Akiva Tor, "BDS and Hopelessness: Response to Moshe Yaroni in *Zeek,"ZEEK,* 13 May 2010. http://zeek.forward.com/articles/116702/; Philip Mendes, "The BDS Movement Cannot So Easily Be Absolved of Charges of Anti-Semitism," *Australian Broadcasting Corporation,* 7 February 2014. http://www.abc.net.au/religion/articles/2014/02/07/3940144.htm

[80] Robert Fine, "Antisemitism and Discourses of Denial", Presentation at the "Colloqium III: Patterns of Excuses for Antisemitism and Forms of Denial" of the Internationales Institut für Bildung-, Sozial und Antisemitismusforschung/International Institute for Education and Research on Antisemitism, London, 28.10.2010.

Hitler's atrocities for the purposes of accusing and silencing those with opposing political viewpoints, including legitimate criticisms of the state of Israel. Such a tactic not only demeans and instrumentalizes the memory of the Nazi genocide, but produces a general cynicism about both accusations of anti-Semitism and predictions of new genocidal possibilities." In a similar vein, JVP Deputy Director Cecilie Surasky argues that BDS opponents "cheapen the charges of anti-Semitism so grotesquely, by throwing the label whenever possible and hoping it will stick, that they should be held responsible for desensitizing an entire generation to real anti-Semitism".[81]

Jewish Identity → ← *Jewish Self-hatred*

Concerning the next colliding frame, "Jewish identity" versus "Jewish self-hatred," one can observe that intra-Jewish debates about identity, representation, and political traditions are often influential in BDS debates. A blogger for the Israeli online magazine *+972* commented after the panel at Brooklyn College, "Often, I feel as though the whole Palestine issue is more about the divisions within the Jewish community than about actual Palestinians".[82] The aforementioned debates within "Hillel" illustrate this divide in the Jewish-American community and reflect struggles over the very meaning of "being Jewish" in America. According to Cecilie Surasky, debates over BDS open a rare arena to talk with other Jews about these issues. Taking as an example a heated divestment campaign at the UC Berkeley in 2010, she writes: "This effort to stifle debate inside our communities has ironically meant that the only way that Jews have been able to speak face-to-face with other Jews about divestment has been at the UC Berkeley hearings. And what the hearings revealed was striking: an authentic crisis in the Jewish community".[83]

---

[81] Cecilie Surasky, "Threatened Lawsuit at Brooklyn College and Abuse of Title VI." Last modified February 22, 2013. http://muzzlewatch.com/2013/02/22/threatened-lawsuit-at-brooklyn-college-and-abuse-of-title-vi/
[82] Lisa Goldman, "Despite Controversy, Brooklyn College BDS Panel Is a Non-event," *+972 Magazine*, 8 February 2013. http://972mag.com/after-a-week-of-controversy-the-brooklyn-college-bds-event-was-a-non-event/65634/
[83] Cecilie Surasky, "Lessons from the UC Berkeley Divestment Effort, Hillel on Campus." Last modified September 30, 2010. http://www.muzzlewatch.com/2010/09/30/lessons-from-the-uc-berkeley-divestment-effort-hillel-on-campus/

→ *Academic Freedom* ←

Regarding academic freedom, we find both sides actually applying the same frame, but—as Butler already noted in 2006—"two separate debates on academic freedom have emerged in the United States".[50] Barghouti goes so far as to claim that "[t]he concept of academic freedom has been abused by opponents of the boycott".[49] Both of the conflicting interpretations ask what the term actually means: The right to free speech? Or the right to free expression within an unbiased framework? And if the latter, then what bias does that framework lean towards? As explained above, BDS advocates perceive a strong right-wing or Zionist influence on campus, BDS opponents a structural liberal dominance. BDS advocates, moreover, debate the notion of Israelis' academic freedom/freedom of speech against the backdrop of Palestinians' lack of human rights and "broader freedoms".[49] Despite these differences, it may be possible to further genuine debate and reconcile divergent frames by opening up for discussion the meaning of academic freedom, freedom of speech and its specific limits on a more general level.[50]

Human Rights→ →

In the same way that neither of the two opposing parties rejects the "Human rights" frame, so too they both accept the frame of "Academic Freedom". Rather, discursive struggles take place *within* this frame, posing questions over the exact meaning of human rights in the context of diverse issues and cases such as Palestinian refugees, the right of return, the Israeli population's need for security, civil rights within Israeli society, and so on. In a similar vein as the "Academic Freedom" frame, some ethical and political common ground can be found here between BDS advocates and opponents that could potentially bridge opposing viewpoints.

CONCLUSIONS: FRAME COALITION NOT FRAME COLLISION?

The panel discussion between Judith Butler and Omar Barghouti at CUNY and the debates surrounding it proved to be a showcase for general features of BDS debates in the United States. Moreover, the dynamics here analyzed are symptomatic of debates on antisemitism and on the Middle East conflict in the United States left in general. They make clear that movements' actors should be aware how they frame their arguments and the effects these frames entail. Today, these strongly divergent frames have created political gridlock; yet most frames reveal analytical shortcomings. Specific theoretical traditions within the political left have resulted in ignorance, if not rejection, of antisemitism as a relevant political issue—among them anti-imperialism and an analysis of racism focused solely on white privilege. This frame ignores that antisemitism *can* be a factor in BDS debates and needs to be challenged, just as racist or otherwise reactionary positions would be. On the other side, hasty accusations of antisemitism by (primarily right-wing) critics result in unwillingness on the part of BDS activists to take criticism seriously. While the clashes illustrated above between frames highlighting antiracism versus antisemitism and Jewish identity versus Jewish self-hatred have proven difficult to transcend, debates which mobilize the potentially shared values of academic freedom and human rights could offer a possible space for dialogue. Rather than seeing the other side's arguments as mere camouflage for either hidden antisemitic or right-wing agendas, or psychologizing them as "self-hating," focusing attention on the actual content of the arguments offers an important starting point, if not a precondition, to better analyze BDS as a current political boycott movement.

CHAPTER 13

The British Summer of 2014: Boycotts, Antisemitism, and Jews

Dave Rich

On 7 July 2014, amidst rising tension following the abduction and murder of four teenagers—three Israeli and one Palestinian—Israeli armed forces launched Operation Protective Edge against Hamas in the Gaza Strip. This military operation, initially prosecuted by Israel's air force and then, after ten days, by its ground forces, continued with varying degrees of intensity for 51 days until a ceasefire on 26 August 2014. By the time of its conclusion, according to the United Nations, 2251 Palestinians were killed, including 1462 Palestinian civilians, and 11,231 Palestinians were injured. Israel disputes these figures, claiming that 2125 Palestinians were killed, of whom at least 44 per cent were combatants. Both agree that 67 Israeli soldiers were killed, as were 5 Israeli civilians and one Thai national in Israel; and around 1600 Israelis were injured.[1] Whatever the exact

[1] United Nations General Assembly Human Rights Council, *Report of the Independent Commission of Inquiry on the 2014 Gaza Conflict*, A/HRC/29/52, (24 June 2015), p. 6, http://www.ohchr.org/EN/HRBodies/HRC/CoIGazaConflict/Pages/ReportCoIGaza.aspx; State of Israel, *The 2014 Gaza Conflict 7 July–26 August 2014, Factual and Legal

D. Rich (✉)
Community Security Trust, London, UK

Birkbeck, University of London, London, UK
e-mail: Dave.R@cst.org.uk

© The Author(s) 2019
D. Feldman (ed.), *Boycotts Past and Present*, Palgrave Critical Studies of Antisemitism and Racism,
https://doi.org/10.1007/978-3-319-94872-0_13

casualty figures, this was a particularly bloody and destructive round of fighting between Israel and Hamas. It was also the trigger for extensive, sustained, and passionate protests in the UK. The story of what occurred in Israel and Gaza during that conflict is not the subject of this chapter, although the fact that those details remain disputed is certainly relevant. Instead, this chapter looks at how boycotts—real, imagined, and accidental—were used by pro-Palestinian campaigners and experienced by supporters of Israel, and particularly by Jewish people, in the UK during the conflict. By taking a range of examples, each with its own context and purpose, it explores how these boycotts were conceived and understood by different actors in Britain that summer and how they connected to perceptions and experiences of antisemitism.

During the summer of 2014, as the conflict in Gaza and Israel began to escalate and then developed into open warfare, the UK Jewish Film Festival was planning its annual showpiece, a three-week celebration of Jewish and Israeli films that takes place in November each year. The festival was due to be held at the Tricycle theatre, an independent cinema in London, as it had been for the previous eight years: except this year was different. First, the Tricycle asked to view any Israeli films in advance in order to approve their inclusion in the festival. The festival rejected this unprecedented demand as censorship and was then hit with another condition: that it should decline the small amount of sponsorship it received from the Israeli embassy if it wanted to go ahead at the Tricycle. The funding from the Israeli embassy was for £1400, which was only a fraction of the festival's overall budget, and the Tricycle offered to make up any financial shortfall. This was about principle, not money: as Indhu Rubasingham, the artistic director of the Tricycle, explained, "The festival receives funding from the Israeli embassy and, given the current conflict in Israel and Gaza, we feel it is inappropriate to accept financial support from any government agency involved." The chairman of the Tricycle, Jonathan Levy, backed her up: "the Tricycle cannot be associated with any activity directly funded or supported by any party to the conflict… The Tricycle will be pleased to host the UKJFF provided that it occurs without the support or other endorsement from the Israeli government." However, the Tricycle found that its principled stand ran into an equally firm and clear principled stand by the Jewish Film Festival to resist any such pressure. The festival's founder and executive director, Judy Ironside, described the Tricycle's decision as a

Aspects, (May 2015), p. A – 1, http://mfa.gov.il/ProtectiveEdge/Documents/2014GazaConflictFullReport.pdf

"boycott" of "what is clearly an apolitical cultural festival... to the great detriment of this celebration of Jewish culture, which is of course intrinsically connected to the State of Israel." The festival refused to comply with the Tricycle's condition that it return the embassy's funding, and the 2014 festival was, as a result, withdrawn from its usual venue.[2]

The reaction to this disagreement, when it became public, was at once both extraordinary and entirely predictable. The row received widespread media coverage and developed into one of the most prominent and divisive issues in British responses to the conflict in Israel and Gaza. The Board of Deputies of British Jews and the Jewish Leadership Council, who comprise the mainstream leadership of the UK Jewish community, described the Tricycle's stand as a "shameful" decision that "shows that boycotts of Israel inevitably lead to the harassment of Jewish culture and individuals."[3] Jewish figures in the arts were divided, with some prominent names condemning the Tricycle and others defending it. Nicholas Hytner, director of the National Theatre, supported the Tricycle and criticised the film festival for having "unwisely politicised a celebration of Jewish culture."[4] The Government intervened, with the Culture Secretary Sajid Javid writing to festival chair Stephen Margolis to offer his support.[5] A disagreement over whether a cultural event should accept state funding—and what this funding even means, in terms of the political neutrality of the event— quickly morphed into a debate over whether the Tricycle's stand was antisemitic. Stephen Pollard, editor of the UK's oldest Jewish newspaper the *Jewish Chronicle*, tweeted that the Tricycle "is now officially antisemitic" because "It is singling out the Jewish state for boycott."[6] Others pointed out that, as the Tricycle had happily hosted the festival for eight years and wanted to continue to do so, and since several of its board members and supporters were Jewish, their decision was unlikely to be motivated by

---

[2] Hannah Ellis-Petersen, 'Tricycle theatre refuses to host UK Jewish Film Festival while it has Israeli embassy funding', *The Guardian* (6 August 2014), https://www.theguardian.com/stage/2014/aug/05/tricycle-theatre-jewish-film-festival-cancelled-israel-gaza

[3] Sandy Rashty, 'UK Jewish Film Festival banned from the Tricycle theatre: But some won't attack boycott', *Jewish Chronicle* (7 August 2014), https://www.thejc.com/news/uk-news/uk-jewish-film-festival-banned-from-the-tricycle-theatre-but-some-won-t-attack-boycott-1.56039

[4] Ellis-Petersen, 'Tricycle theatre refuses to host UK Jewish Film Festival'.

[5] Sandy Rashty, 'Culture Secretary says Tricycle "misguided" over Jewish film festival boycott', *Jewish Chronicle* (12 August 2014), https://www.thejc.com/news/uk-news/culture-secretary-sajid-javid-says-tricycle-theatre-misguided-over-uk-jewish-film-festival-boycott-1.56129

[6] Ellis-Petersen, 'Tricycle theatre refuses to host UK Jewish Film Festival'.

antisemitism.[7] The debate over whether the Tricycle's stance was antisemitic revolved around two issues: firstly, whether double standards were at play in how the festival was treated and secondly, what the impact of the decision would be on British Jews. It is these two factors that created a circumstantial connection between a boycott action and antisemitism, even if the action itself was not motivated by antisemitic prejudice or attitudes.

The allegation of double standards was based on the fact the Tricycle's conditions for hosting the festival were unprecedented. It had never previously objected to the festival's receipt of funding from the Israeli embassy, nor had it ever asked to vet the Israeli films due to be shown in the festival. In fact, the festival always showed a wide range of Israeli films, including some made by Palestinians and others that were critical of the Israeli government. Nobody suggested that its cultural content was influenced, directly or indirectly, by the Israeli embassy or that the festival's programme was designed to promote the policies of the then Israeli government. The Tricycle was itself dependent on funding from the Arts Council, a British taxpayer-funded body, and therefore indirectly funded by the British government. In June 2014 it hosted a London Asian Film Festival that was partly funded by the Indian government. This all suggests that the Tricycle had never before held a principled objection to hosting events that were in receipt of funding from foreign governments, nor did it refuse funding that originated with its own government. This undermined the Tricycle's claim that to host the Jewish Film Festival while it accepted funding from the Israeli embassy would constitute a breach of political neutrality so unacceptable that the theatre could not, in all good conscience, continue to host it. For some, the imposition of a condition on a Jewish film festival that had not been imposed on anybody else was sufficient evidence of antisemitism, whatever the intentions of the Tricycle in doing so. "Of course the theatre would not hold others to the same standard: just Jews," wrote political commentator Nick Cohen, continuing: "Racism consists of demanding behaviour from a minority you would never dream of demanding from your friends."[8] Adam Wagner, a lawyer

---

[7] For example, Archie Bland, 'The Tricycle Cinema's refusal to host a Jewish Film Festival raises issues of immense complexity', *The Independent* (6 August 2014), https://www.independent.co.uk/voices/comment/the-tricycle-cinema-s-refusal-to-host-a-jewish-film-festival-raises-issues-of-immense-complexity-9652414.html

[8] Nick Cohen, 'Anti-Semitic double standards: the arts and the Jews', *The Spectator* (6 August 2014), https://blogs.spectator.co.uk/2014/08/the-double-standards-of-artistic-anti-semitism/

and founder of the UK Human Rights Blog, argued that the Tricycle may have been guilty of unlawful discrimination under the Equality Act 2010 (although no legal action took place).[9]

The question of the impact of the Tricycle's decision on British Jews relates to the close relationship between support for Israel and Jewish identity, and could apply in similar ways to other boycott campaigns and activities. According to a 2010 survey by the Institute for Jewish Policy Research, 95 per cent of British Jews said Israel plays some role in their Jewish identity, while 82 per cent said it plays a central or important role. The same survey found that 95 per cent of British Jews have visited Israel, 90 per cent said they see Israel as the ancestral homeland of the Jewish people, and 87 per cent see British Jews as part of a global Jewish diaspora—while only 19 per cent said that Jews outside Israel are living in exile. A similar survey by City University London in 2015 found that 90 per cent of British Jews support Israel's right to exist as a Jewish state, while 93 per cent said it plays a role in their Jewish identity. Interestingly, both surveys also found majorities of British Jews holding nuanced and critical views about Israeli politics and society, while supporting policy positions that diverged significantly from the policies of the Israeli government at the time the surveys took place. For example, in the 2010 survey, 74 per cent of British Jews said that Orthodox Judaism has too much influence in Israeli society, 67 per cent said that there is too much corruption in Israel's political system, and 56 per cent agreed that non-Jewish minorities in Israel suffer from discrimination. Sixty-seven per cent of British Jews thought that Israel should give up territory in exchange for peace guarantees from the Palestinians, 74 per cent opposed the expansion of existing settlements in the West Bank, and 52 per cent said the Israeli government should negotiate with Hamas to achieve peace. Similar results were found by the 2015 survey.[10]

This suggests that support for Israel, as most British Jews understand it, is not always a case of straightforward political support for, or identification

---

[9] Adam Wagner, 'Have the Tricycle Theatre broken the law by refusing to host the Jewish Film Festival?', *UK Human Rights Blog* (7 August 2014), https://ukhumanrightsblog.com/2014/08/07/have-the-tricycle-theatre-broken-the-law-by-refusing-to-host-the-jewish-film-festival/

[10] David Graham and Jonathan Boyd, *Committed, concerned and conciliatory: The attitudes of Jews in Britain towards Israel* (2010); Stephen Miller, Margaret Harris, and Colin Shindler, *The Attitudes of British Jews Towards Israel* (2015).

with, any particular Israeli government and its policies. Rather, it can often represent an emotional connection to the country, its people and land, which may manifest as political support (especially when the country and people are perceived as being under attack), but also as interest in, and affection for, its cultural output, its sporting success, or other achievements in non-political spheres. Even British Jews who strongly oppose the policies and actions of the Israeli government (whether of left or right, at different points in its history), or who perhaps do not follow Israeli politics at all, generally share this connection to Israel. In short, the diaspora Jewish connection to Israel is not necessarily, or even primarily, a political statement. Some commentators argued that it was the implicit, and probably unwitting, threat to this non-political Jewish connection to Israel that constituted the antisemitic element of the Tricycle's demand that the festival reject Israeli government funding. Anshel Pfeffer, writing in the left-wing Israeli newspaper *Haaretz*, argued that while he did not believe the Tricycle's decision was motivated by antisemitism, it had an antisemitic impact because "while calling on Britain and any other country to boycott Israel is legitimate, targeting Jews and telling them they can't have a connection to Israel is anti-Semitic."[11] An editorial in the *Guardian* newspaper developed this point, arguing that the Israeli embassy "represents Israel itself, its society and its people," as well as the government of the day.[12] As such, to demand that the film festival cut all ties with the embassy "is to tell Jews how they might – and how they might not – live as Jews."

While the Tricycle insisted that its opposition to Israeli embassy funding for the festival was due to its belief that this funding compromised the festival's political neutrality, there may have been a more prosaic reason for its desire to distance itself from Israel. The festival had attracted a small demonstration by anti-Israel protestors the previous year, and one of the Tricycle's board members hinted in an interview with the BBC that they feared much larger demonstrations following that summer's conflict.[13] If this was the case, it backfired, because the Tricycle became the focus of demonstrations by supporters of Israel following the publicity surrounding its decision. Approximately 250 people protested outside the cinema,

[11] Anshel Pfeffer, 'A Theatrical Surrender to anti-Semitism', *Haaretz* (7 August 2014), https://www.haaretz.com/.premium-a-theatrical-surrender-to-anti-semitism-1.5258514

[12] Editorial, 'The Guardian view on Gaza and the rise of antisemitism', *The Guardian* (8 August 2014), https://www.theguardian.com/commentisfree/2014/aug/08/guardian-view-gaza-rise-antisemitism

[13] Wagner, 'Have the Tricycle Theatre broken the law'.

holding signs saying "Don't punish London's Jews" and chanting "Shame on the Tricycle; no to antisemitism; no to racism; no to double standards."[14] After a week of negative publicity, demonstrations, and political pressure, and following private negotiations, the Tricycle reversed its decision and announced that it would host the festival "on the same terms as in previous years with no restrictions on funding from the embassy of Israel in London."[15] However, this was too late to schedule the festival to be held at the Tricycle in 2014 as it had already found alternative venues, and it has not returned to the Tricycle since.

At the heart of this episode lay some common misunderstandings that tend to beset arguments over boycotts of Israel. The first of these is what actually constitutes a boycott. The Tricycle did not consider their decision to be a boycott of the festival, but this is how it was interpreted by many people, and it was widely reported in that language. Connected to this is a fundamental disagreement over political neutrality and whether the acceptance of any government funding, even with no conditions attached to it, breaches such neutrality. The Tricycle argued that it did; the festival argued that to reject Israeli embassy funding that they had previously enjoyed would, itself, be a political statement. Most incendiary was the argument over antisemitism and whether this can be assessed by an objective test or whether it is determined by the subjective impact an action has on those it affects.

By the time the row over the Tricycle's decision became public, British Jews were already expressing strong concerns about antisemitic reactions to the conflict in Israel and Gaza. Antisemitic hate crimes recorded by the Police in England and Wales increased by 97 per cent from 2013–14 to 2014–15, compared with a 26 per cent increase across all hate crime categories.[16] Much of this increase occurred during July and August 2014, the months of conflict in Israel and Gaza, according to the Community

---

[14] Sandy Rashty, 'Demonstrators at Tricycle protest against UK Jewish Film Festival boycott', *Jewish Chronicle* (7 August 2014), https://www.thejc.com/news/uk-news/demonstrators-at-tricycle-protest-against-uk-jewish-film-festival-boycott-1.56104

[15] Caroline Davies, 'Tricycle Theatre does U-turn and lifts ban on Jewish film festival', *The Guardian* (15 August 2014), https://www.theguardian.com/stage/2014/aug/15/tricycle-theatre-u-turn-jewish-film-festival-ban

[16] House of Commons Home Affairs Committee, *Antisemitism in the UK: Tenth Report of Session 2016–17* (13 October 2016), p. 5, https://publications.parliament.uk/pa/cm201617/cmselect/cmhaff/136/136.pdf

Security Trust.[17] Stories about a rise in antisemitism across Europe began to appear in media reporting of the conflict.[18] In Manchester, local attention was focused on Kedem, a shop in the city centre selling Israeli cosmetic products. This had become the target of a local campaign called Manchester Boycott Kedem which held regular protests outside the shop "with the eventual intention of closing the shop down." This was, according to the organisers, because "it is the flagship store for a company in which the Israeli government has a large stake, and whose products are made from Dead Sea salts which are technically properties of the Palestinian Authority." They also hoped to raise awareness of "the humanitarian crisis in Gaza" and "put enough pressure on the Israeli government that it will be forced to reconsider its aggressive policies towards the Palestinian people." They insisted that their protests were peaceful and not linked to any increase in antisemitism.[19]

These demonstrations attracted counter-protests by pro-Israel demonstrators drawn largely from Manchester's Jewish community, and things were becoming disorderly. According to one report, over the weekend of 26 and 27 July, Greater Manchester Police had to deploy 125 officers to police hundreds of demonstrators and made five arrests.[20] Some demonstrators focused their attention on other shops in Manchester that were part of international chains with branches in Israel, including H&M, Marks and Spencer, and Schuh. According to reports received by the Community Security Trust, threats of violence were made to shop workers at the Kedem store, and damage was done to its front door. Some boycott protestors were reported to have made Nazi salutes. A Jewish man reported being asked if he was Jewish and then was called a murderer because he

[17] Community Security Trust, *Antisemitic Incidents Report 2014*, (February 2015), https://cst.org.uk/data/file/5/5/Incidents-Report-2014.1425053165.pdf
[18] For example, Jon Henley, 'Antisemitism on rise across Europe in worst times since the Nazis', *Guardian* (7 August 2014), https://www.theguardian.com/society/2014/aug/07/antisemitism-rise-europe-worst-since-nazis; Melissa Eddy, 'Anti-Semitism Rises in Europe Amid Israel-Gaza Conflict', *New York Times* (1 August 2014), https://www.nytimes.com/2014/08/02/world/europe/anger-in-europe-over-the-israeli-gaza-conflict-reverberates-as-anti-semitism.html
[19] Sairah Ya, 'Statement from Manchester Boycott Kedem' (31 July 2014), https://www.facebook.com/sairah.yassir/posts/10154472578695232
[20] Charlotte Cox, 'Police make five arrests during city centre clash during Gaza protest', *Manchester Evening News* (27 July 2014), https://www.manchestereveningnews.co.uk/news/greater-manchester-news/manchester-gaza-protests-police-make-7516377

was carrying a Kedem-branded bag. Another reported hearing a protestor shout "You Jews are scum and the whole world hates you."[21]

On 30 July, Sir Richard Leese, the leader of Manchester City Council, responded to these protests by warning that "this Council cannot support those who seek to bring this conflict into our city and drive wedges between communities… we cannot support the use of language that would not have been out of place in 1930s Germany." He also warned that the staff and customers at shops in the city were "being subject to abuse and intimidation." Leese stated that he was not willing to "take sides" between Israel and Hamas and criticised both for their actions.[22] The following week, the Chief Constable of Greater Manchester Police, Sir Peter Fahy, added his concerns that the protests posed "a risk to our very good community cohesion" in Manchester.[23] Some local shop workers even held their own small demonstration, organised by the council and city centre retailers, to complain about the behaviour of the demonstrators. Most of the shop workers were young Mancunians with no connection to the Middle East conflict and they were getting fed up with boycott campaigners coming into their shops "with flags and megaphones shouting," according to one. "It is extremists who are preaching revolution here on Market Street," said Pat Karney, a Labour councillor, adding: "they need to read Karl Marx. He said mobilise the workers not attack the workers."[24] The manager of one menswear shop in the city centre claimed to have lost £25,000 in business as a result of the protests. Another said they lost £10,000 in a single day when the main shopping street in central Manchester was closed due to a pro-Palestinian march.[25]

After another week of protests, the main Muslim-Jewish interfaith network in Manchester, the Muslim Jewish Forum, issued a statement in which they warned: "The protest and counter-protest outside Kedem

---

[21] Antisemitic incident reports held by the Community Security Trust and made available to the author.

[22] Manchester City Council, 'The Leader's Blog: Gaza and Manchester', (30 July 2014), http://www.manchester.gov.uk/blog/leadersblog/post/689/gaza-and-manchester

[23] 'Sir Peter Fahy: Gaza protests "threaten cohesion" in Manchester', *BBC News* (4 August 2014), http://www.bbc.co.uk/news/uk-england-manchester-28645331

[24] Dominic Smith, 'Shop workers in Manchester say they are "intimidated" by pro-Palestinian protestors', *The Guardian* (7 August 2014), https://www.theguardian.com/uk-news/the-northerner/2014/aug/07/shop-workers-in-manchester-say-they-are-intimidated-by-pro-palestinian-protesters

[25] Jonathan Kalmus, 'Manchester shop staff hold their own protest over Kedem demonstrations', *Jewish Chronicle* (7 August 2014), https://www.thejc.com/news/uk-news/manchester-shop-staff-hold-their-own-protest-over-kedem-demonstrations-1.56102

together have not been helpful for community cohesion in Greater Manchester. We consider that a more appropriate way for people to engage with such issues would be through dialogue and discussion."[26] On 22 August, five weeks after the protests began, Greater Manchester Police and Manchester City Council made a joint decision to limit the number of protestors to 10 on each side and to move the protests away from the main shopping streets. They justified this on the grounds that "it is the cumulative impact of the daily protests – which is causing significant disruption to the business community on and around King Street and has led to members of our communities experiencing concern, fear and intimidation – that has now exceeded the legal threshold required under the Public Order Act."[27]

To call for the boycott of goods from a state that is believed to be committing human rights abuses is neither new nor exceptional, and need not be antisemitic. The Anti-Apartheid Movement built its entire strategy around the use of boycotts, and while it is the best known example in the recent history of the British left, it is hardly alone. Usually, political boycott campaigns of this nature are designed to bring about a change in a particular policy of the government or company being boycotted. In this case, though, the protagonists explicitly stated that their primary aim was to enforce a boycott of a shop in Manchester, thousands of miles from the conflict itself, "with the eventual intention of closing the shop down."[28] Raising awareness of the situation in Gaza was a secondary goal of the protests, and a vague ambition to pressure the Israeli government into changing unspecified policies was third. There was no clear explanation of how forcing the closure of a shop in Manchester might induce a change of policy from the government of Israel, or an improvement in conditions for the residents of Gaza. There is always a risk that political protests relating to overseas conflicts will have more impact in the UK than they do overseas; in this case, the organisers of the boycott campaign were open about the fact that this was their aim. Given that this was the case, it is not surprising that the campaign had such a strong local impact in Manchester.

---

[26] The Muslim Jewish Forum of Greater Manchester, 'Boycotts and protests directed at the Kedem store in Manchester' (17 August 2014), https://www.muslimjewish.org.uk/Past-events/Statement-on-Kedem-store-boycott.html

[27] Greater Manchester Police, 'Changes to conditions on King Street protestors' (22 August 2014), http://www.gmp.police.uk/content/websitepages/0212C434DC4C019A80257D3C0037E95E

[28] Ya, 'Statement from Manchester Boycott Kedem'.

This impact included alleged antisemitic hate crimes, the obstruction of trade for shops in the area of the protests (including ones with no connection to Israel), and damage to social cohesion more broadly. This went well beyond the limited aims of the protests themselves. It raises the question of whether public protests with the goal of enforcing the closure of a shop, especially one with a connection to a particular minority community, could be conducted in a way that did not have these secondary impacts.

Other cities also saw protests that targeted Israeli goods on sale in shops. In Birmingham, a group of demonstrators lay down on the ground outside a Sainsbury's supermarket on 2 August, forcing it to close its doors and stop trading for the rest of the day. The protest included a Labour Member of Parliament, Shabana Mahmood, who appeared to welcome the fact the shop had been forced to close "for supporting goods from the Israeli settlements which are illegal under international law... the passion here of all of the people campaigning is incredible to see." This action went against Labour Party policy, which did not include the boycott of Israeli settlement goods or the closure of shops that sell them.[29] Later that month, demonstrators entered a different supermarket in Birmingham, took Israeli products off the shelves and threw them onto the floor. Police were called and one person was arrested for assaulting one of the Police officers.[30] These activities were directed at Israeli goods, but the wider impact of the protests did not stop there. Like the Kedem protests in Manchester, by lowering the threshold for illegal or even violent conduct in political activism, they had the potential to contribute to a general increase in tension and fear amongst Jewish people who identified with Israel during the conflict.

These events in Birmingham did not attract as much attention as an incident in London that was not an act of boycott and may even have been intended to protect Israeli goods from anti-Israel protestors. On Saturday,

---

[29] Jonathan Walker, 'Watch: Birmingham MP Shabana Mahmood hauled in by Labour bosses after this video of Sainsbury's Gaza protest', *Birmingham Mail* (20 August 2014), https://www.birminghammail.co.uk/news/midlands-news/watch-birmingham-mp-shabana-mahmood-7643691

[30] Sophie Jane Evans & Emma Glanfield, 'Gaza protesters run amok in Tesco and attack staff and police 'because it stocks Israeli food': Up to 100 demonstrators hunted after shoppers were left terrified by rampage', *Mail Online* (16 August 2014), http://www.dailymail.co.uk/news/article-2726831/Police-officers-attacked-stock-thrown-Gaza-protestors-wreak-havoc-Tesco-store.html

16 August, Colin Appleby was shopping in a branch of Sainsbury's in Holborn, central London, when he noticed that the section of the shop that normally stocks chilled kosher food was completely empty. According to Appleby, who is Jewish, he asked a member of staff why it was empty and was told, "We support Free Gaza." Appleby says he tried to argue that there is a difference between kosher and Israeli goods, but was ignored. Appleby put a photo of the empty shelves on his Facebook page with an account of his conversation with the staff member, and it received enough attention to become a national news story. His account was disputed by Sainsbury's, who said that the manager of the store had temporarily removed the stock from the kosher section to prevent it being damaged by protestors who were holding a small demonstration outside the shop. They also denied that a staff member had said the goods were removed in support of Gaza.[31]

Whichever version is more accurate, this incident was perceived by some observers to either be an antisemitic act by Sainsbury's staff (if they believed Appleby's version), or an antisemitic consequence of anti-Israel boycott campaigns elsewhere (if they believed Sainsbury's). *Jewish Chronicle* editor Stephen Pollard accused Sainsbury's of "giving in to, and colluding with, a form of terrorism" by removing the goods rather than calling Police to protect the store. He went on to argue that this was a form of antisemitism that made it "acceptable to speak or even act against Jews as Jews, under the cover of acting against Israel."[32] Sainsbury's rejected this way of thinking, arguing that the store manager made a reasonable decision in the circumstances. The point, though, is that there is no suggestion that any of the boycott protestors outside the store tried to enter at any point, nor that they intended to damage any goods inside the shop. This was a perceived threat to Israeli produce based on experiences elsewhere. It was based on a misapprehension—even if it was a reasonable

---

[31] See Martin Williams, 'Sainsbury's removes kosher food from shelves amid fears over protesters', *Guardian* (17 August 2014), https://www.theguardian.com/business/2014/aug/17/sainsburys-removes-kosher-food-anti-israel-protesters; Dan Bloom & Lucy Osborne, 'Sainsbury's strips kosher food from its shelves over fear of attacks by anti-Israeli protesters picketing as Gaza demonstrators run amok in Tesco branch', Mail Online (18 August 2014), http://www.dailymail.co.uk/news/article-2727266/Sainsbury-s-strips-kosher-food-shelves-fear-attacks-anti-Israeli-protesters.html

[32] Stephen Pollard, 'Removing kosher food from shelves is giving in to hatred', *Daily Telegraph* (19 August 2014), https://www.telegraph.co.uk/news/uknews/crime/11041391/Removing-kosher-food-from-shelves-is-giving-in-to-hatred.html

misapprehension—about the intentions of the protestors and a confusion between Israeli and kosher produce.

While the boycott campaigns in Manchester, Birmingham, and London did have a practical impact on the availability of Israeli goods (if only temporarily), a peculiar type of boycott announced in Bradford was of largely symbolic value. George Galloway, then the Respect Member of Parliament for Bradford West, called for Bradford to become "an Israel-free zone" at a meeting of Respect activists in early August 2014. According to a report of his speech, Galloway said:

> We have declared Bradford an Israel-free zone. We don't want any Israeli goods; we don't want any Israeli services; we don't want any Israeli academics coming to the university or the college. We don't want any Israeli tourists to come to Bradford even if any of them had thought of doing so. We reject this illegal, barbarous, savage state that calls itself Israel – and you have to do the same.[33]

A few days after Galloway's speech, and in direct response to it, the Israeli ambassador to the UK, Daniel Taub, visited Bradford at the invitation of the local Jewish community. He met local councillors from Labour, the Conservatives and the Liberal Democrats and posted photographs on social media of himself holding an Israeli flag next to a sign saying "Welcome to Bradford." His visit did not attract any protests.

Again, this call for a boycott of Israel provoked an angry reaction from Israel's supporters in Britain. It was Galloway's demand specifically for an indiscriminate boycott of Israeli people, in addition to Israeli goods, that drew particular ire. A spokesman for the Board of Deputies of British Jews described Galloway's comments as "odious" and pointed out: "He doesn't differentiate between an Israeli who supports the Israeli government or an Israeli who doesn't. He doesn't differentiate between an adult and a child – most people are apolitical."[34] The leader of Bradford Council warned that "Galloway is doing something really dangerous because what it does is cause tension within communities in Bradford." He added that Jews in Bradford had reported an increase in verbal abuse.[35] In one incident

---

[33] 'Galloway under investigation over Israel remarks', *BBC News* (7 August 2014), http://www.bbc.co.uk/news/uk-politics-28687233

[34] 'Galloway under investigation over Israel remarks'.

[35] Helen Pidd, 'George Galloway interviewed by police over Bradford "Israel-free zone" speech', *Guardian* (19 August 2014), https://www.theguardian.com/politics/2014/aug/19/george-galloway-interviewed-police-bradford-israel-free-zone

reported to the Community Security Trust on 26 July, a Jewish couple in Bradford were verbally abused by people collecting donations "for Gaza." When they refused to donate, they were called "Jewish bastards." In another incident on 24 August, a group of people on a walking tour of the Jewish history of Bradford were verbally abused by somebody in a passing car when they were near to an old synagogue. The offender, a man of South Asian appearance, shouted, "You're killing our babies in Palestine, why don't you go back to your own country." The choice of language in this incident—describing Palestinian children as "our babies" and Israel as "your own country"—indicates the extent to which some people identified personally with the protagonists in Israel and Gaza.[36]

Zulfi Karim of Bradford Council of Mosques criticised both Galloway and Taub for creating "disharmony among our communities." He advised both of them not to bring political issues "on to the streets of Bradford."[37] These concerns mirror those expressed in Manchester about the potential for the conflict in Israel and Gaza to affect community cohesion in the UK. Galloway was interviewed under caution by the Police following a complaint that he had incited racial hatred, although no charges were brought. While many responses to Galloway's statement were negative, his neighbouring MP, the Liberal Democrat David Ward (in the Bradford East constituency), thought that Galloway had not gone far enough and called for "a national movement" to boycott Israel. Ward had himself been in trouble previously for alleged antisemitism, having used Holocaust Memorial Day in January 2013 to juxtapose the Holocaust and the Palestinian refugee population created in 1948, by claiming that "the Jews, who suffered unbelievable levels of persecution during the Holocaust, could within a few years of liberation from the death camps, be inflicting atrocities on the Palestinians in the new state of Israel and continue to do so on a daily basis in the West Bank and Gaza."[38]

Galloway has long been a politician with a flair for the eye-catching stunt, and this statement was an example of a highly charged political statement that was empty of practical meaning. There was no significant Israeli presence in Bradford to be boycotted. The city had one synagogue,

---

[36] Antisemitic incident reports held by CST and made available to the author.
[37] Pidd, 'George Galloway interviewed by police'.
[38] Lesley Klaff, 'Holocaust Inversion in British Politics: The Case of David Ward', in: *Anti-Judaism, Antisemitism, and Delegitimizing Israel*, ed. Robert S. Wistrich, (2016), 185–196 (p. 191).

with a Jewish population of fewer than 300 people, although a representative of the synagogue pointed out that its members did visit Israel and have relatives there. Rather than Galloway's speech being a trigger for practical action to identify Israelis and prevent them from visiting, it was a rhetorical call to arms that identified the conflict in Gaza as an issue around which Galloway could mobilise politically. He hinted at this purpose after the Israeli ambassador's visit to Bradford, in a tweet that read: "I think Labour's open invitation that 'Israelis are welcome in Bradford' and the ambassador's furtive visit ensured my re-election, no?"[39] This referred to the forthcoming General Election in May 2015, in which Galloway lost his seat to the Labour candidate, a local woman and former Respect activist called Naz Shah. During that election campaign, Galloway again tried to use the issue of the Israeli-Palestinian conflict in his electioneering. Three weeks before polling day, he tweeted an image of Israeli Prime Minister Benjamin Netanyahu, smiling with his arms outstretched, captioned with the phrase: "Thank you Bradford West for electing Naz Shah! Our campaign worked!"[40] Half an hour later he posted a second tweet that juxtaposed celebrating Israelis and celebrating Palestinians, respectively waving Israeli and Palestinian flags. The Israelis were captioned with "Thank you for electing Naz Shah" and the Palestinians with "Thank you for electing George Galloway."[41]

The message in both tweets was obvious: Shah would serve the interests of Israel and Galloway would stand up for the Palestinians. The caption in the first tweet—"Our campaign worked!"—suggested that the Israeli government was actively trying to assist Shah's election campaign. The same day, Galloway retweeted two tweets that appeared to show a man with a Palestinian flag confronting a synagogue in Bradford.[42] It is not known whether Galloway knew that the building in the tweets was a synagogue, or why he retweeted those particular tweets, but the tweets

---

[39] Helen Pidd, 'George Galloway interviewed by police over Bradford 'Israel-free zone' speech', *Guardian* (19 August 2014), https://www.theguardian.com/politics/2014/aug/19/george-galloway-interviewed-police-bradford-israel-free-zone

[40] George Galloway, Twitter post, 14 April 2015, 4:19 am, https://twitter.com/georgegalloway/status/587938164368662528

[41] George Galloway, Twitter post, 14 April 2015, 4:47 am, https://twitter.com/georgegalloway/status/587945160283201537

[42] Baz Hussain, Twitter posts, 4 April 2015, https://twitter.com/ibrarBhussain/status/588087144549376000 & https://twitter.com/ibrarBhussain/status/588084168531308544

themselves are an example of how strongly felt allegiances regarding Israel and Palestine can affect behaviour between people of different communities in the UK. Another interesting feature of Galloway's attempt to the use of the Israeli-Palestinian conflict in this way is that it was not a real point of division between him and his opponent, who was herself active in pro-Palestinian campaigns in Bradford. It is striking that in a domestic British election, in a British city with no significant Israeli or Palestinian populations, Galloway appeared to think that he could exploit voters' sentiments over the Israeli-Palestinian conflict in order to gain votes—and that he could do so by portraying Shah, a Muslim pro-Palestinian activist, as being pro-Israel and backed by the Israeli government. A curious postscript to this story is that Shah herself was accused of antisemitism the following year as a result of messages she had posted on Facebook during the conflict in Israel and Gaza in 2014, and was temporarily suspended from the Labour Party as a result.[43]

The different examples described in this chapter cover a variety of scenarios in which actual boycotts, implied boycotts, anticipated boycotts, and threatened boycotts occurred in the UK in response to the war in Israel and Gaza during the summer of 2014. In Manchester, boycott campaigners tried to enforce the boycotting of an Israeli-owned shop with the intention of closing it down and removing its presence from the city. In Birmingham, campaigners limited their focus to Israeli products in supermarkets, but on one occasion, this still led to the enforced closure of a supermarket for a few hours. In London, a branch of Sainsbury's took an action that some observers assumed was a boycott, but of kosher goods rather than Israeli ones, and which turned out to be intended to protect those goods from boycotters. Even if this was a misguided decision, it was not a conscious boycott action. The Tricycle theatre tried to put pressure on the Jewish film festival to cut its ties to the Israeli government, but insisted this was not a boycott. And George Galloway called for all Israeli people and produce to be denied entry to Bradford, but took no action to implement this.

In each of these cases, the local impact in the UK was greater than any impact on the warring parties in the Middle East. At times this was so severe that Police and politicians felt compelled to intervene. All, in different ways, gave rise to allegations that antisemitism was either a motivating

---

[43] 'MP Naz Shah suspended from Labour', BBC News (27 April 2016), http://www.bbc.co.uk/news/uk-politics-36148704

factor or a consequence of anti-Israel boycotts. This highlights an enduring challenge for anti-Israel boycott campaigners: the gap between their professed motives and intentions, and how their actions manifest in practice, may be an impossible one to bridge. The evidence of the British summer of 2014 suggests that anti-Israel boycotts carry a strong risk of damaging community cohesion and fuelling antisemitic sentiment. This may not be an inevitable consequence of anti-Israel boycotts, but the events of that summer suggest it is a risk that will always be present.

CHAPTER 14

Palestine: Boycott, Localism, and Global Activism

Philip Marfleet

Discussion of the current movement for Boycott, Divestment, and Sanctions (BDS) in relation to Israel takes place in highly charged circumstances.[1] Proponents of BDS frame their efforts as a pursuit of justice for dispossessed, displaced, and marginalised Palestinians. Opponents see their campaigns at best as misguided, often as duplicitous or even malicious. For Israeli Prime Minister Benjamin Netanyahu, those associated with BDS must be "exposed and condemned".[2] The letters B, D, and S, he suggests, "really stand for bigotry, dishonesty and shame", representing

---

[1] In this context, it is important to identify the background of the author. I have been a supporter of Palestinian rights and freedoms since a first direct engagement with the realities of Middle East politics in 1967. I have worked for human rights organisations, focusing on the Middle East, and in universities in Egypt and the UK. I was an early member of the academic boycott campaign vis-à-vis Israel and continue to support the British Committee for Universities of Palestine (Bricup: http://www.bricup.org.uk).

[2] Benjamin Netanyahu, "Full Transcript: Prime Minister Netanyahu's Speech at AIPAC Policy Conference, 2014", *the algemeiner*, 4 March 2014.

P. Marfleet (✉)
University of East London, London, UK
e-mail: P.Marfleet@uel.ac.uk

© The Author(s) 2019
D. Feldman (ed.), *Boycotts Past and Present*, Palgrave Critical Studies of Antisemitism and Racism,
https://doi.org/10.1007/978-3-319-94872-0_14

"simply the latest chapter in the long, dark history of anti-Semitism".[3] On this view, investigation of the BDS movement based on its discourses and practices would confirm that activists are animated by Judaeophobia, that "Anti-Semitism isn't merely an aspect of BDS: it is its essence".[4] In their published work, Israeli academics have been almost unanimous in viewing the BDS movement similarly—as an expression of historic prejudice in which hostility towards Israel converges with antisemitism.[5] The present chapter nonetheless approaches the BDS movement as a social phenomenon that cannot be explained plausibly as a global surge of anti-Jewish sentiment; rather, it should be understood in the context of wider agendas for political and social change focused upon principles of social justice. Here conflicts in Israel/Palestine are among a series of issues addressed by activists worldwide: BDS is a current within movements of contention that challenge the dominant order in the Middle East and across the Global South and the Global North. The chapter also suggests that the scale and energy of the BDS movement is associated with new constituencies of social action in Europe and North America, and with forms of Palestinian agency that reflect a generational change in Palestinian nationalism.

The BDS campaign was initiated formally in 2005 by some 170 Palestinian civil society organisations. They called for implementation of "non-violent punitive measures", with the aim of compelling Israel: (i) to end occupation and colonisation of all Arab lands and to dismantle the [Separation/Apartheid] Wall; (ii) to recognise the fundamental rights of Arab-Palestinian citizens of Israel to full equality; and (iii) to respect, protect, and promote the rights of Palestinian refugees to return to their homes and properties as stipulated in UN resolution 194.[6] The appeal invoked an historic precedent—the concerted international campaign against South Africa that began in the 1960s:

> We, representatives of Palestinian civil society, call upon international civil society organizations and people of conscience all over the world to impose broad boycotts and implement divestment initiatives against Israel similar to those applied to South Africa in the apartheid era. We appeal to you to

---

[3] Netanyahu, "Full Transcript".
[4] Jonathan S. Tobin, "Friedman's Immoral Intifada", *Commentary*, 6 February 2014.
[5] See, for example, the collection of papers, most by Israeli academics, in *Israel Affairs*, vol. 18, no. 3, (July 2012), Special Issue: "War by other means: Israel and its detractors".
[6] BDS Movement, "Palestinian Civil Society Call for BDS", accessed 6 November 2017. https://bdsmovement.net/call

pressure your respective states to impose embargoes and sanctions against Israel. We also invite conscientious Israelis to support this Call, for the sake of justice and genuine peace.[7]

For several years its critics insisted that the movement was certain to fail and would soon peter out. In Israel, there was near-unanimity among political leaders, in the media and in academia, that BDS would be ineffectual internationally and in terms of domestic opinion. Abroad, opponents of the movement saw it as strong on rhetoric but chronically weak in terms of impact.[8] There were signs of unease, however, among strategic analysts. In 2010, the Reut Institute, a think tank linked to decision-makers within the Israeli state, reported that BDS activities were tarnishing Israel's reputation and that even selective partial boycotts could be "a milestone on the road to a comprehensive boycott of Israel".[9] Reut concluded that BDS had developed "a set of ideas that are increasingly sophisticated, ripe [sic], lucid, and coherent"; combined with sustained action, it suggested, these could amount to "a systemic and systematic assault on Israel's political model", amounting to a strategic challenge that was "potentially existential".[10]

By 2014, leading political figures in Israel had modified their approach. On the one hand, they continued to assert that BDS could never succeed; on the other hand, they expressed deepening concern about its influence. Addressing a policy conference of the American Israel Public Affairs Committee in March 2014, Netanyahu insisted, "That movement [BDS] will fail".[11] In devoting much of his speech to the BDS campaign, however, he recognised implicitly its growing impact, including its effects on governments and inter-governmental organisations. In August 2013, US officials had informed Israeli counterparts that in order to advance peace talks with

[7] BDS Movement, "Palestinian Civil Society Call".
[8] Nick Grey, Director of Christian Middle East Watch, described BDS initiatives in Britain as "a complete failure", asserting that "the noise and mess of BDS meetings and demonstrations is empty posturing and publicity": Nick Grey, "The failures of the Israel boycotters", *The Commentator*, 12 July 2012.
[9] Reut Institute, "The BDS Movement Promotes Delegitimization of the State of Israel", *ReViews* 16, June 10, 2010, 9, accessed 6 November 2017. http://www.reut-institute.org/data/uploads/PDFVer/20100612%20ReViews%20-%20BDS%20Issue%2016_1.pdf
[10] Reut Institute, "Building a Political Firewall Against Israel's Delegitimization: Conceptual Framework"; March 10, 2010, 13, 15, accessed 6 November 2017, http://reut-institute.org/data/uploads/PDFVer/20100310%20Delegitimacy%20Eng.pdf
[11] Netanyahu, "Full transcript".

the Palestinian National Authority (PA) they would back sanctions invoked by the European Union (EU) on Israel's settlements in the West Bank.[12] At the same time, US Secretary of State John Kerry warned Netanyahu that failure in the talks would prompt a "boycott campaign on steroids".[13] In December 2013, the Israeli newspaper *Haaretz* quoted European diplomats to the effect that if negotiations with the Palestinians ran aground "you [Israeli officials] should expect a deluge of sanctions".[14] In a detailed assessment of BDS, *Haaretz* concluded that these "dire warnings" were credible, quoting the Molad Center—a liberal Israeli think tank—to the effect that as BDS initiatives spread, Israel suffered general damage to its foreign relations.[15] Molad was particularly exercised by what it called the "silent boycott"—a policy of avoidance of Israel and Israeli institutions that, it said, had "vast" reach in the fields of culture, art, entertainment, and academia.[16] This development, suggested the centre, was "an outcome of the sweeping opposition to Israeli policy towards the Palestinians".[17]

BDS had meanwhile established a modest but vocal presence among Israeli citizens, including Israeli Jews, who declared for boycott measures as "a call from within".[18] When in 2014 activists in the United States compiled a list of Jewish organisations in North America and Europe that backed further BDS action, they concluded: "this wide-ranging support of course reminds us of how nonsensical and futile it is to deploy classic anti-Semitic imagery in an attempt to delegitimize what is a growing international movement for human rights and legal equality".[19]

In 2015, Israeli President Reuven Rivlin identified BDS campaigns among academics and students as a "threat [to Israel] of the first order".[20]

[12] Barak Ravid, "EU Official Says U.S. Quietly Supporting Settlement Sanctions", *Haaretz*, 14 August 2013.

[13] Barak Ravid, "Swell of Boycotts Driving Israel into International Isolation", *Haaretz*, 12 December 2013.

[14] Ravid (2013) "Swell of boycotts".

[15] Ravid (2013) "Swell of boycotts".

[16] Molad Center (2013) *Alliance in Crisis: Israel's Standing in the World and the Question of Isolation*, 2013, 3, accessed 6 November 2017, http://www.molad.org/images/upload/files/Isolation_Report.pdf

[17] Molad Center, *Alliance in Crisis*, 33.

[18] See statements of Boycott! Supporting the Palestinian BDS Call from Within, accessed 6 November 2017, http://www.boycottisrael.info

[19] Paul Duffill and Gabriella Skoff, "Growing Jewish Support for Boycott and the Changing Landscape of the BDS Debate", *Mondoweiss*, June 17, 2014.

[20] Jonathan Lis and Yarden Skop, "Rivlin: Academic Boycotts Against Israel Are First-rate Strategic Threat", *Haaretz*, 28 May 2015.

"The atmosphere in the world is changing", he said, "making it impossible not to see this issue as a strategic threat".[21] Soon afterwards, Prime Minister Netanyahu created a new government office—that of minister of public security, strategic affairs, and information—delegating the appointee, Gilad Erdan, to contest BDS campaigns and other "anti-Israel" activities.[22] The Israeli newspaper *Haaretz* concluded that although the real effectiveness of boycott campaigns had yet to be demonstrated, "It's a BDS world".[23]

Global Audience

The first focused analysis of the BDS movement was produced in 2009 by Abigail Bakan and Yasmeen Abu-Laban. They viewed its initiatives as "positive", "progressive", and "anti-racist"—attempts to contest Palestinian dispossession, discrimination, and marginality that found an unprecedentedly sympathetic response worldwide.[24] This should be understood, they argued, by reference to the new environment in which Palestinian activists sought solidarity. BDS should be seen as "an important component of the transnational popular opposition to neoliberal globalisation and the quest for social justice that marked the first period of the new millennium".[25] Here, BDS was associated with activist networks that emerged fully after protests at the World Trade Organisation conference of 1999—the "Battle of Seattle". In 2001, the networks organised a "convergence"—a World Social Forum (WSF) at Porto Alegre, Brazil. This aimed to co-ordinate "groups and movements of civil society that are opposed to neoliberalism and to domination of the world by capital and any form of imperialism".[26] Pledged to advance the principle that "another world is possible", the Forum resolved, inter alia:

---

[21] Lis and Skop, "Rivlin: Academic Boycotts".
[22] Asher Schechter, "If BDS Isn't a Real Threat, Why Does Netanyahu Make It Out To Be Such a Big Deal", *Haaretz*, 2 June 2015.
[23] Schechter, "If BDS Isn't a Real Threat".
[24] Abigail B. Bakan and Yasmeen Abu-Laban, 'Palestinian Resistance and International Solidarity: The BDS Campaign', *Race and Class*, vol. 51, no. 1, (June 2009), 30, 31, 32.
[25] Abigail B. Bakan and Yasmeen Abu-Laban, "Palestinian resistance", 35.
[26] Fórum Social Mondial, "World Social Forum Charter of Principles", 8 June 2002; accessed 6 November 2017, http://www.forumsocialmundial.org.br/main.php?id_menu=4&cd_language=2

[To] ensure that globalization in solidarity will prevail as a new stage in world history. This will respect universal human rights, and those of all citizens – men and women – of all nations and the environment [sic] and will rest on democratic international systems and institutions at the service of social justice, equality and the sovereignty of peoples.[27]

Further forums took place annually, addressing broad agendas including global poverty, corporate misconduct, environmental issues, land rights, access to water, racism, the claims of indigenous peoples, women's rights, migration, and statelessness. From the first, Palestine featured prominently in discussion on rights and self-determination, and as the Forum's initiatives gathered pace, the Palestine issue was projected to an unprecedentedly large global audience.

The WSF's mode of organisation posed a challenge for academic analysts. Boaventura de Sousa Santos commented that the Forum stood outside familiar political and social categories.[28] It could not be seen as an event or a scholarly conference; it was not a party, an NGO, or a confederation of NGOs, nor even a social movement. Rather, he suggested, it was "a new social and political phenomenon"—a "set of initiatives" among and between social movements and NGOs.[29] These diverse, open-ended, and sometimes chaotic initiatives brought criticism from some participants and sympathetic academic observers[30]; they were nonetheless congenial to those whose concerns had not hitherto engaged sympathetic public discussion, notably Palestinian activists. In December 2002, the WSF organised a thematic forum on Peace in the Middle East, held in Palestine (at Ramallah) with local activists and large delegations from Latin America, North America, Europe, and Asia. Its key aim, said the Forum, was: "To integrate the Palestinian National cause in the Global Agenda of social movements and civil societies, as it is an integral part of the world movement towards human freedom".[31] Palestine subsequently appeared as a key issue at annual convergences and at numerous regional forums.

[27] Fórum Social Mondial, "World Social Forum Charter".
[28] Boaventura de Sousa Santos, *The Rise of the Global Left: the World Social Forum and Beyond* (London, 2003).
[29] Boaventura de Sousa Santos, *Rise of the Global Left*, 7.
[30] See, for example, comments on the World Social Forum held in Nairobi: Frank Kürschner-Pelkmann, "Near chaos in Nairobi", *D+C – Development and Cooperation*, no. 3, (2007), 130.
[31] Relief Web (UN OCHA), "World Social Forum on Palestine (Ramallah – Palestine) – Draft", 26 December, 2002, accessed 7 November 2017, https://reliefweb.int/report/israel/world-social-forum-palestine-ramallah-palestine-draft

Durban and After

Bakan and Abu-Laban observe that the BDS movement inspired civil society actors worldwide to challenge the dominant narrative of the Israel/Palestine conflict, one that for decades had endorsed Israeli claims; in particular, they suggest, BDS challenged "the hegemonic framing of Israel as a victim state in the face of Palestinian 'terrorism'".[32] New approaches to the Israel/Palestine question had in fact been emerging before the launch of BDS and before the WSF initiatives that proved so favourable to the Palestinian cause.

In 1998, the United Nations General Assembly proclaimed 2001 as the International Year of Mobilisation against Racism, Racial Discrimination, Xenophobia, and Related Intolerance and prepared for a World Conference to be held in Durban, South Africa. The event was dominated by intense argument over Israel, the ideology and practices of the Zionist movement, and Palestinian rights to self-determination.[33] A draft closing statement opposed "movements based on racism and discriminatory ideas, in particular the Zionist movement, which is based on racial superiority".[34] After delegations from the United States, Canada, and Israel withdrew, a final statement on Palestine declared (para 5):

> We are concerned about the plight of the Palestinian people under foreign occupation ... We recognize the inalienable right of the Palestinian people to self-determination and to the establishment of an independent State and we recognize the right to security for all States in the region, including Israel, and call upon all States to support the peace process and bring it to an early conclusion.[35]

---

[32] Bakan and Abu-Laban, "Palestinian resistance", 31.

[33] Palestinians were represented by a delegation at the conference on the basis that Palestine was a non-state "entity".

[34] "The Racism Walkout; The Cause and the Effect: Two Excerpts" [World Conference against Racism, Racial Discrimination, Xenophobia and Related Intolerance], *New York Times*, 4 September 2001, accessed 6 November 2017. http://www.nytimes.com/2001/09/04/world/the-racism-walkout-the-cause-and-the-effect-two-excerpts.html

[35] "The Accord on Racism: The Declaration; Regrets for Past Wrongs And Hopes for Peace" [World Conference against Racism, Racial Discrimination, Xenophobia and Related Intolerance], *New York Times*, 9 September 2001, accessed 6 November 2017. http://www.nytimes.com/2001/09/09/world/the-accord-on-racism-the-declaration-regrets-for-past-wrongs-and-hopes-for-peace.html

Israeli officials reacted furiously, describing the conference as "a farce": Israel Ministry of Foreign Affairs, "Briefing by Foreign Minister Shimon Peres and Deputy Foreign Minister

A parallel NGO Forum (often confused with the conference proper) was meanwhile debating similar issues, including in its final declaration (para 20) an affirmation of "the right of the Palestinian people to self-determination, statehood, independence and freedom and the right of return as stipulated in UN Resolution 194".[36]

The immediate effect of the Durban events was to encourage Palestinian activists to seek new forms of solidarity. BDS activist Omar Barghouti notes the importance of the NGO Forum: this, he said, had "condemned Zionism as a form of racism and apartheid", adding that it was "an expression of the views of thousands of civil society representatives from across the globe, whose struggle against all forms of racism, including antisemitism, is mostly informed by humanistic and democratic principles".[37] The references to apartheid at Durban were significant, not only because of analogies with ideas and practices that were widely reviled but also because leading figures of the anti-apartheid struggle in South Africa strongly encouraged Palestinian activists to consider the use of what they called "weapons of the weak"—the strategy of BDS. Among them were veterans of the anti-apartheid movement who, shortly after the Durban conference, presented a statement to the South African parliament highly critical of Israeli policies. This asserted that, "it becomes difficult, particularly from a South African perspective, not to draw parallels with the oppression experienced by Palestinians under the hand of Israel and the oppression experienced in South Africa under Apartheid rule".[38] Authored by Ronnie Kasrils and Max Olinsky, the statement called on "South Africans of Jewish descent" to join an international movement committed to justice for

---

Michael Melchior to the Diplomatic Corps", 4 September 2001, accessed 6 November 2017. http://www.mfa.gov.il/mfa/pressroom/2001/pages/briefing%20by%20fm%20shimon%20peres%20and%20deputy%20fm%20michael.aspx

[36] NGO Forum [World Conference Against Racism, Racial Discrimination, Xenophobia and Related Intolerance], 2001, "Declaration – Guiding Principles", accessed 6 November 2017. http://academic.udayton.edu/race/06hrights/WCAR2001/NGOFORUM/DeclarationIntro.htm

[37] Omar Barghouti, *Boycott, Divestment, Sanctions: The Global Struggle for Palestinian Rights* (Chicago, 2011), 54.

[38] Jon Jeter, "South African Jews Polarized Over Israel: Anti-Racism Leaders Equate Country's Treatment of Palestinians to Apartheid", *Washington Post*, 19 December 2001, accessed 7 November 2017. http://www.mafhoum.com/press2/saj75.htm

Palestine.[39] Archbishop Desmond Tutu, a leading churchman during the anti-apartheid struggle, endorsed their appeal, observing:

> The end of apartheid stands as one of the crowning accomplishments of the past century, but we would not have succeeded without the help of international pressure – in particular the divestment movement of the 1980s. Over the past six months a similar movement has taken shape, this time aiming at an end to the Israeli occupation ... If apartheid ended, so can the occupation, but the moral force and international pressure will have to be just as determined.[40]

PALESTINIAN PREDICAMENTS

The key actors animating BDS initiatives were not at meetings in South Africa, however; rather they were in Israel, in territories under Israeli control and across the Palestinian diaspora. The BDS movement was launched by Palestinian activists as a means of addressing their own existential difficulties, for as international developments offered opportunities to engage with wider audiences, the Arab population of historic Palestine faced an acute crisis.

The Oslo Accords between Israel and the Palestinian Liberation Organisation (PLO), and the "peace process" begun in 1993, had produced little for the majority of Palestinians. In 2000, Palestinian academic Edward Said wrote: "What of this vaunted peace process? What has it achieved and why, if indeed it was a peace process, has the miserable condition of the Palestinians and the loss of life become so much worse than before the Oslo Accords were signed in September 1993?".[41] There was growing anger over territorial arrangements, which fragmented Palestinian territory and made remote the prospect of a meaningful

---

[39] The declaration initially attracted 220 signatories. John Battersby and Jeremy Gordin, "Jewish Declaration of Conscience Launched", *IOL News*, 8 December 2001, accessed 6 November 2017. https://www.iol.co.za/news/politics/jewish-declaration-of-conscience-launched-78160

[40] Ian Urbina and Archbishop Desmond Tutu, "Against Israeli Apartheid", *The Nation*, 15 July 2002, accessed 6 November 2017. https://www.thenation.com/article/against-israeli-apartheid/

[41] Edward Said, 'Palestinians under Siege', *London Review of Books*, vol. 22, no. 24, (10 December 2000).

independent state.⁴² Meanwhile, the Israeli settler population in the West Bank grew rapidly.⁴³ This was the outcome of a sustained project backed by successive Israeli governments: Israeli researcher Gershom Gorenberg describes "a vast investment of state effort and funding" that included integration of settlements into the legal, governmental, and infrastructural networks of Israel proper.⁴⁴ The Israeli economy boomed, boosted by immigration and rapid growth of high-tech industries: the Palestinian economy slumped. Unemployment among Palestinians soared: by 2002, the level was fluctuating between 35% and 50%⁴⁵; key indices of social deprivation in Gaza and the West Bank rose rapidly.⁴⁶

The majority of Palestinians experienced steady deterioration in their circumstances: a minority, however, benefited from both political and economic change. A yawning gap was opening between, on the one hand, historic leaders of the Palestinian national movement led by Yasser Arafat and, on the other hand, the mass of people affected by the settlement

---

⁴² Under the Oslo II agreement, the PA enjoyed direct control over 18% of the territory of West Bank; the Palestinian National Authority (PA) and Israel jointly controlled 22% of the territory (with 70% of the Palestinian population); and Israel retained full control of the remainder.

⁴³ In 1993, Israeli government statistics had recorded 281,800 Jewish settlers in the Palestinian Territories; by 2003, the total was 427,617: Foundation for Middle East Peace, "Comprehensive Settlement Population 1972–201", 13 January 2012, accessed 6 November 2017. www.fmep.org/settlement_info/settlement-info-and-tables/stats-data/israeli-settler-population-1972-2006

⁴⁴ Gershom Gorenberg, *Occupied Territories: The Untold Story of Israel's settlements* (London, 2007), 364. In 1998, Foreign Minister (later Prime Minister) Ariel Sharon told Jewish settlers in areas of the West Bank allocated to the PA, "Everyone should take action, should run, should grab more hills … We'll expand the area. Whatever is seized will be ours. Whatever isn't seized will end up in their hands", Deborah Sontag, "Arafat and Netanyahu Trade Threats as Tensions Rise on the Peace Accord", *New York Times*, 17 November 1998, accessed 6 November 2017. http://www.nytimes.com/1998/11/17/world/arafat-and-netanyahu-trade-threats-as-tensions-rise-on-the-peace-accord.html

⁴⁵ Between 1992 and 1994, the number of permits issued to Palestinians from the Territories to work in Israel fell from 115,000 to 65,000 as they were replaced with workers from the Philippines, Thailand, China, and Eastern Europe: Michael Ellman and Smain Laacher, *Migrant Workers in Israel – A Contemporary Form of Slavery* (Copenhagen/Paris, 2003), 11.

⁴⁶ Fadle M. Naqib, 'Economic Aspects of the Palestinian-Israeli Conflict: The Collapse of the Oslo Accord', *Journal of International Development*, vol. 14, no. 4, (May 2003), 419–512; Sara, 'Why Peace Failed: An Oslo Autopsy', *Current History*, vol. 100, no. 651, (2002), 11–27.

process and by Israel's constraints on movement, employment, and access to resources.⁴⁷ The PA leadership was soon at the centre of new networks of privilege, benefiting from an economic regime imposed on the Territories after 1993 jointly by the United States, the World Bank, and Israel.⁴⁸ This was shaped by a neo-liberal agenda similar to that applied widely across the Global South, combining free-market economics with a self-seeking authoritarian state.⁴⁹ In the case of the Palestinian "entity", the PA elite was supported by a large security apparatus that included multiple police and intelligence forces, implementing what Usher called a "martial mode of governance" responsible for all manner of abuses vis-à-vis the majority of Palestinians.⁵⁰

For decades, the Palestinian national movement had been dominated by leaders determined to contain independent activity among the mass of people. Yasser Arafat and his colleagues in Al Fatah, the core of the PLO, were deeply suspicious of political actions they did not initiate.⁵¹ Fatah was in addition committed to the principle of "non-interference" under which it pledged to inhibit Palestinian involvement in the politics of Arab states. This complemented the approach of Arab regimes anxious to keep the incendiary Palestinian issue at the margin of domestic politics (the quid pro quo being agreement by the regimes to provide arms and money to

---

⁴⁷ Tariq Dana, "Corruption in Palestine: A Self-Enforcing System", *Al-Shabaka*, 18 August 2015.

⁴⁸ Rex Brynen (1995) 'The Neopatrimonial Dimension of Palestinian Politics', *Journal of Palestine Studies*, vol. 25, no. 1, (Autumn 1995), 23–36.

⁴⁹ Neo-liberal policies, pursued aggressively since the mid-1970s by the major international financial institutions, were also taking their effect in neighbouring states—notably in Egypt, where they provided the context for a decade of protests that preceded the revolution of 2011. See Adam Hanieh, *Lineages of Revolt: Issues of Contemporary Capitalism in the Middle East* (Chicago, 2013); Rabab El-Mahdi and Philip Marfleet, *Egypt – The Moment of Change* (London, 2009); and Philip Marfleet, *Egypt – Contested Revolution* (London, 2016).

⁵⁰ Graham Usher, *Palestine in Crisis: The Struggle For Peace and Political Independence After Oslo* (London, 1998), 157. See also Ali Abunimah, *The Battle for Justice in Palestine* (Chicago, 2014).

⁵¹ Concern with management of Palestinian politics and society dominated the agendas of the PA—a key reason why in 1993 Israeli leaders expressed confidence that the Authority would police the West Bank and Gaza more effectively than the Israeli army. Israeli Prime Minister Yitzak Rabin told the newspaper *Yediot Aharanot* (7 September 1993): "The Palestinians will be better at it than we were"; adding, "they will rule by their own methods, freeing, and this is most important, the Israeli army soldiers from doing what they will do." Quoted in Usher, *Palestine in Crisis*, 154.

the PLO). Relations between Palestinians and people of the region were therefore managed formally at the governmental level (the PLO being treated as official representative of the Palestinian people) and the organisation's official quest for solidarity was focused upon governments and diplomatic networks[52]: Palestinian leaders invoked Arab fraternity, calling upon members of the Arab League to enforce a boycott on Israel originally agreed after the war of 1948. The boycott had for years been imposed unevenly, however, and was increasingly ineffective.[53] In an assessment of its efficacy in the mid-1970s, Nancy Turck[54] saw a "practically dormant dimension of Israeli-Arab politics … almost unknown and irrelevant", quoting Israeli Minister of Commerce Chaim Bar-Lev to the effect that: "The Arab boycott means nothing to us. It has no effect on Israel".[55] In a detailed analysis of the boycott in the mid-1990s, Gil Feiler identified a trend from "confrontation to cooperation", concluding that the project was "disintegrating".[56]

In from the Margins

A generation of Palestinian activists who observed the Oslo Process with growing frustration resolved to bring their predicaments to wider attention. The Palestinian national leadership was "unelected, unrepresentative, unprincipled, and visionless", argued Omar Barghouti; it had for

---

[52] On the development of Palestine Liberation Organization (PLO) strategies vis-à-vis Arab states, see Helena Schulz, *The Reconstruction of Palestinian Nationalism: Between Revolution and Statehood* (Manchester, 1999), 23–51.

[53] Estimates of the cumulative cost of the Arab League boycott to the Israeli economy between 1948 and the peace agreement of 1993 vary from $40 billion to $50 billion: Ofira Seliktar, 'The Peace Dividend: The Economy of Israel and the Peace Process', in: *The Middle East Peace Process: Interdisciplinary Perspectives*, ed. Ilan Pelleg, (Albany, 1997), 225.

[54] Nancy Turck, 'The Middle East: The Arab Boycott of Israel', *Foreign Affairs*, vol. 55, no 3, (April 1977), 472–493.

[55] Nancy Turck, 'The Middle East: The Arab Boycott of Israel', *Foreign Affairs*, vol. 55, no. 3, (April 1977), 472.

[56] Gil Feiler, *From Boycott to Economic Cooperation: The Political Economy of the Arab Boycott of Israel* (London, 1998), 5, 1. Egypt withdrew from the boycott in 1979 and following the Oslo Accords the PA pulled out, followed by Jordan and later by the Gulf states.

years been "in total disarray".[57] It was in these circumstances that young Palestinians, members of NGOs rather than of formal structures of the PA, sought new allies. Their interaction with activists from across the Global South at the Durban forum of 2001 soon brought a novel experience—that of engagement in discussion about global affairs in which Palestinians' concerns were integrated uncontroversially into agendas for radical change.

The issue of Palestine had long been viewed as a special case in international affairs—one in which the claims of the Zionist movement made comparison with other examples of dispossession, mass displacement, and exclusion unusually difficult. One catalyst for change was the process of globalisation, which offered new options to reach transnational audiences with what Clifford Bob—using the resources of social movement theory—calls "symbols of oppression and repertoires of contention".[58] By the 1970s, an international regime for human rights had been established at the level of legal instruments and institutional structures. The rise of global communications and media subsequently afforded hitherto marginal groups novel opportunities to project their arguments and to advance these within the context of rights: globalisation amplified claims for justice, providing the possibility of recognition and response, of solidarity and emulation. Intervention by Palestinians within the social justice networks disseminated their accounts of the Israel-Palestine conflict among unprecedentedly large audiences.[59]

---

[57] Barghouti, *Boycott, Divestment, Sanctions*, 7. Comparing the crisis of the PA with that of leaders of the national movement during the mandate period of British rule, Nigel Parsons aptly describes: "a divided Palestinian elite, trapped in a paradoxical framework, compromised by the need for patronage, insecure amid growing socio-economic discontent, fearful amid grassroots rebellion, weary amid the wreckage, desperate for a temporary diplomatic lifeline." Nigel Parsons, 'Palestinian statehood: Aspirations, needs, and viability after Oslo', (review article) *Middle East Journal*, vol. 61, no. 3, (2007), 523.

[58] Clifford Bob, 'Globalization and the Social Construction of Human Rights Campaigns', in: *Globalization and Human Rights*, ed. Alison Brysk, (Berkeley, 2002), 134.

[59] See also the analysis of the Boycott, Divestment, and Sanctions (BDS) movement in the context of social movement theory in Suzanne Morrison, 'The Emergence of the Boycott, Divestment and Sanctions Movement', in: *Contentious Politics in the Middle East*, ed. F. Gerges, (Basingstoke, 2015). For a detailed analysis of BDS campaigns in the transnational context, see: Suzanne Morrison, *The Boycott, Divestment, and Sanctions Movement: Activism Across Borders for Palestinian Justice* [PhD Thesis], London School of Economics, 2015, accessed 6 November 2017, http://etheses.lse.ac.uk/3350/1/Morrison_The_Boycott_Divestment.pdf

The Palestine issue, suggests John Collins, became "Global Palestine"—expressive of "the politics of globalisation in general".[60] In the new millennium, Palestinians could be located at the intersection of two global processes: they had been a target of settler colonialism and of local practices that helped to catalyse an emerging world of pervasive securitisation and intense violence; they were now also important actors in and symbols of an ongoing struggle for global justice.[61] Palestinians were in effect both victims of inequities that were increasingly general and recognisable and active social agents whose resistance prompted solidarity and in some cases emulation.

These developments intersected with the rise of anti-war movements in North America and Europe. Military interventions by the United States and its allies in Afghanistan and Iraq prompted widespread public protest: demonstrations in 2003 in cities such as Barcelona, London, Rome, and New York were some of the largest ever recorded.[62] Mobilisations of the WSF and of anti-war initiatives were mutually reinforcing, prompting demonstration effects and movement "crossovers" that provided space for activists to advance a particularly wide range of issues. In these cycles of contestation, Palestine was increasingly prominent, not only because of the relevance of Middle East conflicts in general but because, as Reitan notes, Palestinians had developed forms of organisation increasingly effective in the global context.[63] There was a feedback effect. In Palestine, a new generation of activists urgently sought means to address the deepening crisis caused by Israeli policy and by acute problems in the national movement: strongly encouraged by the social justice and anti-war networks they achieved unprecedented unity of local organisations in support of the 2005 BDS appeal.[64] In an observation that underlines the impor-

---

[60] John Collins, *Global Palestine* (London, 2011), 1.

[61] Collins, *Global Palestine*, 3.

[62] The scale of protest prompted comment in the *New York Times* that: "there may still be two superpowers on the planet: the United States and world public opinion". Patrick E. Tyler, "Threats and Responses: News Analysis; A New Power in the Streets", *New York Times*, 17 February 2003; accessed 7 November 2017, http://www.nytimes.com/2003/02/17/world/threats-and-responses-news-analysis-a-new-power-in-the-streets.html

[63] Ruth Reitan, 'The Global Anti-War Movement Within and Beyond the World Social Forum'. *Globalizations*, vol. 6, no. 4, (2009), 516.

[64] This was backed by Palestinian trade unions; women's, students', peasants', and refugee organisations; community groups; human rights initiatives; and cultural bodies, including widely differing political currents. Full list at BDS Movement, "Palestinian Civil Society Call".

tance of Palestinian agency in advancing BDS, Nadia Hijab comments that the 2005 appeal was "perhaps the most significant document the Palestinian people have produced since the first national movement emerged in the 1960s".[65]

New Constituencies

Collins suggests that contemporary Palestine has always been more than "a simple location on a map".[66] The displacements of 1948 scattered refugees across the Arab East and the Gulf states; subsequent migrations dispersed Palestinians worldwide. As in other diasporas, refugees made sustained efforts to transmit their experiences within families and community networks, and to non-Palestinian audiences among which they hoped for solidarity and campaigning action. For many decades they were unsuccessful. Outside the Arab region and certain states of Africa and Asia, the Palestinian case went unheard or was received with scepticism, most solidarity initiatives being confined to small groups in which Arab activists and left-wing currents played leading roles. It was particularly difficult to find sympathetic audiences in Europe and North America: John Chalcraft points out that trans-regional solidarity movements focused on the Middle East region and that extended to the populations of colonial or ex-colonial centres had been rare and relatively weak.[67] As the Palestine issue entered social justice networks, however, there was a change: BDS campaigns grew rapidly, engaging new constituencies that included people with their own diasporic experiences. Boycott initiatives were undertaken in diverse ways that, observes Maia Carter Hallward, could be based on local needs and values, and in which activists often acted as "brokers" between groups with related goals and moral frameworks.[68] For the first time a movement focused on Palestinian interests had potential to draw in constituencies

---

[65] Nadia Hijab, 'Reversing defeat through non-violent power', in: *The Failure of the Two-State Solution: The Prospects of One State in the Israel-Palestine Conflict*, ed. Hani Faris, (London, 2013), 273.
[66] Collins, *Global Palestine*, 4.
[67] John Chalcraft, *Popular Politics in the Making of the Modern Middle East* (Cambridge, 2016), 512.
[68] Maia Carter Hallward, *Transnational Activism and the Israeli-Palestinian Conflict* (Basingstoke, 2013), 34.

worldwide: one possibility, suggests Chalcraft, is that would develop "unstoppable momentum".[69]

The Palestinian call for BDS was directed to "international civil society organizations and people of conscience": responses reflected recognition of the Palestinian predicament that drew on widespread experiences of global change. This is particularly clear in the case of support for BDS among churches and faith-based organisations (FBOs) in Europe and North America. For three decades after the Second World War, European states had solicited migrants from former colonies; in the 1980s, further migrations brought large numbers of refugees, among whom many originated in zones of crisis in which dispossession, displacement, and civil conflict were systemic.[70] These experiences, together with the realities of discrimination and marginalisation in Europe, became part of diasporic cultures in which ideas about rights, freedom of movement, self-determination, and refugee return were central.[71] There was a profound effect upon religious institutions. In many European cities, established churches long in decline were revitalised by immigrant congregations[72]; at the same time, migrants established new churches.[73] In both cases, theologies of social activism that originated in the Global South, notably Liberation Theology and radical Pentecostalism,[74] had a major impact. Some churches became centres for advocacy and protection of vulnerable migrants, as during the *sans-papiers* mobilisations that began in France in

---

[69] Chalcraft, *Popular Politics*, 514.

[70] Philip Marfleet, *Refugees in a Global Era* (Basingstoke, 2006).

[71] Wendy Pojmann (ed.), *Migration and Activism in Europe Since 1945* (Basingstoke, 2008).

[72] Peter Brierley, *Pulling out of the Nosedive – A Contemporary Picture of Churchgoing* (London, 2006); Ruth Gledhill, "Church attendance has been propped up by immigrants, says study", *Guardian*, 3 June 2014; accessed 7 November 2017. https://www.theguardian.com/world/2014/jun/03/church-attendance-propped-immigrants-study

[73] Abel Ugba, *Shades of Belonging: African Pentecostals in Twenty-First Century Ireland* (Trenton, 2008).

[74] To be distinguished from politically conservative Pentecostalisms associated with prosperity doctrines and neo-liberal economic agendas. Pentecostalist churches in sub-Saharan Africa, and especially in South Africa, have often identified strongly with struggles for social justice. On the impact of faith-based organisations (FBOs) in migrant communities, see Linda Rabben, *Give Refuge to the Stranger* (Walnut Creek, 2011) and Susanna Snyder, *Asylum Seeking, Migration and the Church* (Farnham, 2012).

1996,[75] and FBOs from Europe were prominent among early participants in the WSF.[76] There were similar developments in Canada and in the United States. In the latter, migrants from Central America had for 50 years been a key component of the US labour force: millions were technically "illegal" and highly vulnerable. FBOs had long played a leading role in networks of solidarity, notably through the Sanctuary Movement, which provided support and sometimes protection for those most at risk.[77] Some churches adopted migrant-centred agendas that combined advocacy in the local context with issues of global social justice—and it was in this context that Palestine was projected more and more insistently into church networks worldwide. Despite the attachment of some Protestant currents to Christian Zionism, and their identification with Israel, by the 1990s, the issue of Palestine was a matter of concern among many congregations. In 2004, the Presbyterian Church, USA, was the first major Christian organisation to debate BDS and to adopt a formal policy of divestment: other denominations in the United States, including Methodists, Quakers, and Mennonites were to follow.

In 2007, the WSF in Nairobi was attended by scores of Christian organisations and by an ecumenical coalition led by the World Council of Churches.[78] Encouraged by these developments, in 2009, Palestinian

---

[75] Jane Freedman, 'The French 'Sans-Papiers' Movement: An Unfinished Struggle', in: *Migration* and *Activism*, ed. Pojmann.

[76] FBOs had already been active in Jubilee 2000, a global advocacy campaign that worked for debt forgiveness—cancellation of debt obligations of states in the Global South. Many embraced broad issues of social justice and later sent representatives to the WSF. See Carole J.L. Collins, Zie Gariyo, and Tony Burdon, 'Jubilee 2000: Citizen Action Across the North-South Divide', in: *Global Citizen Action*, eds. Michael Edwards and John Gaventa, (London, 2001), 135–148.

[77] Rabben, *Give Refuge*.

[78] Among issues under discussion was "the responsibility to protect". The Coalition asked: "if populations are at severe risk and their governments are not protecting them, the international community has a responsibility for doing so. How do churches—which play an important role in prevention, assistance, healing and reconciliation—deal with these issues?" Participants included the All Africa Conference of Churches, the Association of World Council of Churches Related Development Organisations in Europe, Brazil Ecumenical Forum, Caritas International, International Cooperation for Development and Solidarity, Ecumenical Advocacy Alliance, Frontier Internship in Mission, Koinonia, Lutheran World Federation, Pax Romana, World Alliance of Reformed Churches, World Council of Churches, World Student Christian Federation, the Young Women's Christian Association, and the Young Men's Christian Association. Daniel Blake, "Ecumenical Coalition to Participate in 7th World Social Forum", *Christian Today*, January 19, 2007; accessed 7 November 2017, http://www.christiantoday.com/article/ecumenical.coalition.to.participate.in.7th.world.social.forum/9191.htm

churches presented a unified Kairos Appeal,[79] *A Moment of Truth— Christian Palestinians' Word to the World*, calling for divestment and "an economic and commercial boycott of everything produced by the occupation".[80] In 2011, a Kairos Palestine conference held in Bethlehem launched a "Global Kairos Network" based upon what it called "Palestinian liberation theology", making the Appeal available in 22 languages.[81] In 2014, the World Council of Churches announced its support for BDS in the form of "targeted economic measures" vis-à-vis Israel—"an important nonviolent strategy for promoting peace and abating violence".[82]

A similar pattern is clear in the case of labour unions. Both FBOs and labour unions were key participants in actions against the apartheid regime in South Africa. In the case of Britain, the Anti-Apartheid Movement (AAM), founded in 1959, organised campaigns of boycott and divestment

---

[79] In 1985, a Kairos initiative in South Africa (Καιρός – Greek, "the time"/ "the moment"), supported by leading figures across Christian denominations, had called for action against racism and oppression, reflecting a wide engagement of FBOs with struggles against apartheid.

[80] Kairos Palestine, "Kairos Document – A moment of truth, A word of faith, hope and love from the heart of Palestinian suffering", Para 4.2.6, 2009, accessed 7 November 2017, http://www.kairospalestine.ps/index.php/about-us/kairos-palestine-document
See also: Archbishop Atallah Hanna, 'Towards a Just and Lasting Peace: Kairos Palestine and the Lead of the Palestinian Church', in: *Generation Palestine: Voices from the Boycott, Divestment and Sanctions Movement*, ed. Rich Wiles, (London, 2013), 100–108.

[81] Kairos Palestine, "Kairos Document".

[82] Christians, said the Council, were called upon "to take action in support of peaceful solutions to the Palestinian-Israeli conflict. Economic pressure, appropriately and openly applied, is one such means of action": World Council of Churches, "Statement on Economic Measures and Christian Responsibility toward Israel and Palestine", July 7, 2014; accessed 10 November 2017, http://www.oikoumene.org/en/resources/documents/central-committee/geneva-2014/statement-on-economic-measures-and-christian-responsibility-toward-israel-and-palestine (World Council of Churches, "Statement on Economic Measures and Christian Responsibility toward Israel and Palestine", 7 July 2014; accessed 10 November 2017, http://www.oikoumene.org/en/resources/documents/central-committee/geneva-2014/statement-on-economic-measures-and-christian-responsibility-toward-israel-and-palestine).

Among FBOs, it might be expected that Muslim organisations would play a leading role. In fact, their profile in BDS campaigns has been relatively low. This may reflect general problems of social marginalisation in Europe and North America, rising Islamophobia and a reluctance to place Muslim organisations in the front line of political action.

in which trade unions were central.[83] The Congress of South African Trade Unions (Cosatu) was launched in 1985 with a call to intensify international pressure on the apartheid government, including disinvestment from companies active in South Africa. Labour unions worldwide responded: in Europe and North America a host of local, regional, and national union bodies established links with Cosatu and backed its appeals for boycott.[84] Palestinian BDS activist Rafeef Ziadeh comments on the importance of these traditions of solidarity, especially collective actions in which postal workers refused to handle mail from South Africa and dockworkers refused to offload South African produce. "These moments", she suggests, "will stay forever etched in the memories of trade unionists who understand that workers' actions do indeed effect change".[85]

During the 1990s, there was a steady increase in migration to the United States from the Global South, notably from Latin America and Asia, with refugees a significant component among new entrants[86]; there was also marked rise in participation in labour unions by "foreign-born" workers.[87] A similar pattern is evident in Canada[88] and in Britain, where

---

[83] By 1990, 43 British unions were affiliated to the movement: Anti-Apartheid, "Trade Unions Against Apartheid", *Forward to Freedom: the history of the British Anti-Apartheid Movement 1959 to 1994*, nd, accessed 10 November 2017, http://www.aamarchives.org/who-was-involved/trade-unionists.html

For many years the Trades Union Congress (the British federation of labour unions) was reluctant to endorse boycotts, as its sister organisation in South Africa, the white-dominated South African union federation Trade Union Council of South Africa (TUCSA), strongly discouraged sanctions. In 1981, it changed policy under pressure from rank-and-file members and began to campaign for United Nations sanctions on South Africa.

[84] Significantly, the national federation in the United States, the AFL-CIO, remained opposed.

[85] Rafeef Ziadeh, 'Worker-to-worker solidarity: BDS in the trade union movement', in: *Generation Palestine: Voices from the Boycott, Divestment and Sanctions Movement*, ed. Rich Wiles, (London, 2013), 179–180.

[86] Passel and Suro show that the pace of immigration was uneven, with sharp rises and falls. Over the period in question, there was less "white" immigration, more "Hispanic" immigration, and entry from Asian states. Jeffrey S. Passel and Roberto Suro, *Rise, Peak and Decline: Trends in US Immigration 1992–2004*, (Washington, DC, 2005), 4–5, accessed 10 November 2017. http://www.pewhispanic.org/files/reports/53.pdf

[87] Elizabeth Grieco, "Immigrant Union Members: Numbers and Trends", *Immigration Facts*, No 7, May 2004, Migration Policy Institute, accessed 10 November 2017, http://www.migrationpolicy.org/research/immigrant-union-members-numbers-and-trends

[88] Statistics Canada, "Immigrant population by place of birth and period of immigration (2006 census)", 2006, accessed 10 November 2017, http://www.statcan.gc.ca/tables-tableaux/sum-som/l01/cst01/demo24a-eng.htm

more "Black and Black British" workers were likely to be union members than among all employees.[89] People with personal, familial, or community/diasporic experiences of the Global South who were also likely to face inequality, discrimination, and marginalisation in the Global North were more fully involved in shaping union policies.

In North America, a leading role in BDS initiatives was taken by the Canadian Union of Public Employees (CUPE), the country's largest labour organisation with membership concentrated in cities with large immigrant populations. CUPE delegates attended the 2001 Durban forum and participated in successive WSF convergences, placing special emphasis on migrant rights and issues of citizenship. In 2006, its Ontario section was the first major union group in the Global North to endorse the Palestinian call for BDS, prompting endorsements from other labour organisations in Canada and from churches and FBOs. Traditions of international solidarity were confirmed and strengthened by these changes, as the Palestinian campaign for BDS made much faster progress on sanctions than the anti-apartheid initiatives of the 1960s and 1970s. Here, "Global" Palestine was not only a matter of recognition but also of collective response.

"Ripple" Effects

Noura Erekat describes the "mainstreaming" of BDS in the United States.[90] A key factor, she suggests, was the decision by hitherto politically marginal activists to redirect their work towards youthful global social justice groups. By 2006, the US Campaign to End the Israeli Occupation had adopted "an anti-apartheid framework" focusing on corporations that profited from the Israeli presence in the Palestinian territories: by 2011, it could record 375 local groups across the United States.[91] In an assessment of developments over a decade of growth of BDS campaigns, Nadia Hijab, Josh Ruebner and Phyllis Bennis observe:

> There was a time, in the not-too-distant past, during which it was virtually impossible to advocate for Palestinian rights in broader social movements in the United States. Since its inception, the US Campaign has always seen

---

[89] Department for Business, Innovation & Skills, *Trade Union Membership 2012: Statistical Bulletin* (London, 2013) 12.

[90] Noura Erekat, "BDS in the USA, 2001–2010", *Middle East Report*, No. 255, Summer 2010, accessed 10 November 2017, http://www.merip.org/mer/mer255/bds-usa-2001-2010

[91] Erekat, "BDS in the USA".

itself as part and parcel of broader progressive movements for social change in this country and has set itself the task of changing this situation. The US Campaign has undertaken a deliberate strategy to stand with, not apart from, these broader movements.[92]

As elsewhere, BDS campaigns in the United States have been profoundly affected by developments in Palestine and above all by Israel's conduct vis-à-vis the Palestinians and their supporters. Three episodes in particular have produced "ripple effects", amplifying calls for boycott. Military assaults upon Gaza in 2008–2009 and 2014 focused attention on the Palestinian predicament and the failure of the Oslo Process, prompting unprecedentedly large demonstrations of solidarity worldwide and greatly enlarged constituencies of support for BDS. Israel's attack on a flotilla to Gaza in 2010 targeted the solidarity movement itself, emphasising for activists that they too could be a focus for punitive action. Barghouti notes the effect in triggering "mass anger around the world and unprecedented mainstream calls for treating Israel as a pariah state, including through applying boycotts".[93] Israel's Reut Institute identifies the relationship between such events and the advance of BDS, observing that both "Operation Cast Lead" (the invasion of Gaza in 2008–2009) and the flotilla episode of 2010 prompted intensified efforts within global civil society to isolate Israel.[94] Following "Operation Protective Edge" (the invasion of Gaza in 2014), Israel's Institute for National Security Studies (INSS) suggested that, for every such round of fighting, Israel paid a much heavier price in public opinion and in erosion of support for its stand vis-à-vis the Palestinians.[95]

Assessing BDS

INSS suggests that "the movement to boycott Israel is expanding politically and among the public".[96] It notes "worrisome and accelerated developments", including possible sanctions from European governments,

---

[92] Nadia Hijab, Josh Ruebner and Phyllis Bennis, "Looking Back, Moving Forward", (US Campaign to End the Israeli Occupation), 2011; accessed 10 November 2017, https://uscpr.org/archive/downloads/2011conference_lessonslearned.pdf

[93] Barghouti, *Boycott, Divestment, Sanctions*, 206.

[94] Reut Institute, "The BDS Movement Promotes Delegitimization", 1.

[95] Gilead Sher and Einav Yogev, "Image vs. Reality: The Delegitimization of Israel in the Wake of Operation Protective Edge", *Insight* (Institute for National Security Studies), No. 593, 20 August 2014, accessed 10 November 2017, http://www.inss.org.il/index.aspx?id=4538&articleid=7558).

[96] Sher and Yogev, "Image vs. Reality".

concluding: "threats to the legitimacy of the state of Israel are deep, broad, and detailed".[97] Although strongly critical of boycott initiatives and—like Reut—anxious to advance a propaganda response,[98] INSS recognises a relationship between Israel's policies vis-à-vis the Palestinians and growing support worldwide for BDS. In marked contrast, most Israeli politicians have continued to assert that BDS is driven solely by antisemitic sentiment. Sriram Ananth describes an "anti-BDS frenzy" reaching the highest echelons of the Israeli state and including legislation introduced in 2011 as the Law for the Prevention of Damage to the State of Israel through Boycott (the "Boycott Law").[99]

Most analyses by Israeli academics also approach the BDS movement as an expression of widespread antisemitism. In 2012, the journal *Israel Affairs* published a special issue on "War by other means: Israel and its detractors", with ten papers written by academics and researchers in Israel and the United States—then the most focused assessment of BDS by critics of the strategy.[100] In a lead article, Efraim Karsh identifies a "war against the Jews".[101] Mounting criticism of Israel, he proposes, is a manifestation of ancient antisemitic prejudice—"a corollary of the millenarian obsession with the Jews in the Christian and Muslim worlds".[102] Anti-Zionism is "pure and unadulterated racism" and debate in inter-governmental forums such as the United Nations shows the latter "UN-ited [sic] in hate".[103] For Joel Fishman, writing in the same journal, the message of BDS must be seen in the context of a "convergence" of antisemitism and anti-Zionism.[104] Invoking the experience of Nazism, he suggests that "amalgamation of anti-Semitism with anti-Zionism" has provided rationales for

---

[97] Sher and Yogev, "Image vs. Reality".

[98] Israeli think tanks and advisory groups close to the government have advocated intensive campaigns of *hasbara* to challenge BDS initiatives: some are set out in the Reut document of 2010. (*Hasbara* [Hebrew]—"explaining"/"explanation"—is often used as a synonym for Israeli state propaganda.)

[99] Sriram Ananth, 'The Politics of the Palestinian BDS Movement', *Socialism and Democracy*, vol. 27, no. 3, (2013), 134.

[100] *Israel Affairs* 2012, vol. 18, no. 3, special issue: "War by other means: Israel and its detractors".

[101] Efraim Karsh, 'The war against the Jews', *Israel Affairs*, vol. 18, no. 3, (2012), 319.

[102] Karsh, "War against the Jews", 319.

[103] Karsh, "War against the Jews", 321, 327.

[104] Joel S. Fishman, 'The BDS message of anti-Zionism, anti-Semitism, and incitement to discrimination', *Israel Affairs*, vol. 18, no. 3, (2012), 412.

BDS as an attempt to "quarantine" Israel—a step towards its elimination.[105] He continues:

> While the proponents of BDS assert that they seek justice and oppose violence, it is evident that hatred and violence must be part of their programme, particularly if they reach a point when they cannot attain their goals peacefully.[106]

He warns of the danger of such violence, because: "They [BDS activists] are no longer confined geographically to the Middle East but have spilled over into Europe and the American college campus ... despite loud protestations of moral superiority, an ideology that amalgamates anti-Zionism with anti-Semitism has no constraints".[107] Kenneth Levin targets Jewish critics of Israel as "apologists and cheerleaders" for those who wish to translate "Jew-hatred" into action.[108] In a series of ad hominem attacks, he accuses Jewish intellectuals in North America and Europe of defaming Israel and certain Israeli academics—including the New Historians current—of "accommodation to anti-Jewish and anti-Israeli rhetoric".[109] He concludes that they are "fellow travellers in a campaign [BDS] that ultimately seeks Israel's annihilation".[110]

In a more recent collection of papers critical of the BDS movement, more than 30 European, American, and Israeli writers also propose that the underlying element in boycott initiatives is an antisemitic impulse. Introducing *The Case Against Academic Boycotts of Israel*, Paul Berman asserts that the boycott "has gone on forever, as if drawing on inexhaustible sources of rancour and rage".[111] Among contributors to this volume there is striking disinterest in the Palestinians, their specific circumstances and developments that have projected BDS to a global audience. Here, BDS is not a Palestinian issue: rather, in the words of Kenneth Marcus, it

---

[105] Fishman, "BDS message", 416.
[106] Fishman, "BDS message", 417.
[107] Fishman, "BDS message", 417.
[108] Kenneth Levin, 'Jewish defamation of Israel: roots and branches', *Israel Affairs*, vol. 18, no. 3, (2012), 440.
[109] Levin, "Jewish defamation of Israel", 441–442, 446, 448.
[110] Levin, "Jewish defamation of Israel", 452.
[111] Paul Berman, 'Preface' in: *The Case Against the Academic Boycott of Israel*, eds. Cary Nelson and Gabriel Noah Brahm, (2015), 5.

is focused upon Jews.[112] "In the last analysis", he observes, "the BDS campaign is anti-Semitic"—merely another campaign against the Jewish people.[113]

These and similar assessments are disappointingly shallow on analysis of the BDS phenomenon. None mobilise methodologies now widely used to address social movements, notably movements of protest. None considers the roots in Palestine of the BDS movement, its global resonances, constituencies of support, or dynamics of growth. The authors decline to tackle the key issue of periodisation: why did BDS emerge in the early years of the new millennium? What features of the situation in Palestine and in the international/global environment were conducive to its impact at this time? Why did leadership of the movement fall to a generation of youthful activists who challenged traditions of Palestinian nationalism? In avoiding such questions, these accounts decline to consider the impact of Israeli policy vis-à-vis the Palestinians and the latters' action in addressing their predicaments. Rather, they propose that BDS is part of a continuous historic pattern of antisemitism and of discriminatory practices that have recently found many new recruits. Hitherto largely unaffected, millions of people worldwide have abruptly become engaged in "war against the Jews". The proposition is implausible. It is also dangerous—encouraging Israelis and others to believe that relations between Israel and the Palestinians can continue unchanged.

The extent of support for BDS among Israeli academics is a matter of dispute. According to Steven Plaut, "hundreds" of professors and lecturers at state-funded universities in Israel are engaged in activities that threaten

---

[112] Kenneth Marcus, 'Is BDS Anti-Semitic?', in: *The Case Against the Academic Boycott of Israel*, eds. Cary Nelson and Gabriel Noah Brahm, (Chicago, 2015), 257.

[113] In a minor modification of this approach, Steinberg suggests that hostility to Israel is associated with the work of international NGOs that implement a "halo" approach: Gerald Steinberg, 'The centrality of NGOs in promoting anti-Israel boycotts', *Jewish Political Studies Review*, vol. 21, (Spring 2009), 2. Here, organisations present themselves as "altruistic, promoting the common good", assigning virtue to chosen "victims" and condemning others, including the United States and Israel, as neo-colonialist aggressors and "hegemons". The motivation, he argues, is that of "anti-Zionism, demonizing Israel, and the new anti-Semitism" (Steinberg, "Centrality of NGOs", 4). Magen argues similarly to account for "war waged against the Jewish state: Amichai Magen, 'Hybrid War and the 'Gulliverization' of Israel', *Israel Journal of Foreign Affairs*, vol. 5, no. 1, (2015), 59.

A new form of "hybrid war", he argues, embraces "hard" antisemitism, "soft" attempts to deny Israeli rights to self-determination and global campaigns for boycott (Magen, "Hybrid War", 66).

Israel's national interests; within this "domestic academic fifth column", he asserts, are numerous supporters of BDS whose influence has become "near pandemic" at liberal arts universities.[114] As the historian Ilan Pappe observes, however, a commitment of support for BDS by Israelis "remains a drastic act ... It excludes one immediately from the consensus and from the accepted discourse in Israel".[115] Rafael Medoff suggests that backing for BDS among Israeli scholars is rather modest, so that at leading institutions such as Tel Aviv University (TAU) only "a handful" of professors have publicly advocated for boycott.[116] In 2016, the Israeli government asked TAU Philosophy Professor Asa Kasher to draft a code of conduct for academics. Submitted to the government in 2017, Kasher's "Ethical code for the overlap between academic and political activity" proposes, inter alia, that academics should be barred from participating in or calling for academic boycott of Israel and forbidden to collaborate with organisations considered to be political. The draft met strong opposition from Israeli university heads on the grounds that it infringed academic freedom.[117] At the same time, it increased pressure on Israeli scholars to align with government policy, discouraging research on BDS by means of independent critical analyses like those usually employed to examine movements of social protest. With certain important exceptions,[118] academics at Israeli

---

[114] Steven Plaut, 'Israel's Academic Fifth Column', *Middle East Quarterly*, vol. 18, no. 4, (Fall 2011), 61, 62.

[115] Ilan Pappe, "Comment. Ilan Pappé: the boycott will work, an Israeli perspective", *Ceasefire*, 16 May 2012. https://ceasefiremagazine.co.uk/ilan-pappe-boycott-work-israeli-perspective/

[116] Rafael Medoff, "Will pro-BDS professors benefit from Tel Aviv University's new 'anti-BDS' fund?" *Jewish News Service*, 19 September, 2017, accessed 10 November 2017. http://www.jns.org/latest-articles/2017/9/19/will-pro-bds-professors-benefit-from-tel-aviv-universitys-new-anti-bds-fund#.WgdBELacaqA=

[117] Yarden Skop, "Israeli University Heads Blast New Ethical Code as Undermining Academic Freedom", 10 June 2017. https://www.haaretz.com/israel-news/1.794953

For an early assessment of scholarship and academic freedom in Israel in the context of BDS, critical of Israelis supportive of the BDS movement, see Ofira Seliktar, "Tenured Radicals' in Israel: From New Zionism to Political Activism', *Israel Affairs*, vol. 11, no. 4, (October 2005), 717–736.

[118] See, for example, Rachel Giora, "Milestones in the history of the Israeli BDS movement – a brief chronology", U.S. Campaign for the Academic & Cultural Boycott of Israel, 26 January 2010, accessed 10 November 2017. https://usacbi.wordpress.com/2010/01/26/milestones-in-the-history-of-the-israeli-bds-movement-a-brief-chronology/

institutions have not assessed the boycott movement locally or internationally on such a basis.

Israeli scholars abroad have developed some of the most insightful approaches to BDS. For Ariella Azouley, the movement should be understood as an initiative of Palestinians "deprived of their status as political actors both internally and internationally".[119] The movement for boycott should be understood, she argues, "as addressed to the international community" after decades during which local means of resistance to occupation proved largely fruitless.[120] Eyal Weizmann (2015: 106) argues similarly; the BDS movement, he suggests, has potential to unite political actors in Palestine and abroad—"to open democratic platforms for co-resistance".[121] "Through rupture", he argues, "it can connect the separate actors within a field it creates".[122]

Endorsing and promoting BDS, Palestinians have attempted to move out of the isolation imposed by their historic predicament and by the leadership of the national movement. Here, boycott is an orientation on the wider world and an engagement with people who have their own agendas for social justice. In Israel, by contrast, BDS has brought strong reassertion of localism and of ethno-nationalism. In an era of global change these exclusivist claims may find a shrinking audience.

---

[119] Ariella Azouley, "We,' Palestinians and Jewish Israelis: The Right Not to Be a Perpetrator', in: *Assuming Boycott*, eds. Kareem Estefan, Carin Kuoni, and Laura Raicovich, (New York, 2017), 82.

[120] Azouley, together with Adi Ophir, Dov Michaeli, Itamar Mann, and Galit Eilat contributed to a special issue of *South Atlantic Quarterly*, "Against the Day: Israeli Jews Address the Palestinian Boycott Call", published in 2015, in which Israeli scholars assessed the BDS movement as a meaningful expression of social protest. *South Atlantic Quarterly*, vol. 114, no. 3, (July 2015).

[121] Eyal Weizman and Kareem Estefan, 'Extending Co-Resistance', in: *Assuming Boycott*, eds. Kareem Estefan, Carin Kuoni, and Laura Raicovich, (New York, 2017), 103, 106.

[122] Eyal Weizman and Kareem Estefan, 'Extending Co-Resistance', in: *Assuming Boycott*, eds. Kareem Estefan, Carin Kuoni, and Laura Raicovich, 106.

CHAPTER 15

The Boycott, Divestment, Sanctions (BDS) Movement and Radical Democracy

John Chalcraft

Introduction

On 25 June 2015, the high-profile magazine *Newsweek* reported that Foreign Direct Investment in Israel was nearly 50% lower in 2014 than in 2013. The drop was attributed to "the fallout from the Israel Defence Forces (IDF) Operation Protective Edge [of July-August 2014] and international boycotts against the country for alleged violations of international law".[1] Research on the Boycott, Divestment, Sanctions movement (BDS), nonetheless, is still in its infancy, and opinion is highly divided as to its nature and role. This chapter takes the view that the movement cannot be dismissed as just another form of antisemitism. It argues that the BDS movement instead exhibits a number of important similarities to recent radical democracy movements. It is a non-hierarchical and non-doctrinal movement that is networked, de-centralized, multitudinous, and trans-local. The movement seeks to address and change political society without aiming to take up an established position of power within political society itself,

[1] Jack Moore, "Foreign investment in Israel drops by 50%," *Newsweek*, 25 June 2015.

J. Chalcraft (✉)
London School of Economics and Political Science, London, UK

© The Author(s) 2019
D. Feldman (ed.), *Boycotts Past and Present*, Palgrave Critical Studies of Antisemitism and Racism,
https://doi.org/10.1007/978-3-319-94872-0_15

through inclusionary, direct-action mobilization rooted in universal rights. The chapter argues that it is precisely these radically democratic features that can help account for the movement's increasing potency in recent years.

This chapter is based on participant observation in the movement over nearly a decade, and is offered by an academic with a commitment to the movement. Some are bound to discount contributions from those who have stakes in the movement or its suppression as overly interested and politicized; others will maintain a more open-minded position, grasping the complexity of the relationship between politics and scholarship, the problems lurking behind claims to objectivity,[2] and understanding that in an unresolved and profoundly polarizing conflict, neutrality and detachment is a difficult stance for any contemporary actor to maintain credibly, or even usefully.

Radical Democracy

New forms of radically democratic theory and activism emerged after the late 1960s in various parts of the world. Theories bearing family resemblances appeared in diverse sites. Jacques Rancière's work on new forms of democratic politics was launched after May 1968 with a critique of Left doctrinalism and authoritarianism.[3] In the wake of the military defeat of 1967, Anwar Abd Al-Malek wrote a major criticism of Egypt's military society and the failure of an authoritarian Left to generate popular democracy in the Arab world.[4] He was joined by others in the region who sought a democratic form of socialism.[5] Elsewhere, a seminal critique of Marxist economism put the struggle for a reformulated hegemony involving radical democracy at the centre of a new normative political theory for the Left.[6] In a different register, anarchist and autonomist philosophers Hardt and Negri invoked not a working class seeking to seize the means of production, but a networked multitude capable of creatively generating a

---

[2] Peter Novick, *That Noble Dream: The 'Objectivity Question' and the American Historical Profession* (Cambridge, 1989).

[3] Jacques Rancière, *Hatred of Democracy* (London, 2006).

[4] Anwar Abd Al-Malek, *Egypt: Military Society: The Army Regime, the Left, and Social Change Under Nasser* (1968).

[5] Fadi A. Bardawil, "When All this Revolution Melts into Air: The Disenchantment of Levantine Marxist Intellectuals". Unpublished PhD Thesis. Columbia University, 2010.

[6] Ernesto Laclau and Chantal Mouffe, *Hegemony and Socialist Strategy: Towards a Radical Democratic Politics* (London, 1985).

revolutionary form of democratic politics.[7] French post-structuralists deepened the idea of networked forms of identity involving multiple non-hierarchical entry and exit points through their concept of the rhizome.[8] Revivals in anarchist theorizing also regularly placed radically egalitarian and stateless visions at the centre of their normative theory.[9] A number of scholars have sought to theorize deliberative, pre-figurative, and participatory forms of democracy.[10] Others have put forward notions of activism and direct action that eschew appeals to the state or the use of a vanguard and enjoin the construction of new forms of social order that bypass state and capital.[11]

Since the 1960s, uprisings and movements have exhibited homologies with radically democratic normative theory. People power uprisings, "relatively nonviolent demonstrations in which hundreds of thousands simply showed their disgust, lack of fear, and unwillingness to cooperate with the old regime in massive demonstrations in urban public spaces"[12] without disciplined hierarchical organization, and without necessarily proposing an alternative ideological blueprint for state and society, were seen in 1986 in

---

[7] Michael Hardt and Antonio Negri, *Multitude: War and Democracy in the Age of Empire* (New York, 2005).

[8] Gilles Deleuze and Felix Guattari, *A Thousand Plateaus: Capitalism and Schizophrenia* (Minneapolis, 1987).

[9] Jon Beasely-Murray, *Posthegemony: Political Theory and Latin America* (London, 2010); Richard Day, *Gramsci is Dead: Anarchist Currents in the Newest Social Movements* (London, 2005); Saul Newman, *The Politics of Post-Anarchism* (Edinburgh, 2011).

[10] Carl Boggs, 'Marxism, Prefigurative Communism, and the Problem of Workers' Control'. *Radical America*, vol. 11 (November 1977); A. Dhaliwal, 'Can the Subaltern Vote? Radical Democracy, Discourses of Representation and Rights, and Questions of Race', in: *Radical Democracy: Identity, Citizenship, and the State*, ed. D. Trend, (New York, 1996), 42–61; Donatella Della Porta, *Can Democracy Be Saved?: Participation, Deliberation and Social Movements* (Cambridge, 2013); John Dryzek, *Deliberative Democracy and Beyond* (New York, 2000); Sara Motta, 'Notes Towards Prefigurative Epistemologies', in: *Social Movements in the Global South: Dispossession, Development and Resistance*, eds. Sara C. Motta and Alf Gunvald Nilsen, (Basingstoke, 2011).

[11] John Holloway, *Change the World Without Taking Power: The Meaning of Revolution Today (Get Political)* (London, 2010); Hilary Wainwright, *Reclaim the State: Experiments in Popular Democracy* (London, 2003).

[12] Doug McAdam and William H. Sewell Jr., 'It's About Time: Temporality in the Study of Social Movements and Revolutions', in: *Silence and Voice in the Study of Contentious Politics*, ed. Ronald R. Aminzade et al., (Cambridge, 2001), 89–125.

the Philippines, the Occupied Palestinian Territories in 1987–1991,[13] Eastern Europe and China in 1989, in Mexico under the Zapatistas after 1994, in the independence intifada in Lebanon in 2005, and in South East Asia in the 1980s and 1990s.[14] A highly networked and trans-local movement contributed to the fall of apartheid in South Africa in 1994. The movement of landless workers in Brazil since 1984 eschewed the use of a party and has invoked themes of de-centralization, non-hierarchy, and consensus; *piquetero* movements of the unemployed in Argentina similarly emphasized themes of autonomy and de-centralization[15]; the term "horizontalism" (*horizontalidad*) was coined in Argentina to describe the movements that emerged in December 2001, in Argentina, after the economic crisis. This activism was distinctive in its rejection of political programmes and its attempts to create directly democratic and deliberative spaces and new social relationships.[16] The alter-globalization and global justice movements emerging in the 1990s set considerable store by non-hierarchical, consensus-seeking, and participatory decision-making processes in opposition to Left doctrinalism and sectarianism.[17] The global spread of demonstrations against the Iraq War of 2003 strongly evoked transnational themes.[18] Participatory and anarchist elements have been at work in Israeli and Palestinian activism against the separation barrier in Israel/Palestine since 2002.[19] Horizontalism, understood to involve decentralized and networked organizing, 'leaderfulness', and creativity, and an emphasis on consensus and deliberation, was at work in the Arab upris-

---

[13] Mazin B. Qumsiyeh, *Popular Resistance in Palestine: A History of Hope and Empowerment* (London, 2011).

[14] George Katsiaficas, *Asia's Unknown Uprisings: Vol 2: People Power in the Philippines, Burma, Tibet, China, Taiwan, Bangladesh, Nepal, Thailand, and Indonesia, 1947–2009* (Oakland, 2013).

[15] P. Chatterton, 'Making Autonomous Geographies: Argentina's Popular Uprising and the 'Movimiento de Traebajadores Desocupados (Unemployed Workers Movement)', *Geoforum*, vol. 36, no. 5, (2005), 545–61.

[16] Marina Sitrin (ed.), *Horizontalism: Voices of Popular Power in Argentina* (Oakland, CA, 2006).

[17] Marianne Maeckelbergh, *The Will of the Many: How the Alterglobalisation Movement is Changing the Face of Democracy* (London, 2009).

[18] Sidney Tarrow, *The New Transnational Activism* (Cambridge, 2006), xiii.

[19] Joel Beinin, "High-Risk Activism and Popular Struggle against the Israeli Occupation of the West Bank" Public Lecture. LSE (4 November 2014).

ings of 2011, especially among urban youth.[20] Since 2011, Occupy movements in Spain, Greece, London, New York, Iceland, and more recently protests in Turkey, Brazil, France, and Hong Kong, have also placed considerable weight on horizontalist logics, eschewing vertical and "arborescent" structures.[21]

Radically democratic mobilizing projects are diverse but exhibit family resemblances. They invoke "[p]refiguration, horizontality, diversity, decentralisation and the network structure".[22] They aim to pre-figure the alternative orders that they envisage through the forms of action and styles of organizing that they themselves embody. This is the sense in which such movements declare that the movement is the message. These movements are non-doctrinal in that they do not seek to apply an ideological blueprint (classical liberalism, communism, fascism, nationalism, or Islamism)— seen as conformist, essentialist, hierarchical, repressive, and undemocratic—and pointless because new political orders do not arise from blueprints in any case, but from the actions of the many. Rather than imposing doctrine, these movements strive to seek out consensus. Their most crucial enemy is not capitalism, globalization, or discourse as such, but coercive, authoritarian, exclusionary, intersectional, and totalizing systems of power, systems that often combine discursive, military, legal-administrative, economic, gendered, or other aspects of domination. They aim to deconstruct dominant arrangements and bring into being alternative systems of egalitarian (re)production and meaning which go well beyond the reformulation of the sphere of formal politics. The mode of integration and identification is more or less explicitly held not to be that of the traditional collective subject: "the people", "the nation", "the proletariat", the "woman", the "Jew", the "Muslim", and so on. These categories are seen as essentialist and conformist. The "we-ness" of the movement is instead supplied by the notion of a motley multitude in the tradition of Spinoza and Hardt and Negri. The multitude is the "living

[20] Aly El-Raggal, "Generation Rev and the Struggle for Democracy: An Interview [by Linda Herrera] with Aly El-Raggal," *Jadaliyya*, 15 October 2011. http://www.jadaliyya.com/pages/index/2869/generation-rev-and-the-struggle-for-democracy_inte; John Chalcraft, 'Horizontalism in the Egyptian Revolutionary Process'. *Middle East Report*, no. 262, (Spring 2012), 6–11.

[21] Manuel Castells, *Networks of Outrage and Hope: Social Movements in the Internet Age* (Cambridge, 2012); David Graeber, *The Democracy Project: A History. A Crisis. A Movement* (London, 2013).

[22] Marianne Maeckelbergh, *The Will of the Many: How the Alterglobalisation Movement is Changing the Face of Democracy* (London, 2009), 145.

alternative" that grows within Empire. It "might ... be conceived as a network: an open and expansive network in which all differences can be expressed freely and equally, a network that provides the means of encounter so that we can work and live in common"; it is not like "the people" or "the working class" but "composed of innumerable internal differences that can never be reduced to a unity or a single identity – different cultures, races, ethnicities, genders, and sexual orientations". Production here is seen as not just being about the working class and must not be conceived purely in economic terms "but more generally as social production – not only the production of material goods but also the production of communications, relationships, and forms of life. The multitude is thus composed potentially of all the diverse figures of social production".[23] The "we" is thus a multiplication of singularities, cultivating an "ethic of dissensus".[24]

Radically democratic movements regularly make use of networked and rhizomic (lattice-like) forms of organization, emphatically rejecting sole or charismatic leaders such as a Nasser, a Khomeini, or a Chavez. Instead, they prefer to unlock the power of the diverse, multicoloured, and multitudinous subjectivities that make up the movement, eschewing the party or vanguardist forms, with an emphasis on spontaneity more than on the building up of resources or organizational structures. Such movements are thus leaderless or, better still, leaderful, with many points of creativity and "intelligent" decision. In this sense, these movements are 2.0 movements, in the sense that "users" create content rather than passively consuming content provided by others, just as many new media users do in their everyday lives. The rhizome is supposed to work with creativity and personal autonomy, and even pleasure, although procedures, forms of "facilitation", and skills there are aplenty. Instead of policing boundaries, rhizomic organization thinks in terms of multiplying points in a network. Radically democratic movements stress deliberation, not representation, and the de-centralization of decision-making capacity. The idea is that the demos (rewritten as the multitude) is not easy to separate from its representatives, and such a separation brings about distortion and "speaking for" and "speaking over" rather than "speaking with". Characteristic

---

[23] Michael Hardt and Antonio Negri, *Multitude: War and Democracy in the Age of Empire* (New York, 2005), xiii–xv.
[24] Ewa Ponowska Ziarek, *An Ethics of Dissensus: Postmodernity, Feminism, and the Politics of Radical Democracy* (Stanford, 2001).

organizations are thus general assemblies, popular committees, and coordinating networks, rather than parties, unions, or established NGOs.

Direct and unmediated action, rather than supplication before the powers that be, is a common feature of the strategies and tactics of these movements. In place of persuasion, negotiation, and representation comes direct action, civil disobedience, and institutional disruption. In place of the demonstration, seen as ineffective and passive, comes the continuous and defiant occupation of symbolically important public space. In place of complaining to customer services, we find hacktivism.[25] In place of demands, one finds "misbehaviour",[26] and the do-it-yourself construction of alternatives. Traditional forms of claim-making are seen as problematic. They presuppose a failure to problematize existing forms of authority, and they may smuggle in statism by authorizing state actors to take charge or to co-opt. Conventional forms of the state, multi-party democracy, constitutions, elections, and parliaments are regularly seen as inadequate levers of transformation, corrupted, rigged, and controlled by corporate power, international financial institutions, alliances with the US hegemon, and saturated by Public Relations. Rather than seizing the state, the aim is often to bypass it, make it irrelevant, or remake it in some basic way.

THE BDS MOVEMENT

In May 2011, Ehud Barak, an ex-prime minister of Israel, who had also been Chief of General Staff in the Israeli army, spoke to the left-leaning Israeli daily *Haaretz*:

> There are some pretty powerful elements in the world that are active in the matter … in various organisations of workers, academics, consumers, green parties … And this drive boils down to a large movement called BDS, which is what they did with South Africa. It won't happen all at once. It will begin, like an iceberg, to advance on us from all quarters. (Ehud Barak, 9 May 2011, interview in *Haaretz*, cited in Wiles[27]: 222)

---

[25] Peter Krapp, "Terror and Play, or What Was Hacktivism?" Posted Online March 13, 2006. https://doi.org/10.1162/152638105774539770. MIT Press. No. 21 (Fall 2005), 70–93.
[26] Gemma Edwards, *Social Movements and Protest* (Cambridge, 2014), 213–234.
[27] Rich Wiles (ed.), *Generation Palestine: Voices from the Boycott, Divestment and Sanctions Movement* (London, 2013).

In the early 2010s, Israeli politicians started to take notice of the BDS movement more than in passing. Whether or not the movement is an iceberg which can hole the Israeli Titanic below the waterline, it is certainly highly de-centralized, with initiatives coming from many quarters and countries. By the 2010s, activists had been at work for almost a decade. With the lack of progress made by the second intifada, the Israeli reinvasion of cities such as Jenin in April 2002, the search for new kinds of politics that could break the impasse of Israeli domination, the failure of the Palestinian Authority, and Islamist armed struggle, a number of Palestinian academics and students, along with half a dozen or so like-minded academics in Britain and France, started to raise the question, in secular and democratic terms, of boycotting the institutions of the Israeli state that were complicit in colonization and occupation.[28] Activists were certainly heavily inspired by, and made constant reference to, what the international Anti-Apartheid Movement had achieved in bringing down apartheid in South Africa in 1994–1995.[27] From early calls, discussions, union, and associational activity in both Palestine and the UK and to a lesser extent France between 2002 and 2004, well over a hundred Palestinian associations, unions, and committees endorsed a general call for BDS on Israel in 2005. Over the next decade, academics, consumers, students, church groups, workers, unions, co-operatives, campaign groups, and professional associations from Palestine, the UK, the USA, France, and to some extent in other countries such as Spain and Australia, their ranks swelling in the wake of Israeli military actions in 2006, 2008–2009, and 2014, built a movement with thousands of activists against occupation, colonization and attendant violations of human rights and international law.[29] The movement scored some success in provoking debate, and generating boycotts of Israeli academic and cultural institutions, notably by world-famous

---

[28] Suzanne Morrison, "The Palestinian Boycott, Divestment, and Sanctions Movement." *Bulletin of the Council for British Research in the Levant* 8, No.1 Research Reports Part I (October 2013), 51–52; Suzanne Morrison, 'The Emergence of the Boycott, Divestment, and Sanctions Movement', in: *Contentious Politics in the Middle East*, ed. Fawaz A. Gerges, (London, Forthcoming).

[29] Omar Barghouti, *Boycott, Divestment, Sanctions: The Global Struggle for Palestinian Rights* (Chicago, 2011); T. Hickey and P. Marfleet, 'The 'South Africa moment': Palestine, Israel and the boycott', *International Socialism*, no. 128, (2010). http://www.isj.org.uk/index.php4?id=680&issue=128; Suzanne Morrison, 'The Palestinian Boycott, Divestment, and Sanctions Movement.' *Bulletin of the Council for British Research in the Levant*, vol. 8, no. 1, Research Reports Part I (October 2013), 51–52.

scientist Stephen Hawking in 2013. It also caused divestment in some cases, such as the major Dutch pension fund, PGGM in January 2014, and a loss of contracts worth billions in Europe for companies such as Veolia whose reputations were tarnished by campaigners because they operated in the Palestinian occupied territories. It has been less successful in changing facts on the ground.

Opinions on the BDS movement are as far apart as those of Harold Brackman, who in a study written for the Simon Wiesenthal Centre, characterizes the BDS movement as a "thinly-veiled, anti-Israel and anti-Semitic "poison pill", whose goal is the demonization, delegitimization, and ultimate demise of the Jewish State"; a "movement that does not help better the life of a single Palestinian and which is oblivious to major human rights disasters erupting throughout the Middle East and beyond".[30] At the other end of the spectrum is the view of one of the chief architects of the movement, the Palestinian Omar Barghouti, who argues that "[t]he global BDS movement for Palestinian rights presents a progressive, anti-racist, sophisticated, sustainable, moral and effective form of civil, non-violent resistance ... affirming the rights of *all* humans to freedom, equality and dignified living".[31] This chapter offers some evidence on the nature of the BDS movement by considering various elements of the movement's mobilizing project in turn: its identity, principles, goals, organization, strategies, and tactics.

Identity

What is the identity of the BDS movement? There is an obvious sense in which Palestinian nationalism is at play: the boycott speaks in terms of the rights of Palestinians in the Occupied Palestinian Territories, Palestinian refugees, and Palestinians living in Israel, and speaks a good deal about self-determination. Palestinian flags are found at BDS events. Whether or not boycotters declare "we are Palestinian nationalists", there is at least a

---

[30] Harold Brackman, "Boycott, Divestment, Sanction (BDS) Against Israel – An Anti-Semitic Anti-Peace Poison Pill". Simon Wiesenthal Centre (March 2013) http://www.wiesenthal.com/atf/cf/%7B54d385e6-f1b9-4e9f-8e94-890c3e6dd277%7D/REPORT_313. PDF

[31] Omar Barghouti, 'Palestine's South Africa Moment has Finally Arrived', in: *Generation Palestine: Voices from the Boycott, Divestment and Sanctions Movement*, ed. Rich Wiles, (London, 2013), 216–232.

sense that the act of boycotting is an act of solidarity with a nationalist movement that has not yet found its state.

Palestinian nationalism is not as central to the movement's "we-ness", however, as might be assumed. If we compare the literature on the boycott to that of the national liberation movements of the 1960s and 1970s, we find a relative lack of ideational depth or emphasis on the question of nationalism. Very powerful in anti-colonial and Third Worldist nationalist movements of the "short" twentieth century was the construction of, and membership within, a central, national subjectivity, whether Palestinian, Egyptian, Indian, Chinese, pan-Arab, pan-African, or otherwise. The well-known intellectual progenitor of Ba'thist pan-Arabism, Michel Aflaq, for example, enunciated a romantic and heavily acculturated Arab national identity involving 'one Arab nation with an eternal mission'.[32] Vitally important were the existence of commonalities – a common history, language, spirit, destiny, and so on. Ba'thists identified with this powerful, overarching identity, which was supposed to be rooted in long experiences of togetherness, and very much defined the 'we' of the movement. The liberation of the nation as such was freighted during much of the twentieth century with the belief that national emancipation was a guarantor of social rights, economic development, self-determination, social progress, and liberation in a more metaphysical sense. Nationalism takes a different place within the BDS movement: it does not serve by any means such a central function or deep meaning in defining the "we-ness" of the BDS movement.

On the contrary, many BDS supporters would find themselves in some measure of agreement with Gilbert Achcar's strictures against nationalism:

> Nationalism is too often ... a very deadly disease. Superseding nationalism is a precondition for the achievement of real peaceful coexistence between nations.[33]

This rejection of a strong form of nationalism chimes with much of the movement. Even in the articles, statements, and exhortations put out by

---

[32] Michel Aflaq, *Choice of Texts from the Ba'th Party Founder's Thought* (Florence, 1977).

[33] Gilbert Achcar, "The Holocaust & the Arab-Israeli War of Narratives: Critical Dialogues with Gilbert Achcar." Center for Middle East Studies. Occasional Paper Series, No. 3 (2014). University of Denver. http://www.du.edu/korbel/middleeast/media/documents/cme-soccasionalpaperachcar.pdf, p. 19.

Omar Barghouti, there is a clear downplaying of nationalism. This might be viewed as the mere instrumental usage of an existing metropolitan ennui with nationalism; or it might, and probably should, be taken more seriously. The BDS movement encapsulates a more active form of participation than the idea of "solidarity with" implies. It is not that pre-existing unions, NGOs, parties, churches, and so on now declare solidarity with an externalized Palestinian nationalism. It is instead that they incorporate the principles enunciated by the boycott, with regard to human rights, international law, global justice, and so on, into their own internal functioning. While it is true that such a rejection of nationalism is amenable to long-standing Left traditions, the fact is that class is not central to the identity of the movement, which although containing socialists, anti-capitalists and alter-globalization activists, is not built around a working class identity.

Adherents to the BDS movement are from highly diverse ethnic, religious, national, and class backgrounds. They include Muslims, Jews, and Christians, Israelis, British, French, Indians, Egyptians, Americans, and so on. They are racially and ethnically mixed. There are wealthy, male celebrities such as Elvis Costello and white pensioners living in cul-de-sacs in the suburbs of Sheffield. There are those who do self-identify as working class, as well as those on low incomes who do not, or those who would see themselves as middle or even upper class, as well as those with high incomes and status. Boycotters maintain a motley patchwork of different forms of social identity—from Pakistan to Los Angeles. This does not mean that the movement is integrated as a mosaic: we note that the movement is not composed of lesser, unitary identities, unlike the nationalism of the 1950s and 1960s. There are no "toiling masses" described as having specific components: workers, peasants, students, fighters, and women—with their respective organizations and unions. Instead, the networked form of integration does not rely on an aggregate of essentialized identities. BDS "relies on the voluntary participation of people at all levels of society, regardless of their national or ethnic identities, and without geographical limitations".[34] The BDS movement, however, does not enunciate very explicitly a "we-ness" that would encapsulate all these differences. It does not explicitly state "we are a multitude"—although in many respects the resemblances with the multitude are many.

---

[34] Richard Falk, 'International Law, Apartheid, and Israeli Responses to BDS', in: *Generation Palestine: Voices from the Boycott, Divestment and Sanctions Movement*, ed. Rich Wiles, (London, 2013), 85–99.

Principles

What does the BDS movement stand for? What are the principles that define the cause? The lead note in the language of the BDS movement is that the Palestinians are human beings whose basic rights have been violated and on whom dispossession has been practised.

The pre-figurative idea, to my knowledge, is not especially developed—the self-conscious claim that the very mode of organizing pre-figures the alternative society that the movement wishes to construct. The movement is more outward-looking and goal-focused, one might argue. Nonetheless, there are claims that what the BDS movement does is democracy in action. Indeed, BDS supporters at the Fourth National BDS Conference, held in Bethlehem on 8 June 2013, made exactly this claim. The networked form of the BDS movement allows a rare space for democratic forms of organizing and participation and can open up such spaces in Palestine and perhaps beyond. There are clearly those that see non-violence in this light; a non-violent movement is inherently a democratic form that generates deliberative space and pre-figures a desirable society. Non-violence is elevated to a principle, and not just a tactic.

Barghouti insists that the BDS movement adopts a rights-based approach. The idea is that boycotters are those who support Palestinian rights: the right of return (referring above all to the Palestinians in the diaspora), the right of freedom from occupation (referring above all to Palestinians in Gaza, the West Bank, and East Jerusalem), and the right to civil equality (referring above all to Palestinian citizens of Israel).

The rights invoked by the BDS movement are closely identified with universal rights—self-determination, freedom, and equality—which do not belong only to Palestinians or Arabs. They are supposed to be inalienable rights to which anyone would sign up. They are thus capable of being linked to other struggles.[31] These rights are not seen as the special property of one or other category of citizens, or nationals, Muslims, or Jews, civilized or backward, proletarian, or bourgeoisie. On the Israeli-Palestinian stage, it is Jewish-Israelis that enjoy them as a matter of course, and Palestinian-Arabs who should now obtain them, having been deprived of them. This vision is not seen as a zero-sum game.

The insistence on international law and human rights is very much part of the discourse of the movement, especially its Palestinian sections. Substantial intellectual labour and practical activism around the Israeli court system has gone into this question, involving thinkers, activists, and legal scholars (Nasreer Aruri, Raja Shehadeh, and Richard Falk are some of the names involved). Falk traces a genealogy of these Palestinian rights since the First World War. In the Balfour declaration, he writes, it was "clearly understood that nothing should be done which may prejudice the civil and religious rights of existing non-Jewish communities". The responsibility for this protection was then transferred to the United Nations (UN) in 1948. Neither Britain nor the UN upheld these rights.[35] This approach, which characterizes aspects of the BDS movement, is in stark contrast to the dismissal of UN resolutions that characterized the Palestine Liberation Organisation during the period of the *thawra* from 1968 to 1982.

Arguably, nationalism serves more as a principle than as an identity. It is invoked less for its own sake, and less as an identity and community that must be constituted, and more in order to establish the importance of and warrant for rights. Likewise, the movement does not adopt an ideological blueprint or programme for the transformation of society, neither liberal capitalism, Islamism, socialism, nor fascism. Rights are not derived from ideology, but are inalienable. The implicit model of emancipation is rather distinct: neither to constitute an unrealized national community, or instantiate an unrealized ideology, but to establish, through action rooted in civil society but directed at political society, the conditions of existence for the flourishing of diverse subjectivities—considered as factors in the (re)production of the social as a whole.

Opponents

If the BDS movement's de facto mode of identification is multitudinous, and if it stands for basic and inalienable rights—then what is it against? Who are its opponents, systemic or otherwise, and what does it see as the obstacles to its progress?

The movement does not say: we are those who hate, fear, or harbour prejudices or wariness about Jews. It invariably claims that Zionism is completely distinct from Judaism. Barghouti insists on the "crucial distinction between Israel and Jews worldwide, which rejects the racist claim that Israel or Zionism represents all Jews".[31] The British Employment

---

[35] Ilan Pappé, 'Colonialism, the Peace Process, and the Academic Boycott', in: *Generation Palestine: Voices from the Boycott, Divestment and Sanctions Movement*, ed. Rich Wiles, (London, 2013), 124–138.

Tribunal's March 2013 judgement in the case of *Fraser v. the University and College Union* (UCU) to the effect that Zionist political beliefs are not the same as Jewishness as a protected characteristic under the Equality Act 2010 was an important moment for the BDS campaign in the UK, as it gave legal backing to their position distinguishing sharply Jewishness from Zionism.[36] Antisemitism as a discourse, a set of clichés, a form of racism or cultural essentialism, a sentiment, or an ideology plays no meaningful role in the BDS movement. Those who levy the charge of antisemitism either use simple misrepresentation or rely on notions of sub-conscious influences, hidden motives, or coded language or argue that the antisemitism is an effect, but not an intention.[37] Such claims are notoriously difficult to falsify or verify. Rather like propaganda against Jews, such as that carried on by Hamas especially in its earliest pronouncements, claims of this kind are resistant to rational procedures of proof because they rely on the attribution of hidden motives and dark subterranean forces.

The BDS movement is characterized by its rejection of communalism. Unlike other parties to the conflict, it is acutely opposed to the neo-Orientalist idea of a Judeo-Christian West opposed to an irrational and hostile Arab and Islamic East; it does not endorse the nativism of Hamas, with its opposition to "Jews and Crusaders"; it vigorously opposes ethnocratic forms of Zionism, which assert with state-backing that the Jews are a congenitally constituted racially and ethnically marked group apart and thus have a peculiar destiny to live together in a single state in which Jews are dominant.

We obtain a stronger sense of what the movement is against by considering the World Conference against Racism held in Durban in 2001. There, occupation was equated with racism and apartheid, and a call went out for the international community to sanction Israel with the intention of bringing about an end to these illegal practices, and "ensuring compliance with international law".[38] The opponent here is thus conceived less as a military practice of direct domination and violence (occupation) but as

---

[36] BRICUP, "Abusing the Law: Fraser v. UCU". Bricup (2013), www.bricup.org.uk/FraservUCU.pdf

[37] Judith Butler, 'No It's Not Anti-semitic' *London Review of Books,* vol. 25, no. 16, (21 August 2003), 19–21. http://www.lrb.co.uk/v25/n16/judith-butler/no-its-not-anti-semitic

[38] Raji Sourani, 'Why Palestinians Call for BDS', in: *Generation Palestine: Voices from the Boycott, Divestment and Sanctions Movement,* ed. Rich Wiles, (London, 2013), 61–71.

"racism" and "apartheid". It is interesting to note that the opponent here is precisely the opposite of the multitudinous form of collective identification. Insofar as Durban-like statements in regard to apartheid and racism, not to mention actions, are to be found aplenty in the BDS movement, the opposition is to totalizing, permanently fixed, and essentialized forms of identity.

There is a powerful echo here of Laclau and Mouffe's programme as set out in the 1980s in *Hegemony and Socialist Strategy*.[6] The real enemy in this work is totalizing and closed forms of identity, any attempt to represent the social as an invariant and finally fixed totality. The radically democratic struggle for hegemony that Laclau and Mouffe endorse is a struggle for open and non-totalizing and non-essentialist forms of collective integration and representation.

The target for the BDS movement is not a race or an ethnicity—the Jews, Crusaders, Christians, infidels, and so on. The target here differs markedly, for example, from the enemies perceived by Hamas. But nor is the opponent simply a totalizing mode of representation. The enemy is instead a system of oppression that organizes rights according to ethnic and religious privilege. The implication is that the enemy is not even Israel as such. To say so is an important imprecision. The BDS movement opposes violations and seeks to instate rights.

The BDS movement often identifies Zionism as a racist settler colonial project—as a form of apartheid.[39] The enemy is not above all capitalism—although corporate profits are involved; the enemy is not an imperialism of exploitation, although militarism and US foreign policy is hardly a friend; the movement is focused on Zionism itself, its racialism and its violations of law and rights. Hence we find Barghouti defining BDS as

> a global struggle for Palestinian freedom, justice and self-determination against a powerful, ruthless system of oppression that enjoys impunity and that is intent on making a self-fulfilling prophecy of the utterly racist, myth-

[39] Abigail B. Bakan and Yasmeen Abu-Laban, 'Israel/Palestine, South Africa and the 'One-State Solution': The Case for an Apartheid Analysis' *Politikon: South African Journal of Political Studies*, vol. 37, no. 2–3, (2010), 331–351; Daryl Glaser, 'Zionism and Apartheid: A Moral Comparison', *Ethnic and Racial Studies*, vol. 26, no. 3, (2003), 403–21; Gabriel Piterberg, *The Returns of Zionism: Myths, Politics and Scholarship in Israel* (London, 2008); Oren Yiftachel, *Ethnocracy: Land and Identity Politics in Israel/Palestine* (Pennsylvania, 2006); Oren Yiftachel, 'Voting for Apartheid: The 2009 Israeli Elections', *Journal of Palestine Studies*, vol. 38, no. 3, (Spring 2009), 72–85.

laden, foundational Zionist dictum of 'a land without a people for a people without a land'.³¹

The central component of the oppression in the above quotation is racism and how it is put into practice: impunity is not the source of oppression itself. Barghouti elaborates what this racism actually involves—that is, a system and not simply a set of misguided attitudes: it involves an apartheid system "of bestowing rights and privileges according to ethnic and religious identity" which "fits the UN definition of the term [apartheid] as enshrined in the 1973 International Convention on the Suppression and Punishment of the Crime of Apartheid and in the 2002 Rome Statute of the International Criminal Court".³¹

Pappé identifies the source of oppression in similar terms. He writes that the problem in

> Israel was not a particular policy or a specific government. There was a principled problem rooted deeply in the ideological infrastructure that fed Israeli decisions on Palestine and the Palestinians ever since 1948 – an ideology, which elsewhere I described as a hybrid dogma that fuses together colonialism and romantic nationalism.³⁵

It is important to note that the source of oppression Pappé identifies here is not capitalism or imperialism but a form of discursive closure: a deeply rooted "ideological infrastructure", a "hybrid dogma". The problem, for Pappé, then, is that over time there was a weakening of the opposition, as fewer and fewer Israelis were willing to question this "ideological infrastructure".³⁵ This infrastructure had a whole apparatus of power at its disposal: "a state that was willing, using the most lethal weapons at hand, to crush any resistance to its control and rule over what used to be historical Palestine".³⁵ Again, the opponent is depicted as a form of discursive closure, not an abstracted one, but one stitched into a system of domination secured by state and military direct domination by one set of persons over another. Direct domination, therefore, is not completely displaced as the figure of oppression. The form of dispossession invoked, nonetheless, clearly has cultural dimensions. Israeli state-sponsored cultural forms are seen by cultural boycotters as privileged sites enjoyed only by and through the erasure of Palestinian history, culture, and national existence. The cultural boycott announces, as the Palestinian performance poet and War on

Want activist Rafeef Ziadah stresses, that there is a fundamental and iniquitous inequality at work where Zionist culture develops its own narratives and sense of Self while Palestinian culture is denigrated, fragmented, and stifled through Israeli-Zionist access to the media as well as through physical and economic chokeholds on Palestinian communication and expression.[40]

Objectives

What are the goals of the movement? The BDS movement is not defined by the idea that it is through the establishment of a state congruent with the nation that the Palestinians will be emancipated. The notion of a Palestinian state tends to imply in the current conjuncture a two-state solution. The downfall of the Oslo Process, however, for many activists, Palestinian and non-Palestinian, has broken the idea of the two-state solution. It is said that the two-state solution has been tried, and it has failed. For Edward Said, who presciently opposed Oslo from the outset, it was bound so to do.[41] Morrison's doctoral research in particular is finding that the failure of Oslo to be central among the reasons for mobilization offered by Palestinian protagonists of the BDS movement[42]: these figures see it as an alternative to both the corruption and statism of Fatah and the essentialism and communalism of Hamas. Many among the ranks of the BDS movement are one-staters. In other words, they believe that the only way to end genuinely the forms of oppression in Israel-Palestine is to create one democratic state, a result of a civil rights struggle by Arab-Palestinians, who seem to be on the way to becoming a demographic majority in the territories controlled by Israel. This is a contested area, but official statistics show, for example, that at the end of 2014, there were more Palestinian-Arabs living between the Mediterranean and the Jordan

---

[40] Palestine Solidarity Campaign, "The Case for Cultural & Academic Boycott of Israel with intro by Ken Loach" (20 November 2012). https://www.youtube.com/watch?v=CPvV8QZE35w

[41] Edward Said, 'The Morning After', *The London Review of Books*, vol. 15, no. 20, (21 October 1993), 3–5.

[42] Suzanne Morrison, 'The Emergence of the Boycott, Divestment, and Sanctions Movement', in: *Contentious Politics in the Middle East*, ed. Fawaz A. Gerges, (London, Forthcoming).

river (6,270,668) than there were Jews (6,219,2000).[43] We note here that emancipation is not achieved through the consummation of the nation but through federal or binational arrangements, or those in which sovereignty is deterritorialized.[44] Others in the movement, sensitive to the problems of majoritarian ethnic democracy, consider consociational arrangements, or are undecided on the contours of the final settlement—beyond insisting on fundamental Palestinian rights.

Just as among horizontalist movements, the goal is not the imposition of a new collective or ideological blueprint. It is the achievement of basic inalienable rights and the dismantling of forms of racism, and apartheid that are actualized in forms of occupation, colonization, and spectacular violence and humiliation visited by the Israeli state on the bodies of rightless Palestinians—and the continuous violations of international law and human rights that are attendant on this intersectional violence, siege, massacre, and closure. Unlike some of the Occupy movements of recent times, the goals of BDS nonetheless are concrete and specifiable. The movement calls for an end to occupation, apartheid, colonization, and discrimination. The call remains in existence until Israel "fully complies with its obligations under international law".[31]

Organization

What modes of organization and coordination are involved in the BDS movement? The BDS movement does not entirely self-identify as horizontalist. To my knowledge, activists do not continuously make heavy play of their status as "horizontals" in opposition to other activists seen as "verti-

[43] Central Bureau of Statistics [Israel] 2015. http://www.cbs.gov.il/reader/shnaton/templ_shnaton_e.html?num_tab=st02_01&CYear=2015; Palestinian Central Bureau of Statistics. 2015. http://www.pcbs.gov.ps/Portals/_Rainbow/Documents/gover_e.htm; The Israeli CBS estimates that the de jure population of Israel, in what it calls Jewish and non-Jewish localities (i.e. everywhere from the Mediterranean to the Jordan river, including Golan), included 6,219,200 Jews at the end of 2014. It records that the Palestinian-Arab population, excluding the West Bank and the Gaza Strip, but including pre-1967 Israel, the Golan Heights, and East Jerusalem, stood then at 1,720,300 Arabs. The Palestinian CBS records 4,550,368 Arab-Palestinians in the West Bank and Gaza. These figures, which are not definitive for a number of reasons including measurement issues, are used to give the estimates above.

[44] Ephraim Nimni, *The Challenge of Post-Zionism* (London, 2003); Ephraim Nimni (ed.), *National Cultural Autonomy and Its Contemporary Critics* (London, 2005).

cals": contrariwise, such talk was certainly present in, for example, Occupy Wall Street.[45] Nonetheless, some of the conflicts that have played themselves out within the movement have to do with this distinction. The prescriptive, ideological, and hierarchical mode of organizing has come into some conflict with BDS networks. In the UK, for example, the relationship between the BDS movement and political parties such as the Socialist Workers Party and the trade unions has occasionally been difficult to negotiate. Boycotters have resisted vigorously the idea that they are being used as a pawn or taken over by those with pre-conceived ideas on programme and party. These relationships—between existing parties and the BDS movement—have worked productively only when they are constituted as equal nodes in a larger network. As Marfleet's chapter in this volume emphasizes, unions, parties, and workers' organizations have played an important role in the progress of the BDS movement as a whole. The relationship between the BDS movement and some of the established political factions, authorities, and parties in the OPT has also had points of conflict and of productive coordination. The BDS movement has always been sufficiently distinct from Fatah, the PLO, Hamas, not to mention the Palestinian Authority. At the Fourth National BDS Conference, 8 June 2013, Bethlehem, for example, by far the stormiest session pitted Dr Taisir Khaled, member of PLO Executive Committee, and Dr Jawad Naji, Palestinian Minister of the National Economy, against BDS supporters who had little time for the failures of the established political parties and the authorities to deliver on basic Palestinian rights.

There is no admissions process to the BDS movement, and no central authority. One does not join the BDS movement like one joined the Palestinian Communist Party in earlier parts of the century.[46] One cannot be expelled in any formal or official sense from the movement. There are no formal membership criteria or dues to be paid or formally established hierarchical processes. This style of organizing therefore has rhizomic characteristics. There are places of intersection to be sure: conferences, leading networks such as the Boycott Israel Network (BIN) or the Palestinian Academic and Cultural Boycott Initiative (PACBI), significant

---

[45] David Graeber, *The Democracy Project: A History. A Crisis. A Movement* (London, 2013), 3–54; Marianne Maeckelbergh, *The Will of the Many: How the Alterglobalisation Movement is Changing the Face of Democracy* (London, 2009), 39–66.

[46] Musa Budeiri, *The Palestine Communist Party, 1919–1948: Arab and Jew in the Struggle for Internationalism* (Chicago, 2010).

academics or intellectuals such as an Ilan Pappé, and particular organizations such as the British Committee for the Universities of Palestine (BRICUP) in the UK; there are membership organizations and specific campaigns; and there are numerous overlaps with church groups, trade unions, some political parties, student groups, and NGOs; these should not be underestimated. But it is hard to counter the thesis that the boycott movement is in organizational terms an open-ended network that continually adds new nodes and connections that spread in de-centralized ways. Nonetheless, joining BDS is not a free for all. There are plenty of guidelines as to how to act, how to position oneself, and how to cope with the deluge of charges and polemics that inevitably follow the decision to openly declare boycott.

The de-centralized form is clearly evident in the rise of the movement, which did not start from a vanguardist organization, or a state-based initiative. The movement emerged from many streams in diverse global locations: the call in 2002 for a moratorium on EU funding by academics Hilary and Steven Rose in the UK, initiatives from among Palestinian academics in Birzeit and Al-Quds Universities around the same time in the OPT, the Durban conference of 2001, the global justice movement in the USA, to the beginnings of divestment campaigns in churches, and the actions of student groups and trade unions in diverse locales. The movement emerged gradually, trans-locally, and according to no pre-conceived plan, and came with various false starts and modifications, including for example, in regards to the developing line taken by the movement after 2004 on the fact that the academic boycott was of institutions and not of individual Israeli academics.

The leaderless/leaderful formula should not be pushed too far. The movement remains in many ways under the more or less flexible direction of the Palestinian coordinating networks. This gives a certain direction to the movement as implied in its fundamental goals, while allowing for the differences that emerge over tactics and strategies in different national contexts. As Falk states, "it is important for non-Palestinian supporters to accept that its [the BDS movements'] direction and political approach should always remain under the direction of its Palestinian organisers".[34] Clearly some forms of leadership remain. Even highly networked and seemingly horizontal activism, as Nunes has recently argued, involves leadership, strategic interventions, structure, coordination, mobilization, and well-defined ends.[47]

---

[47] Rodrigo Nunes, *Organisation of the Organisationless: Collective Action after Networks* (Lüneburg, 2014), 41–3.

Strategy and Tactics

How is the boycott movement to achieve its goals? Implementing a broad, global campaign of BDS is supposed to strike at and undermine the system of oppressive rights violations at which the movement takes aim. The idea is to do so not through armed struggle, nor simply through debate and negotiation, or through a difficult-to-sustain and highly costly mass uprising (these means are held to have failed), but through the powers of institutional disruption that the movement mobilizes. BDS is supposed to weaken the structure of colonization and occupation through ostracism, economic divestment, and ultimately state-based sanctions.

Boycotts, enacting ostracism, aim to undermine legitimacy and weaken oppressive institutions. When business-as-usual is withdrawn, debates about the rights and wrongs of boycott, and the forms of complicity of the institutions boycotted, are far harder to ignore than when such debates are not backed with action. But the boycott is not only about legitimacy. Moral opprobrium does not have an entirely clear record on stopping atrocities—as cases from Chechnya to Iraq confirm. Boycott is centrally about weakening the capacities of complicit institutional and state-based forms. "Since convincing a colonial power to heed moral pleas for justice is, at best, delusional", writes Barghouti, "many now understand the need to 'besiege' Israel through boycotts, raising the price of its oppression and thus *compelling* it to comply with international law".[31] Non-cooperation is in principle replicable across many domains of social life and suited to diverse, de-centralized, and direct-action initiatives. It is a many-headed tactic that can minimize direct conflict between elements of the movement and more powerful and centralized organizations. Resistant elements have some protection because they are numerous and dispersed. This many-headed-ness was an important factor in the capacities of the civil rights movement in the USA in the 1960s.[48]

Divestment is supposed to strike at the economic bases of occupation and colonization. It hits companies and investments profiting from occupation or settlement, whether because they situate their production and capital in occupied territory, or whether they export products from occupied territory, or whether they profit from the arms, transport infra-

---

[48] Kali Akuno, 'The US Civil Rights and Black Liberation Movement: Lessons and Applications for the Palestinian Liberation Movement', in: *Generation Palestine: Voices from the Boycott, Divestment and Sanctions Movement*, ed. Rich Wiles, (London, 2013), 47–58.

structure, and heavy-equipment that the occupation requires to function. The strategy does not require that businessmen become moral. It simply requires that they see reputational risks through their association with Israeli human rights violations. Veolia, because of its activities in the Occupied Territories, has already lost billions of dollars in contracts and tenders, and divested completely from the Israeli market in 2015.[49] Where business competition is global, and where capital and production can be moved, and where even small risks can influence commercial decision-making, the strategy should not be dismissed as entirely unrealistic.

These pressures are expected to be more effective because they are less polarizing than armed struggle, while giving moderates among Israeli-Jews, Jews living outside Israel, and other relevant parties the chance to push for and bring about civil rights for Palestinians and new political arrangements. It is not necessarily to be expected that Zionist-Jews will be convinced in the short-term of the morality of the cause, but they may increasingly take account of the institutional costs of failing to compromise, and seek new arrangements. Dividing opponents, the boycott tactic is supposed to be inclusive, mobilizing, and able to unite supporters from a wide variety of backgrounds. Inclusionary mobilization was important in the use of boycott and non-cooperation in the movement for Indian independence,[50] as well as in the anti-apartheid movement.[51] Inclusiveness is particularly important in the Palestinian case because Palestinian civil society alone, still less Palestinian labour, on which the Israeli economy does not depend, does not have the capacity to institutionally disrupt the Israeli economy: this lesson was learnt during the first intifada, when Israel depended far more on Palestinian labour than now. This fact makes all the more important a movement strategy that goes well beyond labour withdrawal, and harnesses forms of non-cooperation and ostracism at the level of global civil society.

---

[49] Shir Hever, 'BDS: Perspectives of an Israeli Economist', in: *Generation Palestine: Voices from the Boycott, Divestment and Sanctions Movement*, ed. Rich Wiles, (London, 2013), 109–123.

[50] Prabir Purkayastha and Ayesha Kidwai, 'India's Freedom Struggle and Today's BDS Movement', in: *Generation Palestine: Voices from the Boycott, Divestment and Sanctions Movement*, ed. Rich Wiles, (London, 2013), 34–46.

[51] Ronnie Kasrils, 'Boycotts, Bricks and the Four Pillars of the South African Struggle', in: *Generation Palestine: Voices from the Boycott, Divestment and Sanctions Movement*, ed. Rich Wiles, (London, 2013), 18–33.

BDS has been activated to some extent amid the failure of interstate diplomacy: it "is a mechanism used by individuals when their States fail them".[38] The failure of political society certainly has provided reasons for mobilization. For example, the well-known film director Ken Loach and others write that "[g]iven the failure of international law, and the impunity of the Israeli state, we believe there is no alternative but for ordinary citizens to try their best to fill the breach".[52] The signal is very strongly that civil society must take direct action to protect Palestinian rights. On the other hand, the movement does not, in the manner of some contemporary state-eschewing movements, shy away from the attempt to draw in the state through the application of sanctions stemming from pressure from civil society. It is not therefore an anti-statist movement, even if it does not seek political power, or specify political arrangements. If it is radically democratic, it is not so in any straightforwardly anarchist sense but in the sense of a movement that aims to change political society while retaining at least one foot in civil society, to change the world without taking power.

Conclusion

The evidence presented in this chapter suggests that the BDS movement should not be dismissed as antisemitic. It can more appropriately be compared with recent radically democratic movements. In terms of the movement's "subject-ness", its identities, principles, goals, and styles of organization, this chapter argues that the movement is highly diverse and multitudinous, rooted in universal rights, opposed to fixed and totalizing forms of ascriptive privilege, and organized in networked, de-centralized, and non-hierarchical ways. Strikingly, the movement deploys nationalism less to establish the truth and emancipation of a pre-existing and richly elaborated national identity, and more to provide a warrant for universal rights. I have also provided evidence for the view that the asymmetric strategies and tactics of the movement, in a search for the desired institutional disruption, are based around inclusion, diversity, trans-locality, many-headedness, direct action, and the idea of changing the world without taking power. This last feature refers to the important, directly democratic idea that movements can stay rooted in civil society while changing

---

[52] Ken Loach, Rebecca O'Brien, and Paul Laverty, 'Why We Back the Boycott Campaign', in: *Generation Palestine: Voices from the Boycott, Divestment and Sanctions Movement*, ed. Rich Wiles, (London, 2013), 153–58.

the contours of political society, without becoming just another established actor in political society itself. The key features of the movement's mobilizing project, both in terms of "subject-ness" and in terms of strategy, therefore, bear a number of similarities to the characteristics of radical democracy movements. It is worth adding that the institutional and systemic targets of the BDS movement, which has invariably been driven forward by civil society actors, stands in strong contrast with boycotts that historically targeted Jews or particular categories of people on a religious or racialized basis, and which were often, but not always, led by the state, politicians, or established institutions.

The radically democratic features of the movement can help explain its appeal among progressive constituencies in the alter-globalization and global justice movements. If we consider the internal morphology of the movement's mobilizing project, moreover, as this chapter has endeavoured to do, we can add that a key strength of the movement is its internal cohesion. Identities, principles, and styles of organization based around universal rights, networks, and the multitude cohere at a fundamental level with an inclusionary, civil society-based, and many-headed strategy for change. Only through a multitudinous we-ness frame, and through networked forms of organization, can the movement hope to be as inclusive as it needs to be to acquire wide adherence and the requisite asymmetric leverage. Movement principles and identities, therefore, cohere with a particular kind of transnational asymmetric strategy. Just as importantly, horizontal networks are not just a means to an end, but invested by movement adherents with moral value in themselves. The idea of the motley multitude, moreover, is not just seen as a value in itself, but also a strategically viable way to achieve change. In this way, the movement weaves together instrumental-rational logics with value-rational logics, a powerful form of internal cohesion which can help account for its agency and capacity on the contemporary scene.

CHAPTER 16

Moral-Historical Questions of the Anti-Israel Boycott

Jeremy Krikler

There is a paradox that lies at the heart of Israel's emergence. A notable feature of the Israel/Palestine tragedy is that it resulted from the rise, consolidation, and extension of a settler state in the post-Second World War period. That is to say, at the very moment that the historic process of decolonisation began, the rise of Israel in many respects ran counter to this process. It is quite true that the establishment of Israel is unthinkable without European antisemitism. The process of Jewish settlement of what was historic Palestine was driven forward by persecution and discrimination and was not part of imperialism in the classic way in which the building of European settler colonial states was. Indeed, notwithstanding the crucial support given by British imperial power to the project of establishing a Jewish national home in Palestine,[1] the creation of Israel was ultimately to entail a struggle against British imperialism, although it

---

[1] For this, its context and ramifications, see Avi Shlaim, *Israel and Palestine: Reappraisals, Revisions, Refutations* (London, 2009), chapter 1.

J. Krikler (✉)
University of Essex, Colchester, UK
e-mail: krikjm@essex.ac.uk

© The Author(s) 2019
D. Feldman (ed.), *Boycotts Past and Present*, Palgrave Critical Studies of Antisemitism and Racism,
https://doi.org/10.1007/978-3-319-94872-0_16

became—in certain central ways—a *settler* struggle against imperialism.[2] Indeed, although it might be discomfiting for some to hear this, there is something analogous in the historical processes that gave rise to Israel and those which gave rise to Rhodesia, a state that was also distinguished by settler rebellion against an imperial power and the suppression of indigenous nationalists.[3] As in Palestine/Israel, those indigenous nationalists also then took up arms against the order fashioned by settlers and their descendants.

The world into which Israel was born, then, just as the world into which white Rhodesia emerged, was a world in which colonisation and the settler displacement of original populations was construed as one of the great moral problems of the age. Israel cannot escape that fact. A colossal, epochal shift against the settler state was taking place at the very time that Israel established itself, displaced large numbers of Palestinians, expanded its borders, subjected still more Palestinians to military occupation, and sent increasing numbers of settlers to colonise newly conquered territory. It was inevitable that the myriad peoples who emerged from imperial or settler control in the post-war world were bound to see correspondences between their historical experience and that of the Palestinians. It was therefore perfectly logical for the very first speech ever made by a Palestinian leader to the UN General Assembly to contain rhetorical emphases that reflected this: hence its allusions to, inter alia, the 'heroic Algerian war of national liberation', to states that had had only recently acquired their independence from Portugal and Britain, to the need for 'a world free of colonialism, imperialism, neo-colonialism and racism in each of its instances', and hence the reference to subordinated peoples in Southern Africa, including what was then Rhodesia, whose situations and struggles were described as akin to those of the Palestinians.[4] It is

---

[2] *All* Jewish nationalist organisations in Palestine participated in armed attacks against the British at various points between 1944 and 1947: for a sketch of these, see Benny Morris' *1948. A History of the First Arab-Israeli War* (New Haven and London, 2008), 29–30, 31, 35, 38–9.

[3] It is interesting that a major study of settler states, that focuses in great part on Rhodesia, should refer repeatedly to Israel for comparative purposes: see Ronald Weitzer's *Transforming Settler States: Communal Conflict and Internal Security in Northern Ireland and Zimbabwe* (Berkeley, 1990), 25, 26, 27, 28–9, 31, 33, 35, 40, 44, 98, 131.

[4] See 'Yasir Arafat, Speech to the United Nations General Assembly, New York, 13 November 1974', reproduced as Appendix 8 of *The Palestinian-Israeli Peace Agreement. A Documentary Record* (Washington, 1994); quotations from pp. 212 and 213.

unthinkable that had the United Nations in 1947 been configured in the way it was in 1974 when this speech was made—that is, had the UN been much more fully representative of the peoples of the world, especially the scores of nations of Africa and Asia who were excluded from the organisation in 1947—that there would have been a vote in favour of establishing a Jewish state in Palestine. The process of decolonisation has been fundamental to why many have called into question the legitimacy of Israel.

Israel's history as a settler state emerging in the period of decolonisation inevitably means that, for large numbers of people, a moral question was—and is—posed by its establishment. Insofar as Israeli policy is complicit—as it has often been—in a process of increased settlement and displacement in territory occupied since 1967, it sharpens that initial moral question. It is a question that simply cannot be avoided, although the place of extreme antisemitism in the birth of Israel and the fact that the state commands the democratic allegiance of most of the people within its (1967) borders—a crucial difference from the settler state of Rhodesia—is part of the context in which that moral question has to be addressed.

Some of those discomfited by the anti-Israel boycott and divestment movement that has developed in civil society in parts of the West are apt to reduce it to antisemitism. Certainly, the outpouring of anti-Jewish abuse from some elements of the Left during the crisis in the British Labour Party on the issue of antisemitism in 2018 provides a salutary lesson in this regard.[5] It suggests that a constituency (the Left) that is central to the boycott campaign regarding Israel does contain some who hold antisemitic prejudices.[6] These could be expressed and masked in an anti-Israel boycott and, insofar as they are, the moral force of the boycott movement is weakened and corrupted. Clearly, that movement has to be alert to the deep implantation of antisemitic tropes and beliefs in national cultures in which it operates, and to battle against their finding a place in its campaigns.

---

[5] Momentum, the grassroots organisation linked to the Labour Party, conceded that antisemitism was 'more widespread in the Labour party than many of us had understood', with the leader of Momentum himself having been treated to antisemitic abuse: see Jessica Elgot, 'Momentum: antisemitism claims are not conspiracy', *The Guardian*, 3 April 2018, p. 2.

[6] The socialist writer and Labour Party supporter, Owen Jones, in commenting on the Labour antisemitism furore is forthright about the existence of '[t]he poison of antisemitism...among a minority on the left': see Owen Jones, 'Labour has so much to do. It can't let bigotry get in the way', *The Guardian*, Journal section, 4 April 2018, p. 3.

However, the process of identifying antisemitic idioms and beliefs and combatting them is hardly to be furthered by a blanket equation of antisemitism with opposition to militaristic and discriminatory policies of the Israeli state. This equation can run the gamut from implications that supporters (including Jewish supporters) of Palestinian rights might simply be deluded by a sophisticated antisemitic propaganda machine[7]—a curious inversion of the more familiar Jewish conspiracy theory—to extreme accusations that a Jewish critic of Israeli policy is peddling 'viciously anti-Semitic' work, and is responsible for 'a modern-day version of the notorious...forgery *The Protocols of the Elders of Zion*'.[8] Proof should be demanded in all cases: as David Feldman has argued, criticism of Israeli policy cannot be construed as antisemitic if it is not tinged in some way with any of the characteristic stereotypes, beliefs, and tropes of antisemitism.[9] Moreover, whether or not some antisemites participate in calls for a boycott does not negate the concerns raised by those offering a genuine moral critique of Israeli policy. By way of analogy, one might note that there are Islamophobes who are determined to keep as many Muslims out of Europe as possible by preventing Turkey from joining the European Union. They have at times supported the demands of those who—for honourable reasons—campaign to pressure Turkey to recognise its responsibility for the Armenian genocide. It would be cynical and dishonest to use this fact to besmirch the values of those who demand recognition of a genocide for the right reasons, or to use it to absolve Turkish governments of their responsibility to acknowledge and reckon with the ramifications of the mass murder of the Armenians.

Most of those supporters of Palestinian rights in the West calling for forms of boycott of and divestment from the Israeli state—they include some Jewish people—do so because they see the plight of the Palestinians

---

[7] Illustrative of this would be the letter by Judy Samuel of London in *The Guardian*, 17 February 2015, p. 32. She was writing in opposition to the artists, including Jewish artists, who had declared a cultural boycott of Israel a few days before. Her response: 'Could these British artists possibly be the target of sophisticated anti-Israel propaganda shrouding its antisemitic message under the cloak of liberal rhetoric?' The boycott declaration had appeared in *The Guardian* on 14 February.

[8] These are the comments of Alan Dershowitz in his (unsuccessful) campaign to prevent the publication of a work by Norman Finkelstein by the University of California Press: see Avi Shlaim, *Israel and Palestine*, 369–370.

[9] This was argued by David Feldman in a paper he delivered in Cambridge in 2015.

in terms of colonisation, discrimination, military subjection, and disproportionate armed action. When opponents of the boycott hope that somehow the intense moral focus on Israel/Palestine will diminish, they are being unrealistic: first, because the conflicts in the Middle East will continue to draw the world's attention and second, because the Israel/Palestine tragedy bears upon some of the central values in Left and liberal culture in the post-war world. A vast tide of history—colossal nationalist struggles, anti-imperial campaigns, decolonisation—has made international civil society peculiarly sensitive to issues of dispossession and displacement by settlers. That is not going to change.

There is, therefore, at least one sense in which the present boycott movement directed against Israel bears a similarity to the great international boycott movements of the past. If the anti-slavery boycotts resulted in part from a profound shift in international civil society regarding notions of rights and freedom,[10] the present boycott movement related to Israel, as did that regarding apartheid South Africa or white-ruled Rhodesia, similarly expresses a profound shift relating to colonisation, settler states and the discrimination intrinsic to them. This moral-historical fact calls into question attempts to tar the present boycott movement in the West with the brush of the Nazi boycott of Jewish professionals and businesses in Germany in the 1930s. An utterly persecutory, racist campaign against Jews—one in which the state was so involved that, as Christoph Kreutzmüller demonstrates in this volume, it is questionable whether the term 'boycott' should be used to refer to the policies of blockade and attack employed—[11] is manifestly not the same as a campaign emerging within civil society and that is trying to shift state policies regarding a subject population. There needs to be much more care taken in the invocation of the history of boycotts in the Nazi period: there was also a boycott of German goods internationally by those seeking to alter Nazi policies towards Jews, the subject of another of the papers presented at the conference out of which this book has emerged.[12]

---

[10] The classic study of the massive historical shifts underpinning the rise of abolitionism, of which the boycotts were a part, is Davis Brion Davis' *The Problem of Slavery in the Age of Revolution 1770–1823* (Ithaca, 1975).

[11] See Christoph Kreutzmüller, 'The blockade of Jewish owned businesses in Nazi Germany – a boycott?', a chapter in this volume.

[12] Gideon Reuveni, 'The good, the bad and the marketplace: buycott, boycott and Jewish consumers in post-1933 Germany', paper delivered at the 'Boycotts – Past and Present'

In another respect, recent history has made the manner of Israel's birth and consolidation problematic in sections of international civil society. Since the dissolution of Yugoslavia and the vicious processes of 'ethnic cleansing' associated with it, a general horror has emerged in the conscience of the West—the political world to which Israel particularly appeals—with regard to policies that have aimed at denuding territories of peoples deemed as undesirable by those holding decisive coercive force. Israeli revisionist scholarship has proved beyond doubt the systematic policies of this kind directed at Palestinians at the moment of Israel's founding. Aside from Benny Morris' general and magisterial demonstration of this,[13] there is—for example—Ari Shavit's unflinching and moving evocation of how the tens of thousands of Arabs of the city of Lydda, which neighboured Tel Aviv, were forced into exile through 'occupation, massacre, and psychological pressure'. An 'indirect threat of slaughter', Shavit writes, hovered before a community that was given less than two hours to leave forever their homes.[14] The establishment of Israel, then, is indissolubly linked not only to the rise of a settler state but to 'ethnic cleansing' that occurred in the midst of civil and, then, impending and actual interstate war.[15] One should reject the idea of a long-term conspiracy regarding the expulsion of the Palestinians, but one should equally not deny what enormous labours of research have demonstrated: that within Zionist discourse in the first half of the twentieth century, there was always a stream of thought—it jostled with others—that hoped for what was euphemistically termed the 'transfer' of Palestinian Arabs from an envisaged Jewish state; that the situation of crisis and the military exigencies of 1947–1948 in Palestine set the forced exodus in motion; that the military actions and threats of the forces of the nascent Jewish state were fundamental to this; and that once the so-called transfer was achieved, the new state of Israel immediately refused

---

conference, Pears Institute for the Study of Antisemitism, Birkbeck College, University of London, 2014.

[13] See Benny Morris, *The Birth of the Palestinian Refugee Problem Revisited* (Cambridge, 2004).

[14] See Ari Shavit, 'Lydda, 1948', *The New Yorker*, 21 October 2013, pp. 40–46; quotations from p. 44.

[15] As demonstrated by Morris in *The Birth of the Palestinian Refugee Problem Revisited*.

the refugees the right to return to their homes.¹⁶ It is both unrealistic and morally questionable to hope, as some supporters of the Israeli state do, that the deep ethical questions arising from a history of what would now be called 'ethnic cleansing' are not going to lead large numbers of people who are not antisemitic, including many Jews, to demand that Israel recognises the responsibilities flowing from this history. When one writer despairingly alleges that 'some well-intentioned, well-meaning people' have been duped into seeing Israel as a state that requires sanctions,¹⁷ he would do better to recognise the degree to which the phenomena associated with the dispossession, expulsion, and plight of the Palestinians under Israeli rule inevitably touch deeply the ethical sensibilities that have been fashioned by momentous post-war historical developments.

It is, of course, undeniable that many atrocities have been perpetrated against Israelis by Palestinian nationalists: examples would be the killings of Israeli athletes in Munich, or the suicide bombings of the second intifada. This list could be extended considerably. However, those who deplore such atrocities but who remain opposed to Israeli policies of colonisation, discrimination, and displacement will view them as emanating from the despair and hatred arising from a historic and continuing victimisation. For such people, violence arising from those who are relatively powerless, and who are discriminated against or oppressed, will be viewed differently from violence pursued by the powerful maintaining or advancing discrimination and oppression. In this respect, those in favour of Palestinian rights are likely to take the same view as did many abolitionists in the nineteenth century to Nat Turner's revolt in the slave south of the USA. Turner's movement saw the murder of unarmed people, with a

---

[16] The statements provided in the text above will be accepted by those who take the full force of the massive weight of evidence provided by the so-called revisionists. There are debates and disputes that have arisen, not least amongst the revisionists themselves, which have helped to refine and amend some of their findings. However, most non-partisan scholars would consider the statements in the text above to be beyond historical dispute. The key historians whose work made this possible are: Simha Flapan, Benny Morris, Nur Masalha, Ilan Pappé and Avi Shlaim. Shlaim provides a survey and adjudication of key works in his *Israel and Palestine*, chapter 4.

[17] See Benjamin Pogrund, 'Israel has many injustices. But it isn't an apartheid state': *The Guardian*, 22 May 2015, p. 37.

significant majority of the nearly threescore people slaughtered by the rebels being women, teenagers, and children, including infants.[18] But the most committed of abolitionists, William Garrison, still described Turner's actions in terms of the quest for freedom and 'a dreadful retaliation' impelled by what he had endured.[19] Clearly, no instances of murder by slaves led people like Garrison to cease their opposition to the structural and systemic violence and oppression of slavery.

A reasonable argument can be made by boycotters that their movement is necessary. After all, Israeli politics and society might be democratically framed and capable of giving rise to many radical critics of state policy, as also to brave and powerful exposés of the cruelty perpetrated against Palestinians,[20] not to mention brilliant evocations in art of the brutal ramifications of Israeli militarism.[21] But the country has nevertheless found it very difficult to find the internal resources to address meaningfully the Palestinian tragedy that has resulted from the establishment of Israel and its policies. In this case, Israel bears a certain similarity to apartheid South Africa, rather than to a discriminatory order such as segregation in the USA. In the latter case, a protest movement, an existing constitutional and legal structure, as also political and legislative developments proved capable of removing the segregationist order; in the South African case, insurrection and international ostracism proved necessary to force white South Africa to abandon apartheid. We do not yet know if there is going to be some kind of agreeable solution to the Palestine/Israel dispute but, if there is, it is hard to imagine that future historians will not consider international pressure as fundamental to ending Israel's military occupation, its denial of sovereignty to the people of the West Bank and Gaza, and the reduction or ending of those elements of second-class citizenship which Palestinians in Israel suffer. There are, after all, Israelis who themselves

---

[18] See Mary Kemp Davis, *Nat Turner Before the Bar of Judgment. Fictional Treatments of the Southampton Slave Insurrection* (Baton Rouge, 1999), 1.

[19] Stanley Harrold, *The Abolitionists and the South, 1831–1861* (Lexington, 1995), 57.

[20] Consider the journalism of Gideon Levy of the Israeli newspaper, *Haaretz*, collected together in his *The Punishment of Gaza* (London, 2010).

[21] See, for example, Ari Folman and David Polonsky, *Waltz with Bashir* (London, 2009) and the animation documentary to which it relates.

support forms of boycott and who see a demand for justice as intrinsic to the boycott movement in the West.[22]

Certainly, if something approximating a just order in Israel/Palestine emerges, it is highly unlikely to emerge solely through the democratic will of the Israeli electorate which for most of Israel's existence has produced governments that have followed, to varying degrees, a combination of some if not all of the following policies against the Palestinians: dispossession, expulsion, colonisation, annexation, discrimination, military occupation, and blockade. Such policies should not be seen as the monopoly of the right-wing governments in which Likud has played so notable a part. Before Likud ever had a claim on government, they were followed by Labour, whose Golda Meir was not merely opposed to the idea of a Palestinian state but who denied that the Palestinians existed.[23] Decisive movement away from opposition to a Palestinian state (as exemplified by the Peace Now movement and the Rabin-Arafat negotiations of the 1990s) has tended to result in an extreme reaction from the wider electorate: the Rabin/Peace Now moment was terminated through political assassination and the removal of his party from power. Those who argue against a boycott and divestment movement might be asked to consider if there are sometimes tragic situations within regions that simply cannot be solved solely by the contending parties involved.

Arguably, then, a boycott and divestment campaign to compel Israel to make decisive concessions to the Palestinians will be seen by many as morally required, and this not only because Israeli history reveals that its state and electorate have found extreme difficulty themselves in finding the concert and resources to do this on their own. It is also because the failure by successive generations to alleviate the situation of the Palestinian people can only compound their historic tragedy and inevitably drive more and more of them into a destructive hatred. The more extreme of the political tendencies within Palestinian society welcomes the indiscriminate

---

[22] See, for example, Gideon Levy, 'A Just Boycott' (4 June 2006) in his *Punishment of Gaza*, 3–6.

[23] An excellent introduction to the fact that pre-Likud Israeli governments—these were always Labour Governments—espoused and followed policies of discrimination, dispossession, expulsion, and annexation after 1967 is Noam Chomsky's *Peace in the Middle East?* (London, 1975), which was published before Likud first came to power: see pp. 16, 93–94, 99–100, 103–104, 105, 108, 110–111, 116, 125, 150, 152–153, 155, 171 (n. 72), 177 (n. 2). For Golda Meir's statements regarding the Palestinians as referred to in the text above: see pp. 104, 140.

killing of Israelis, just as the most extreme of the political tendencies in Israeli society feels itself to be justified in something similar with regard to Palestinians. Such tendencies have found tragic symbols in those infamous massacres in places of worship that have occurred on both sides, but there is much other evidence for it.[24] A situation which produces such toxic responses is intolerable, which—of course—does not mean that it will not persist. However, the presence of such corrosive hatreds in sections of *both* Israeli and Palestinian society will not lead those in the West who support a boycott of Israel to lessen their pressure on the Israeli state. The reasons for this relate to the fact that the conflict has resulted in a radical inequality of casualties on the two sides, to the distribution of power amongst the contending forces, and to the history that has produced this. The Israeli state, because it is the holder of decisive and overwhelming power in the territories taken from the Palestinians, and because its rise, establishment, and policies are fundamental to what is widely accepted as the tragedy of the Palestinian people, will inevitably be viewed by the boycott movement as bearing the primary responsibility for the situation.

Opponents of the boycott have sometimes sought to trump this history by gesturing at the Holocaust: surely, they implicitly argue, genocide justifies Israel's rise, even if this entailed what befell the Palestinians. But this argument raises very disturbing moral questions. One cannot possibly justify an injustice done to one people in the name of an injustice done to another. Thus, there is little doubt that religious persecution, including murder, drove large numbers of Europeans to what became the USA. Those Europeans then dispossessed and marginalised Native American populations in a set of events that included atrocity. Persecution of the denominations in Europe who went on to found colonies in North America can be used to explain a pattern of migration and a seeking of refuge; they cannot explain or justify what befell the Native Americans. That is to be explained in terms of the policies and ideologies of the settlers. To keep gesturing at the reasons for migration would be a way of sloughing off responsibility for those policies and ideologies. Moreover, to justify a state in terms of the

---

[24] Unfortunately, too much evidence for this could be provided. Here is some of it. One of the leaders of Hamas called a knife attack in which Israelis were indiscriminately attacked on a Tel Aviv bus as 'brave and heroic': see *The Guardian*, 22 January 2015, p. 18: 'Four seriously injured in Tel Aviv bus stabbings'. A good example of the culture of indiscriminate murder would be the kidnapping and murder of Israeli teenagers in 2014 by Palestinians, which was followed by the kidnap and killing of a random Palestinian teenager by Israelis. David Remnick sketches the events in 'The One State Reality', *The New Yorker*, 17 November 2014, pp. 47–8.

genocide that has befallen a people can lead some to view the genocide as a necessary precondition for the state and, therefore, if one sees the establishment of the nation state as the ultimate good—as nationalists tend to— the genocide can be implied to have had a positive outcome. To view the Holocaust in terms of the rise of Israel is not to view the Holocaust in its own terms. It runs the danger of elevating the nation state above the victims of genocide, who are enlisted as ghostly founders and reasons for the state. The French Jewish philosopher, Emmanuel Levinas, whose family perished in the Holocaust, appears to have succumbed to this line of thinking and thereby violated that basic precept of his own philosophy: that a victim must always be looked at in his or her own terms and situation and not in the terms, context, and interests of somebody else.[25]

One can and should note the important role of antisemitism as a motor of Jewish emigration to historic Palestine, and one can and should note that refugees or survivors from the Holocaust undoubtedly found a sanctuary in what was to become Israel. All of this is a matter of historical fact. What is historically and morally problematic is to convert the Holocaust into something positive for Jewish nationalism.

Does the anti-Israel boycott movement in the West have moral-historical questions of its own to consider? Yes. The first relates to a point made earlier: the need to pursue campaigns in a way that fully recognises the long history of anti-Jewish prejudice and the need consequently to be vigilant against the smuggling of antisemitism into boycotts. Obviously, such vigilance will be weakened by assumptions that any Israeli body or individual is a supporter of discriminatory policy against the Palestinians. Moreover, historically some boycotts have been utterly open-ended, particularly when they are related to nationalist movements. In this regard, consider three economic boycotts, two of them analysed in this volume: that of Germans by Czech nationalists in late nineteenth-century Bohemia, that of Jews by Polish nationalists in the early twentieth century, and that of Arab workers as demanded by Jewish workers in early twentieth-century Palestine.[26] What could Germans, Jews, and Arabs do

---

[25] I have explored some of the problems that have arisen in applying Levinas' theory to Holocaust studies in Jeremy Krikler, 'Voice, Face and Holocaust', *The Holocaust in History and Memory*, vol. 2, (2009), 91–2. In this, I was strongly influenced by the work and findings of Howard Caygill, *Levinas and the Poltical* (London, 2002).

[26] The Czech nationalist boycott referred to is dealt with in this volume in Michael Miller, 'In Defence of Nation: Protectionism and Boycott in Central and Eastern Europe'; the Polish nationalist boycott is also dealt with in this volume in Grzegorz Krzywiec, '*Swój do swego po swojeł*' ('Stick to your own for all you own'). The Anti-Jewish Boycott: Polish and

to get the nationalists to lift their boycott? Nothing. They would have had to cease to be Germans, Jews, and Arabs for this to occur. Implicit in such boycotts is a desire for the non-existence of a group, which should make any participants in a boycott linked to nationalism vigilant about its implications. It may be that the anti-Israel boycott movement in the West is not primarily inspired by nationalism and that it is linked more to a humanitarianism aroused by the plight of a people and, notably, by the excesses of Israel's repeated military actions in Gaza, the West Bank, and in Lebanon. Nevertheless, this boycott movement has some links to a nationalism—that is, Palestinian nationalism. And, as suggested above, because of the possibility of boycott movements linked to nationalism inclining to the construal of people of the 'enemy' nation as somehow irredeemable, it is incumbent upon those who support a boycott strategy with respect to the Israeli state to answer the question: 'At which point would the boycott be called off?'

The question is not easy to answer because the boycott movement is composed of many different strands and tactics. Some supporters of forms of boycott are focused on the occupied territories and Israeli policy in them: their aim is to bring Israel to the negotiating table and allow—with whatever mutually agreed compromises—the creation of an independent Palestinian state on the basis of the boundaries that existed prior to 1967. They are not calling into question the Israeli state as it emerged in its pre-1967 borders. Such boycotters might argue that the objectives of the boycott are to secure decisive movement on the following: withdrawal of Israel to pre-1967 borders (including dismantling of the wall), with East Jerusalem recognised as the capital of a Palestinian state; Israel's recognition of major responsibility for the Palestinian refugees of the late 1940s and their descendants, this to entail some meaningful, but nevertheless symbolic, conferral of the right to resettlement within the borders of Israel proper, and compensation to those not resettled; and removal of any discriminatory laws or policies in Israel that, in effect, make into second-class citizens Israeli nationals who are not Jewish, albeit—and this is not insignificant—second-class citizens with full franchise rights.

East-European politics in the early twentieth century'; for the Jewish boycott of Arab labour, see Uri Ram, 'The colonization perspective in Israeli sociology', in: *The Israel/Palestine Question*, ed. Ilan Pappé, (London, 1999), 65, 70 and Gershon Shafir, 'Zionism and Colonialism: a comparative approach', in: *The Israel/Palestine Question*, ed. Pappé, 88, 89.

Other boycotters, however, will go further. They will condemn not merely what has happened and is happening in the occupied territories but will call into question the legitimacy of the Israeli state as it exists within the borders that emerged from its War of Independence. We pass here from one kind of boycott—one with limited aims—to another, one that can have as an aim the effacement of the Israeli nation state and its replacement by a state—no longer called Israel—that incorporates present day Israel and the occupied territories, a state that will be the home for both present day Israeli Jews and all Palestinians, whether those in Israel, in the occupied territories, or in the Palestinian diaspora, especially in the refugee settlements in the Middle East: in short, the state ideal formally envisaged by the Palestinian national movement until the Palestine Liberation Organization (PLO) recognised Israel in 1988.[27] That is an aim and a boycott movement that is calling for the end of the Israeli nation state.

Does that entail a moral question? To my mind it does. After all, what does demanding the end of the Israeli nation state mean in our very non-utopian period of history? If boycotters are aiming at this, they will inevitably draw suspicions from some that they incline to an idea of 'the destruction of Israel'—a concept that has frequently been mooted by politicians in the Middle East and one that can still be heard from some Palestinian nationalists. While one can concede that it is a desperate tragedy that often impels the articulation of such extreme views amongst Palestinians, there are two other factors that one should recognise. First, that the view is not merely a marginal attitude: it was, after all, a foundational element of modern Palestinian nationalism. It was evidenced, for example, in that that call—issued a few years after Israel occupied the West Bank and Gaza and subscribed to by every organised Palestinian political

---

[27] The formal state ideal to which I refer was proclaimed by Yasir Arafat to the UN General Assembly in 1974: 'In my formal capacity as Chairman of the Palestine Liberation Organization and leader of the Palestinian revolution I proclaim before you that when we speak of our common hopes for the Palestine of tomorrow we include in our perspective all Jews now living in Palestine who choose to live with us there in peace and without discrimination. ...We offer them the most generous solution, that we might live together in a framework of just peace in our democratic Palestine'. See 'Yasir Arafat's Address to the UN General Assembly', 13 November 1974 as reproduced in Charles D. Smith, *Palestine and the Arab-Israeli Conflict*, 6th edn. (Boston, 2007), 348–351; quotations from pp. 350–351. For the formal recognition of Israel in 1988 and the immediate US signal of its significance, see 'Statement by Yasir Arafat, Geneva' and 'Statement by George Shultz, Washington, D. C.', both dated 14 December 1988: reproduced in Smith, *Palestine and the Arab-Israeli Conflict*, 448–9.

tendency—for the necessity to liquidate Israel's 'political, military, social, syndical, and cultural institutions'.[28] Second, as Noam Chomsky long ago pointed out, such a project, given the force and resistance it will encounter would be either suicidal for those who attempt to implement it or, if it was successful, 'would involve the destruction by force of a unified society, its people, and its institutions'.[29] Such a project would be so undiscriminating and violent that it will inevitably lead some to see it as a species of extreme antisemitism. This is why the boycott movement in the West has to make clear its attitude to the legitimacy of the Israeli nation state within its pre-1967 borders.

A boycott campaign that is truly historically grounded, then, has to pay respect to two incontrovertible facts: first, the dispossession and tragic plight of the Palestinians through the rise, expansion, and policies of the Israeli settler state and the need to address that in a way found meaningful by most Palestinians; and, second, the fact that the historical process—including a murderous antisemitism—has delivered into existence a nation (in the main no longer made up of settlers) democratically bound up with the present Israeli state. This is not to say that an Israeli withdrawal to the borders of 1967 and its acceptance of responsibility for the Palestinian refugees along the lines I suggested earlier means that all criticism and even campaigns against Israeli policy will become unjustifiable. Insofar as discrimination or the abridgement of rights of Palestinians in Israel remains, focused campaigns around those issues may well be felt to be necessary. But they will now be taking place on a quite specific basis: they will be aimed at the granting of full and equal citizenship rights to Palestinians living within the 1967 borders of Israel.

If, after the achievement of a two-state solution based on the 1967 borders, an international protest movement came to restrict itself to this—that is, to a campaign for full and equal rights for all citizens in Israel—it would imply two things: first, that it was expecting a colossal concession on the part of the Palestinian national movement—namely that it no longer consider as basic to its cause a right to return to their historic homeland for the great majority of the Palestinian refugees and their descendants. (Such a concession would affect not merely the millions of Palestinians

---

[28] Quotation from the programme of the Unified Command of the Palestinian Resistance Movement, 6 May 1970: quoted in N. Chomsky, *Peace in the Middle East?*, 84. As Chomsky wrote, the Unified Command 'included all the Palestinian organizations'.

[29] Chomsky, *Peace in the Middle East?*, 85.

who are accredited as refugees by the UN and who live in Lebanon, Syria, and Jordan, but also substantial numbers of Palestinians in Gaza and the West Bank. For the West Bank and Gaza Strip were—along with the states mentioned above—the chief territories in which the Palestinian refugees of 1947–1950 sought sanctuary.)[30] But a two-state solution as sketched above would also be aiming at a major concession from the Israeli national movement—namely that Israel no longer allow policies that discriminate in favour of Jews, which must have a bearing upon Israel's definition as a specifically Jewish state. For those policies dictate that citizens of Israel who are not Jewish do not have the same rights as those who are.[31] Netanyahu's announcement before the Israeli elections of 2015 that there could be no settlement with the Palestinians until they recognised Israel as a specifically Jewish state, is—in effect—a demand that Palestinians accept that their compatriots within Israel will always be second-class citizens.[32] Definition of a state in exclusivist terms—whether racial, religious or ethnic—will always imply second-class citizenship or non-citizenship for those who do not (or who are made not) to conform to the definition. This is certainly the case for Palestinians within the borders of Israel proper. As long as the state is defined as Jewish, it allows legislation such as the Basic Law: Israel Lands of 1960 which, in effect, reserves to people of Jewish origin rights to more than 90% of the land.[33] This is a law incidentally that bears some similarity to the notorious 1913 Land Act in South Africa which drastically curtailed rights to the land for black people: the percentage of the country's land from which black people in South Africa were officially forbidden ownership or leasing rights was remarkably similar to the percentage of Israel's land from which Arabs were excluded

---

[30] Benny Morris, *The Birth of the Palestinian Refugee Problem Revisited*, 1.

[31] Many years ago, Noam Chomsky trenchantly described the corrosion of the democratic ideal and the discrimination resulting from defining the Israeli state in ethnic-religious terms: see Chomsky, *Peace in the Middle East?*, 16–17, 37–38, 72, 100, 101, 109–111, 116, 117–118, 128–9, 150–151, 152, 153.

[32] Linked to Netanyahu's announcement was an Israeli cabinet endorsement of a bill, which alarmed even the Israeli President and Attorney-General, to declare Israel a specifically Jewish nation state. This was recognised immediately as running counter to the formal cast of the Israeli Declaration of Independence and a demotion of its democratic commitment: see *The Guardian*, 29 November 2014, p. 42, 'With a bill for narrowly Jewish nationhood, a democracy is on the brink of downgrading itself'. The article was right to accord a significance to these developments but reveals an ignorance of the degree to which Israel was already defined, not merely in its policies, but in Israeli law as a Jewish state.

[33] See Chomsky, *Peace in the Middle East?*, 21. Note also the discussion on p. 110.

from such rights.[34] Put simply, the Basic Law: Israel Lands of 1960 is incompatible with a non-discriminatory state.

At any rate, for those who accept the argument presented here, the conclusions would be the following. A boycott movement aiming at the withdrawal of Israel to its pre-1967 borders, the termination of policies of control over the West Bank and Gaza, and the ending of discrimination in Israel itself would not be aiming at the dismantling of the Israeli nation state. It would, however, be aiming to alter the character of that state. It would be aiming for that state no longer to be defined in exclusivist terms, allowing all those within its borders equal rights of citizenship. If such a boycott movement achieved its objectives, the state that emerged would still however have an overwhelming Jewish majority. How that state evolved, how it related to the states around it, and to the Jewish and Palestinian populations outside Israel, would be unclear. What is clear is that a boycott movement linked to a strategy that insists on much more than this—that is, to dissolve the Israeli nation state—is potentially linking itself to an objective that could be achieved in the short and medium term only through a hurricane of violence that would simply compound the tragic histories of Palestinians and Jews. This does not mean that the aspirations of some in the boycott movement—a vision of a democratic state comprehending Israel proper, the West Bank, and Gaza—has to be dispensed with. However, it does mean that those who hold this view concede that it can only be meaningfully and democratically achieved after the withdrawal of Israel to its 1967 borders, and after the ending of discriminatory policies, structures, and laws in Israel—that is, after the point at which a boycott movement has lost its rationale and has, therefore, ended.

---

[34] For the 1913 Land Act and the history to which it relates, see—for example—Colin Bundy, *The Rise and Fall of the South African Peasantry* (London, 1979), chapter 7; Tim Keegan, *Rural Transformations in Industrializing South Africa. The Southern Highveld to 1914* (Basingstoke, 1987), chapter 6; and various articles in *Journal of Southern African Studies*, vol. 40, no. 4, August 2014, which has a special focus on the Land Act. An instructive comparative essay could be written comparing the Land Act and its subsequent fate under apartheid with the Basic Law: Israel Lands. This might help to offer some genuine (as opposed to rhetorical) similarities and differences between the segregation/apartheid order in South Africa and the elements of discrimination that exist in the Israeli state. Another fruitful area of analysis would be the forced removal of communities and individuals who do not have the full rights of citizenship. A further one would be the right to bear arms for the country, and also the recourse to detention without trial in both orders. The place of the franchise, obviously and crucially, would be another area to explore and here, of course, there is a key difference between apartheid South Africa and Israel.

At that point, competing visions for the future would have to take their chances in the evolving politics of the Middle East, and they would have to convince a majority of the populations in both Israel and Palestine. In some respects, the once tortured politics of Northern Ireland—these also arose through the establishment of a settler state—have resolved themselves in such a frame.

The history that has produced the Israel/Palestine tragedy does not admit of a utopian resolution. But if there is to be any hope for something approaching an adequate solution, it has to recognise the historic processes that have produced it and been entailed by it. A boycott movement might consider how its own demands can facilitate this. This requires an approach which identifies clearly the points of reversal of the historical processes that it is aiming at, and stressing the point beyond which it feels it is undesirable and dangerously utopian to go. This might better facilitate the movement linking up with sections of Israeli society who support withdrawal to the 1967 lines and the removal of all forms of discrimination within those lines but who are unsure if what is demanded of them is much more fundamental than that, that is, the dissolution of their state.

There are a set of tremendously difficult questions—moral-historical questions, as I have called them here—with which those concerned with the Israel/Palestine tragedy have to grapple. Identifying the historical processes one has to accept, which one has to try to reverse, and to what extent is no easy task. A sense of the moral dangers that lie in the way of those who seek to grapple with these questions will be apprehended when it is remembered that one of the incendiary strategies utilised in occupied territory by those seeking a Greater Israel has been to 'create facts on the ground', seen by those who sponsor them as irreversible faits accomplis of colonisation.[35] If one sets the bar of 'historic processes that cannot be reversed' too low, one would be acquiescing in or supporting the flouting of international law intrinsic to illegal settlement and dispossession on the West Bank. This is obviously incompatible with the dignity and rights of the Palestinian people and cannot be a road to peace or justice. (Even so, a meaningful two-state solution would still have to face the question of

---

[35] Ariel Sharon, that 'fiercely aggressive advocate of Greater Israel' is perhaps most associated with this idea: see Shlaim, *Israel and Palestine*, 108, 288–9, 291, 293–4. Quotations from pp. 108 and 289. However, it is important to bear in mind that this policy has a very long history and was followed in the decade after the occupation of the West Bank and Gaza, both in those places and indeed in the Golan Heights: see, Chomsky, *Peace in the Middle East?*, 31–32; for Jerusalem, see pp. 99–100, 111.

how ethically to deal with the by now very sizeable population of Israelis on the West Bank.) On the other hand, if one sets too high the bar of 'historic processes that must be reversed', the road to peace is likewise blocked. As argued in this paper, demanding or implying the necessity for the replacement of the Israeli nation state as a sine qua non for peace and the ending of a boycott is morally fraught, running the risk of implicitly subscribing to a wish for the disappearance of Israeli society.

The problems that will have to be confronted are enormously complex and are far from exhausted by the analysis provided. For example, this paper has not explored the ramifications for any protest movement in support of Palestinian rights of the possibility that ongoing developments—the consolidation of policies of annexation and settlement, avoidance of meaningful negotiations—might put a viable Palestinian state and, therefore, a two-state solution permanently beyond reach. For it is quite true, as a US Secretary of State commented not long ago, that 'the two-state solution is now in serious jeopardy'.[36]

Finally, a boycott movement that is true to the history that produced the Israel/Palestine tragedy is bound to be concerned with demands regarding the Palestinians originally displaced and also their descendants? No peace or restorative justice is possible without this. This was recognised, for example, by President Bill Clinton who, whatever his faults, and as suggested by his stance during the Northern Ireland peace process, cannot be accused of a lack of insight into the enormous emotion attached to particular symbols.[37] In his final attempt at a peace settlement just before his Presidency ended, Clinton's proposals to Israelis and Palestinians included the status of the refugees as part of the settlement. (The proposal that an independent Palestinian state in the West Bank and Gaza be 'the focal point for the Palestinians who choose to return to the area' obviously left open the possibility of some resettlement in Israel proper.)[38] Even the more realistic and far-sighted members of the Israeli security establishment

---

[36] *The Guardian*, 29 December 2016, p. 13, 'Kerry accuses Israel of undermining peace hopes as Trump pledges strong US support'.

[37] One of the great symbols of discrimination and, indeed, oppression for republicans and Catholics in Northern Ireland had been the policies and Protestant domination of the police force. Clinton, with his knowledge of discriminatory policing in the South of the USA, was clear on the need to transform the police force in Northern Ireland so that it commanded confidence amongst Catholics.

[38] For the quotation, for Clinton's last effort and its complete unravelling after Ariel Sharon and George Bush came to power in 2001, see Shlaim, *Israel and Palestine*, 259–260.

recognise that Israel has to take responsibility for the Palestinian refugees. Thus, a former head of the Shin Bet, the Israeli security service, pointed to this in a startling interview, whose ambiguities can only be read as favouring some return of refugees but in a way that did not threaten the idea of a Jewish state: 'We reject the return of refugees. But we can only reject that if Israel recognizes unambiguously its role in the suffering imposed on the Palestinians and its obligation to participate in the solution to the problem. Israel must accept the principle of the right of return and the PLO [then the principal voice of Palestinian nationalism] must commit itself to not challenge the Jewish character of our state'.[39]

How is Israel, in the words of one of its former security chiefs, to recognise 'unambiguously its role in the suffering imposed on the Palestinians'? Substantial compensation could be offered to the families of those who lost their property and were forced to leave their country in the late 1940s. This would be one road of recognition and redress that the Israeli state could offer to Palestinians in the refugee settlements who were not allowed to return to the land of their people that lies within the pre-1967 borders of Israel. Others that would be appropriate might be educational programmes in Israeli schools that adequately registered the tragedy of the Palestinians and the degree of Israeli responsibility for it, and the enshrinement of the dispossession and displacement of the Palestinians in museums and memorials. There would also have to be rights to some resettlement in Israel proper of Palestinians who wished to return to their historic homeland. Whilst this would be symbolic—complete rights to return of the Palestinian diaspora imply too drastic a reversal of the historic process and would be viewed by an overwhelming majority of Israelis as a profound existential threat to their nation state—it would nevertheless have to be substantive. That is to say, it would go beyond what the Israeli Prime Minister Ehud Barak was offering at the Camp David negotiations of 2000 when he proposed that only 500 Palestinians be admitted to Israel each year but only on the grounds of reunifying families.[40] It is hard to see how Palestinians could not view such a proposition as tokenism: most of the people who would have been eligible for a right to return on this basis are now dead; it is, after all, 70 years since families were torn asunder by the

---

[39] See the Interview with Ami Ayalon, 22 December 2001: reproduced in Smith, *Palestine and the Arab-Israeli Conflict*, 547–549; quotation from pp. 548–549. Until May 2000, Ayalon led Shin Bet.

[40] Avi Shlaim, *Israel and Palestine*, 206.

convulsions of 1947–1950. The proposal was obviously framed by the highly discriminatory state demographic project followed by Israel since its establishment: the project—it has racial overtones—which has aimed at boosting the numbers of the ruling Jewish group vis-à-vis those of the subordinate Arab population.

This nationalist demographic project is the fundamental flaw in Israeli democracy. If one should not make a desert and call it peace, one should equally not empty a country of almost half of its population and call it democracy. This is undeniably what happened. By the end of 1948, the region that became Israel was converted very rapidly from one that had an Arab majority to one that had a very sizeable Jewish majority.[41] This was the great unspoken fact of the Declaration of the Establishment of the State of Israel, which was proclaimed in the midst of this transformation. The Declaration's insistence on giving 'complete equality of social and political rights to all…irrespective of religion, race or sex' expressed a democratic tradition,[42] but it also rested upon the radical reduction of the numbers of Palestinians who could exercise them. This was not the first time in history that grand statements shrouded fundamental inequalities and deprivations that made for later conflict. The USA in its Declaration of Independence happily evaded the overwhelming fact of slavery in making its classical Enlightenment statement of the freedom and equality of all; it proved unable to evade the cruel and violent history, including civil war, that flowed from this flawed conception of freedom. And Israel, likewise, has not been able to evade the consequences that flow from subordinating democracy to an ethnic-demographic project.

The Israeli ethnic-demographic project hinges on the Law of Return and there can be no adequate addressing of the Palestinian tragedy without broaching its implications. As is well known, the Law of Return allows any Jew anywhere in the world rights to settle and become a citizen of Israel in a context in which this is forbidden to Palestinians in their diaspora, despite the fact that these are people who actually have much more immediate historic ties to the area comprehended by Israel than do most

---

[41] Consider the statistics pertaining to 1948 as 'provided by Onn Winckler, 'Fertility Transition in the Middle East: the Case of the Israeli Arabs', in: *The Israeli Palestinians: An Arab Minority in the Jewish State*, ed. Alexander Bligh, (London, 2007), 41 and 56.

[42] The Declaration of the Establishment of the State of Israel, 14 May 1948, is reproduced as Document 5.5 in Smith, *Palestine and the Arab-Israeli Conflict*, 223–225; quotation from p. 225.

Jews outside of that country. A non-discriminatory immigration policy in Israel would be guaranteeing the same rights to Palestinians and Jews: that might entail a Law of Return for both groups, or for neither, or equal quotas of immigrants for each group. At any rate, while a Law of Return applies to Jewish people outside of Israel who cannot trace ancestors to the Holy Land, while Palestinians are refused the right to return to the place in which their family trees are so obviously rooted, a fundamentally discriminatory policy will remain. It allows one part of the population to be joined by their compatriots, but not another. The policy will remain a profound symbol of the displacement and exclusion of the Palestinians. However, for the purposes of this analysis, the important point to note is that a boycott movement opposed to discrimination in Israel and calling for either the end of the Law of Return, or its application to both Palestinians and Jews, as part of its campaign is compatible with defending the right of the Israeli nation state to exist. It would simply be calling for purging that state of policies of discrimination. Some will inevitably damn such a call as antisemitic. For many, including Jews such as this writer, there will be a deep and tragic irony in this. After all, those who would oppose a campaign for the full equality of all citizens of Israel, whether they be Jewish or not, are staring into the mirror of history. Reflected back at them are those many antisemites of the past who refused Jews the full rights of citizenship.

Index[1]

A
Abd Al-Malek, Anwar, 288
Abe, Shinzo, 24
Abu-Laban, Yasmeen, 265, 267
Academic boycott, 211, 261n1, 285, 306
  Palestinian Campaign for the Academic and Cultural Boycott of Israel, 222
Achcar, Gilbert, 296
Adámek, Karel, 48
Aflaq, Michel, 296
African National Congress (ANC)
  BDS and South Africa, 199–202, 207, 209, 210
  1955 Freedom Charter, 200
  Marxism, 200, 201
African Union, 176
Agricultural industry (US)
  agricultural workers' unionization, 160
  Bracero Program, 160
  children, 128, 160
  Latino and immigrant farm workers, 174
  media, 158, 161
  pesticides, 128, 160, 162, 166, 169
  wage and working conditions, 32
  See also United Farm Workers (UFW); United Farm Workers Organizing Committee (UFWOC)
Agricultural Workers Organizing Committee (AWOC), 161
Albrecht, Catherine, 45, 48
Allende, Salvador, 124, 125, 132, 171
American Israel Public Affairs Committee (AIPAC), 229–231, 261n2, 263
Ananth, Sriram, 282
Anti-apartheid movement (AAM), 14, 125–127, 198, 201, 268, 278
Anti-Defamation League, 223

---

[1] Note: Page numbers followed by 'n' refer to notes.

Antisemitism
  antisemitic hate crime, 249
  antisemitic propaganda, 117
  BDS and, 16, 221, 222, 237
  as BDS frame, 230
  BDS Movement and opponents, US, 231, 234, 240
  Britain, 2014 summer boycotts and, 243–259
  British Labour Party, 313
  'Campus Antisemitism,' 221
  Congress Poland, 47, 67, 70, 71
  cooperative movement, 45, 46
  denial of, 318
  European antisemitism, 2, 94, 311
  Habsburg Empire, 43, 45, 46, 51
  Jewish businesses in Nazi Germany, 3, 14
  Middle East conflict and, 226, 227, 229, 237
  popular culture and, 68, 71
  stereotypes, 16, 235, 314
  trivialization of, 235, 237
  West Germany, radical Left boycotts, 115–118, 120, 129, 135, 137, 138
Anti-slavery boycott/campaign
  abolitionists, 158, 226
  Britain, 6, 12, 26
Anti-war movements (against wars in Afghanistan and Iraq), 222n14, 274
Arab League, 272
Arab-Palestinians
  'buy national' campaign, 76, 77, 80, 86–88, 95
  nationalist movement, 75, 80, 296, 321
  See also Zionist 'buy national' campaigns
Arab Revolt, 84–86, 95
Arafat, Yasser, 270, 271
Arms embargo, 185, 202, 211

Azanian People's organization (AZAPO), 183
Azoulay, Ariella, 286

B
Bakan, Abigail, 265, 265n24, 265n25, 267, 267n32, 301n39
Ball-Kaduri, Kurt Jakob, 113n94
Bam, Brigalia, 126
Barak, Ehud, 293, 329
Barghouti, Omar
  BDS, definition of, 301, 302
  Boycott, Divestment, Sanctions, 226–230
  Butler/Barghoutiat Brooklyn College, 222–226
Barkai, Avraham, 107
Ba'thists, 296
Baton Rouge bus boycott (US)
  Baton Rouge City-Parish Council, 140
  black churches, 141, 145, 156
  boycott end, 155
  bus drivers strike, 144, 145, 151
  Civil Rights Movement, 139n1, 140, 148n36, 154, 157
  fare hike, 141, 155
  First Ward Voters League, 152, 153
  Free Ride program, 145, 151
  Jim Crow laws, 151
  Jones, Johnnie, 151, 153, 155
  Louisiana Weekly, 139n1, 142, 144, 155
  Mt. Zion Baptist Church, 141, 148
  Ordinance 222, 142
  Ordinance 251, 151, 154
  Reed, Willis, 140, 152, 153
  segregation on public transport, 11, 155, 157
  success, 154, 155
  support for the boycott, 148

Thompson, Horatio, 148, 150, 153
violence, 146
White, Martha, 143, 144
women, 139n1, 141, 149, 149n39
See also Jemison, Theodore J., Reverend; Montgomery bus boycott (US); United Defense League (UDL)
Baudouin de Courtenay, Jan, 58
BDS actors
  churches and FBOs, 276, 280
  civil society/NGOs and, 177, 179, 207, 297
  Israeli Jews as activists/supporters, 264
  opponents, 17, 19, 179, 219–242, 299–303
  Palestinian activists, 203, 265, 268, 269
  See also BDS
BDS features
  antisemitism and, 2, 17, 18, 221, 222, 231, 236–239, 241
  definition, 116, 296, 301, 302
  goals, 1, 3, 15, 19, 199, 203, 206, 208–217, 295, 298, 307
  human rights and, 1, 14, 227, 228, 240, 295
  identity, 17, 19, 241, 295–297, 301
  nationalism, 262, 296, 297
  non-violence and, 18, 295, 298
  organization, 295, 297, 304–306
  principles, 18, 262, 295, 298–299, 309
  racism and, 15, 219, 300, 301
  radical democratic features, 18
  social justice and, 262, 265, 286
  targets, 18, 201, 209, 214, 216, 230, 301, 310
  as universalist movement, 14
  See also BDS
BDS Fourth National Conference, 298, 305
BDS frames

'academic freedom' frame, 229, 230, 233, 240
anti-BDS frames, 230–234
'anti-colonialism/anti-imperialism' frame, 226, 227, 230, 235, 237–239
'anti-colonialism/anti-imperialism' *vs.* 'antisemitism,' 226, 230, 235, 237–239
'antiracism' frame, 226, 230, 235–237
'antiracism' *vs.* 'antisemitism,' 235, 236, 241
'antisemitism' frame, 231, 235–239
frame analysis, 225
frame coalition instead of frame collision, 240–241
'freedom of speech' frame, 228–230
'human rights' frame, 228, 230, 240
'Jewish identity' frame, 228, 230, 232, 239
'Jewish identity' *vs.* 'Jewish self-hatred,' 232, 239, 241
'Jewish self-hatred' frame, 232, 239
pro-BDS frames, 236
See also BDS Movement and opponents, US
BDS Movement and opponents, US
  antisemitism, 18, 222, 231, 235, 236, 241
  BDS advocates, 207, 222, 230, 233, 234, 240
  BDS opponents, 222, 226, 228, 230, 232, 240
  Butler/Barghouti at Brooklyn College, 222–226
  data/interviews, 222, 222n14
  debates on BDS, 222, 228, 239–241
  US college/university support for BDS, 220, 222
  US Left, 227, 237
  US Right, 227
  See also BDS frames

BDS, South Africa/Palestine
    comparison
  ANC's views on BDS, 200–203
  Palestine, BDS as means to create
    mass struggle, 200, 207
  Palestine, incoherence in goals and
    tactics, 208–215
  Palestine, liberation movement
    weakness, 203–216
  Palestine, means-ends confusion and
    'success' claims, 215–216
  South Africa, BDS as supplement to
    mass struggle, 199, 202, 217
  South Africa, clarity on goals and
    strategy, 199
  See also BDS strategies
BDS strategies
  addressing the Israeli public, 212
  compellance, 209, 210
  divestment, 220, 226–230, 278,
    307
  incoherence in, 199, 204, 216
  lacking a defined strategy, 15, 199
  normative communication, 209,
    210
  ostracism, enactment of, 307
  political fracture, 209, 210, 212
  resource denial, 209–211
  two-stage strategy, 210, 214, 215
  See also BDS; BDS, South Africa/
    Palestine comparison
Benford, Robert, 225
Bennis, Phyllis, 280, 281n92
Berliner, Cora, 109, 110
Berlin, Isaiah, 137
Berman, Paul: *The Case Against
  Academic Boycotts of Israel*, 283,
  283n111
Berzanskis, Jonas, 14
Billington-Greig, Teresa, 38
Blobaum, Robert, 53n1, 58n12, 69
Bob, Clifford, 273, 273n58

Botha, Pieter Willem, 187, 191–193
Boycott
  anti-colonial struggle and, 23
  civil society and, 3, 8, 12, 15, 23,
    27, 29, 39, 197, 220, 262,
    265, 267, 281, 299, 308–310,
    313, 315
  definition, 24, 35, 51, 91, 98, 99,
    112, 115, 215, 226, 325, 326
  economic warfare and, 98–100, 134
  effectiveness of, 50, 157, 163, 265
  expressive and instrumental goals,
    10
  features of, 3, 5, 6
  goals, 3, 10
  history of, 3, 4, 33, 315
  international perspective of, 11
  moral-related issues, 53–72, 100,
    102, 106, 119, 138, 150–154,
    163, 174, 175, 193, 227, 253,
    258, 278, 307, 308, 313, 319
  nationalism and, 41–52, 102, 116,
    313
  political goals of, 3, 9
  popularity of, 30
  revolutionary dimension of, 6
  selectivity of, 12
  'silent boycott,' 264
  state and, 3, 18, 23, 26, 32, 102,
    323
  targets, 10, 12–14, 17, 115, 119,
    132, 133, 135, 137
  tension between constitutionalism
    and revolution, 19
  the term, 4, 10, 99, 111, 112, 122,
    315
  violence, 113, 120, 122
  See also Academic boycott;
    Consumer boycott; Economic
    boycott; Sports boycott;
    Tourism boycott
Boycott, Charles, Captain, 7, 112

Boycott, Divestment and Sanctions (BDS)
  assessing BDS, 281–286
  BDS Call, 207, 208, 226
  global audience, 265–266, 283
  impact of, 200, 263
  Israeli academia on, 262, 282, 284
  Israel on, 230
  justification of, 15
  moral-related issues, BDS, 233, 237, 280, 282
  neoliberalism, 265
  new constituencies, 262, 275–280
  origins, 179
  Palestine and, 204, 216, 226, 281, 284, 286, 298
  'ripple effects,' 280–281
  rule of law and social revolution, 18, 19
  singling out Israel, 15–17
  South Africa, sanctions against apartheid and, 179, 180
  as 'the South Africa strategy for Palestine,' 2, 198
  success, 180, 199, 204, 215–216, 219, 220
  tensions within, 19
  US and, 232, 237
  violence, 16, 216, 283, 304
  Zionism and, 268, 299–301
  See also the entries below for BDS; UNWCAR (2001 UN World Conference Against Racism, Durban)
Boycott Israel Network (BIN), 305
Brackman, Harold, 295
Bráf, Albín, 48, 49
Brandt, Willy, 118, 132
Breen, Tim, 5
Brinkley, Douglas, 154, 156
Britain
  anti-slavery boycott, 11, 315
  BDS in, 263n8
  consumer boycott, 25, 35, 37
  'East India Sugar not made by Slaves,' 27
  2010 Equality Act, 247, 300
  fair trade, 27, 38
  inter war period, 311
  Labour Party, 253, 258, 313
  left-wing politics, 231
  Stamp Act, 4
  Zionist 'buy national' campaigns, 73–95
  See also Britain, 2014 summer boycotts
Britain, 2014 summer boycotts
  anti-Israel boycotts and community cohesion, 251, 256, 259
  antisemitic hate crime, 249, 253
  antisemitism, 243–260
  Birmingham boycott, 253, 255
  Bradford boycott, 255–258
  British Jews, 245–247, 249, 255
  2014 conflict in Israel and Gaza, 245, 249, 258
  Galloway, George, 255–257
  Javid, Sajid, 245
  Karim, Zulfi, 256
  Leese, Sir Richard, 251
  London, Sainsbury's incident, 253, 254, 258
  Mahmood, Shabana, 253
  Manchester Boycott Kedem, 250
  media, 245, 250, 255
  non-political Jewish connection to Israel, 248
  political neutrality, 245, 246, 248, 249
  Shah, Naz, 257, 258
  Taub, Daniel, 255, 256
  Tricycle theatre, 244, 245, 258
  UK Jewish Film Festival, 244, 246, 258
  Ward, David, 256
British Committee for Universities of Palestine (BRICUP), 261n1, 306

338 INDEX

British Palestine Solidarity Campaign, 135, 303n40
Bus boycott, *see* Baton Rouge bus boycott (US); Montgomery bus boycott (US)
Buthelezi, Mangosuthu, 184, 208
Butler, Judith, 226, 227, 230–233, 237, 240
  Butler/Barghoutiat Brooklyn College, 222–227
'Buy national' campaign
  economic nationalism, 76
  1908 Ottoman campaign against Austro-Hungarian products, 76
  See also Zionist 'buy national' campaigns

C
Camp David negotiations (2000), 329
Canadian Union of Public Employees (CUPE), 280
Carter Hallward, Maia, 275
Central/Eastern Europe
  cooperative, 13, 45
  economic nationalism, 41, 45, 73, 74, 76
  World War I, 76
  See also Habsburg Empire (1844–1914); Hungary; Poland
Central Verein deutscher Staatsbürger jüdischen Glaubens (CV), 100
Chalcraft, John, 3, 15, 18, 275, 276, 287
Chavez, Cesar
  death, 173
  jail, 170
  lettuce boycott, 158, 170
  See also United Farm Workers Organizing Committee (UFWOC)
Chesler, Phyllis, 232

Chile, 11, 12, 124, 125, 171
China, 11, 23, 24, 99, 270n45, 290
Chomsky, Noam, 222, 319n23, 324, 325n31
Church
  Baton Rouge bus boycott and, 139–156
  BDS and, 201, 219, 276–278, 280, 294, 297, 306
  Kairos Appeal, 278
  Liberation Theology, 276, 278
  Pentecostalism, 276
  Presbyterian Church, 277
  See also Faith-based organisation (FBO); World Council of Churches
Citizenship
  equal rights, 324, 326
  second-class citizenship, 318, 322, 325
City University of New York (CUNY), 223, 226, 229, 231, 233, 237, 240
Civil rights movement (US), 140, 150, 154, 157, 170, 226, 228, 307
Civil society
  BDS and, 2, 15, 195, 220, 265, 267, 268, 276, 281, 299, 309, 310
  boycott and, 2, 3, 8, 12, 15, 23, 27, 39, 197, 220, 262, 265, 281, 308, 310, 313, 315
  state and, 3, 23, 27, 39, 177, 179, 276, 281, 309, 310, 315
  See also Non-governmental organisation (NGO)
Clinton, Bill, 328
Cobden, Richard, 42
Cohen, Nick, 246
Cohn-Bendit, Daniel, 122
Cohn, Georg, 97, 98, 98n5

INDEX 339

Cohn, Selma, 98
Cold War, 115–138, 181, 193, 195, 198
Collins, John, 274, 275
Colonialism
'anti-colonialism/anti-imperialism' BDS frames, 226, 227, 230, 235, 237–239
boycott and, 15, 94, 183, 226, 227, 238
Israel, 15, 226, 227, 237–239, 302, 312
Congress of South African Trade Unions (COSATU), 190, 279
Congress Poland (Kingdom of Poland/Russian Poland)
1912 anti-Jewish boycott, 70, 71
anti-Litwak hysteria, 62–64
antisemitism, 2, 57–64, 68, 70, 71, 228, 231, 233, 239, 262, 268, 282–284, 287, 300, 311, 313, 314, 321, 324
Catholic press, 57, 68
1907–1909 economic crisis, 69
elections to the Fourth Duma, 53n1, 69
Endecja/Endeks, 54, 55, 60–62, 67, 68, 70
left-wing politics, 231
National Concentration, 55
National Democracy, 54–62, 69, 71
nationalism, 21, 23, 41, 43, 45, 60, 73, 74, 76, 83, 93, 94, 262, 284, 291, 295–297, 299, 302, 309, 321–323, 329
nationalist press, 54, 56, 57, 61, 68
1906–1907 Łódź uprising, 61
Party of Real Politics, 58, 64
Polish Progressive Party, 58
Polish Progressive Union, 58, 63
Polish Socialist Party—Revolutionary Faction, 63
press, 54, 56, 61, 62
1905 Revolution, 59, 60, 61n19
right-wing politics, 53–71, 223
Rozwój/Society for the Development of Industry, Crafts and Trade, 56
Swój do swego po swoje/'to each his own,' 47, 51, 56, 73, 321n26
Warsaw, 53, 54, 58, 63, 67, 68
xenophobia, 71, 174, 267
Conservative Party, South Africa (CP), 64, 123, 187
Consumer boycott
aim and target, 21, 128
Britain, 37
boycott, 12, 26, 28, 30
choice and, 29, 32, 35, 37, 38, 116, 131, 158
clothing, 24, 36
consumer activism, 12, 23, 26, 27, 31, 32, 34, 35, 115
consumer rights movement, 159
definition, 21, 115
domestication of products, 34
globalisation, 30–34
Habsburg Empire, 43, 45, 46, 51
Hungary, 50
morale economy, 216
political action, 21–39
politicisation of consumption, 29
state and, 21–39
sweatshop labor, 28, 29
US, 3, 21, 28, 115, 157, 294
wage and working conditions, 32
women and, 79, 162, 164
See also 'Buy national' campaign; Fairtrade; United Farm Workers (UFW); United Farm Workers Organizing Committee (UFWOC)

Consumer capitalism, 129
Cooperative/cooperative movement, 13, 14, 45, 46, 51, 91
Cosmopolitanism, 42, 52
Crawford, Neta C., 185n32, 209
Critical Whiteness studies, 235, 237
Cultural boycott, 12, 201, 215, 302, 314n7
   Palestinian Campaign for the Academic and Cultural Boycott of Israel, 222

D
Daily Herald, 101
Daily Mail, 106
Davis, Uri, 135
Decolonization, 188
De Klerk, Wilhelm, 182
Deák, István, 44
Denmark, 30
Dershowitz, Alan, 223, 233, 314n8
Der Stürmer, 104, 108, 109
Discrimination
   BDS, 236
   Israel/Palestine conflict, 267
   See also Baton Rouge bus boycott (US); Montgomery bus boycott (US)
Dmowski, Roman
   antisemitism, 57, 59, 60, 62, 67
   Myśli nowoczesnego Polaka/'Thoughts of a Modern Pole,' 60
   See also Congress Poland (Kingdom of Poland/Russian Poland)
Doherty, Lewis, 142

E
Earl of Erne, 7–9
Economic boycott
   Arab League boycott, 272
   boycott of Jewish businesses in Eastern Europe, 14
   impact of, 51
Economic nationalism
   Habsburg Empire, 43
   Hungary, 43
   nation-building, 43
   protectionism, 74
   Zionist 'buy national' campaigns, 73–76
Egypt, 11, 21, 23, 24, 81, 271n49, 288
Erakat, Noura, 208
Erdan, Gilad, 265
Evans, Richard, 105

F
Fairclough, Adam, 151
Fair trade, 12, 30–32, 37, 38, 129
   See also Consumer boycott
Fair Trade (ethical consumer movement), 37
Faith-based organisation (FBO), 276–278, 277n76, 278n79, 278n82, 280
   See also Church
Falk, Richard, 209, 212, 299, 306
Fatah, 135, 271, 303, 305
Federal Republic of Germany, 11
Feiler, Gil, 272
Fichte, Johann Gottlieb, 52
Fine, Robert, 238
Finkelstein, Norman, 222
Fischer, Joschka, 122
Fishman, Joel S., 282
Flapan, Simha, 317n16
Fox, William, 6, 35
France, 34, 99, 276, 291, 294
Frankl, Michal, 48, 49
Freeman, Hazel, 145, 151, 155
Free trade, 25, 37, 42, 51, 73
   criticism, 41

Frick, Wilhelm, 100, 101
Friedman, Monroe, 115
Fromm, Bella: *Blood and banquets. A Berlin social*, 110

G

Galtung, Johan, 185, 186, 188
Gandhi, Mahatma, 24, 99, 161
Garrison, William, 318
Gaza/Gaza Strip
  2008–2009 Israeli Operation Cast Lead, 281
  2010 Israeli attack on a flotilla to Gaza, 281
  2014 Israeli Operation Protective Edge, 243, 281, 287
  See also Britain, 2014 summer boycotts
Genschel, Helmut, 101
Germany, 18, 28, 33, 34, 38, 46, 87–90, 99–102, 105–109, 111–113, 121, 133, 138, 232, 251, 315
  Berlin Wall, 117–119, 188
  See also Nazi Germany; West Germany boycotts
Gerstenfeld, Manfred, 233, 236
Giddens, Anthony, 35
Gladstone, William, 9
Globalisation
  alter-globalisation, 290, 297, 310
  consumer boycott, 31, 34
  neoliberalism and, 32, 265
  Palestine and, 274
Goebbels, Joseph, 101–103, 106, 110, 113
Goering, Hermann, 111
Goffmann, Erving, 225
Golan Heights, 304n43, 327n35
Goodman, Alan, 236n74
Gorenberg, Gershom, 270

Grendyszyński, Ludomir, 58
Grey, Nick, 263n8
The Guardian, 106, 248, 314n7

H

Haaretz, 248, 264, 265, 293
Habe, Hans, 121
Habsburg Empire(1844–1914)
  anti-Czech boycott, 47, 49
  anti-German boycott, 43, 47
  antisemitism, 46, 48, 49
  Bohemian Lands, 45–48
  boycott tactics, 47, 49
  consumer boycott, 50
  credit/trade cooperative, 45, 46, 51
  dissolution of, 45
  economic liberalism, 41, 45, 49, 51
  economic nationalism, 41, 43, 45
  Jews in, 46–49
  Kauft nur bei den Deutschen/'buy only from Germans,' 47
  nationalism, 45
  self-help, 45, 47, 49, 51
  Svůj k svému/'Each to his own,' 47–49, 51
  See also Protectionism
Hamas
  Israeli Operation Protective Edge, 243
Hani, Chris, 175, 191
Hardt, Michael, 288, 291
Harlan, Veith, 117, 118
Harpers Monthly Magazine, 33
Helleiner, Eric, 42
Hever, Shir, 214
Hijab, Nadia, 275, 280
Hillel, 230, 230n52, 239
Histadrut (General Federation of Labor), 91
Hitler, Adolf, 87, 100–102, 104, 239
Hitler Youth, 109, 110

Holocaust
  2013 Holocaust Memorial Day, 256
Hooghe, Marc, 36
Horáček, Cyril, 49
Horizontalism, 217, 290
Human rights
  BDS and, 1, 14, 15, 227, 240
  as BDS frame, 228
Hungary
  boycott of imported goods, 43
  economic nationalism, 43
  National Defense League/*Országos Védegylet*, 43, 44, 48
  nationalism, 43
  People's Bank, 13

I
Imperialism
  'anti-colonialism/anti-imperialism' BDS frames, 226, 230, 235, 237
  Britain, 7
  Israel, 237
  US, 301
India, 11, 24, 81, 177, 178
International Jewish Anti-Zionist Network (IJAN), 226
International Monetary Fund (IMF), 124, 189
Ireland
  Ballinrobe, 7–9
  Irish Land League, 7
Israel
  anti Israeli Apartheid movement, 179
  as apartheid state, 1n1, 179, 195, 197
  1948 Arab–Israeli War, 138
  Basic Law, 325, 326, 326n34
  on BDS, 285
  Boycott Law, 282
  colonialism, 227
  creation of, 15, 311
  Declaration of the Establishment of the State of Israel, 330
  democracy, 330
  demographic project, 330
  discrimination by, 326, 331
  economy, 133, 207, 214, 216, 270, 272n53, 308
  end of the Israeli nation state, 323
  'ethnic cleansing' by, 316, 317
  hasbara, 238, 282n98
  'hybrid war' against, 284
  Israeli fruit as target of boycotts, 133, 134
  as Jewish state, 16, 247, 325, 325n32
  Law of Return, 330, 331
  legitimacy of, 209, 282, 313, 323, 324
  moral-historical questions, 327
  population, 240
  pre-1967 borders, 322, 324, 326, 329
  responsibility for Palestinians' suffering, 278n80
  sanctions against, 263
  settlement process, 207, 253, 264, 270, 313
  as settler-colonial state, 16
  US aid to, 210, 211
  See also Antisemitism; Gaza/Gaza Strip; Palestine; West Bank; Zionism
Israel Affairs, 282
Israel's Institute for National Security Studies (INSS), 281, 282
Italy, 99

J
Jabotinsky, Vladimir (Ze'ev), 89
Japan, 21, 99
Jaworski, Rudolf, 50

Jedlicki, Jerzy, 69
Jemison, Theodore J., (Reverend), 141–147, 148n36, 149–154, 156
See also Baton Rouge bus boycott (US)
Jewish businesses in Nazi Germany
  picketing of; aims of, 57; antisemitism, 233, 283; 1933 'April boycott,' 101, 113; atrocity propaganda and, 102; blacklist, 105; a boycott?, 97–113; boycott by the state, 3; consequences of, 3, 107; as 'counter boycott,' 102; 1938 'Crystal Night,' 111; economic warfare/ *Wirtschaftskrieg*, 99; 'Judenaktion,' 104, 112; media, 112, 113; nationalism, 14, 105; Nazi Party, 100, 102; 1938 pogroms, 111; as racist blockade, 100; SA/SS storm troopers, 102, 104–106, 110, 136; targets, 14; violence, 85, 101, 113; 1934–1935 violence, 108
Jewish Voice for Peace (JVP), 228, 229, 238
Jews
  British Jews, 245–249, 255
  distinction between Israel and, 299
  Habsburg Empire, 43, 45, 46, 51
  Israeli Jews as BDS activists/ supporters, 283
  Jewish identity, 75, 80, 93, 228, 230, 232, 239, 241, 247
  'Jewish identity' as BDS frame, 222
  Jewish Leftists, 228
  Jewishness, 92, 228, 300
  'Jewish privilege,' 235
  'Jewish self-hatred' as BDS frame, 232, 239, 241

Litvaks, 63, 63n22, 64, 65, 67, 68
Polish Jews, 53, 54, 58n12, 59–63, 68, 69

K
Karsh, Efraim, 282
Kasher, Asa, 285
Kasrils, Ronnie, 268
Kelley, Florence, 28
Kerry, John, 264, 328n36
King, Martin Luther, Jr., 146, 153, 156, 161
Klemperer, Viktor, 102
Klotz, Audie, 209
Koizumi, Junichiro, 24, 24n4
Kossuth, Lajos, 43, 44, 51
Krzywicki, Ludwik, 58
Kucharzewski, Jan, 55

L
Labor
  female worker, 128
  labor boycott, 163
  labor market, 190
  labor strike, 157, 174
  sweatshop labor, 22, 29, 33, 35
  wage and working conditions, 32
  Zionist 'buy national' campaigns and labor segregation, 73–95
  See also Agricultural industry (US); United Farm Workers (UFW); United Farm Workers Organizing Committee (UFWOC)
Laclau, Ernesto, 301
Laepple, Klaus, 122, 123
Lange, Józef, 55, 58
Late modernity, 22, 35, 36
Lauder, Ronald, 2

Leftwing politics
  British Left, 252
  Congress Poland, 14, 47, 51, 54,
    61, 62, 67, 70, 71
  Jewish Leftists, 228
  Left doctrinalism, 288, 290
  US Left and BDS Movement, 227,
    237, 293–295
  See also West Germany, radical Left
    boycotts
Levinas, Emmanuel, 321
LeVine, Mark, 212
Liberalism, 57, 71, 291
  economic liberalism, 41, 42, 45, 49,
    51
Likud, 319, 319n23
Lipton, Merle, 183
List, Friedrich, 41–44, 48, 51, 52
  *The National System of Political
    Economy*, 41, 43
Lithuania, 14, 62, 65, 88
Loach, Ken, 309
Lorenz, Torsten, 45
Lubińska, Teresa, 58
Lüth, Erich, 117–120
Lydda, 316

M

Maira, Sunaina, 18
Manchester Guardian, 101
Mandela, Nelson, 175, 176, 192
Marcus, Kenneth, 1n1, 17, 221n9,
  283
Marx, Karl, 198, 199, 217, 251
Masalha, Nur, 317n16
Mbeki, Thabo, 176, 176n1, 177, 178,
  181, 182, 191–194, 201
  See also South Africa: sanctions
    against apartheid

McAdam, Doug, 289n12
Media
  Britain, 2014 summer boycotts,
    243–259
  Congress Poland, 14, 47, 51, 54,
    61, 62, 67, 70, 71
  Congress Poland, nationalist press,
    54, 56, 57, 61, 68
  Jewish businesses in Nazi Germany,
    3, 14, 101, 105, 112, 113
  newspaper, 5, 8, 10, 36, 50, 99, 102,
    103, 106, 109, 119, 139n1,
    142, 146, 171, 245, 248, 264,
    265, 271n51, 318n20
Medoff, Rafael, 285
Meir, Golda, 319, 319n23
Micheletti, Michele, 22n2, 30n9, 36,
  36n20
Middle East conflict, 226, 227, 237,
  240, 251, 274
Mill, John Stuart, 42
Minty, Abdul, 202
Molad Center, 264
Montgomery bus boycott (US), 139,
  140, 150, 156, 157
  Parks, Rosa, 156
  See also Baton Rouge bus boycott
    (US)
Moral-related issues
  BDS, 15, 16, 180, 197, 206, 209,
    210, 217, 275, 283, 295
  boycott and, 53–71, 100, 102, 106,
    119, 138, 150–154, 163, 173,
    175, 193, 227, 253, 258, 278,
    307, 308, 313, 319
  consumer boycott and moral
    economy, 12, 21–39, 75, 116,
    122, 129, 131, 132, 159
  Israel, moral-historical questions,
    311–331

Morris, Aldon, 139n1, 145, 146, 148n36
Morris, Benny, 312n2, 316, 317n16
Morrison, Suzanne, 273n59, 303
Moszczeńska, Izabella, 65
Mouffe, Chantal, 301

N

National Consumers' League (NCL), 22n2, 28
National Farm Workers Association (NFWA), 161
Nationalism
  BDS and, 262, 284, 286, 295–297, 309
  boycott and, 41–52, 102, 116, 133, 175, 313
  'buy national' campaign, 73–95
  clothing and, 24, 36, 109
  Congress Poland, 14, 47, 51, 54, 61, 62, 67, 70, 71
  Habsburg Empire, 43, 45, 51
  Hungary, 13, 43, 44, 48, 50, 51, 99
  Jewish businesses in Nazi Germany, picketing of, 97–113
  Palestinian nationalism, 262, 284, 295–297, 322, 323, 329
  Zionist 'buy national' campaigns, 73–95
  See also Economic nationalism
National Party, South Africa (NP), 186, 191, 193
Nation-building, 3, 43, 45, 89, 195
Nazi Germany
  Jewish boycott of, 88, 90
  1936 Olympic Games, 109
  See also Jewish businesses in Nazi Germany, picketing of
Negri, Antonio, 288, 291

Neoliberalism
  globalisation and, 30, 32, 265
  South Africa, 129, 190, 194, 276n74
Nestlé, 12, 129
Netanyahu, Benjamin, 2, 231, 257, 261, 263–265, 325, 325n32
  on BDS, 2, 231, 261, 263–265
Niemojewski, Andrzej
  Myśl Niepodległa, 64–66
NGO Forum, 1n1, 268, 268n36
The Netherlands, 38, 125
Nevel, Donna, 229
Nevinson, Henry, 33
Newsweek, 287
New York Times, 101, 107, 110, 112, 113
Non-Aligned Movement, 178n8
Non-governmental organisation (NGO)
  promoting anti-Israel boycotts, 284n113
  United Nations World Conference Against Racism (UNWCAR), 177, 180
  See also Civil society
Northern Ireland, 327, 328, 328n37
Nunes, Rodrigo, 306

O

Occupy movement, 232, 291, 304
Occupy Wall Street, 220, 222n14, 231, 305
Oksza-Grabowski, Ignacy, 56, 67
Olinsky, Max, 268
O'Malley, John, Father, 9, 10
Oslo Peace Accords (1993), 204
  failure of, 281, 303
Ottoman Empire, 76

P

Palacký, František, 48
Palestine, 3, 73–95, 198, 199, 204, 207, 208, 210, 211, 215–217, 222n14, 226, 239, 256, 258, 261–286, 290, 294, 298, 302, 311–313, 315, 316, 318, 319, 321, 327, 328
   Balfour Declaration, 76, 83, 299
   BDS and, 286
   economy, 84, 270
   first intifada, 135, 207, 308
   globalisation and, 274
   'Global Palestine,' 274, 280
   Israeli military occupation of, 229
   Jews in, 90
   Occupied Palestinian Territories, 179, 290, 295
   'one-state solution,' 19, 208
   opposition to a Palestinian state, 319
   Palestinian nationalism, 262, 284, 295–297, 322, 323, 329
   Palestinian national movement, 207, 212, 270, 271, 323, 324
   Palestinian predicament, 269–272, 276, 281
   peace talks/process, 204, 216, 263, 269, 328
   population, 256, 258, 269, 326
   self-determination, 204, 237, 266, 267, 276, 295, 298, 301
   social justice, 262, 273, 275, 277, 286
   South Africa and, 180, 199
   'two-state solution,' 208, 303, 324, 325, 327, 328
   wall, dismantling of, 1, 322
   See also Gaza/Gaza Strip; Israel; Palestinian National Authority (PA/PNA); West Bank; Zionist 'buy national' campaigns
Palestine Liberation Organisation (PLO), 133, 204, 205, 209, 269, 271, 272, 305, 323, 323n27, 329
Palestinian Academic and Cultural Boycott Initiative (PACBI), 305
Palestinian National Authority (PA/PNA)
   crisis of, 59
   martial mode of governance, 271
   Oslo II agreement, 270n42
Palestinian refugee
   1948 Palestinian exodus, 316
   right of return, 1, 208
Pappé, Ilan, 212, 285, 302, 306, 317n16
Parnell, Charles, 7–9
Parsons, Nigel, 273n57
Pawelski, Jerzy, 68
Peal, David, 46, 51
Perez, Izhak, 69
Pfeffer, Anshel, 248
Pieńkowski, Stanisław, 56, 57, 67
Pinochet, Augusto, General, 124, 125, 132, 171
Plaut, Steven, 284
Poland, *see* Congress Poland
Politics
   consumer boycott and political action, 21–39
   formal politics/boycott relationship, 36
   political boycott, 241, 252
   political identity, 5, 9, 11, 19
   political mobilisation, 2, 5, 6, 160, 208
   political party, 60, 63, 126, 305, 306
   politicisation of consumption, 29
Pollard, Stephen, 245, 254
Popular Front for the Liberation of Palestine (PFLP), 133, 134
Postone, Moishe, 227

Propaganda
   antisemitic propaganda, 62, 66, 117, 314
   atrocity propaganda, 102, 104, 112
   hasbara, 238
Protectionism, 41–52, 74

R
Rabin, Yitzak, 271n51, 319
Racism
   'antiracism' BDS frame, 230–234
   BDS and, 287–310
   racialization of the boycott target, 13
   Zionism as form of, 268, 301
   See also South Africa
Radical democracy, 18, 287–310
   BDS, radical democratic features, 18
Raiffeisen, Friedrich Wilhelm, 46
Raiffeisen movement, 46
Rancière, Jacques, 288
Redpath, James, 9, 10
Reimer, Eduard, 99, 112
Reitan, Ruth, 274
Relly, Gavin, 191
Reut Institute, 263, 281
Revolutionäre Zellen (RZ), 127, 128, 131, 133–135
Rhodesia, 312, 313, 315
Ricardo, David, 42
Right-wing politics, 53–71, 223
   US Right and BDS Movement, 223
Rivlin, Reuven, 264
Ruebner, Josh, 280
Rule of law, 5, 18, 19
Runte, Gerhart, 112
Russian Empire, 45, 51, 54

S
Said, Edward, 205–206, 212, 269, 269n41, 303
Samuel, Judy, 314n7

Sanctions
   Burma, 198
   mechanisms by which sanctions might work, 209
   political change and, 187, 202, 209
   revolutionary model, 187
   'the thumb-screw approach,' 188
   See also South Africa, sanctions against apartheid
Sanctuary Movement, 277
SA/SS (Sturmabteilung/Schutzstaffel) storm troopers, 102
Self-determination
   BDS, 204, 296, 298, 301
   Palestine, 204, 237, 266–268, 295
Sempołowska, Stefania, 58
Sewell, William, H., 289n12
Shapira, Anita, 79, 91n70, 93n82
Sharon, Ariel, 270n44, 327n35
Shavit, Ari, 316
Shertok, Moshe, 82
Shlaim, Avi, 317n16
Simon Wiesenthal Center, 180, 231
Singer, Bernard, 68
Smilansky, Moshe, 85
Smith, Adam, 42
Snow, David, 225
Social justice
   BDS and, 262, 265, 286
   Palestine, 262, 273–275
Social protest, 285
Sourani, Raji, 216
Sousa Santos, Boaventura de, 266
South Africa
   African Renaissance and, 176, 176n1
   apartheid, economic cost of, 189
   Cold War, end of, 181, 193, 195
   democratization of, 177, 181, 188, 193
   1985 Kairos initiative, 278n79
   neoliberalism, 129
   Palestine and, 2, 198, 199

South Africa (*cont.*)
  The Path to Power, 194
  1960 Sharpeville massacre, 202, 208
  South African miracle, 175–182, 194, 195
  1976 Soweto uprising, 202
  See also Anti Apartheid Movement (AAM); African National Congress (ANC); Congress of South African Trade Unions (COSATU); Conservative Party, South Africa (CP)
South Africa, boycott against apartheid
  1960 boycott campaigns, 201
  armed struggle, 15, 175, 182–183, 198
  Autonomen/autonomists, 124, 127
  banking campaign, 126
  fruit boycott campaign, 129
  REWE, attack on, 128
  violence, 127
  West Germany, radical Left boycotts, 115–138 (*see also* RZ)
South Africa, sanctions against apartheid
  ANC, 184, 199
  BDS and, 198, 199
  black opposition to the sanctions, 184
  efficacy of sanctions, 179, 180, 182–190
  Inkatha Freedom Party, 184
  Israel, sanctions against, 263
  naïve theory of sanctions, 185, 188
  non-white elites, 193, 200, 203
  South African economy, resilience of, 182, 185, 186
  South African elite, 190, 193
  white population in South Africa, 186, 188
  See also Azanian People's organization (AZAPO); Mbeki, Thabo; National Party, South Africa (NP); South African Communist Party (SACP)
South African Communist Party (SACP), 182–183, 194, 194n52
South African Non-Governmental Organization Coalition (SANGOCO), 219
Sports boycott, 12, 201
Springer, Axel, 118
State
  boycott as instrument of power, 23
  boycott of Jewish businesses in Nazi Germany, 3–4, 97–113
  civil society and, 39, 315
  consumer activism and, 27
  consumer boycott and, 21–39
  state sovereignty, 23, 27
  welfare reform, 33
Steinberg, Gerald, 284n113
Stepphuhn, Fritz, 103
Stojałowski, Stanisław, 71
Stolle, Dietlind, 36
Streicher, Julius, 104
Students for Justice in Palestine (SJP), 222–223, 236
Stultz, Neville, 187, 188
Surasky, Cecilie, 239
Sweden, 31, 36, 38

T
Tambo, Oliver, 191, 192, 201
Taraki, Lisa, 212
Tel Aviv, 76, 84–86, 87n51, 89, 90, 316, 320n24
Tel Aviv University, 285
The Times, 8, 12, 101
Tinsman, Heidi, 171
Tishby, Nahum, 77, 84
Tourism boycott, 211
Trade union

AAM, 201
  BDS and, 201, 305
  boycott and, 11, 126
  South Africa, 190, 279
Turck, Nancy, 272
Turner, Nat, 317
Tutu, Desmond, Archbishop, 184, 185, 187, 194, 198, 269

U
UN General Assembly, 312, 323n27
United Defense League (UDL), 145, 150–152, 154
United Democratic Front (UDF), 200, 203, 207, 208
United Farm Workers (UFW), 171–174
  1973 boycotts, 171
  children and students, 171
  1980s grape boycott, 172–173
  1979 strike-boycotts, 172
  See also Agricultural industry; United Farm Workers Organizing Committee (UFWOC)
United Farm Workers Organizing Committee (UFWOC), 157
  boycott success, 157
  consumer boycott, 157–158, 168
  DiGiorgio Corporation, 161
  farmworkers' labor rights and conditions, 157
  fasting, 161, 164
  Giumarra Vineyards, 161, 166
  grapes boycott, 162, 163, 166
  grocery store/supermarket boycott, 158, 162, 173
  Huerta, Dolores, 157, 160–162, 168
  InterHarvest, 167, 169
  labor strike, 157, 174
  lettuce strike and boycott, 166, 170
  Lopez, Hope, 163–164
  New York boycott, 165
  pesticides, 160, 162, 166, 169, 170
  Philadelphia boycott, 158, 163, 164, 166, 168
  pilgrimage, 158, 161
  Salinas Valley, 166–170
  shop-ins/pray-ins, 165
  tactics, 158, 165
  Teamsters Union, 166
  women, 159, 162–164
  See also Agricultural industry; Chavez, Cesar; Consumer boycott
United Kingdom (UK), *see* Britain; Britain, 2014 summer boycotts
United Nations (UN)
  1955 Bandung conference, 178
  1968 Teheran conference, 178
  UN Resolution 194, 219, 262, 268, 299
United States (US)
  9/11 attacks, 227, 236
  American Revolution and boycott, 4, 6, 9
  antiracism, 226, 230, 235–237, 241
  BDS and, 219–241
  Boston Tea Party, 4
  consumer boycott, 115
  labour boycott, 13
  See also Baton Rouge bus boycott; BDS Movement and opponents, US; Montgomery bus boycott
Unszlicht, Juljan, 66
UNWCAR (2001 UN World Conference Against Racism, Durban), 177–178, 180
  NGOs, 177, 180
US Campaign for the Academic and Cultural Boycott of Israel (USACBI), 220

US Campaign to End the Israeli Occupation, 215, 227, 280
Handbook for Student Divestment Campaigns, 227
Usher, Graham, 271

V

Van Zyl Slabbert, Frederik, 193
Vinton, Arthur Dudley, 10
Violence
  Baton Rouge bus boycott, 140, 153, 155
  BDS, 16, 216, 283, 298, 304
  BDS and non-violence, 298
  boycott and, 55, 106, 119, 138
  Israeli/Palestinian conflict, 208, 257, 258
  Jewish businesses in Nazi Germany, 3, 101, 105, 112, 113
  South Africa: boycott against apartheid, 195
  West Germany, radical Left boycotts, 116, 117, 120, 122
  Zionist 'buy national' campaigns, 75–77
Von Bethmann-Hollweg, Martha, 28
Von Knebel-Doeberitz, Elisabeth, 37, 37n22

W

Wagner, Adam, 246, 247
War on Want, 1
Warschawski, Michael, 212
Washington Post, 113, 168n19
Wasilewski, Leon, 63, 64, 66
Wasiutyński, Bohdan, 68
Weizmann, Eyal, 286
West Bank, 206, 247, 256, 264, 270, 270n44, 271n51, 298, 304n43, 318, 322, 323, 325–328, 327n35
  Israeli settlements in, 207, 270
West Germany boycotts
  boycott against East German-run Berlin S-Bahn, 118, 132
  boycott against Harlan's *Immortal Beloved*, 117
  boycotting as communicative strategy, 136, 138
  comparing boycott campaigns, 132
  Federal Constitutional Court, 117–119
  Federal Court of Justice, 119
  freedom of expression, 118–121
  1950s–1960s, 116
  regime-of-provision perspective, 116
  Springer/*Blinkfüer* boycotts, 118, 119, 132
  See also West Germany, radical Left boycotts
West Germany, radical Left boycotts
  anti-apartheid campaign, South Africa, 120, 125
  anti-nuclear energy protest/boycott, 129, 130
  antisemitism, 2, 14, 91, 137, 138, 231, 238, 243–259
  anti-Springer campaign, 120, 121
  anti-Zionist boycotts, 116, 133
  Autonomen/autonomists, 124, 127, 135
  boycott against electricity companies, 120
  boycott against multinational companies and countries, 120, 124
  Chile, 11, 120, 124, 125
  Evangelische Frauenarbeit in Deutschland, 125
  Green Party, 131, 293
  Hafenstraße mural, 135
  legal treatment of boycotts, 118, 120

public transport boycott, 122, 132
RZ, 127, 128, 133
sit-in blockade, 122
the *Spontis,* 122
violence, 106–108, 111, 113, 120, 122, 127
See also West Germany boycotts
Wiener, Alfred, 100, 113
Wildt, Michael, 107
Women
   Baton Rouge bus boycott, 141, 147, 149
   consumer boycott, 79, 162, 164
   Evangelische Frauenarbeit in Deutschland, 125
   UDL, 145, 146, 150–152, 154
   UFWOC, 159, 162–164
   Zionist 'buy national' campaigns, 77, 79
World Bank, 124, 189, 271
World Council of Churches, 126, 277, 277n78, 278, 278n82
World Jewish Congress, 2
World Social Forum (WSF), 265–267, 274, 277, 277n78
World Trade Organisation, 1999 conference, 265
World War I, 73, 76, 299
World War II, 87–90, 160, 228, 235
World Zionist Organization, 88, 89

X
Xenophobia, 1n1, 71, 174, 267

Y
Yiddish press and literature, 62
Yugoslavia, 99, 316

Z
Zakrzewski, Adam, 58
Ziadeh, Rafeef, 279
Zionism
   anti-Zionism, 17, 282, 283, 284n113
   BDS and, 16, 277, 299–301
   distinguishing Jewishness from, 92, 300
   as form of racism and apartheid, 268, 300, 304
   as racist settler colonial project, 301
   West Germany, anti-Zionist boycotts, 116, 122, 133, 136–138
Zionist 'buy national' campaigns
   Arab-Palestinian nationalist movement as rival, 75, 86
   Arab Revolt, 84–86, 95
   Arabs, 76–87, 92, 94, 95
   blacklisted products, 80
   the British, 76, 77, 80–83, 88, 90, 94
   economic nationalism, 73–76, 83, 93, 94
   ethnonational separatism in consumption, 80, 84
   goal, 93
   Ha'avara agreement, 90, 91, 94
   Hebrew labor and, 77, 79, 80
   Iggud Lema'an Totseret Ha-arets/ Union for the Products of the Land, 77, 79, 80, 86, 91, 92
   labor segregation, 78
   Mandate government, 84
   Merkaz Lema'an Totseret ha-Arets/ Center for the Products of the Land, 85
   mid-1930s, 84, 86, 87, 90, 91, 93–95

Zionist 'buy national' campaigns (*cont.*)
    nationalism, 73–81, 83, 93, 94, 291
    Nazis and other Germans, 87–91
    other Jews and 'Jewishness' of products, 92
    Templers, 89–91
    totseret ha-arets/products of the Land, 77, 79, 80, 85, 89, 91, 92
    Va'ad Le'ummi, 85
    violence, 79, 85, 86, 94, 95
    women and children, 79
    World War II, 87–90
    Yishuv, 77, 78, 80, 84, 87, 91
    Zionist ideology, 78
    See also 'Buy national' campaign
Zionist Organization of America (ZOA), 224, 231

GPSR Compliance

The European Union's (EU) General Product Safety Regulation (GPSR) is a set of rules that requires consumer products to be safe and our obligations to ensure this.

If you have any concerns about our products, you can contact us on

ProductSafety@springernature.com

In case Publisher is established outside the EU, the EU authorized representative is:

Springer Nature Customer Service Center GmbH
Europaplatz 3
69115 Heidelberg, Germany

www.ingramcontent.com/pod-product-compliance
Lightning Source LLC
LaVergne TN
LVHW020340260326
834688LV00045B/1454